Reconstruction and Peace Building in the Balkans

ADST-DACOR Diplomats and Diplomacy Series
Series Editor: Margery Boichel Thompson

Since 1776, extraordinary men and women have represented the United States abroad under all sorts of circumstances. What they did and how and why they did it remain little known to their compatriots. In 1995 the Association for Diplomatic Studies and Training (ADST) and Diplomatic and Consular Officers, Retired, Inc. (DACOR) created the Diplomats and Diplomacy book series to increase public knowledge and appreciation of the role of American diplomats in world history. The series seeks to demystify diplomacy through the stories of those who have conducted U.S. foreign relations, as they lived, influenced, and reported them. Robert William Farrand's *Reconstruction and Peace Building in the Balkans,* 47th in the series, is an apt example of the genre.

OTHER TITLES IN THE SERIES

Herman J. Cohen, ***Intervening in Africa: Superpower Peacemaking in a Troubled Continent***

Charles T. Cross, ***Born a Foreigner: A Memoir of the American Presence in Asia***

Brandon Grove, ***Behind Embassy Walls: The Life and Times of an American Diplomat***

Paul Hacker, ***Slovakia on the Road to Independence: An American Diplomat's Eye Witness Account***

Parker T. Hart, ***Saudi Arabia and the United States: Birth of a Security Partnership***

Edmund J. Hull, ***High-Value Target: Countering Al Qaeda in Yemen***

Cameron R. Hume, ***Mission to Algiers: Diplomacy by Engagement***

Dennis Kux, ***The United States and Pakistan, 1947–2000: Disenchanted Allies***

Jane C. Loeffler, ***The Architecture of Diplomacy: Building America's Embassies***

William B. Milam, ***Bangladesh and Pakistan: Flirting with Failure in Muslim South Asia***

William Michael Morgan, ***Pacific Gibraltar: U.S.-Japanese Rivalry over the Annexation of Hawaii, 1885–1898***

David D. Newsom, ***Witness to a Changing World***

Ronald E. Neumann, ***The Other War: Winning and Losing in Afghanistan***

Richard B. Parker, ed., ***The October War: A Retrospective***

Nicholas Platt, ***China Boys: How U.S. Relations with the PRC Began and Grew***

Howard B. Schaffer, ***The Limits of Influence: America's Role in Kashmir***

James Stephenson, ***Losing the Golden Hour: An Insider's View of Iraq's Reconstruction***

Ulrich Straus, ***The Anguish of Surrender: Japanese POWs of World War II***

William G. Thom, ***African Wars: Recollections of a Defense Intelligence Officer***

Reconstruction and Peace Building in the Balkans

The Brčko Experience

Robert William Farrand
in collaboration with Allison Frendak-Blume

ROWMAN & LITTLEFIELD PUBLISHERS, INC.
Lanham • Boulder • New York • Toronto • Plymouth, UK

Published by Rowman & Littlefield Publishers, Inc.
A wholly owned subsidiary of The Rowman & Littlefield Publishing Group, Inc.
4501 Forbes Boulevard, Suite 200, Lanham, Maryland 20706
http://www.rowmanlittlefield.com

Estover Road, Plymouth PL6 7PY, United Kingdom

British Library Cataloguing in Publication Information Available

Library of Congress Cataloging-in-Publication Data

Farrand, Robert William, 1934–
  Reconstruction and peace building in the Balkans : the Brcko experience / Robert
William Farrand, in collaboration with Allison Frendak-Blume.
     p. cm. — (ADST-DACOR diplomats and diplomacy series)
  Includes bibliographical references and index.
  ISBN 978-1-4422-1235-0 (cloth : alk. paper) — ISBN 978-1-4422-1237-4 (electronic)
  1. Peace-building—Bosnia and Hercegovina—Brcko. 2. Postwar reconstruction—
Bosnia and Hercegovina—Brcko. I. Frendak-Blume, Allison. II. Title.
  DR1313.7.R42F37 2011
  949.703—dc23

                                    2011026287

㊀™ The paper used in this publication meets the minimum requirements of American
National Standard for Information Sciences—Permanence of Paper for Printed Library
Materials, ANSI/NISO Z39.48-1992.

Printed in the United States of America

For Pam

Contents

Figures, Maps, Photos, Tables, and Textboxes

TABLES

TEXTBOXES

Preface

April 11, 1997. The first thing that struck me as our helicopter began its descent onto the football pitch at the edge of town was how different it all appeared from the images endless briefings had etched in my mind about the dangerous state into which the municipality of Brčko (pronounced BIRCH-koh) had fallen. Before the Bosnian War of 1992–1995 broke out, Brčko had been a thriving small city on the right bank of the Sava River. By war's end, the city and its environs had been transformed into a cauldron of interethnic hatred that threatened to tear apart the Dayton Peace Accords of 1995. To salvage the Dayton agreement and to resolve—or at least reduce to workable proportions—the seemingly irreconcilable differences between Serbs, Croats, and Bosniaks (Muslims) that had long lived side by side in this Balkan municipality, the international community imposed an outside administrator, or "supervisor," on Brčko.

For the first time in my life, I witnessed a spectacle of wanton destruction of property so vast it nearly took my breath away. One reliable estimate had set at ten thousand the number of Bosniak and Croat houses that units of the Yugoslav People's Army, abetted by Serbian paramilitary forces, had laid waste during and after their nighttime attack of April 30, 1992. Looking out from the chopper to the west and south of the city, where by design Serbian forces had concentrated their fury, I asked myself how in heaven's name I could ever pull together the resources necessary to enable the return of thousands, literally thousands, of internally displaced Muslims and Croats to their homes by March of the coming year as stipulated in my mandate.

Having lived as a child through World War II and served as an officer in the U.S. Navy between the Korean and Vietnam conflicts, I had read widely about war and its aftermath but had experienced neither up close. In Brčko,

I would come on a daily basis over the next three years face-to-face with the human pain, both physical and psychic, that violent interethnic conflict leaves in its wake. No briefing can prepare you for the empty looks on people's faces, or the suspicion and distrust in their eyes. On that first day, furtive glances met our cavalcade as we passed through the streets on our way to the supervisor's new headquarters. You could sense the danger of renewed violence below the outward calm.

This was an assignment like none other I had been given in three decades of diplomatic service. In other postings, for example, I could normally walk the streets unobserved—except, perhaps, in Cold War Moscow. But in Brčko, I went from common man to *the man to watch.* More significantly, the typical diplomat's duties to represent, observe, analyze, report, and carry out instructions were supplanted by a new set of operating principles: more demanding, forceful, and fraught with consequences. In Brčko, I was given the authority—and responsibility—to exert direct control over the governance of a divided city and its surroundings.

Faced with circumstances unlike any I had encountered before, the question arose as to whom I could turn for guidance. The high representative in Sarajevo had assigned to my office a remarkably able and experienced multinational staff to which I could turn for tactical advice; but when it came finally to settling on a course of action, that decision would be mine.

This question would have particular relevance when we began to address the thorny tasks of restoring freedom of movement in the area, facilitating the return of displaced persons to their homes, establishing a multiethnic administration, and, bringing up the rear, infusing life into the local economy. There were no textbook answers to the questions that would arise in dealing with these challenges. Lamentably, it seemed that writings devoted to the elusive concept of civilian administration (supervision) of modern post-conflict war zones were few. It was thus an easy sell for Professor Michael Doyle, then of Princeton University, who came by one day after spending a month in Brčko to urge me to "fill a gap in the literature" by writing about my experiences. My hope is that this work does in fact contribute to that lofty goal. But, as important, I wish it to be a useful reference for those whose fate it is to take on such poorly understood, professionally risky hybrid operations as was the international supervision of the ethnically divided city of Brčko.

Acknowledgments

I owe thanks to many for helping bring this writing project to fruition. Before I turn to the pleasant task of thanking them individually, however, I must first mention two fine organizations that supported me throughout: the U.S. Institute of Peace (USIP) and George Mason University (GMU). In appreciation of USIP's generous support, I strove to meet the professional standards of this congressionally funded, nonpartisan body devoted to the dissemination of knowledge, skills, and resources, including the study of specific post-conflict peace interventions, for the enhancement of peace around the world.

My gratitude is boundless to George Mason University's School of Public Policy, under Dean Kingsley Haynes, for welcoming me aboard as an affiliate professor and distinguished fellow, thus providing me with an essential base of operations. Professor David Davis, founder of the Peace Operations Policy Program (POPP) at GMU, kindly brought me under his wing and assisted me in ways too numerous to count. My primary editor and goad, the ever-resourceful and prodigiously hardworking Dr. Allison Frendak-Blume, was POPP's academic director during the drafting period. I am particularly grateful to Allison for her keen editorial eye and for smoothing my writing into coherent prose, which lent a vital sense of order and logic to my, at times, unruly narrative. With Allison's blessing, I was permitted to tap into the energies and insights of research assistants at EMU—Rebecca Deux, Kimberly Formo, Burcin Cevik, Callie LeRenard, and Maral Noori-Moghaddam.

Let me also profoundly thank Margery B. Thompson and the Association for Diplomatic Studies and Training (ADST) for adopting this book for their series and arranging for its publication.

As this book took form, I owe a debt of gratitude to those who offered wise counsel, advice, and essential input. Presiding Arbitrator of the Brčko

Arbitration Tribunal, Roberts B. Owen, was always available at the end of a telephone line to keep me, in his kind and gentle way, free of loose reasoning and wayward facts. He graciously gave of his time to read and lend his wisdom to the draft manuscript. His wise, even Solomonic, solution to the impasse over Brčko's political status will surely go down in the annals of peacemaking as one of its finer moments.

Pride of place must go to my indefatigable and unflappable office manager, Doris Hoffmann. As one of the U.S. Department of State's veteran "roving" secretaries, Doris brought brains, grit, and common sense to our multinational team of professionals. While no one can be called indispensable, Doris came close. On call 24/7, she tailored a system for tracking, cataloguing, and archiving papers and cyber communications in this one-of-a-kind hybrid peace operation. Doris's steadiness in moments of high tension and equipment outages is the stuff of legend. She managed the steady stream of people flowing in and out of my office with a firm but caring hand.

The late Samuel Edwin Fry, a Foreign Service pal since our days in the former Soviet Union of the late 1960s, gave generously of his time and acumen to "cold read" the entire text and to suggest key improvements. Sam was a steady source of encouragement: bucking me up, making me laugh, pushing me on.

Ian McLeod, boon companion and courageous partner in Brčko, read applicable parts of the manuscript and provided photographs from his ever-ready camera.

Ambassador Gennadiy Ivanovich Shabannikov, veteran Russian diplomat, was away in New Zealand representing his nation while this book was being drafted. Although unable physically to comment on the manuscript, Gennadiy's loyal support and enthusiastic spirit inspired my thinking at every turn.

Michael G. Karnavas, lawyer and friend, read over the chapter on rule of law and carefully edited the section that described the work of the Brčko Law Revision Commission.

Sophie Lagueny, senior advisor and elections expert, cast her critical eye on relevant portions of the draft manuscript, pointing out areas where my memory was either faulty or downright wrong. Sophie was unmatched when it came to electoral numbers and their interpretation. She kept me honest.

Claire O'Riordan arrived in Brčko as a junior staff member and in two years rose to head our economics division. To the chapter on the economy, she applied both her keen knowledge of Brčko's then struggling commercial sector and her born gift for language.

Donald Grady, Brčko commander of the UN International Police Task Force (UN/IPTF), read those portions of the manuscript touching on police matters. His clear-eyed, no-nonsense approach to the recounting and analysis of events gone by was an invaluable check on my tendency to embellish memory with wandering facts.

Warmest thanks go to Colonel Robert "Bob" Sundberg, U.S. Army Reserve, who having spent a year on my staff as a civil-affairs lawyer, became a dedicated and lifelong supporter of the Brčko mission. No matter where the army assigned Bob after Brčko, the good colonel stayed in touch with local translators who provided him—and, through him, me—with weekly media updates across the years. Sundberg's steady flow of fresh news from the district was, and continues to be, a rich source of current information on trends set in place during our time together in Brčko.

Finally, to the dedicated officers and soldiers of SFOR (Stabilization Force) garrisoned at Camp McGovern in Brčko and at Eagle Base in Tuzla, my deepest respect and gratitude for maintaining an environment in which we civilians had the freedom to work in safety with the local population. And to the many citizens of Brčko who displayed uncommon courage in supporting our efforts to bring them peace and stability, my highest affection and esteem. Thank you all for taking a chance on peace.

Needless to say, such errors of fact and interpretation of events as remain are mine alone.

Abbreviations

ABiH	Army of Bosnia and Herzegovina (*Armije Bosne i Hercegovine*)
AMWG	Arizona Market Working Group
BiH	Bosnia and Herzegovina
BLRC	Brčko Law Revision Commission
CA	Civil Affairs
CAFAO	Customs and Fiscal Assistance Office
CAPT	Captain
CIMIC	Civil-Military Cooperation
CIRP	Community Infrastructure Repair Project
CIVPOL	Civilian Police
COL	Colonel
COMSFOR	Commander SFOR
CRPC	Commission on Real Property Claims
DEM	Deutschmarks
DFID	Department for International Development
DMT	District Management Team
DP	Displaced Person
DPA	Dayton Peace Agreement (or Accords)
DPKO	Department of Peacekeeping Operations
EASC	Election Appeals Sub-Commission
EBRD	European Bank of Reconstruction and Development
ERIC	Elections Results Implementing Committee
FOB	Friends of Bill
FRY	Federal Republic of Yugoslavia
GDS	Civic Democratic Party (*Gradjanska Demokratska Stranka BiH*)
GFAP	General Framework Agreement for Peace

GTZ	*Deutsche Gesellschaft für Technische Zusammenarbeit*
HDZ	Croatian Democratic Union (*Hrvatska Demokratska Zajednica*)
HVIDRA	Croatian Homeland War Disabled Veterans Association (*Hrvatskih Vojnih Invalida Domovinskog Rata*)
HVO	Croatian Defence Council (*Hrvatsko Vijeće Obrane*)
IAPG	Inter-Agency Planning Group
IBRD	International Bank for Reconstruction and Development
IDP	Internally Displaced Person
IEBL	Inter-Entity Boundary Line
IFI	International Financial Institutions
IFOR	Implementation Force
IMF	International Monetary Fund
IO	International Organization
JIC	Joint Implementation Council
JNA	Yugoslav People's Army (*Jugoslovenska Narodna Armija*)
JWG	Judiciary Working Group
KM	Convertible Mark
LEC	Local Election Commission
LNO	Liaison Officer
LTC	Lieutenant Colonel
LTG	Lieutenant General
MAJ	Major
MDMP	Military Decision-Making Process
MG	Major General
MoD	Ministry of Defense
MND	Multinational Division
MRX	Military Readiness Exercise
MZ	*Mjesna Zajednica* (singular) / *Mjesne Zajednice* (plural)
NATO	North Atlantic Treaty Organization
NGO	Nongovernmental Organization
NHI	New Croat Initiative (*Nova Hrvatska Inicijativa*)
OECD	Organization for European Cooperation and Development
OHR	Office of the High Representative
OSCE	Organization for Security and Cooperation in Europe
PEC	Provisional Election Commission
PIC	Peace Implementation Council
PKSOI	Peacekeeping and Stability Operations Institute
PNG	Papua New Guinea
RS	Serb Republic (*Republika Srpska*)
SBiH	Party for Bosnia and Herzegovina (*Stranka za Bosnu i Herce-govinu*)

SDA	Party of Democratic Action (*Stranka Demokratske Akcije*)
SDP	Social Democratic Party of Bosnia and Herzegovina (*Socijaldemokratska Partija Bosne i Hercegovine*)
SDS	Serbian Democratic Party (*Srpska Demokratska Stranka*)
SDS-SZ	Serb Democratic Party-Serb Country (*Srpska Demokratska Stranka-Srpskih Zemalja*)
SEED	Support for East European Democracies
SFOR	Stabilization Force
SITREP	Situation Report
SNS	Serbian People's League (*Srpski Narodni Savez RS*)
SPRS	Socialist Party of Republika Srpska (*Socialisticka Partija Republike Srpske*)
SPS	Socialist Party of Serbia (*Socialisticka Partija Srbije*)
SRS	Serb Radical Party (*Srpska Radikalna Stranka*)
SRSG	Special Representative of the Secretary General
UK	United Kingdom
UN/IPTF	United Nations International Police Task Force
UNCITRAL	United Nations Commission on International Trade Law
UNHCR	United Nations High Commissioner for Refugees
UNMIBH	United Nations Mission in Bosnia and Herzegovina
UNTAES	United Nations Transitional Administration for Eastern Slavonia, Baranja, and Western Sirmium
USAID	U.S. Agency for International Development
USIA	U.S. Information Agency
VRS	Army of Republika Srpska (*Vojska Republike Srpske*)
ZOS	Zone of Separation

Chapter One

Introduction

Brčko is a microcosm of Bosnia and Herzegovina (BiH). Every issue that confronted the international community throughout BiH could also be encountered there. Brčko is a municipality (*opština*) covering approximately 490 square kilometers situated in the lowlands of northeastern BiH known as the Posavina Corridor. The seat of government is located in a city (*grad*) bearing the same name. The municipality is divided into thirty-four wards or local communities (*mjesne zajednice*). The Sava River separates Brčko from the Republic of Croatia to the northeast. To the northwest through east, in counterclockwise fashion, lie the BiH municipalities of Orašje, Ločari, Gradačać, Srebrenik, Čelić, Lopare, and Bijeljina.

Established during the fifteenth century, Brčko developed over time into an agricultural and transportation hub with the *grad* serving as an important stop along the Sava River. A rail bridge had been constructed in 1894 and took on automobile traffic several decades later when a modern railway bridge was constructed. Port (*luka*) facilities were built in 1964, and Brčko continued to grow as a regional economic center. Prior to the outbreak of hostilities, several large manufacturing enterprises were located in the *grad* and surrounding area. In 1990, approximately seventy-seven thousand metric tons of goods passed through BiH's sole multimodal port (Arbitral Tribunal 1997, 14–15).

Brčko was richly multiethnic for most of its history. The *grad* traditionally mirrored the distribution of peoples in the region—Croats, Serbs, Muslims, gypsies, and others. The population in outlying villages, particularly in the south and west of the *opština*, was more homogeneous and typically non-Serb in character. The last census conducted prior to the breakup of the Socialist Federative Republic of Yugoslavia, of which Bosnia and Herzegovina was

1

one of six republics, took place in 1991. Table 1.1 demonstrates the population totals for Brčko.

The war, which initially had erupted in the Yugoslav republics of Slovenia and Croatia in 1991, broke out in Brčko on April 30, 1992, when Serb forces blew up the vehicular and railroad bridges and shelled communities in which Muslims and Croats were residing. These elements of the Yugoslav People's Army (JNA, *Jugoslovenska Narodna Armija*), locally mobilized Serbs, and Serbian paramilitary groups, notably Mirko Blagojević's *Mirkovi četnici* and Ljubiša Savić's Panthers, then carried out "ethnic cleansing" (*etničko čicenje*) against non-Serbs. As these actions transpired, other population centers in eastern BiH were similarly attacked. After only a week, the Serb forces had effectively eradicated all non-Serb residents from both the Brčko *grad* and a large horseshoe-shaped swath of the *opština* to the south and west of town. Many citizens were summarily executed. Thousands more were rounded up in collection centers or imprisoned in concentration camps, with the systematic killing of mostly Muslim detainees predominantly taking place at or near the Laser Bus Company, the Brčko police station, and Luka camp. In the *Final Report of the United Nations Commission of Experts*, published in May 1994, twenty-eight camps were identified throughout the Brčko municipality (United Nations 1994, par. 86).

Those non-Serbs who were driven out of Brčko *grad* and its surrounding suburbs and settlements dug in along a line a few kilometers to the south and west that, with few adjustments, they were able to defend until the end of the war. The General Framework Agreement for Peace (GFAP), more colloquially referred to as the Dayton Peace Agreement (or Accords) (DPA), or simply "Dayton," was negotiated in November 1995 at Wright-Patterson Air Force Base in Dayton, Ohio, by representatives of the parties involved in the war in BiH, including the neighboring Republic of Croatia and the Federal Republic of Yugoslavia (FRY). On November 21, the parties successfully concluded the negotiations and, on December 14, signed the agreement in Paris. The Republic of Bosnia and Herzegovina was

Table 1.1. Population Breakdown for Brčko *Grad* and *Opština*, 1991

	Muslim	Serb	Croat	Other	Total
Grad (5.93 sq km)	23,089 (56%)	8,254 (20%)	2,869 (7%)	7,134 (17%)	41,346
Opština	38,771 (44%)	18,133 (21%)	22,163 (25%)	8,265 (10%)	87,332

Source: Arbitral Tribunal (1997, 14, quoting *Statisticki Godisnjak Jugoslavije* 1991).
Note: Individuals who refused to identify with any of the three ethnic groupings utilized the designation "Other" ethnic group or "Yugoslav."

annexes that followed in its stead.[3] In fact, the arbitration process for Brčko memorialized at Dayton did not run smoothly. The Federation appointed Dr. Ćazim Sadiković to serve its interests, and the RS appointed Dr. Vitomir Popović. However, the two failed to appoint a third arbitrator for the tribunal within seven months of the signing of the agreement. On July 15, 1996, the president of the International Court of Justice appointed American attorney Roberts B. Owen as third, and presiding, arbitrator. Rather than the award reflecting the opinion of the majority of the arbitrators, the parties subsequently agreed to change this standard UNCITRAL rule for decision making so that the rulings of the presiding arbitrator would be treated as decisive. Owen issued a pre-hearing order on August 14, 1996, requiring both parties to submit written statements for consideration by the tribunal in rendering its decision. Dr. Popović and political officials of the RS assumed a nonparticipatory stance toward the tribunal through mid-November, when they provided a Statement of the Republika Srpska as part of other filings. On November 27, 1996, the one-year date for completion of the arbitration was extended from December 14, 1996, to February 15, 1997. In December, Serb officials stated they would not participate further in the proceedings and wished to revoke Dr. Popović's appointment. Owen indicated that such actions would violate the RS's treaty obligations under Dayton and encouraged their future participation. All three arbitrators met in Rome between January 8–17, 1997, where written and evidentiary submissions were presented. Final deliberations were conducted in Washington, D.C., with an award issued February 15, 1997.

First Arbitration Award (February 15, 1997)

Throughout the January 1997 Rome proceedings, both parties sought to establish their own fundamental and exclusive right to jurisdiction over the Brčko area. Federation representatives argued Brčko historically had been dominated by Bosniaks and Croats and that for the RS to retain exclusive possession of a city Serbs had captured and ethnically cleansed during the war was unconscionable. Further, Brčko served as a vital northern opening between central Bosnia and Europe. RS officials contended the corridor connected the two halves of their entity and any change in its exclusive possession would be inconsistent with the alleged principle of "territorial continuity." Additionally, it would violate the terms of Dayton, where it had been agreed the RS was to control 49 percent of BiH territory. Owen commented in his February 1997 decision, which will also be referred to in this text as the First Award, that the jurisdictional debate tended to obscure considerations for the welfare of the Brčko community. Surveying "a host of historical, economic and psychological factors" that served to mold perceptions on both sides, the tribunal conceded that given the complexity of such factors it was "unable . . . to say that either side is 100% right in its position or 100% wrong" (Arbitral Tribunal 1997, 25). Owen concluded "that any 'simple solution' must be rejected in favor of an approach that is consistent with *law and equity and is designed gradually to relieve the underlying tensions* and lead to a stable and harmonious solution" [emphasis mine] (25). Thus, given "ongoing failures to comply with the Dayton Accords in the RS area of the Brčko Opština (particularly in terms of freedom of movement and the return of former Brčko residents to their Brčko homes), and the high levels of tension resulting therefrom," Owen found there was a "clear need to establish a program for implementation of the Dayton Accords in the area" (40). He called on the Office of the High Representative (OHR)[4] to "establish an office and staff in Brčko under the leadership of a Deputy High Representative . . . (a) to supervise Dayton implementation throughout the Brčko area for a period of not less than one year, and (b) to strengthen local democratic institutions in the same area" (40). The Brčko supervisor was expected to perform the following duties:

(1) The Supervisor will have authority to promulgate binding regulations and orders in aid of the implementation program and local democratization. *Such regulations and orders shall prevail as against any conflicting law.* [emphasis mine] All relevant authorities, including courts and police personnel, shall obey and enforce all Supervisory regulations and orders. The parties shall take all actions required to cooperate fully with the Supervisor in the implementation of this provision and the measures hereinafter described.

(2) The Supervisor should consider assembling an Advisory Council and include within its membership representatives of OSCE [Organization for Security and Cooperation in Europe], UNHCR [United Nations High Commissioner for Refugees], SFOR [Stabilization Force],[5] IBRD [International Bank for Reconstruction and Development], IMF [International Monetary Fund], the Institutions of Bosnia and Herzegovina, local ethnic groups, and such other official and unofficial groups as the Supervisor may deem appropriate to provide advice and liaison in implementation of this Award.

(3) The Supervisor in close liaison with SFOR should coordinate with IPTF [International Police Task Force] and such other international police mechanisms as may be established in the Brčko area to provide services with two principal objectives in mind:

(a) To ensure freedom of movement, through highway patrols and otherwise, for all vehicles and pedestrians on all significant roads, bridges and port facilities in the relevant area from (and including) the Donja Mahala–Orašje Road (the so-called "Arizona Road") on the west to the eastern boundary of the Brčko Opština.

(b) To ensure that the relevant authorities will undertake normal democratic policing functions and services for the protection of all citizens
of Bosnia and Herzegovina within the relevant area.

(4) The Supervisor should establish, with advice and assistance from
UNHCR, the Commission for Displaced Persons and Refugees, and
other appropriate agencies, a program (which may incorporate previously established procedures) to govern the phased and orderly return of
former residents of the relevant area to their homes of origin and for the
restoration, construction, and allocation of housing as necessary to accommodate old and new residents.

(5) The Supervisor should (a) work with OSCE and other concerned international organizations to ensure that free and fair local elections are conducted under international supervision in the relevant area before the end
of the international supervision; and (b) following such elections, issue
such regulations and orders as may be appropriate to enhance democratic
government and a multi-ethnic administration in the Town of Brčko. The
parties will fully implement the results of the municipal elections according
to the rules and regulations of the PEC [Provisional Election Commission].

(6) Given the significance of economic revitalization (particularly in terms
of easing ethnic and other tensions in the area), a concerted effort at
economic reconstruction is considered essential to the reduction of such
tensions, the Supervisor therefore should assist the various international
development agencies to develop and implement a targeted economic
revitalization program for the Brčko area.

(7) Since revitalization of the Sava River port in Brčko is of paramount
interest to both parties, all land now publicly or socially owned within
the port area shall be placed under the exclusive control of the Bosnia
and Herzegovina Transportation Corporation (an entity established under GFAP Annex 9, Article II(1)). Both parties are directed to use their
best efforts—and the Supervisor is invited and encouraged to guide such
efforts—to attract public and private investment (e.g., through leasing
space) to revive the port through physical reconstruction, river dredging,
and other appropriate measures.

(8) The Supervisor should, in the interests of fostering commerce and international economic development, assemble a group of international customs
monitors to work with appropriate authorities of the parties (including Bosnia and Herzegovina) toward the establishment of efficient customs procedures and controls in the relevant area. (Arbitral Tribunal 1997, 40–42)

An extraordinary meeting of the Steering Board for the Peace Implementation Council[6] was held in Vienna, Austria, on March 7, 1997, to outline
modalities for successful implementation of the Brčko arbitral award. A
statement was issued establishing the supervision of the Brčko area under
the direction of Robert W. "Bill" Farrand. A nominee from the Russian Fed-

eration and Ian McLeod of the U.K. were to serve as deputies. Supervision was to commence March 22, 1997, and implementation was expected to include overall international coordination, economic revitalization, presence of a robust international civilian police force, freedom of movement, return of refugees and displaced persons, and installation in the area of a new multiethnic administration, including the police, based on the result of elections held according to the rules and regulations laid down for the nationwide local elections.

The First Award authorized either party to make an application for further action with respect to allocation of political responsibilities in the Brčko area between December 1, 1997, and January 15, 1998. The Federation did so in a timely manner, and a schedule for written submissions and oral hearings was prepared. Eight days of hearings were conducted in Vienna from February 5–12, 1998. Final written submissions were presented to the tribunal on March 4, 1998. Owen promulgated a supplemental award on March 15, 1998.

Supplemental Award (March 15, 1998)

Continuation of the Brčko supervisory regime was the theme of the Supplemental Award. Owen remarked that since April 1997 the supervisor and his staff had pushed forward with programs to establish freedom of movement, return people to their homes, create a multiethnic municipal government, and revitalize the Brčko economy. However, evidence presented during the hearings revealed that the RS authorities in Brčko, directed by the Serbian Democratic Party (*Srpska Demokratska Stranka*, SDS) headquartered in the hard-line stronghold of Pale, had defied all attempts to implement Dayton in the area. Federation authorities also were cited for lack of compliance. Positive changes had been occurring on the RS political landscape during the latter half of 1997, culminating with the January 18, 1998, appointment of the more moderate Milorad Dodik (1998–2001) as prime minister, to the outrage of the SDS. The tribunal acknowledged that until this transformation, Brčko's assignment to Federation control seemed the proper solution. The changed circumstances, though, warranted an extension of time to ensure in the long run that the most just and equitable result be achieved. Thus, the following text was drafted:

VI. Supplemental Award
   23. For the foregoing reasons the Tribunal adopts the following orders and provisions, which shall form part of the Award, shall be binding upon all Parties to GFAP Annex 2, and with which all Parties shall comply and cooperate in full.

24. The supervisory regime established by the Award (at Para. 104(I)(B)) shall continue in existence, with the powers and responsibilities therein provided. The Supervisor, being Deputy High Representative for Brčko, shall enjoy in the Brčko area powers equivalent to those conferred upon the High Representative by the Bonn Conference of December 1997, including the power to remove from office any public official considered by the Supervisor to be inadequately cooperative with his efforts to achieve compliance with the Dayton Accords, to strengthen democratic institutions in the area, and to revitalize the local economy.

25. The Supervisor is authorized and encouraged to take appropriate measures toward economic revitalization, including steps
    a. to re-integrate the economy of that portion of the pre-war Brčko Opština that lies north of the IEBL with the economies of surrounding regions,
    b. to create in the Brčko area a duty-free or special economic zone to stimulate the region's economy,
    c. for the same purpose to establish a program of privatization of state-owned and socially-owned enterprises in the area, and
    d. looking toward the re-opening of the Sava River port in Brčko, to activate the Bosnia and Herzegovina Transportation Corporation and facilitate international support for the port program.

26. Pending further action by the Tribunal, to be taken upon the request of either party, the IEBL within the pre-war Brčko Opština shall remain unchanged. The Tribunal will entertain and act upon any such request that is received between 15 November 1998 and 15 January 1999. A further decision by the Tribunal in response to such a request will be rendered as soon as possible after the request has been received.

27. The Tribunal hereby gives notice
    1. that any further Tribunal action is likely to be significantly affected by the degree to which the respective parties have acted in good faith to comply with the Dayton Accords and the Tribunal's orders, and
    2. that among the alternative solutions that will be seriously considered by the Tribunal, upon proper request, will be
       a. the location or relocation of the IEBL in such a way as to place Brčko and its surroundings within the territory of one party or the other, and
       b. the conversion of the pre-war Brčko Opština into a "neutral district" beyond the exclusive control of either Entity.

The parties met once again in Vienna for hearings on the matter February 8–17, 1999. The tribunal issued its final award one month later.

Final Award (March 15, 1999)

The changed circumstances on the 1998 RS political front failed to have the desired result of promoting positive implementation of the Dayton Accords in Brčko. While Owen noted the parties agreed the supervisory regime should remain in effect, he believed a definitive ruling on Brčko's status was necessary to move the peace process forward. The Final Award was issued on March 15, 1999.

I. Summary of Conclusions

6. During the 1999 Vienna hearings the RS failed to make the kind of showing required by the Supplemental Award of 15 March 1998. Instead of suggesting "a very vigorous and consistent program of correction and compliance [with Dayton and the prior arbitral rulings] throughout 1998," the evidence showed instead (as more fully described below) that throughout 1998, notwithstanding the good intentions of RS Prime Minister Milorad Dodik, the Serb political leaders exercising immediate local control in Brčko—especially individuals aligned with the anti-Dayton SDS and SRS [*Srpska Radikalna Stranka*, or Serb Radical Party] parties both locally and entity-wide—tolerated and apparently encouraged a significant level of obstruction against the attainment of Dayton's and the Tribunal's objectives, particularly as against the goals of (a) encouraging and enabling displaced persons and refugees to return to their pre-war homes, (b) helping to develop democratic multi-ethnic institutions, and (c) cooperating with the international supervisory regime.

7. The Tribunal has further concluded that it is very unlikely that the level of local obstructionism will effectively diminish so long as anti-Dayton political elements—particularly the SDS and SRS parties led by newly elected RS President Nikola Poplasen—are allowed to remain dominant in that portion of the Brčko area that is in RS custody. Indeed, if pro-Dayton elements had been able to implement their programs in the Brčko area during the last year, the Tribunal's present decision to require a change of government might not have been necessary but SDS/SRS intransigence has left the Tribunal with no choice.

8. With all parties in vigorous agreement that the international supervisory regime must continue in force indefinitely in the Brčko area, it is appropriate to allow the necessary change to be brought about on an orderly schedule, thus avoiding the kind of abrupt change that may unnecessarily aggravate the situation. The Supervisor will have responsibility for scheduling and implementing the changes described below over the next several months, and severe penalties will be imposed for any failure to cooperate with his implementation program, including the ultimate remedy of placing Brčko in the exclusive control of one entity or the other. See 65–68, infra. In the meantime, pending implementation of the District plan by the Supervisor, the Inter-Entity Boundary Line ("IEBL") will continue in place without change, and existing laws and governmental arraignments (including those related to payment of salaries to employees) will remain in force. See 39, infra.

9. Pursuant to the commitments made by BiH and both entities to "implement without delay" the Tribunal's decision, upon the effective date to be established by the Supervisor each entity shall be deemed to have delegated all of its powers of governance within the pre-war Brčko Opština to a new institution, a new multi-ethnic democratic government to be known as "The Brčko District of Bosnia and Herzegovina" under the exclusive sovereignty of Bosnia and Herzegovina. The legal effect will be permanently to suspend all of the legal authority of both entities within the Opština and to recreate it as a single administrative unit.

10. As an institution existing under the sovereignty of Bosnia and Herzegovina, the new District government will be subject to the powers of the common institutions of BiH as those powers are enumerated in the BiH Constitution. All other powers of governance within the Brčko Opština, having been delegated by the two entities, will be exercised exclusively by the District government, subject, however, to supervised coordination with the two entity governments. See 43, infra. Responsibility for overall coordination, and for issuing any needed directives to ensure that the entities fulfill their obligations with respect to the new District, will be that of the Supervisor, who may delegate that responsibility to an appropriate BiH institution. *The entities are hereby ordered to implement without delay any such directive, regulation or order issued by the Supervisor or his delegate.* [emphasis mine] The Tribunal is satisfied that these arrangements are fully consistent with the BiH Constitution. See 58–62, infra.

11. Upon the establishment of the new District, the entire territory, within its boundaries (i.e., the pre-war Brčko Opština) will thereafter be held in "condominium" by both entities simultaneously: The territory of the RS will encompass the entire Opština, and so also will the territory of the Federation. Neither entity, however, will exercise any authority within the boundaries of the District, which will administer the area as one unitary government. Existing entity law will continue to apply as appropriate within the District until modified by action of the Supervisor or the District Assembly, and the IEBL will continue to exist within the District until the Supervisor has determined that it has no further legal significance and may cease to exist. See 39, infra. No subdivision of the District on any ethnic basis shall be permitted.

12. Having considered all of the evidence, the Tribunal has concluded that the new District plan will adequately protect the legitimate interests of both of the two entities and those of the international community. See 50–57, infra.

13. The Dayton Accords require that the entities "implement without delay" this "final and binding" Tribunal award. In the event of non-compliance, the Supervisor will have authority to issue remedial orders. In addition, this Tribunal will remain in existence until such time as the Supervisor, with the approval of the High Representative, has notified the Tribunal (a) that the two entities have fully complied with their obligations to

facilitate the establishment of the new institutions herein described, and (b) that such institutions are functioning, effectively and apparently permanently, within the Brčko Opština. Until such notification, the Tribunal will retain authority, in the event of serious non-compliance by either entity, to modify this Final Award as necessary—e.g., by placing part or all of the District within the exclusive control of the other entity.

The Final Award was supplemented by an annex dated August 18, 1999. The Annex addressed the status of present and future Brčko citizens, including the vesting of all Brčko District legislative powers in a district assembly and executive functions in an executive board; creation of judiciary and penal institutions; establishment of the Law Revision Commission to produce a uniform set of district laws; formation of the District Law Enforcement Agency and Customs Service; taxation and financial matters; voting; symbols; integration of the district's educational system; administration of public properties; and movement of military forces for nonaggressive purposes.

Chapter Two

Supervisor's Authority

I received a tap on my shoulder in Embassy Riyadh's darkened theater, and pulled my eyes from the screen where Nicholas Cage was locked in mortal combat with Ed Harris in the thriller *The Rock*. Just at that moment, a flight of navy jet fighters was screaming in from the Pacific Ocean under—yes, under—and over the Golden Gate Bridge with orders to bomb the island of Alcatraz before the protagonist could execute his evil plot. "Sir, the State Department asks you to call urgently," whispered a marine guard, handing me a slip of paper with a number scribbled on it. "How urgently?" I muttered. "Urgently," the marine replied. So, like a kid called from his favorite TV show, I reluctantly got up and made for the door as Cage frantically flailed his arms to wave off the fighters.

It was near midnight in Saudi Arabia, on February 27, 1997. The ten-person team I had been leading from the State Department's Office of the Inspector General had been in the country for two weeks to inspect, as part of the normal three-year cycle, the U.S. Embassy in Riyadh and two American consulates in Jeddah and Dhahran. When the call came through, the voice on the other end of the line in Washington was that of Bill Montgomery, an old Foreign Service friend and at the time special advisor to the president and secretary of state for Bosnian Peace Implementation. "Do we have a deal for you," he said in a sunny voice. It had been a long workday and I shot back, "Stuff it, Montgomery, if there was a deal to be had one of you clowns back there would have taken it. So what kind of detail do you want me to do?" "It's Bosnia," Montgomery answered. "The big one." "The big one?" I asked. "Yes, the big one—Brčko. You know about Brčko, right?" "Sure," I said, lying through my teeth, "I know all about Brčko, but tell me about it anyway." Montgomery explained that the Dayton talks that ended the war in BiH had nearly broken down over the political status of a little city named Brčko. After a year of hard trying, a tribunal established to arbitrate the impasse had decided to place Brčko under international supervision to break the logjam. "If we can get it right in Brčko," I remember Montgomery saying, "we might have a chance of making the Dayton peace process work throughout Bosnia and Herzegovina. But if we fail to turn the corner in Brčko, the Dayton process will almost certainly fail elsewhere." He quickly described the role of the proposed supervisor for Brčko and ended on this note: "We want you to consider taking this on. It will involve breaking you out of the Inspection Corps immediately so that you can come home, get briefed, and go out to Brčko right away. We need your answer by morning. Let me know." Thus began the most demanding and wildest ride of my three decades in the Foreign Service.

I arrived in Washington, D.C., the following day and subsequently attended meetings over the next few weeks with multiple actors and agencies addressing the Bosnia issue as a means to prepare myself, a time-honored approach by State Department standards. This was truncated by attendance at the conference held by the steering board of the Peace Implementation Council in Vienna, where I was presented officially as supervisor on March 7. The final stage in the process of readying to work in Brčko began March 27 when I arrived in Sarajevo, the capital of Bosnia. The next two weeks were spent in as many or more dawn-to-dusk meetings and calls as those in Washington. This time, however, my interlocutors were not only Americans but ranged across a wide spectrum of experts and officials from many nations involved in bringing peace and stability to this nation torn by war and ethnic hatred.

In the United States and abroad, I viewed each of my meetings as an opportunity to open channels of communication and, where possible, reach some preliminary understanding of the sort of cooperation that would be pivotal in attaining our common objectives in Brčko. I heard each organization's thoughts on the parties to the conflict and what issue was paramount to bringing about peace. Many people offered advice. Throughout my preparatory time, I would reflect back on the day's proceedings. I was soon convinced that Brčko was a pivotal issue whose resolution was at the top of the international agenda. A peaceful resolution of the dispute was vital to the establishment of a sustainable peace in Bosnia. This realization served both to intimidate and inspire me, with emphasis on the former. As each layer of the onion was pulled back, revealing more of what I was about to face, I began to question whether I was really the person for this job— whether I could handle it. I dealt with this uncertainty by using the awards as my guideposts.

PRESSING FLESH

When I arrived in Brčko on April 22, 1997, the beautiful sunny day was not reflected in the grim faces of several hundred Serbs who filled the street in front of OHR-Brčko's office. The crowd was anything but festive. As I stood for a moment taking in the scene from the top of the steps, former Swedish prime minister and then High Representative Carl Bildt (1995–1997) grabbed me by the arm and pulled me down the steps onto the street and into the crowd. When I asked where we were going, Bildt exclaimed over his shoulder, "Come on, I'm a politician don't forget!" The next thing I knew, we, along with our startled security details, were in the midst of the disgruntled crowd. People began firing questions at Bildt because they recognized him. One man with a fierce mustache and missing teeth shouted out that he would never live with "them" again because "they" had burned down his home. Bildt asked the man if he knew exactly who had burned down his home. The fellow said a neighbor had done it. Bildt then asked the angry fellow why he did not confine his hatred to his neighbor rather than blame his neighbor's entire ethnic group for burning down the house. The hubbub of the crowd drowned out the fellow's response, but I learned a valuable lesson from this brief encounter—it was good and proper to "press the flesh," to engage directly with the man in the street, to show no fear. People respond to people and Bildt's action that day was a "people thing" to do. In establishing and maintaining my authority I realized I need not—indeed, should not—be totally austere and aloof from the people of Brčko.

This policy was translated into my approach with the local leaders. Early on, Ian McLeod,[1] my British deputy, and my newly appointed Russian deputy, Gennadiy Ivanovich Shabannikov,[2] and I agreed we needed to size up the neighborhood, and get to know the people and those that passed for their leaders to get a better feel for the situation on the ground. I deemed it important to meet local actors in their own environment. Some on my staff argued this was the wrong approach. In their view, I should summon Brčko's *three* mayors, first singly and then as a group, to my office to lay down a marker about who was who. A lifetime of working with people, however, had persuaded me of the utility of meeting people first on their own turf, where they would be at home and marginally more comfortable in receiving a stranger. My deputies and I traveled together as a sign of cohesion and unity of purpose when meeting local leaders. The arrangement served to ensure that our initial impressions of the personalities with whom we would be interacting grew in parallel and at the same pace. Although I did most of the talking, Ian, Gennadiy, and I shared perceptions before and after each of these early meetings so that our message of intent to implement the Dayton peace process, while constant and unbending, could be adapted subtly for each audience.[3] Gradually, as our separate workloads grew and we began to hear the community referring to us as the "Three Musketeers," we dropped the joint meetings, except where circumstances required them. This policy of meeting representatives of all three ethnic groups and their religious counterparts—Serbian Orthodox, Muslim, and Roman Catholic clerics, both locally and away in Bijeljina, Tuzla, and Sarajevo, as appropriate—regularly and on rotational basis *in their own offices* continued during my tenure in Brčko.

Pressing flesh allows one to hear the parties' different messages. When I first arrived in Brčko, Miodrag Pajić was serving as Serb mayor in the area north of the IEBL. He was full of reasonableness and tried to get us to believe he was ready to cooperate in any way, despite the fact the Serbs had deep reservations about the First Award. Munib Jusufović's message was different from that of Pajić—the Bosniaks of the Rahić-Brčko community south of the IEBL would hang tough. If, at the end of the period of supervision, the arbitral tribunal awarded final authority over Brčko to the Serbs, his people would refuse to submit to RS laws and regulations. He himself would not go back to Brčko *grad* if the Serbs remained in power, and indicated at some point there would be a line of principle he would be unable to cross. Mijo Anić, mayor of the Croat region of the Brčko prewar *opština* now known as Ravne-Brčko, provided an overview of the situation from his community's point of view and left us with the impression the Croats would let the more numerous Serbs and Bosniaks duke it out over Brčko *grad*. Then, under the cloud of dust this

Photo 2.1. Brčko's Three Mayors, with Secretary of State Madeleine Albright (second from left), and Bill Farrand (far right), 1997 (Photograph by Ian McLeod)

created, his people would quietly slide back into their villages to the west of town. My intention was to use these meetings with the local leadership as starting points for the long process that lay ahead in trying to understand the fundamental differences between the three factions and to identify over time areas of agreement. To reduce the former and expand the latter was, of course, the goal here. I was in no hurry during our early encounters with the mayors and their deputies to press for solutions. Essentially, I used these first meetings to listen carefully to what each mayor had to say, keeping my comments to a minimum. We thought it important to let the mayors vent their grievances and frustrations—for they all harbored both—and to stay in the mode of empathetic listeners until they got it all out. At some point, of course, we would have to move, but I wanted to be in as strong a position as possible in terms of understanding local attitudes when that moment came.

The pressing of flesh must be consistent. As an example, a few short weeks after I arrived in Brčko one of my staff members, Anna Nylander, reported that the local Bosniak leaders south of the IEBL were complaining loudly and publicly that I was ignoring them. For some time, a dozen or so Bosniak *mjesne zajednice* (MZ) leaders had been routinely meeting on Monday mornings in the conference room in the Rahić-Brčko municipal

Photo 2.2. The "Three Musketeers," 1998 (Bill Farrand, Gennadiy Ivanovich Shaban-nikov, and Ian McLeod; photograph from the author's collection)

building to exchange views and let off steam on the current situation. This weekly meeting was closely monitored by representatives of the international community—especially OHR, SFOR, and aid agencies concerned with returns—as a bellwether of anxieties and emotions south of the IEBL. The room was generally packed with observers as the MZ leaders vented their frustration and complaints to the chairperson, Mayor Jusufović. Anna said at that week's meeting one vocal MZ leader stood up and loudly declaimed: "The supervisor is ignoring us! He's spending all his time up in Brčko *grad* eating lamb and chasing women!" Anna said the rest of the MZ leaders nodded vigorously in agreement. A few weeks later I set aside a Monday morning to go south down the deep-rutted, potholed, mud-covered road the military had renamed Route Kiwi to appear at the weekly gathering of MZ leaders. I spoke for twenty minutes and answered questions for nearly an hour. Grudging smiles and handshakes were given all around—lesson learned. Unless civilian peace implementers follow the simple rule of meeting frequently and in a more or less sequential way with all parties in the disputed area, they will find themselves accused by one faction or the other of either favoritism or of playing games. That is a sure recipe for losing one's authority and descending into irrelevance.

Pressing the flesh also translated into dining out in the darkened city on many an evening, moving from one "mom and pop" restaurant to the next. This simple act seemed to be an effective means of connecting with the local populace and setting the rumor mills in motion with tidbits on what I did and did not like to eat. Sometime later I learned that the word had gotten around that the supervisor was not a monster, that he was heard to laugh out loud, and that he enjoyed a light moment with friends and strangers alike. And, get this, he drank local instead of imported beer and downed a glass of *šljivovica*, the ubiquitous Balkan plum brandy, after the meal! This delicate weaving of goodwill, of course, could be expected to do little more than create an image of someone who chose not to inhabit an ivory tower, aloof and imperious.

Finally, given the level of distrust and suspicion held by opposing communities in a postwar setting, civilian decision makers should consider the benefits to their image that can accrue from making a good-faith effort to learn simple phrases and even a few stock sentences to sprinkle about in formal and informal settings. Often, simply learning the sound system of the local language permits the peace implementer to mouth whole sentences even where fluency is a distant dream. Language is the great leveler, and if you can show your audience that you are trying to speak their tongue, they will warm to you in intangible but real ways. Having formally studied the Russian language and informally the Czech language, both of which are in the family of Slavic tongues that includes, of course, Serbo-Croatian, I was able with some adjustment to adapt myself to the sound system. While I am sure my accent grated on many ears, it slowly but surely improved to the point that I was not embarrassed to use it sparingly in public, which I did whenever the situation seemed ripe for it. On the whole, I think people were somewhat mollified by the fact that I made the effort to learn the language at all. However, there are dangers in flirting with a tongue that is not your own. Among the phrases I found useful to commit to memory was the sentence "*Drago mi je da to čujem!*" translated into English as "I am very happy to hear it!" I found I could use this simple expression in both formal and informal settings when I knew, through my interpreter, what was being said. I would not overuse it, but rather sprinkle it casually once or twice in a long conversation. One day, however, my glib phrase tripped me up. An elderly Serb woman had dropped by our office to make a request of some sort or other and I bumped into her in the passageway. "*Dobar dan!*" (Good day!) I said cheerily and she replied, "*Dobar dan!*" mistaking my greeting for an invitation to unload her problems and concerns on me. Wishing not to seem unresponsive or in a hurry, but knowing she needed to address her entreaties to the experts on our staff, I tarried a moment before directing her to the proper office. At one point in her peroration she confided that in addition to all her other problems, just the other day her companion of fifteen years, a black-and-white spaniel, had died. In my haste to move on, but still wanting to appear empathetic, I blurted out my favorite phrase: "*Drago mi je da to čujem!*" Not one of my shining moments . . .

WORK-STYLE DIFFERENCES

In discussing work styles I need to first point out this assignment was truly unlike others I had experienced in the Foreign Service. As a professional diplomat, I well understood the goals and objectives of my trade to represent the interests of the United States in whichever host country I was assigned. Like most diplomats, my authority rarely had extended beyond observing, analyzing, and reporting on developments in a host country; suggesting policy options where necessary; and once a policy line was decided upon, supporting it in face-to-face meetings with host-country officials. Taken together, these functions were essentially passive in nature, at least insofar as the host country's government was concerned. Put another way, none of them involved interfering in the internal affairs of the host country. In contrast, when I delved into the First Award and learned what I was called upon to do as supervisor, it dawned on me with stunning clarity that not only was I expected to interfere directly in the affairs of the Brčko *opština*, but I was also meant to run the place as a sort of proconsul. To implement peace, I was given the authority to promulgate binding regulations and orders, which would prevail against any conflicting law. I was expected to ensure freedom of movement; establish a program to govern the return of former residents; ensure the conduct of free and fair elections and follow this up with directives to enhance democratic governance and the creation of a multiethnic administration; and assist international development agencies to implement an economic revitalization program for Brčko. As an implementer rather than an architect of the peace accords, I faced the practical problem of translating goals and objectives into actual, palpable change on the ground—*real* results in *real* time under *real* conditions. This required a sharp shift in approach from passive observer to active participant.

Not only is there a difference in professional work styles between what I had performed as a diplomat and this civilian administrator position, marked differences exist between operating as a civilian in a post-conflict environment as opposed to a member of a military force. It is not my purpose in these pages to undertake an exhaustive comparative critique of civilian versus military approaches to mission management but to underscore for those who are about to embark on peace operations where both military and civilian components are in the same place, working toward the same goal—and for the life of me I cannot imagine where both would *not* be together on the ground—that such differences exist and are deeply embedded in both systems. While they may converge over time in small ways, they are unlikely to change at the core. Unless this fact is generally understood and accepted by players in both camps, a significant degree of dissonance will arise to complicate communications between the two communities.

Few civilians in or out of government have even a bare understanding of the complex process military planners go through in deploying forces. This is especially the case since the draft was ended in 1974 and few civilians active in American government today can point to military service at an earlier point in their lives. Civilians have little idea of the level of complexity to which the U.S. Army—the force generally called upon to perform these longer-term peace operations—must go in every aspect of its manifold functions. Little or nothing is left to chance. If an operation needs doing, the army will need to train repetitively and often to do it. Depending on the level of criticality, doctrine will be written to define and delimit the operation and to prescribe the training required for its fulfillment. The key point is, however, that the capability will be covered from all angles. Every effort will be made to fill the preparatory gaps between training for a mission and its execution.

This highly structured approach to problem solving has several positive qualities. It inspires a "can-do" attitude, especially when the objective is clearly defined. It breaks large problems down into their component parts so they become more amenable to solution. Finally, it creates an aura of finiteness to all problems—they have a beginning and, most important, an end. But there is a negative side to the military technique for addressing problems. For example, the need for clearly spelled out objectives fosters a sense of impatience with ambiguity that can lead to a certain narrowness of outlook and unwillingness to contemplate alternative—less direct, less structured—ways of addressing complex issues.

Civilian decision makers, on the other hand, proceed in a somewhat more open and less structured way. In the State Department, for example, a tasking will come down from higher levels to the regional or functional desk to draft a plan, or memorandum, laying out the essential facts of an issue, its history, and options for addressing it. The "tasker" will contain a deadline for submission and will direct the drafting office to "clear" its concept paper with other selected bureaus and offices within the State Department. Once a draft product has been fully cleared and all objections and emendations have been taken into account, the memorandum will move to higher levels—not infrequently to the Secretary of State—for decision. If the matter is of sufficient magnitude to require interagency coordination, the National Security Council will be drawn in to perform the coordinative function. At this point, the clearance process, as it now involves other agencies, will become more complex and time-consuming.

Apart from procedures established for moving paper along, however, the process is relatively free-flowing with many "off-line" conversations in person and by phone. The odd staff meeting may be convened to focus on the topic but such will be, in comparison, small and characterized by informal, loose-flowing debate that, while grade will be taken into account, is not wholly dominated by hierarchy. First names, not titles and ranks, are the order of the day. In the interagency arena, differences will often be horse-traded away so that a balanced policy position can, if necessary, go before the president. The civilian decision-making process is, therefore, often suffused in ambiguous and subjective criteria that may at times be rooted in political ideology. Recommendations for action are often fashioned to accommodate a wide array of competing interests and may emerge as the lowest common denominator. Gone is the crisp language of the military operation's order with its precise timelines and quantified objectives. The State Department, for example, tends not to proceed on doctrine. Indeed, department publications and manuals disseminated over the years to guide diplomats in the rudiments of their trade are generally, with the exception of consular and administrative manuals, gathering dust on shelves.

The foregoing is a frightfully truncated description of the decision-making process at State. Although it shamelessly overlooks the myriad informal relationships between civilian actors at all levels and largely ignores the role of personalities that is always at work, it nonetheless gives a sense of the difference between the civilian and military approaches to decision making. Thus, to a military observer, civilians—especially in a conflict zone—can seem disorganized, unfocused, and, worse, downright frivolous in their attitude toward mission accomplishment. By the same token, the civilian practitioner tends to perceive in his or her military counterpart a comparatively rigid and unbending mindset in adjusting to new and changing conditions.

This is a factual rather than argumentative point I am making here, and it helps explain the strong reaction to our work by Camp McGovern's battalion commander, who entered my office a week or so after we arrived in Brčko.[4] The supervisor's two-story headquarters building was a leased structure that had housed a commercial trading enterprise under the Yugoslav system before the war. The top floor consisted of offices. The main floor had been designed as a sales showroom, which meant the "wall" facing the street was little more than a row of plate glass windows. The lower floor, partly below ground, had additional office space. Near the end of April, the commander of McGovern Base, Lieutenant Colonel (LTC) Jim Greer, had come to our building to attend a joint meeting chaired by one of my senior staff members. As the meeting progressed, the commander reportedly became distressed by what he was seeing and hearing. After several minutes, according to a junior staffer who ran upstairs to inform me, Greer exclaimed that we—the supervisor and his staff—were going to fail, indeed, were already failing in our mission. Later, others who were present at the meeting told me they interpreted Greer's outburst to mean he was unhappy not to hear the outlines of a grand strategy, nor to see an operations room up and running à la standard military practice.

At the time, I faulted LTC Greer for his outburst, but after three years working cheek-by-jowl with the U.S. Army—an experience that has been enriched and deepened by heavy exposure to the army as a civilian consultant since I returned from Brčko —I can now fully empathize with how he reacted that day. For my part, I called in a U.S. Army Civil Affairs officer who had been assigned to my staff under the Civil-Military Cooperation (CIMIC) program[5] and asked if he knew how to set up an operations center. LTC James Rogers, who had a doctorate in operations analysis, replied that he did, and I commissioned him to establish such a room without delay. By the end of the week, we had an operations center replete with maps, colored pins, and status boards supposedly measuring progress in all sorts of areas. From that point on, when visitors—especially military visitors—came to call, I invariably ended my briefing with a stroll through our operations center. Greer must have been mollified, because we never heard another peep out of him about our trajectory toward failure. Personally, however, I never used the operations center for any serious purpose other than show—yet another object lesson in the different approaches to problem solving between the civilian and military worlds.

Work-style differences may be linked to, or reflections of, our respective concepts of time. Simply put, concerns over the pace of progress had already begun to arise among military commanders and their logistics planners at the time of the Greer outburst, principally because, as I now see clearly in retrospect, they were coming under severe pressure from Washington to begin putting in place a plan—an "exit strategy"—for complete withdrawal of U.S. forces from Bosnia by the summer of 1998.[6] The June 1998 target date for withdrawal had been widely put about in capitals and was, therefore, well known to the indicted war criminal and Bosnian Serb leader Radovan Karadžić (1992–1996) and his colleagues, who were doing all they could to obstruct Dayton implementation from their headquarters in the village of Pale, located in the hills some fifteen kilometers east of Sarajevo just inside the RS.[7] From my perspective, a more self-defeating policy could hardly be imagined than that of announcing publicly and often your plans for leaving a crisis zone. Yet that was how the Clinton administration (1993–2001) chose to find a way between those who saw the need for military engagement in Bosnia and those, mostly Republicans, who held firmly to the view that the U.S. military was to be used solely for fighting wars—period. Such announcements reinforce

Photo 2.3. The Supervisor's Office, 1997 (Photograph by Ian McLeod)

the hard-liners' view that they can outlast the international community and at the same time demoralize those in the indigenous populace who are silently rooting for the international community to stay the course in imposing peace on their tortured land. I literally cringed whenever I heard that yet another four-star general in the Pentagon had said publicly that U.S. forces would be withdrawing from Bosnia on a certain date. Both Karadžić and his mentor, FRY president Slobodan Milošević (1997–2000), understood English well and had full access via satellite TV and the Internet to such statements. In the game of poker what do you gain by showing a card needlessly?

FORM POSITIVE AND OPEN RELATIONSHIPS
WITH YOUR MILITARY COUNTERPARTS

About two weeks after I had arrived in Brčko, General William W. Crouch, the commander of Allied Land Forces Central Europe, invited me to dinner at SFOR headquarters in Ilidža, a municipality in Sarajevo. Several others were in attendance including Major General (MG) Montgomery Meigs, commander of Multinational Division-North (MND-North);[8] a newly arrived general from the German Army named Werner Widder; Deputy High Representative Michael Steiner, accompanied by OHR's new chief of staff, Admiral Ian Forbes; and OHR political advisor Christian Clages. The purpose of the dinner, Steiner had informed me beforehand, was to cement relations between my office and SFOR. Apparently, there was a feeling we needed to be in closer touch. While I had no argument with that sentiment as a going-in proposition, I saw two problems. First, SFOR, in its need to have everything wrapped up before June 1998—exactly twelve months off—wanted my mission in Brčko to succeed greatly. Second, I had only twenty-four hours in a day, like everyone else. I could only surmise that, up to that point having smothered me with offers of help and advice, SFOR was disappointed with my less than totally responsive stance and, thus, a sense of anxiety was rising in headquarters that somehow the Brčko undertaking, now nearly a month old, was going off the rails. When I gently broached this point of view during the meal, our SFOR hosts assured me this was not the case at all.

In any event, I sought to reassure those present that we had matters reasonably well in hand and that I would certainly call upon them for advice and counsel, even personnel, when appropriate. But—and this goes to the establishment of authority theme of this chapter—I explained that what I wanted to avoid was the impression that my small organization was overwhelmed with uniformed military personnel coming to "help" me and, in the process, transforming the supervisor's office from a civilian implementation unit into an organization with large military overtones. It would not, in my view, serve either SFOR's or our interests for that to happen, since SFOR would not be able, in the end, to follow through on initiatives mandated in the First Award for civilians to implement. That said, I hastened to add that the civilian operation in Brčko depended fundamentally on the presence of a palpable, disciplined, well-equipped military force to provide the secure environment so necessary for our work.

The conversation ended on a positive note with all present agreeing that more could and should be done to maintain closer contact between OHR-Brčko and SFOR in the future. Indeed, a practical outgrowth of this meeting was that General Meigs and I agreed to get together on a regular basis each week at either Camp McGovern, or Tuzla Main, for a complete review of where matters stood in Brčko. These meetings gradually induced an element of trust between our two different cultures. Without this basic, nay, *essential*, level of trust between senior civilian and military officials in a post-conflict theater, the likelihood of a successful peace implementation campaign *will* be cast into serious doubt.

The following story is offered to illustrate this level of trust, plus perhaps how—once understood—the predictability of the military system of management may serve as a positive aspect for the civilian administrator. One day I was invited to the Croat village of Krepsić, four kilometers west of Brčko *grad*, to speak to the Serbs who had been squatting there for a couple of years. Most of the Serbs had been driven from their homes in the predominantly Croat city of Jajce, about a hundred kilometers southeast of Brčko in the Federation. I had been briefed by my chief of staff, Tim Yates, that the Serbs in Krepsić were angry—no surprises there—and worried about their homes in Jajce. Although it was a warm Sunday afternoon under a perfect sky, our hosts ushered us into what appeared once to have been used as a small cattle barn. Our eyes struggled to adapt as we stepped from the sunlight into the barn's dark interior where upwards of fifty sullen-faced men were sitting on benches or leaning against the walls, waiting to hear what I would have to say. After attempting some light banter with a few of the men, I walked to the center of the room where the sun was shining through the only window, introduced myself, and began by saying that I was there not so much to talk as to listen. At that, a nervous fellow rose from his bench on my left and asked me in a loud, menacing voice what I intended to do about the SFOR soldiers that were harassing children along the highway and destroying crops with their tanks. I asked the man for particulars and he said a soldier at an SFOR checkpoint outside of Krepsić had attempted in broad daylight to lure his twelve-year-old daughter away by offering her a piece of candy the other day. Also, an SFOR tank had driven straight over an elderly lady's garden, ruining her crops. "What," he cried, "do you intend to do about those outrageous acts?" I asked the man whether he had reported both incidents to the police. He made no reply. After a pause, I told the fellow he should submit a detailed, written report on both occurrences to the police without delay. I said while I would be happy to see a copy of the police report, my initial reaction was to reject his charge about the soldier luring his daughter with a piece of candy and, as regarded the story of an SFOR tank running its treads over someone's garden, SFOR would both repair the garden and compensate the lady for her loss if the incident could be proven to have happened. At this, the fellow seemed to lose his voice and sat down. We then went on with the meeting, exploring every twist and turn of their program for return to Jajce.

The point of the foregoing vignette lies in the complete confidence I had in the discipline and professional behavior of the U.S. Army troops stationed within a stone's throw of my area of supervision. Because I was fully informed about the SFOR battalion's rules of engagement and its local code of conduct, I had no qualms, as a civilian, in stoutly defending SFOR against charges of misconduct before an angry crowd, in press conferences, in front of TV cameras, or in one-on-one interviews. I never once had to eat my words. And on those rare occasions where I did not fully agree with a SFOR action or decision, I sought to fashion my public remarks so that there would be no hint of daylight between SFOR's position and my own.

In the vast majority of cases, SFOR and my office got on just fine and sang from the same broad sheet of music. This constructive relationship depended in large part on frequent but irregular contact between the SFOR liaison officer (LNO) on my staff and his counterparts at Camp McGovern;[9] weekly meetings scheduled between the battalion commander and myself; and monthly meetings between the commander of MND-North and me, either at SFOR headquarters in Tuzla or at the smaller Camp McGovern. It would be hard to exaggerate the importance I attached to keeping lines of communication between my office and MND-North, at its two command levels, wide open and amenable to immediate access. When problems arose, I sought to resolve them as quickly as possible and preferably face-to-face with my military counterparts so that lingering questions could be ironed out on the spot. This is the hard nugget of advice I would encourage the reader, civilian or military, to take away from this discussion.

FORM POSITIVE AND OPEN RELATIONSHIPS
WITH YOUR CIVILIAN COUNTERPARTS

Thrust into the middle of a nearly chaotic crisis zone that had few antecedents to serve as models for action, I immediately began shoring up my rickety grasp of local ethnic power relationships by turning for tactical guidance to my staff and the representatives of other international agencies, all of whom were more familiar with the lay of the land than I. From the outset I wanted to be seen and understood not only as the man in charge but as a person open to advice, eager to communicate with one and all. My intuition led me to a conclusion, aptly put into words two years later by Ian McLeod's successor, Andrew Joscelyne: "Although you can govern by diktat, you don't want to." Truth to tell, I would not have known how to govern by diktat had I tried, since as a diplomat accustomed to negotiation and compromise, my instincts led me in other, less Draconian, directions. So I set out to supervise with light strokes at first, testing the ground as I went along. Later, as and when the hammer was needed, I turned to the supervisory order to effect changes needed.

As the head of a multinational staff in a multiethnic crisis zone, I was intent on getting to know personally every member of my staff and the senior staffs of all international agencies, in order to share with them my vision and plans for tackling the manifold problems that lay ahead. It was vital, in this connection, to insure that information would flow freely among us and as close as possible to real time. Since we were operating in a multinational, and therefore unclassified, world, I judged there to be little need for excessive secrecy—to what end? With several international organizations and nongovernmental organizations (NGOs) operating in the Brčko area of supervision, each with its own agenda and set of internal goals and objectives, there needed to be a point of coordination, and I took it to be the supervisor who should perform that role. After wrestling with how most efficiently to tap into the enormous pool of expertise available to me, and following a few false starts with the format for daily staff meetings, Ian McLeod and my special assistant, Karen Decker, designed a plan to improve time management and internal communications, and to bring people and organizations together for maximum effect. First, we prevailed upon OHR-Sarajevo to establish a small Brčko working group that would, in addition to the normal obligations of its members, follow events in Brčko reasonably closely and stand ready to facilitate—and, where necessary, expedite—*within* OHR-Sarajevo matters related to Brčko and its needs. The chief of staff was by then Judge Patt Maney, a U.S. Army Civil Affairs officer who, having understudied under then deputy high representative Jock Covey, was an enthusiastic backer of the Brčko mission. Maney, like Covey, "got it." Second, we decided to tighten up on morning staff meetings so that what had degenerated into hour-long rambling group discussions would henceforth focus only on operational and administrative issues confronting us that very day. Longer-term questions involving major decisions were to be kept off the table. Daily staff meetings would be rigidly held to thirty minutes, in and out. Since we had been meeting for an hour or more six mornings a week, the new format would save us three hours a week, which we gave back to ourselves in a once-a-week strategy session. Third, an hour before the truncated daily staff meeting, Ian, Gennadiy, and I met with representatives of the other international organizations in town—UN/IPTF, OSCE, UNHCR, UN Civil Affairs, SFOR, the Customs and Fiscal Assistance Office—in my office to review overnight events and their plans for the day. Fourth, and finally, we scheduled weekly strategy sessions to be held at 3:00 p.m. on Saturday afternoons, to be attended by department heads and selected others, a dozen persons in all.[10] We discussed strategies for dealing with the larger questions that required policy decisions and formal positions by the supervisor. The agenda was usually limited to three and no more than four topics agreed to beforehand. We encouraged comprehensive, wide-ranging debate and occasionally invited outsiders with special expertise to take part. Special Assistant Decker, and her successors David Greenberg and William Cammett, circulated notes to participants after the meeting, including actions to be taken.

This scheme, arrived at in August 1997 after three months of groping about, permitted information to flow relatively unimpeded while keeping staff frustration with meetings to a minimum. In addition, of course, I attended several weekly and bimonthly meetings that I either chaired or co-chaired: a weekly gathering of heads of international agencies in my office on Tuesday evenings; a monthly gathering of regional heads of all international agencies in MND-North at SFOR headquarters in Tuzla; as well as the previously mentioned meetings at Camp McGovern with the commander of MND-North to discuss security-related matters.

I have taken the time here to describe the format and schedule of meetings because they are so very essential to an effective and well-coordinated peace operation. Absent such meetings, the overall effort will quickly descend into confusion, disorder, and eventually organizational entropy will set in. Despite the firewall embedded in the DPA between the military and civilian sectors of responsibility, there could be no question of the need for consultation—close, continual consultation—between the leadership on both sides of this divide if progress was to be made. Simple common sense dictated that consultation and information sharing of the freest kind occur regularly and often, both among civilian implementing agencies and between them and the military. To do less was to court failure and even disaster. Progress in a complex contingency operation such as Brčko depends crucially upon each international organization "staying in its lane" and performing its assigned function in the most effective way it can. As Ian McLeod often reminded me: "If one agency strays into the lane of another, then who will do that agency's work?" As regarded Brčko, a large part of the modest success we attained in restoring a semblance of order and the early glimmerings of reconciliation to a community had more than a little to do with the practice we consciously promoted of sharing information, as well as the criteria for decisions, on an open and nonexclusionary basis among local representatives of the international community.

In making this point, my relations with two key UN offices in Brčko, UN/IPTF and the United Nations Mission in Bosnia and Herzegovina (UNMIBH), come to mind. From the first day, I invited both the commander of the 258-person UN/IPTF and his putative superior, the Civilian Police (CIVPOL) advisor from UNMIBH, to attend our early morning staff meeting with other agency representatives. Since I was blissfully unaware of the internal pecking order within the UN hierarchy, and as I encountered no resistance to my desire to hear from both men each morning, the arrangement held for two years under two Special Representatives of the Secretary General (SRSGs) and multiple changes of personnel in each job. Both SRSG Kai Eide (Norway) and Elizabeth Rehn (Finland) were professionally committed to the Brčko arbitration issue and concerned that the supervisor be given all the backing he needed to move the process along. It was also true that the people involved—from the SRSG, to the CIVPOL advisor, to the UN/IPTF commander—were of one mind regarding the overriding need to support the Brčko mission. Such personality differences as may have existed within the UN family were submerged for the common good.

Riding on this benevolent wave of cooperation, I was able directly to tap into the expertise of both local UN offices virtually around the clock. This resulted in a much defter handling of two major riots that occurred in the Brčko *grad*, as well as the installation of the first multiethnic—indeed triethnic—police force in all of BiH. The formation of the multiethnic government following the elections of September 1997 and then, again, after the handing down of the Final Award in March 1999 were in good part attributable to advice UN Civil Affairs officers Salman Ahmed and Eric Scheye, both superb young political analysts with practical bents, gave my staff and me from their reading of the local political tea leaves.[11] On the UN/IPTF side, Commander Donald Grady, the former chief of police of Santa Fe, New Mexico, who held a doctorate in public administration from Walden University, ably and courageously led his force of police advisors in overcoming the resistance of local Serb police to doing their job in tight spots and, when the time came, in transforming the Brčko police force from a collection of ex-Serb war fighters to a burgeoning body of professional policemen and -women. Because of our amicable daily interaction, not only with me but also with key members of my staff, I was, as supervisor, able to extend my operational reach significantly while projecting an image of unity and solidarity on these crucial issues. This latter effect was most important, given the well-known proclivity of local obstructionists to "play the crease"—to ferret out policy differences between international agencies and, by exploiting those differences, seek to play agencies off against one another. So easy and fluid became our working relationship that I began to look upon both UN offices as extensions of my office in our daily struggle against local diehards and obstructionists. UN Civil Affairs officer Scheye once confided to me that because of the mutual trust we enjoyed, he made it a point routinely to drop by my office late on Sunday afternoon, when he knew I would be working alone and in a relatively relaxed frame of mind, to chew the fat on a range of police-related issues, freely and without constraint. I also vividly recall a conversation with UN/IPTF Commander Grady, who had dropped by to say hello late one Saturday evening, turning into an informal skull session on how to introduce modern policing to Brčko's soon-to-be multiethnic police force. We parted company at 3:00 a.m. Sunday morning! As a newcomer to city government, I was uncommonly grateful for these impromptu exchanges with real-life experts on civilian policing, a topic about which I had little knowledge and even less experience.

Partial confirmation that my take on the efficacy of open versus closed sharing of information (at a minimum) and engagement in decision making (as the ideal) came several months later when, back at my home in Virginia, I received a phone call one day from Ed Joseph, a former colleague who had served for nearly a year as head of the OSCE regional office in Brčko. It seems that after leaving Brčko and decompressing for a few months in the United States, Joseph had signed on to head up the operations of a large NGO in Kosovo. Besides calling to inquire how I was adapting to life in the slow lane, Joseph said he wanted to share with me some thoughts about Kosovo and how his life there compared to his experience in Brčko. Joseph said his routine inclusion—even more, welcome—at the supervisor's table in Brčko stood in sharp contrast to the exclusive, tight-lipped working climate among international agencies he encountered in Kosovo. Brushing aside my demurrer that Kosovo was different from Brčko and may have called for a tighter approach, Joseph said our modus operandi in Brčko was unquestionably a more enlightened way of managing post-conflict crises anywhere. He lamented its absence in Kosovo.

I can say without apology that I found my first brush working within an organization staffed with experts from two dozen countries one of the more fascinating and rewarding experiences of my diplomatic career. It also had its surprises. The first major difference to jar my sensibilities—habituated as I was to working in a world where words like "top secret," "confidential," "secure facility," and the like filled my day—was the absence of classified documents and a secure communications system. All operational instructions and information were passed over telephone lines, speaking in the clear for oral communications and sending by fax for written communications, which were only slowly being restored from war damage. A nascent system of e-mail also depended on access to the poorly configured telephone system. In fact, for our first year in Brčko, OHR's e-mail server was physically located in the OHR support office in Brussels, Belgium. So, to dial up your e-mail account, you needed first to connect with the Brussels server, a process that entailed entering a long cyber queue since there were always others in the OHR system waiting to get online. Once in the queue, you then had to hope that the arm of a construction crane operating on a building site next door to OHR's Brussels office had not swung around in such a way as to block your cyber pulse, which traversed its last few miles by radio beam! If the crane's arm stood between the last radio relay and OHR's receiver station, you were out of luck. If, on the other hand, the arm remained out of the way, your pulse would enter the Brussels server and instantly be routed back to the intended addressee at OHR headquarters in Sarajevo, only 150 miles (225 kilometers) south of Brčko! It took several months for this crude system to be streamlined so that our computers could stay permanently online and free of mundane obstacles like construction cranes. Every situation is unique, of course, but the practitioners of peace operations need to be prepared to contend with such bewildering eventualities, even in this high-tech age, so that they are not thrown unduly off stride. For the military reader of these pages, it will be enough simply to be aware that glitches of this type occur more often in the civilian than in the military world and can become impediments to civilian decision making.

Another interesting phenomenon in these types of operations, and one that the civilian peace administrator must accept and become thoroughly comfortable with, is the fact that members of your multinational staff will be sending their home governments, on a more or less regular basis, appraisals of developments in the organization and its mission. This may take place openly and in full view or quietly and behind the scenes, but you may count on its happening one way or the other. Some administrators will see in this practice a threat to their role and mission and may, therefore, unwisely seek to put a crimp in such communications in the name of organizational integrity and cohesion. I say "unwisely" because it is a hopeless task and to pursue it will only result in frayed nerves and a frustrated, diminished administrator. Better by far, in my view, openly to accept the practice and embrace it. In Brčko, my Russian deputy, Ambassador Gennadiy Ivanovich Shabannikov, would routinely spend several hours a week preparing a report to Moscow for transmission through the headquarters of the Russian SFOR contingent at Ugljevik, some fifty kilometers away to the southeast. Normally, as an ex-Soviet hand in the U.S. diplomatic corps, I would have been highly suspicious of such communications, not to say paranoid about them. But in the changed international circumstances following the collapse of communism, and knowing Gennadiy and his devotion to the arbitral process in Brčko, I had no qualms whatsoever about his reports, nor did I ever ask to see them. Hard to believe, perhaps, but I trusted him as a colleague and friend to report professionally, candidly, and in a manner that would advance our mutual interests. Whether it was those reports or other factors at work I cannot say, but the fact that the then Russian deputy foreign minister, Igor Ivanov, and the Russian special envoy for the Balkans, Viktor Chernomyrdin, visited Brčko (the latter, three times) for fruitful and pointed conversations with all three factions—but most importantly, given Russia's historic ties, with the Serbs—may be attributed at least in part to Gennadiy's back-channel reporting. In the proper atmosphere of trust and cooperation, such circuitous communications can work wonders in supporting your mission. Relax and let them wash over and around you. They are a fact of life.

GETTING YOUR WORD OUT: USE OF THE MEDIA

As I mentioned earlier, I made it a point to get out of the office and move around town as often as my schedule permitted. In late April 1997, a journalist for *Ekstra Magazin*, a Serb weekly, interviewed me in my office. Since this was my first one-on-one encounter with a local journalist, I used his questions as vehicles for wide-ranging answers that I hoped would come across as candid, open, and fundamentally friendly in tone. Threaded through the young Serb's questioning was an overriding solicitude for the immediate welfare of the town's Serb inhabitants as supervision commenced in earnest. Clearly, the rumor mill was alive with dire predictions, and enormous anxiety was building in the Serb community. The prime question on everyone's mind: Just who is this powerful new outsider who has come to live among us and run our lives? The journalist's questions honed in on my plans and priorities. Would I retain Serb policemen on Brčko's streets? What would be the pace of return of Bosniaks and Croats to their Serb-occupied homes? How did the situation in Brčko compare with that in Mostar? How would the world's "bad impression" of the Serbs affect the supervisor's attitude toward them? I tried to answer each query in as straightforward a manner as possible to show I had no agenda other than that laid out in the Dayton Accords and the First Award. Both were open documents that all could read, digest, and against which judge my performance.

On April 25, the article hit Brčko's sparse newsstands. Its opening paragraph, with apologies for inelegant translation, read: "After long announcements and previous introductions to the public, the supervisor for Brčko has finally arrived. The dull, customary performance of the foreign diplomat—typical of those who have formerly run through the town and to which we have become accustomed—has been shaken in this case for at least two reasons: First, he is not a passerby, but the boss (*hozjajin*) of this town whose words will have to be listened to whether we want to or not. And second, on a personal level, he has taken care to win over others with his directness— walking into stores and a nearby *burek*[12] place, wearing a smile and making a bow." The two-page article closed on the following note: "The idea of a stiff, cold, and restrained supervisor, who brings only anxiety and troubles to the Serbs, collapsed the moment he entered the nearby *burek* shop without an escort and with a smile on his face. Had he so chosen, he could have had a snack at some better place, but he wouldn't have drawn so many sympathies, while at the same time destroying possible prejudices about his mission being at the expense of the Serbs. The ice is melting, the conversation more spontaneous, and he is more talkative."

Civilian peace administrators need constantly to remind themselves that they are creating images both in what they do and in what they do not do. Since administrators cannot be everywhere at once, the media becomes for them an essential tool to lean on in getting out their message. There are real dangers in this, of course, especially if you become entangled with a hostile interviewer who will twist your words and their meaning. Nonetheless, in this one case, it worked for me. A simple, unannounced noontime visit to an eatery down the street had the unexpected—and salutary—effect of portraying me as someone who did not hold a deep grudge against the Serbs in town. In fact, I did not. Assigning guilt to every member of an ethnic or religious group for the sins of a few did not strike me as a particularly useful way to go about the complex process of lowering tensions in a community weary with war and at odds with itself. But my views on collective guilt were not known when I arrived in Brčko.

It is a simple truth that a civilian administrator's every word and action will be dissected for hidden meaning. Rightly or wrongly, mostly the latter, such speculations will be magnified in the invisible discourse that permeates the watching populace and washes over your person and office. Used wisely, this natural human phenomenon can be turned to your advantage. But to do that reliably you will need your own means of communicating with the general public, where necessary—and it will nearly always be necessary—over the heads of local power brokers. That is the ideal situation. But as luck and lack of prior planning would have it, our office in Brčko did not have, either in the beginning or throughout my period of supervision, a proprietary radio or television facility to broadcast our own version of events and our policy line. We thus were forced to rely on local media—such as they were, with all of their entrenched biases, hostile prejudices, and stunning lack of professionalism—to get our word out. In fact, since journalists from all three ethnic factions were pursuing me for interviews, I came to realize that the biases of one group would play off against the biases of the others. Thus, assuming their various publics were reading or hearing at least some of the others' reporting (admittedly a poor assumption given the levels of mutual hatred and suspicion), a certain rough balance might possibly emerge. Not much to count on, I knew, when accuracy in disseminating the word was at an absolute premium; but we were limited in time and circumstance.

In a great stroke of luck, I had been able to pull bureaucratic strings before leaving the United States and recruit Razvigor "Raz" Bazala, a former Foreign Service officer in the now-defunct U.S. Information Agency and speaker of Serbo-Croatian, to join my staff in Brčko as chief of our media and press section. As a professional information officer, Raz brought years of experience to the task of monitoring, analyzing, and responding to local media reporting, as well as arranging and preparing me for radio, print, and television appearances and interviews. Since we had no robust media outlets under our control, it became of paramount importance to track local news media either for sloppy mistakes or downright lies in reporting about supervisory actions, plans, or decisions, so that we could quickly correct the record.

Raz arranged biweekly press conferences in our premises that, in addition to me, included spokespersons for SFOR, UN/IPTF, OSCE, and UNHCR. Raz modeled this biweekly media event on a similar outreach effort taking place in Mostar, where the same lineup of international agencies met the press every other week under the auspices of OHR. Hostile in the beginning and dominated by Serbs, the press conferences gradually became, once freedom of movement across the IEBL was restored, events that attracted news people from the Federation as well as the RS. Occasionally, Western news media would attend, such as the U.S. Army's newspaper *Stars and Stripes*, Voice of America, and the like. Normally, I would kick off the press conference with a prepared five-minute statement on a topic or topics of particular relevance to the day. As my competence in the local language grew, I would read whole sentences and even paragraphs from my scripted speech, suitably translated in large block letters, in the local language. Inevitably, those would be the excerpts chosen for sound bites on TV elsewhere in BiH. I say "elsewhere" because Brčko had no television station, and in fact, TV transmitters in other parts of the country were not strong enough to reach Brčko, which sat in what technicians called a "TV shadow," caused partly by the physical configuration of the hills surrounding the municipality. As luck would have it, such TV signals as were able to reach Brčko emanated not from within BiH but from Belgrade, 150 kilometers to the east. As you might guess, Belgrade was far from a helpful source of news in those days.

On a good day, the supervisor's press conference might attract as many as seven TV stations from as far away as Banja Luka to the west and Tuzla to the south. Frequently TV crews from Sarajevo would turn up, resulting in portions of our press conference being carried in the Federation's (and BiH's) capital. Representatives from the radio and print media normally filled the room; in all, some forty or so news organizations carried away information and impressions from the conference. With the passage of time, our biweekly press conference became a fixture in the lives of local newspeople. For this reason, I prepared for it carefully by spending several hours consulting with staff, drafting the opening statement, coordinating the statement with other agency representatives, and selecting key passages from it for rendering in the local language.

Bazala also worked closely with the communications wing of the nearby SFOR base at Camp McGovern to utilize the U.S. Army's portable radio transmitter, complete with a mobile antenna, in developing a weekly radio show devoted to civilian administration that would feature in-depth interviews with the Brčko supervisor. The idea was to give me a radio forum that I would largely control, with SFOR's complete agreement. This initiative fit neatly into SFOR's in-theater mandate to facilitate civilian implementation of the DPA. Local commanders understood in a way their Pentagon superiors seemed either unwilling or unable to that the military's exit strategy from Bosnia was directly linked to the success of civilian peace implementers in completing their mission as well. To paraphrase the words of my friend Ambassador (ret.) John McDonald: "The only exit strategy that will work over time is to make sure you are leaving behind a safe, secure community whose economy is self-sustaining under the *rule of law*" [emphasis mine]. The transmitter's range was probably no more than fifty kilometers, and the frequency assigned to Radio Mir (peace) was not in a sweet spot on the local dial. Nonetheless, I would at long last have the capability, in an unhurried and controlled setting, to sound off on issues that all groups—Serb, Bosniak, and Croat—needed to hear about directly from me. So I jumped at the chance.

For what seem to have been countless weeks I carefully prepared a ten-minute opening statement for our Thursday evening rendezvous with what I hoped, on the basis of little evidence other than oral assurances, were hundreds of radio listeners in the makeshift studio of Radio Mir. The captive interviewer and emcee was an army warrant officer who worked out his questions with Bazala beforehand. Our respective interpreters separately interpreted the emcee's questions and my replies for the listening audience. In time, I began to detect flaws in the Radio Mir setup. For one thing, my host was an American soldier who had been a deejay in civilian life. An expert on neither the Balkans nor foreign policy, his questions were scripted beforehand and, like my answers, had to be interpreted for the radio audience, a process that chewed up several minutes in an hour-long program. Second, the army's portable transmitter and antenna had a limited broadcasting range, although I was assured we were covering most parts of the Brčko *opština*. Third, the normal fare of Radio Mir was popular Western music. While it may have been true that young local listeners preferred "turbofolk" over the more traditional music of their heritage, I was quite sure their parents, who were part of my target audience, were less drawn to the loud, pounding noise that made up the CD repertoire of SFOR's deejays. So, after nine months of spending most Thursday evenings being interviewed on Radio Mir, and never once receiving a direct indication from the local populace that my message was getting through, I gave it up.

Near the end of our first year, Bazala was pulled away for another assignment. A young British woman named Jennie Pierce took his place. She was followed by Montserrat Radigales in mid-1998. An experienced reporter from the Madrid daily *El Diario*, Montserrat was a close student of the Bosnian conflict and a human sponge for information. She provided me with encyclopedic daily updates on the news, not only as it related to Brčko, but from around all of BiH. While of exceptional value, the news can also be a trap for a decision maker who is strapped for time in moving his or her agenda forward. In fact, I would argue—and consistently did—that the decision maker needs someone on staff who can craft speeches and messages so that the endless flow of news coming in can be balanced, or at a minimum partially offset, by an outflow of newsworthy information. When you are on the receiving end of bad reporting and worse, your need is for a propagandist capable not only of drafting speeches for you to deliver, but also of developing and sustaining a media campaign over time—in short, someone who can help you manage the news. I was never able to satisfy this need. Essentially, we gave up this ground to the opposition who continued to attack us. The good news is that I learned how to write speeches over meals, in moving vehicles, and even while I was delivering them.

LOCAL CHALLENGES TO AUTHORITY

Let me relate a couple of stories to put flesh on two of my behavioral rules. The first rule has to do with opening informal lines of communication to those who wished neither the Dayton peace process nor me well. Left to my own instincts, I would have shunned these people, who were hell-bent on obstructing us at every turn. But Ian McLeod immediately sat me down and educated me about the utility of getting to know everyone, including our enemies. Having served two tours with the British Army in Northern Ireland, McLeod had experienced the importance of at least establishing lines of communication with the adversary so that in times of maximum threat you could make contact with him to divine his true intentions and demands. By the very act of communicating, you stood a chance of deflecting the potential for violence. It was, in any case, worth a try.

From then on, I welcomed opportunities to meet not only with SDS hard-liners, who actually pulled the strings behind Brčko's Serb mayors and their deputies, but also with their even harder-line counterparts in the SRS.[13] As Ian predicted, I found it highly useful to become personally acquainted with these characters so I could put faces to names when assessing our options for responding to threats. As an example, I was introduced to the local leader of the SRS, an ineffective fellow in his mid-forties named Jovo Jeftić, whom I came to know and, ironically, to like. This interaction gave me more confidence when the time eventually came in 1999 to exclude the SRS from participating in the formation of the new district government. I judged Jeftić and his lieutenants to be empty blusterers and their party a paper tiger, thus there would be no serious backlash.

Of all the local troublemakers none was more shadowy and sinister than the Serb ultranationalist Boško Maričić. Somewhere in his late forties, with black hair and small black eyes, he dressed in black from his shoes to his turtleneck sweater. Maričić operated out of Brčko's formerly state-owned furniture factory, where he held the title of director. Several months passed before I became aware of the role he was playing behind the scenes, fomenting violent resistance to the return of Bosniaks among Serb residents. But Maričić was well known on the street, as well as by SFOR, as Pale's organizer in Brčko, controlling a gang of thugs—mostly homegrown, but also recruited from Bijeljina and points east—whose sole aim was to disrupt life.

Suspecting that Maričić had a leading role organizing and hyping local Serb participation in riots that took place in Brčko on August 28, 1997, as well as in other less violent but nonetheless dangerous confrontations, we began to look for ways to flush him out. For starters, several of us paid an unannounced call on the industrial compound at the edge of town where Maričić's furniture factory was located. It was late in the afternoon and the factory appeared to be closed. In the failing light, however, we were able to peer through the shut factory's windows on a scene of overstuffed chairs and couches collecting dust. Nothing was moving, no lights were burning, and no workmen were in evidence. The place was empty, so we drove on.

Some days later, I sent word to Maričić through our economic unit that I would like to meet with him to discuss his business plans. Accordingly, a few days later, he came by the office in the evening accompanied by two heavies. Gennadiy and I received him in our conference room, and since Maričić spoke no English, we conversed through an interpreter. Having directed the U.S. Commercial Office in Moscow for two years (1976–1978), I knew how to talk with people like Maričić who knew little about the technical aspects of their industry and even less about the market for its products either at home or abroad. Such people were factory executives only because of membership in a political party—in this case, the SDS. We fenced for twenty minutes or so about the furniture industry in Bosnia, with me asking questions about his plans for restarting production with its implications for creating jobs, and Maričić dully replying "Yes" or "No" and only occasionally with a full sentence, never more.

Clearly, he was as uninterested in the world of furniture making as I was. After a decent interval, and to show me he was under no illusions about why I had called him in, Maričić asked whether I had learned enough about his furniture business. He suggested perhaps it was time to conclude our conversation. I thanked him for his time and said while I had certainly gained a better understanding of his plans for the furniture factory, I was more than a little concerned over the damage that events such as those of August 28 would do to the long-run prospects for peace and stability in Brčko. At that, Maričić came alive. His coal-black eyes lit up and he launched into an animated monologue about the precariousness of life for Serbs in Brčko in the face of a tidal wave of non-Serb returnees. No longer slumping arrogantly in his chair, Maričić was now leaning forward as he made no bones about the fact that the riots were a sign of the frustration of the people. After he had ranted on for several minutes, I stood and told him that further outbreaks of violence of that kind would not be tolerated. Reluctantly, he shook Gennadiy's and my hand and departed. So far as we were concerned, the meeting had gone well. Maričić now knew our eyes were on him.

I asked Gennadiy to take a special interest in Maričić, whom we now called "The Prince of Darkness." As SFOR was equally concerned about his ability to instigate turbulence in the Brčko area of responsibility, we further began routinely to share information on him. In the weeks following our conversation, Maričić quietly left his cushy job at the furniture factory only to reemerge in late December 1997 as head of the special police unit in the police headquarters downtown. This, just as UN/IPTF Commander Donald Grady was putting the finishing touches on his plan to install a restructured, multiethnic police force based on ethnic showings in the September elections. At the same time, several newly certified policemen informed Grady we could expect an orchestrated attempt to obstruct implementation of our October 13, 1997, Supervisory Order regarding multiethnic policing. According to our informants, this obstruction would take the form of a work slowdown, demonstrations, and physical intimidation of Bosniak and Croat policemen on patrol. Thus was Pale moving to ensure that no matter how we restructured the Brčko police department, the Serbs would remain in clandestine control.

On hearing all of this, Gennadiy swung into action, first calling on Maričić's brother, who lived next door to his flat, to relay a not-so-subtle message that we were on to the game Boško Maričić was playing. Second, we asked SFOR to support Gennadiy's message with its own not-so-subtle tactic of rumbling a four-vehicle Humvee patrol into Maričić's cul-de-sac to reconnoiter his neighborhood. As anyone familiar with the fully armed Humvee knows, it is a somewhat cumbersome vehicle with a wide turning circle. Thus, the maneuvering required to turn four lumbering Humvees around in a cramped cul-de-sac is noisy and takes a considerable amount of time. No soldiers had to dismount, no guns had to be flashed to achieve the desired effect, especially when the patrol was repeated several times a week. In the end, Maričić, although never a benign influence over Brčko, became Gennadiy's regular interlocutor and the two would often meet over lunch to exchange views. On balance, this was an excellent example of how we addressed one exceptionally charged threat to our mission, as well as how civilian and military tactics can be meshed intelligently to neutralize, if not to bring under total control, a dangerous actor without resorting to life-threatening methods.

I need to share with the reader some things I learned about Boško Maričić as time passed. Through a Bosniak acquaintance, I learned that before the war he had many Muslim friends. As the owner of a coffee shop in the village of Brka (Rahić-Brčko), Maričić was known and liked by Muslims. At some point around 1991, however, he turned sour, sold his coffee shop, and began to spout extremist Serb views. Then, during the war, several members of his family—perhaps as many as five or six—were killed, presumably by Bosniak forces, and later found buried in shallow graves near the bucolic village of Bukvik where heavy fighting had taken place. Not surprisingly, I found that persons who held extremely nationalist views had often lost members of their immediate family under particularly gruesome circumstances. This was not always the case, of course, but in the main I found a high correlation between tragic private loss and a wider generalized hatred of the ethnic group that the survivor, fairly or unfairly, held responsible for the loss. Thus my second behavioral rule: Simply to recognize and express sympathy for an interlocutor's personal loss would sometimes help me in opening the gates to dialogue—not always, but sometimes. Although Maričić had apparently begun to spout extremist views before the war began, by taking into account his personal loss during the war, we were better able to understand him during ensuing conversations.

CHALLENGES TO AUTHORITY FROM WITHIN

This next section is very sensitive. One can imagine that hard-liners inevitably will challenge the civilian administrator during the course of his implementation of a peace agreement. Their power is at stake! Over my tenure in Brčko, I experienced two forms of challenges to my authority from my *own* kind—those in other international civilian organizations also attempting to bring peace to Bosnia. The first seemed more specific to this situation. As an example, on June 29, 1997, I was awaiting the arrival by helicopter of Robert Gelbard, U.S. Secretary of State Madeleine Albright's recently appointed special envoy to the Balkans, and an entourage of ten assistants, on his first visit to Brčko. I had been professionally acquainted off and on with Gelbard for many years going back to our serving as midgrade officers in adjoining offices in the State Department—he on French affairs, and I on Eastern European affairs. On a personal level we had always gotten along fine. Having spent the bulk of his career working on Latin American affairs, with early assignments in Western Europe, he had had no prior experience in the formerly Communist Slavic world. That said, Gelbard was known as someone who "got things done" and that quality, among others, had reportedly commended him to Secretary Albright to replace John Kornblum as State Department's top man for the Balkans.

After heliport formalities at Camp McGovern, we drove together into Brčko where his delegation and my senior staff all crowded into our modest conference room. Not having agreed beforehand on protocol for the meeting, as was my custom with visitors, I led off by welcoming Gelbard and those accompanying him to my office. As I then began a few remarks describing where we stood, he interrupted and asked whether he might be allowed to speak. After several minutes, Gelbard then turned back to me for an assessment of our needs, which I briefly outlined and to which he very helpfully replied that he would do all in his power to find the resources we needed to achieve our objectives in Brčko. He then asked for my views on removing police checkpoints that were hindering freedom of movement at the time. As I was describing our position on checkpoints,[14] which I said we were trying to remove without loss of life, Gelbard again interrupted to say there should be no slackening from the hard line. I responded that while we certainly intended to be hard-line, I hoped at the same time to avoid casualties—especially fatalities—because given local tensions even one death would complicate our lives enormously no matter who was in the right. At that, he slammed his hand on the table and in a raised voice told me with a hard stare that this was U.S. policy and that was that. I instantly reacted by asking Gelbard in a loud voice whether he had just shouted at me. My Russian deputy clenched my arm under the table and hissed, "Calm down!" Such open discord in a hierarchy was rare in the old Soviet Union. A chill fell over the room.

Gelbard, angry and caught off guard, sputtered some forgettable comments about lines of authority and we quickly returned to our agenda, which, in the awkwardness of the moment, we ran through in short order. Later we patched up our differences, although months later someone on his staff told me he had wanted to fire me on the spot but cooler heads had prevailed. Be that as it may, I made up my mind then and there not to be browbeaten by individuals coming cold to Brčko with preset ideas on how we were to proceed in our delicate mission. Had Gelbard succumbed to his impulse to get rid of me on the spot, the entire Brčko operation, so carefully planned up to that point, would have been thrown into confusion. A useful, if highly situational, point you might take away from this cameo event is that at some stage you may need to establish your authority even among your own kind and in your own hierarchy. Clearly, this point has wider application in a civilian context than it would in a military setting, although that is my assumption only.

The second form of challenge I equate to both the passage of time and the tension that exists between the center and peripheries of an organization. With regard to the former, I am reminded of a quote by Chester A. Crocker of the U.S. Institute of Peace: "Intervention in the affairs of others is a serious business. It is not an arena for mere posturing or for being seen as 'doing something.' It should be attempted with the best, most committed, and perseverant people and pursued with a relentless intensity" (1996, 195–96). Frankly, I cannot envisage a level of effort short of these tough words for those who intervene in others' affairs in the hope of bringing about a change for the better. Unless qualified people are willing to step forward and commit themselves to the cause—whatever the cause may be—in the manner Crocker describes, the enterprise is doomed to fail before it is launched. It is perhaps in the nature of post-conflict crises like Bosnia that, especially in the initial stages of response, a surplus of capable civilians will sign up either for the task of rebuilding or, if a new order is needed, building from scratch a civil society shattered and broken by war. In the same vein, and just as predictably, when the sense of immediacy has passed, you should not be surprised to find in the echelons that follow a detectable retreat from the total, whatever-it-takes commitment to the mission characterized by the first wave of experts.

Frequently people ask why, at my age, did I agree to go to Brčko and, once there, to stay on for over three years under such conditions? Andrew Joscelyne once described Brčko as one of the more charmless places he had ever encountered and after only six months moved on to a bigger job in Kosovo. I frankly did not blame him. Persons unfamiliar with peace operations and the demands they place upon practitioners may find my response to the opening question less than gratifying. But as I neared the end of my diplomatic career, I found the idea of one last big challenge intriguing, especially since it would call on all my experience working on Soviet and Eastern European affairs over some fourteen years. Having been a small part of the U.S. government's long struggle against the harsh reality of communism, it would be fitting, I thought, to end my career as part of an international effort to instill democracy and the rule of law in a spot where quasi-Communist Yugoslavia had come crashing down in such an unforgiving way. The chance to be in a pivotal post, implementing an untried peace plan in Europe's most unstable corner, held great attraction for me. Although Dean Acheson's words "present at the creation" applied in a far, far larger setting half a century earlier, I got a faint whiff of the same aroma going into Brčko for the first time. As to why three years and not one or two, it was, as I explained to a friend, a sort of "in for a dime, in for a dollar" sort of thing. Once the arbitral tribunal found itself unable within a year to decide Brčko's political status, I felt it incumbent to stay on so that valuable momentum was not lost as a new supervisor was groomed for the job.

At this juncture I must share a widely held perception in the international community that because Brčko was located in MND-North (the American sector), arbitrated by an American lawyer (Roberts Owen), and supervised by an American diplomat (me), it was an *American* problem to solve. The story, perhaps apocryphal, had it that during the final days of peace talks at Dayton, when Brčko threatened to become a deal breaker, the British Foreign Office instructed its delegation to do all in its power to ensure that Brčko fell squarely into the American lap. Whether true or not, that, in fact, is where Brčko ended up falling. But it was a perception that I came only slowly to recognize and accept as reality. This was neither openly spoken about nor written down anywhere. It was simply one of those subliminal ideas that gained currency in the aftermath of the Dayton peace talks and hung on ever since. This raises the question of why, in such circumstances, an American senior civilian needed to be part of an organization whose head was European, especially as that organization became more and more centralized and more and more bureaucratic.

The adverse effect on a civilian administrator's ability to make clear-eyed decisions when all these factors come together is not to be minimized. For the military student of peace operations, the message here is that civilian leaders will nearly always encounter frictions internal to their organizations as they seek to build, maintain, and provide for their staffs—essential to the process of meeting objectives in pursuit of the common goal. Contrary to the military stereotype of civilians as disorganized and feckless in confronting crises, however, it is not always for lack of will, acumen, or competence that the civilian side of peace operations sometimes lags behind when judged by military criteria for attaining defined objectives. As has been shown, the very challenge of working within a multinational organization whose various members have differing levels of commitment and understanding is daunting in and of itself. Add to that the real possibility that persons in top executive positions within the multinational body of which you are a part may actually, either through ignorance or inclination, oppose both the timing and terms of a decision to resolve a crucial issue like Brčko, and you have a serious problem on your hands.

During more than three years in Brčko, I worked with three high representatives who had contrasting styles of management. Carl Bildt preferred to stay above day-to-day squabbles within the international community and to conserve his energy for issues requiring a political and strategic overview. His role as senior civilian in theater was to establish OHR in its formative days and to insure conformity of its policies and actions to the letter and spirit of the DPA. Administrative matters were pushed down and out, so that deputy high representatives in Mostar and Brčko, for example, had nearly full sway over their staffs and how their regional budgets would be spent. He largely left the running of OHR and its coordinative function in the hands of his capable principal deputy, Michael Steiner, and chief of staff, Jock Covey. Bildt's special assistant, Bjorn Lyrvall, was an exceptionally competent young Swedish diplomat, who made it a point to be always reachable. When I needed his advice or assistance, Lyrvall would unfailingly relay my request to Bildt, who, just as unfailingly, would get back to me within a day—not a week, a day. He traveled with a laptop computer and cell phone so that wherever he was he could promptly read and respond to his e-mail messages. He kept very, very long days. In reflecting on this situation now, it seems clear to me that while Carl Bildt stayed in the saddle as high representative, every member of his multinational staff, top to bottom, gave Brčko their unstinting support. He saw the importance of getting Brčko right and conveyed that message clearly to his staff. Because I was one of his deputies, I chose to work within and through the Office of the High Representative, both to establish critical lines of communication and supply, and to allay suspicions that I would somehow be working at cross purposes behind Bildt's back.

So long as OHR-Sarajevo under Bildt perceived Brčko as "mission impossible," a perception, by the way, I was slow to recognize, I could count on its support in countless ways, large and small, that masked how uncoordinated and piecemeal were the commitments of donor organizations to the Brčko mission. Because ethnic antagonisms in Brčko remained at or near the boil, all eyes were focused in our early days on whatever happened there. Thus, if a grenade went off in town, we could be assured that an attentive and responsive audience in Sarajevo and beyond would read our report about it and be ready to react in helpful ways. In those days, everyone with whom I had serious dealings was closely familiar with the forty-three-page First Award and its provisions. As the months passed, however, and people came and went, it became clear that fewer and fewer of my counterparts in Sarajevo were taking time to read through the First Award, not to mention the Supplemental and later Final Award. New people coming in had their own portfolios to master. It was asking a lot to expect them to devote the extra time needed to become truly conversant with the Brčko phenomenon. For many newcomers, it was simply all too confusing and sui generis to warrant their time and attention. Thus, it became harder as time wore on to find persons in the international community with a clear knowledge of the Brčko mission and what it entailed. Added to that basic lack of understanding, there appeared to be a growing suspicion of and resentment toward the Brčko implementation process, especially as it began to pass from a state of "mission impossible" to one of—maybe, just maybe—"mission doable."

Bildt's successor, Carlos Westendorp (1997–1999), had no equivalent of a Bjorn Lyrvall in his executive suite. Quite understandably, he recruited his staff largely from the Spanish Foreign Office in Madrid, where he had for a time served as acting foreign minister. As an ex-cabinet minister and, before that, university professor, Westendorp was familiar with, but no expert on, the Balkans as his predecessor had been. Warm and engaging as a conversationalist, he knew how to work a room, full of smiles and good humor. His grasp of the issues, however, was less than total and he seemed to rely for advice on a personal confidant named Fernando Mansito, a highly intense but ill-informed man who fluttered around like a hummingbird and was given to sprinkling his conversation with expressions like: "How interesting!" "Really!?" "Can that be true?" I found it nearly impossible to rely upon Mansito to convey my specific concerns coherently to Westendorp. So I would either try to speak to him directly, which, given his long weekends in Madrid, was not easy to arrange on quick notice; or to send him e-mails, copying his American secretary of Puerto Rican descent who, by prearranged agreement, would print them out and flag them for the high representative. It was not, as you might surmise, a particularly rapid channel of communication. I appealed to Westendorp to stay on top of the arbitral process—and during his first (and only) visit to my area of supervision stated that with his personal support we

might together move more rapidly toward success in Brčko, a key ingredi-
ent to success elsewhere in BiH.[15] Faced with reality though, my staff and
I increasingly worked the system at lower levels within OHR, which made
better sense anyway, so long as the lower levels remained broadly responsive
to Brčko's needs. At the same time, of course, the PIC continued to express
concern with the slow pace of implementation while calling for economies in
OHR operations. The scope for regional freedom of action began to narrow as
a succession of persons whose instincts for policy were less honed than those
for instilling bureaucracy came to hold the title of "chief of staff."

With the arrival of Wolfgang Petritsch (1999–2002), an ex-ambassador of
neutral Austria to Yugoslavia, the process of centralizing control over policy
as well as over administrative affairs in Sarajevo moved into high gear. Immediately, an echelon of young Austrian diplomats descended upon OHR's
front office; and the satellite offices in Mostar, Banja Luka, and Brčko soon
gave the new crew the collective label of "munchkins," because of their
proclivity for circling protectively around the new high representative. To be
fair, by the time he came on board the size of OHR had grown by two or more
orders of magnitude from Bildt's day. That said, the distance between the
front office and branch offices in the field began to widen perceptibly under
Petritsch. Whereas I often met with Bildt—and even with Westendorp—one-
on-one, either in his office or over a meal, I can only remember one occasion
in which Petritsch received me alone in his office and that was near the end of
our association when our relations had, for all practical purposes, completely
broken down. On all other occasions, he invited one or more of his munchkins—his principal deputy high representative, Ralph Johnson, a retired
American career diplomat and long acquaintance of mine, or a lawyer—to be
in the room when I called upon him. A classic European diplomat, he dressed
impeccably at all times and, while outwardly polite and charming, treated me
much as he would an outsider to OHR whenever we met. In the beginning,
I chalked his officiousness up to his middle-European origins and manner
since, having served five years in Czechoslovakia, a neighboring country to
Austria, I was familiar with the type. But over time I came slowly (too slowly,
as I look back on it now) to see that Petritsch, under the daily influence of his
legal, economic, and front office advisors, was, in fact, less than enamored of
my role in Brčko and, perhaps, of the whole idea of Brčko itself.

To future civilian peace implementers and practitioners, I pause to under-
score that in the intricate and jumbled process of bringing order to a complex,
post-conflict peace operation like Brčko—a process that by its nature requires
extraordinary patience and time—you need to maintain tight relations in
all directions within your own hierarchy. In other words, both physical and
operational nearness to the "center," however the center is defined, mat-

ters a very great deal. At the risk of repetition, you simply cannot assume that because the common mission has been reduced to writing and is duly incorporated in a formal document on file somewhere that everyone in your organization is familiar with its contents and therefore singing from the same sheet of music. Nothing is an adequate substitute for staying in close touch to keep misunderstandings from hardening into disputes whose boundaries, once set, are difficult to soften.

With respect to the physical, because surface travel to Sarajevo in good weather took over three hours on substandard—even dangerous—roads, I was not able to visit as often as I would have liked. Occasionally, SFOR would provide me with a helicopter for the forty-minute ride, but this was far from the norm. Besides, I rather naïvely clung to the view that since my objectives in Brčko were openly spelled out and made abundantly clear in the wording, logic, and force of the awards, all honorable men everywhere understood and supported those objectives. What more needed to be written or said? That this was not the case became clear to me during the period in which I sought to implement the March 1999 Final Award and its August 1999 Annex. Looking back, however, I recall sitting late one afternoon in the office of George Bartsiotas, a senior American Foreign Service officer whose strong reputation as an administrator led Bob Gelbard to recruit him for the task of bringing OHR's finances under control, which included reviewing Brčko's resource needs with a view to reducing them. At one touchy point in our conversation, I told Bartsiotas I was sure OHR's front office would support my position on the matter over which we were at odds. At that, he looked me in the eye incredulously and said: "Really? You better watch your back, Bill." In that moment, a number of remarks of recent weeks fell suddenly into place. I took it from Bartsiotas's comment that my position within the OHR hierarchy was eroding and I had been slow to read the signals.

Perhaps, given Sarajevo's negative feelings against the Final Award itself, little could have been done to stem the rising tide against my stewardship role of Brčko, but certainly being so far away from the center and physically located on the very periphery of BiH had done little to ease the situation. Words that Federation president Ejup Ganić (1997–1999, 2000–2001) had uttered during one of our periodic meetings some weeks earlier leapt into memory: "Supervisor Farrand, you really should spend much, much more time here in Sarajevo. You need to be here to protect your and Brčko's interests!" In any case, whatever the merits of this example, the message to future practitioners is clear: Stay close to the center so that the chances for ironing out policy differences up front will be improved. Like a garden, your relationships with and among people in the center need constant tending. The center is also the best place periodically to take the pulse of the overall mission and to reassess where your role fits in at the moment. At a minimum, you will not be blindsided as I was by a growing wall of low-grade suspicion and opposition to your mission. It hardly needs saying that ill feelings, particularly those emanating from the top, are surely evident to observers—including the conflict parties.

Tight relations must be fostered to maintain operational cohesion. I discovered that failure to do so affected my staff, relations with other implementing bodies, and our ability to carry out in a coordinated fashion my Final Award and Annex directives. In his bestseller *The Tipping Point*, author Malcolm Gladwell writes perceptively that big trends are often triggered by little events when "the moment of critical mass, the threshold, the boiling point" may have been reached (2000, 12). While perhaps not the perfect analytical tool to describe my experience, Gladwell's hypothesis struck a chord as I reflected on when and why my personal relations with the center began seriously heading south.

As regards staff, essentially, the drift begun under Westendorp to bring the OHR field offices in Mostar, Brčko, and then Banja Luka, under Sarajevo's control became a stampede under Petritsch. As an example of how this not-so-subtle transformation affected Brčko, whereas before Petritsch's arrival the head of my legal department, a young British-educated lawyer from Greece, Ilias Chatzis, responded directly to me as supervisor, he now came under pressure to report as well to the head of OHR-Sarajevo's legal department, which was, unfortunately, no friend of the Brčko arbitral process. The same held true for every other department in my small office: the head of my economic division now answered also to the senior economic officer in Sarajevo, my press officer reported to the head of OHR media affairs, my administrative officer to the chief administrative officer in headquarters, and so on and so forth. Brčko's senior staff was reduced to a veritable hodgepodge of employees working for two masters. And as if that were not dysfunctional enough in managerial terms, the worst aspects of it were manifested when OHR-Sarajevo wished to slow the rate of progress in Brčko as, collectively, they were increasingly wont to do, especially as regarded legal and judicial reform, economic revitalization, and customs border modernization. The putative senior officer in a given department would merely suggest to his or her "subordinate" in Brčko that perhaps the supervisor's approach to whatever issue was at hand was not the ideal way to proceed. So what, in such circumstances, was the hapless employee to do? Most, to their credit, reported such conversations quickly to me so I could register my concerns over mixed signals at the appropriate higher level in Sarajevo. Frequently, the Brčko staff member was left confused and caught between two bosses—only one of whom (the one from Sarajevo) ultimately controlled his or her contract and its terms of renewal. And when it came time to make personnel allocations within departments, the regional offices in Mostar, Banja Luka, and Brčko were no longer given pride of place in the bidding process for talented candidates, but rather relegated to the same status as other placeholders in the central office. Thus, the regional offices were forced to stand in queue—and often at the very end of it—with rarely anyone at the table in Sarajevo to look after their interests. Had senior division chiefs themselves understood operations in the field this might (barely) have passed muster as an operational approach to staffing, but they tended not to travel outside of Sarajevo and thus were poorly disposed to give the regional offices the priority they deserved and needed.

In the face of increased fiscal discipline, decreased personnel allocations, and calls to achieve the goals of Dayton—in my case the Brčko arbitral process—we streamlined existing staff in minor ways and continued working closely with local offices of the OSCE, UN/IPTF, SFOR, and the larger, more stable NGOs to ensure that every possible avenue for coordinating and synergizing our activities in Brčko was exploited. Regrettably, when other agency headquarters in Sarajevo began to harden bureaucratically and fall under increasingly turf-conscious leadership, we began to encounter friction with our policy of inclusiveness. Returning to my civilian policing example from earlier in this chapter, the reader will recall I thought it necessary to collocate the office of the UN/IPTF commander within our building, a move I hoped would both improve our physical security and make it easier to coordinate policy regarding police affairs. As a spin-off, I included the UN/IPTF uniformed police commander in our morning staff meetings, as well as his superior, the UN-appointed CIVPOL political advisor. Although I did not realize it at the time, the normal practice (if one could call much of anything normal under the circumstances) would have been for me to have invited *only* the UN political advisor into these meetings and count on him or her to brief the uniformed commander later on what transpired. This vital link was broken when Jacques Paul Klein (1999–2002) took over the reins as SRSG during my final year of supervision.

Having served for two years as Westendorp's principal deputy—and thus technically above me in OHR's internal chain of command—Klein had a management style that favored command decisions, especially if he was the one making them. Intelligent to the point of brilliance, he saw his mission in BiH through a prism focused on him. During our two years of uneven collaboration, Klein visited Brčko only once, spending the bulk of his time lecturing the Serb mayor on his myopia, and the rest of the time on his cell phone to General Wesley Clark at Supreme Allied Commander Europe headquarters in Belgium, and to Washington. He had no interest in hearing from me about Brčko. As SRSG, his first step in Brčko was to reassign, over my sharp objections delivered to him personally, UN Civil Affairs officer

Scheye to a secondary job in Mostar and to replace him with a UN officer who had served under him when Klein led the UN Transitional Administration for Eastern Slavonia, Baranja, and Western Sirmium (UNTAES) operation in eastern Croatia. Robert Gravelle, a Canadian citizen, arrived in September 1999 and immediately called on me to pledge his support to the common agenda. He then interposed himself between me and the then UN/IPTF commander, a Dane, confining the latter to attending our morning meetings only. Henceforward, Gravelle informed the UN/IPTF contingent all communications between the UN/IPTF and my office were to be funneled through him, a procedure that almost instantly posed problems, since he, as time would show, spent the bulk of his time at UN headquarters in Sarajevo. All of this happened at the very moment we were preparing to announce the lineup for the newly trained and reconstituted Brčko police force. Scheye, who had served nearly a year in Brčko, had been working long hours to help me identify a slate of ethnically balanced leaders for the new district police force—an exquisitely difficult task. Gravelle, on the other hand, came new to the game and had few insights beyond those he gained working for UNTAES in Croatia, which was an altogether different situation. He arrived in Brčko ostensibly to work with me, but his underlying agenda was to impose the new SRSG's views and authority over the Brčko police force. As an advisor on candidates for the new police leadership, Gravelle had nothing to offer. Thus, at a critical time, I was largely thrown back on my own resources to select candidates for that leadership.

I will refrain from testing the reader's patience with more details of this regressive state of affairs, except to note that these changes led not only to an effective breakdown in the productive and mutually supportive relationship we had enjoyed with UN offices in Brčko but also to a rupture in the collaborative atmosphere between UN Civil Affairs and the UN/IPTF itself, although I am certain little of this was ever reflected in reports back to the SRSG. Gone were the days of open discourse—freewheeling agreement and disagreement—between my office and the vitally important UN contingent in Brčko. Nor do I exclude myself from part of the blame for this deterioration in relations. I admit to reacting with barely disguised unhappiness over a turn of events I judged to be destructive of a good working relationship—and unnecessarily so. The essential point is, however, that the working climate went from one of openness and inclusion, to one of closed mouths and exclusion virtually overnight.

Finally, this last story speaks to how failure to maintain operational proximity can negatively affect one's ability to implement. During the fall of 1999, my legal staff led by Ilias Chatzis, ably assisted by Goran Duka, a Bosnian Serb lawyer of moderate bent, and a Bosniak student of law worked long hours together to create a draft statute, or basic law, for the new Brčko District, as called for in the August 1999 Annex. Although I am not a lawyer, I nonetheless closely monitored the drafting process to ensure its conformity with our overarching policy goals under the Final Award. The job of creating a basic statute for a jurisdiction the size of the Brčko District would have been no mean task for a legal staff three times larger than ours, but, although we had requested additional personnel for this (and other) purposes, they were not, as previously discussed, approved in OHR-Sarajevo. So we had to make do with our small staff. Chatzis and his colleagues labored through long days to complete the job. To expand their drafting capability, Ilias suggested, and I agreed, that we take advantage of the Venice Commission to critique our work so that it would be in line with modern democratic statutes that the commission had helped create for the states emerging from the breakup of the former Soviet Union and its satellites in Eastern Europe. That, along with advice from the Council of Europe and wording from the Rambouillet Agreement (1999) went far in assuring our draft statute's concordance with democratic legal thinking in the West. To ensure its relevance to Balkan legal traditions, we even drew language from the municipal statute for Sarajevo.

When our first draft of the new district statute was complete, we sent it to OHR-Sarajevo for review and comment as we did with every official document, including each of the twenty-five supervisory orders I promulgated over three years in Brčko. In the past, our drafts were accorded a reasonably quick turnaround, but this time we heard nothing. Given that we were working under an abbreviated time frame—as the Final Award intoned, "It is the Tribunal's hope and expectation that the various components of the new District government will be operational, for the most part, by 31 December 1999 or within a few months thereafter"—I helicoptered down to meet with Petritsch on October 18 in an attempt to dislodge the draft statute from OHR headquarters. I wanted to be personally on hand to engage with him on whatever arguments regarding the new district and its constitutional underpinnings he was receiving from his advisors.

In particular, I recognized there were differing opinions regarding delegation of powers. First, we in Brčko took the words of the Final Award at their face value: "The basic concept is to create a single, unitary multi-ethnic democratic government to exercise, throughout the pre-war Brčko *Opština*, those *powers previously exercised by the two entities* and the three municipal governments. . . . The District derives its powers of local self-government by virtue of each Entity having delegated all of its powers of governance as previously exercised by the two Entities and the three municipal governments [Brčko *grad*, Rahić-Brčko, and Ravne-Brčko] within the pre-war opština, as defined in Article 5, to the District Government" [emphasis mine]. As we interpreted those words, the entities simply delegated their powers over the Brčko *opština* to the new Brčko District without an intermediary step—a one-step process. OHR-Sarajevo's legal team, however, held the process involved two steps. First, the entities devolved their authority over the Brčko *opština* to the state of BiH and, second, the state then bestowed those powers on the new district. To the casual reader this may seem like a distinction without a difference, a tempest in a teacup, but in fact the disparity between the two positions went to the very heart of the new district's raison d'être. Stripped to its essentials, the argument came down to one of control—if my interpretation of the Final Award was correct, then the district derived its powers to govern directly from the two entities of which it was simultaneously a part in condominium. If, on the other hand, OHR-Sarajevo's interpretation of the Final Award were correct, then the two entities devolved their powers to govern the territory of the Brčko District first to the state of BiH, which then passed on those powers to the district government. By inserting the state of BiH in the devolution process, OHR-Sarajevo also, in effect, injected *itself* between the entities and the district, in contravention to the letter and the spirit of the Final Award. Both processes are depicted in Figure 2.1.

Lurking just below the surface of this (for me) sterile debate was the issue of who in the end would oversee and control the arbitral process in Brčko—the supervisor or the high representative in Sarajevo. The unspoken rationale behind OHR-Sarajevo's position in adopting a two-step analysis for the delegation of entity authority was that, if accepted, then OHR-Sarajevo, analogous to the state of BiH (both had seats in Sarajevo), would assume control over the supervision. At the risk of repetition, the tacit arrangement between our two offices that had worked so smoothly during the first two years of supervision—a habit of fluid consultation—apparently no longer satisfied

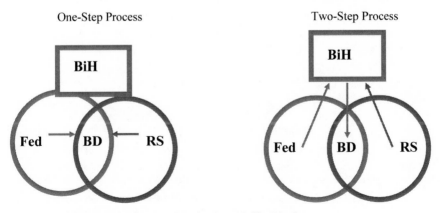

Figure 2.1. Delegation of Entities' Authority to Brčko District

members of the center that the high representative maintained an adequate level of control over developments in Brčko.

Despite my own meetings with Johnson and Petritsch in late October 1999, and my legal staff's efforts to reach agreement with their superiors in OHR-Sarajevo, this crucial point of law remained open and I sought counsel with Roberts Owen in early December. Present in my office when I made the call was my legal team, including Judge Finn Lynghjem and his senior deputy, Michael Karnavas of the Brčko Law Revision Commission (BLRC). After hearing us out, Owen responded that our understanding of the intent of the words used in the Final Award was proper and correct. He said he thought what we had done thus far, what he had seen, "made a lot of sense." Owen agreed to look at our latest negotiated changes to the draft statute; and, at my request, to write a letter to that effect to Johan von LaMoen, head of OHR-Sarajevo's legal division. Much cheered to know we were on firm ground, I took the informal Owen "ruling," if it can be called that, as dispositive and therefore a green light to proceed on our way.

My sense of elation was short-lived, however. First, I did not count on the endless ability of lawyers to confound an issue. In this case, OHR-Sarajevo lawyers advising the high representative simply reverted to their fallback position—never publicly stated—that the Final Award was *illegal* and that it did not matter how anyone chose to interpret it. Second, the fact that Owen agreed with our position meant little unless he was prepared to weigh in with the executive branch of the U.S. government on our behalf. But I sensed that Owen, much like a judge in any court proceeding, saw himself above and outside the executive structure that was entrusted, in theory at least, with helping the supervisor enforce the Final Award. Fair enough, but with many eyes turned to address post-conflict Kosovo that executive structure was not there when I needed it. Third, I needed to recognize that absent a strong, visible U.S. government backing for the Final Award, my insistence on the draft language in question—even though I had the oral (and moral) support of the presiding arbitrator—would lead to a Pyrrhic victory only. Without adequate administrative and technical resources, the supervisor could not go very far; and such resources, by December 1999, were increasingly under the control of OHR-Sarajevo.

With the high representative due to arrive in Brčko within days for the last meeting of the Joint Implementation Council (JIC) where we were expected to present the final—repeat *final*—version of the Brčko District Statute, I personally engaged in a last-ditch effort with his legal advisors the weekend before to bring them around to our position on this Article I, Paragraph (2) issue. At a minimum, I urged them to alert Petritsch to our differences before he departed. This was critical—the statute was to become the basic law when, I hoped, either at the end of February or early March, we would be able to bring it into force and announce the interim government and get moving. But on December 7, 1999, the high representative came to town accompanied only by Sandra McCardle, his Canadian special assistant, and his security detail. None of his legal team was in the party. Thus, the issue was left to the two of us to decide, although at first I think Petritsch was genuinely unaware of the exposed position his lawyers, in my view purposefully, had left him.

After a few pleasantries in my office, I indicated to Petritsch that we had an important issue to resolve before we made public the text of the new statute in just two hours. Although Judge Lynghjem was with me, I asked McCardle to leave the room, which she did in a state of near shock. When the high representative and I sat facing each other across the table, I explained to him in briefest terms the nature of the problem before us. He responded with what I took to be genuine surprise that the matter had not been ironed out between the lawyers. I told Petritsch that unfortunately it had not and that his trip would end in embarrassment if we were *not* to go before the JIC with a united view and an agreed text. The high representative asked how, without legal counsel, he could be expected on the spot to resolve a question with such far-reaching consequences. At this, I simply told Petritsch that I had exhausted every means I knew to bring the matter to an amicable conclusion, that I was satisfied that my position was based on an accurate understanding of the intent of the Final Award, and that, finally, for me the question had become a "matter of principle." With that, he went silent for a moment and then asked if he could use my telephone.

Judge Lynghjem and I waited in an outer office while Petritsch conferred behind my closed office door with his staff for nearly twenty minutes. As we cooled our heels, I reflected that what we really could have used in this situation was a higher authority, or at least a forum of peers, to arbitrate between us. When he finally emerged it was to say, "OK, we'll go with your version, now let's get on with the day!" Relieved, and in the flush of the moment, I almost surely ascribed to Petritsch's decisive tone more assent to my position than he intended to convey. However that may be, we sat side by side early that afternoon and presented to the JIC the final version of the district statute, which they had seen in each of its earlier draft forms, noting that it would go into force when the district was formally established. Perhaps I should have taken closer notice of Petritsch's words thanking *JIC members*, essentially, for having labored long over the drafting of the statute, while mentioning the foundational work of our BLRC staff only in passing.

As the next few days showed, however, the battle over the meaning of Article I, Paragraph (2) to the district statute raged on. On December 9, I found myself again in Sarajevo defending our position with which two days earlier the high representative had ostensibly agreed. The ultimate irony was that while these differences within OHR were complicating progress, the two entities—the Federation and RS—were both *complying* with the terms of the Final Award! Sitting in Brčko, it was difficult see why OHR-Sarajevo's legal team found it necessary to undermine the work before us. Some on my staff suggested there might have been an element of institutional envy involved and certainly an element of the need to control. The trouble with that interpretation was that control over Brčko from Sarajevo was not a workable option. So it was difficult to deduce from their tactics where they were going in the larger picture.

In light of the foregoing, however, I was forced to reassess the high representative's decision to go along with my position on December 7 as but a tactical move on OHR-Sarajevo's chessboard to let me have my way in the short term, since time was on their side. Having been in Brčko at that point for nearly three years, I had more seniority in terms of time served than other senior civilian implementers. So the advice Petritsch received from his advisors, political and legal, was more likely to have been something like this: "Let him have this one, it's not the end of the world. After Farrand is gone, we will appoint as his successor a person less truculent and more amenable to our views. Things that go around, come around." Whatever the truth may be, I am now persuaded that in forcing my position regarding the district statute on Petritsch, I earned his enmity (or, better said, intensified the enmity that was already growing) from that moment on. In other words, I triggered a tipping point in our relations.

"So what," the civilian student of peace operations may ask, "might I have done differently to have avoided this rupture, this falling-out, with my putative superior?" I have thought long and hard on that question and have concluded, "Not much more than I did." Without becoming overtly defensive, I am reasonably content that within the restricted time constraints under which we all operated, I made an honest effort to educate two high representatives and their staffs to the crucial role the Brčko arbitration process played in the larger picture. There were several problems. Until the Final Award—the final decision—was handed down, Brčko could safely be relegated to a second- or even third-order concern in the back of people's minds in Sarajevo. So long as Brčko had a supervisor on scene that seemed to be handling things tolerably well, it was not an immediate problem and could therefore be safely ignored. Anyhow, in order truly to understand the Brčko mess one had to spend time reading the arbitral awards, and that was a real pain, given all the other pressing items on OHR-Sarajevo's agenda. So, come up with a few easily remembered slogans as to why the Brčko resolution was flawed (e.g., the Final Award was "illegal"), repeat those slogans until they became accepted wisdom, and that is all one really needed to satisfy the low threshold of debate on Brčko within OHR-Sarajevo as time passed. Against such an institutional mindset, it was a major challenge to keep Brčko at or near the top of anyone's agenda—except mine, of course, and that of the two entities. Washington's attention focused on Kosovo, and the American Embassy in Sarajevo was embroiled mainly in the Federation and its problems. I faced an uphill struggle in funneling OHR-Sarajevo's resources toward Brčko. Further, the legal staff provided Westendorp and Petritsch, neither of whom were technically trained in the law, with flawed arguments on the Final Award and then faded into the background when the political ground began to shake. OHR headquarters and my office—the center and the periphery—had descended into a condition that *New York Times* columnist Thomas L. Friedman (2000) noted anthropologists label "systemic misunderstanding"—a condition that "arises when your framework and the other person's framework are so fundamentally different that it cannot be corrected by providing more information" (par. 4). In the long run, it was I who paid the bill.

CONCLUSION

Establishing one's authority is neither a quick nor simple process. The foregoing pages attempt to bring out some of the real obstacles one may encounter in attempting to impose one's influence on a post-conflict environment where societal wounds are still in their rawest state, both literally and figuratively. While I have never considered myself a brave, nor even a particularly adventuresome, man the experience of leading a civilian peace implementation process in an ethnically divided municipality where intercommunal anger was still boiling drove home to me the point that such endeavors should not be undertaken by the fainthearted. If that seems a contradiction in terms, well there you have it.

In fact, the elusive question of authority—especially civilian authority—remains at the heart of most serious peace operations. In the chaotic aftermath of war, military oversight of the conflict zone must at some point give way to civilian oversight. That is in the very nature of things, since a military force is not by its nature endowed with all the skills and tools necessary for standing a war-ravaged society on its feet again, such as rebuilding the human, as opposed to the physical, side of civil institutions. By that I mean working closely with the local populace and its leaders, even those who may be a legacy of the old wartime regimes, to identify persons who either show promise or can be worked with in the short run, in such spheres as police, public health, education, administration, law, judiciary, public works, and so on—the building blocks of civil society. A broad spectrum of international organizations and NGOs, all staffed by civilians, are well established to tackle each of these areas and others more closely defined. However, civilian peace operations cannot proceed without strong military support to maintain or impose, in the words of Dayton, a "safe and secure environment" in which civilians may be free to do their work. It is a myth to think civilians can do the job alone without friendly, armed protection. Depending on the crisis, the time for military involvement may be long or short. As a rule, however, the period of military participation will generally tend to be longer—often much longer—than that for which the outside crisis managers planned.

The important exercise of power, especially on a scale that will have an immediate and perhaps long-lasting effect on the lives of others, should be a sobering prospect. It should also be a humbling prospect, especially for a person like me who never particularly thought of himself as a seeker of power. That said, power and its proper exercise were organic to the Brčko peace effort. Thus, power seeker or not, one had to become comfortable with the idea and gradually to prepare oneself for it. Antecedent to the exercise of power is the need to establish one's living authority as distinct from its formulation on paper. Perhaps this is only another way of saying the same thing, but I think not. The establishment of one's authority requires, inter alia, clarity of purpose, openness to the views of others, patient reaction, and steadiness under fire. And even these may not always be enough, as I was to be reminded on several occasions.

The bad news is that authority, once established, can also easily be lost through miscalculation, overuse, mistakes, or sheer stupidity. This narrative will be unsparing in casting light on my errors in judgment and planning. The cameo occurrences described above will also come up again in other wider contexts as this account unfolds. I close this chapter on a note of optimism for others who, like me, may find themselves in the ambiguous and occasionally awkward position of one asked to assume a civilian leadership role in a high-visibility, post-conflict circumstance where the wounds of war are still open and running. Will you make mistakes? Yes, of course. But if you will act, and be seen to be acting, in the broad interests of the community and in strict accordance with your mandate, your efforts will be noticed and your well-intentioned mistakes forgiven. Can you avoid making mistakes? Probably not. But the greatest mistake of all would be to hang back, hide behind your formal authority, and take as few risks as possible to keep within your comfort zone. It is fair to say that under those circumstances those who do not wish you well from all quarters will soon move to fill the vacuum left by your relative inaction. And you will lose authority. As F. Kenneth Iverson, former

CEO of Nucor Corp. Inc., a highly successful steel firm at a time when most steel producers were failing in the United States, often stated, "My goal is to make the right decision about 60 percent of the time" (Wayne 2002, par. 9). Just as the indiscriminate use of authority will damage your mission, so by the same token, authority not used will atrophy to the same end. U.S. president Harry Truman (1945–1953) said it best: "If you can't stand the heat, stay out of the kitchen"—apt advice for those contemplating civilian leadership roles in peacekeeping operations.

Chapter Three

Freedom of Movement

The task of restoring freedom of movement in a place where the dogs of war have only recently been leashed needs to be approached with immense caution. The process is likely to put lives in danger. False moves will have tragic consequences, especially since the enmity and hatred between former belligerents—both ex-combatants and civilians—rages on beneath the surface. In such circumstances, the underlying emotion that pervades society at all levels, except perhaps among its top leadership, is fear—of the "Other," of the present, and, most of all, of the future. In the case of Brčko, to these was added one more—fear of the new supervisor and what his coming would mean for the community.

Brčko in early 1997 was an *opština* dissected across the middle from east to west by the IEBL. There existed two nearly equal geographic sectors, one north and one south of the line. Whereas before the war Brčko's population of eighty-seven thousand had been distributed throughout the *opština* within more or less loosely defined ethnic areas, there were few, if any, communities so ethnically circumscribed that one group dominated to the exclusion of all others.[1] In the absence of a formal census, we found it impossible to know with any degree of precision the postwar total number of persons, particularly north of the line. An educated guess, considering the widespread destruction of dwelling units, would be in the neighborhood of twenty-five thousand individuals. Whatever the true number, however, we could be certain of one thing—those north of the IEBL were almost exclusively Serbs.[2] Frankly, in a perverse way, I found the very ambiguity inherent in not knowing the precise number of inhabitants was a source of some comfort. In tight situations, ambiguity can be your ally when wisely used.

There were two types of Serbs in the area of supervision. Some 20 percent had been born in Brčko—*Brčak* (singular) or *Brčaci* (plural). The remaining 80 percent had arrived from homes elsewhere in Bosnia, the larger number of whom had voluntarily left Sarajevo and other urban centers, or had been driven from those places by Serb—yes, Serb—forces implementation of Dayton as commenced on the ground in the spring of 1996. They found themselves living precariously and illegally in houses and apartments owned by Bosniak and Croat prewar residents of Brčko, in what appeared to be part of a considered strategy by Bosnian Serb leader Radovan Karadžić and his hard-line SDS. These Serb displaced persons (DPs) were understandably concerned not only about their current circumstances but about what the future held in store for them and their families. Angry, resentful, and afraid, the great majority of newcomers to Brčko had had nothing to do with the grisly crimes that had been committed in the municipality. As I often observed to visitors, they were part of the flotsam and jetsam of war, just as much victims in their own way as were Bosniaks and Croats who had been forced under threat of death to flee from Brčko in 1992. And, because of this, the Serb newcomers were easily manipulated by fearmongers in Pale and from among their own number. As their fears mounted, the very thought that the supervisor might allow members of the other factions to travel in and through their territory became anathema to them.

Serb civilians who might have cooperated with the JNA and paramilitary forces from Serbia in the ethnic cleansing of Brčko were more likely to be found among the *Brčaci*. These Serb natives not infrequently took advantage-of the emptied-out city between 1993 and 1995 by helping themselves to vacated properties. It was not uncommon for them to simply move into one, two, or in the rare case, three houses left empty by their former Muslim and Croat friends and neighbors. This pernicious phenomenon, known as "multiple occupancy," was to greatly complicate the process of reinstating Bosniaks and Croats into their prewar homes in the *grad*. So, apart from fear of the "Other," there was a natural desire on the part of many Serbs not to see owners of the homes they were occupying illegally come back to claim their properties. Greed, too, played a large role in blocking freedom of movement and return.

In addition to the psychological factors above, a brief description of the physical attributes of the Brčko area as these relate to the topic in question is in order. As regards roadways, Brčko has three main arteries leading into and out of town. First, there is the two-lane Belgrade–Banja Luka road that runs east-west through downtown and extends for roughly twenty kilometers to the *opština* boundaries each side of town, known to the international community as Route Texas. Second and third were two narrow two-lane roads running north-south from the *grad*, known respectively as Route Kiwi and Route Kansas. A third and more important artery, the Donja Mahala–Orašje

Road, ran north-south between Orašje and Srebrenik. Popularly known to the international community as the Arizona Road, this was the main road to Sarajevo, four hours to the south.

As previously noted, Brčko had been one of very few intermodal (road, rail, and river) transportation centers of regional significance in Bosnia before the war. However, the war had closed the Sava River itself to waterborne traffic. Two massive rail-mounted cranes in the Brčko *luka* stood silent, naked, and rusting against the sky. The vehicular bridge had been effectively out of commission for use by the local citizenry since April 30, 1992.³ As for rail traffic, one of Bosnia's two north-south rail lines ran through Brčko, but the destruction of the railroad bridge shut down yet another mode of travel, and an important source of revenue, for the region.

The ability to move about freely in Brčko *opština*, and BiH as a whole, was practically moribund due to these psychological and infrastructure issues. In a large sense, even if one were to address the latter there still might be little impact due to the former. For instance, in another divided *opština* to the south of Brčko, SFOR had repaired a small roadway to permit travel from Federation Goražde to Srpska Goražde. Those few attempting to make the trip, however, were subject to stoning and taunting by Serbs along the route. In 1996 UNHCR attempted to alleviate restrictions on freedom of movement by establishing bus lines for interentity travel, but even these initiatives were frustrated by local authorities (Rehn 1996, par. 11). The freedom of movement issue was further complicated by lack of democratic policing. Serb police established illegal checkpoints and harassed, fined, or even detained members of other ethnic communities. Families attempting to visit grave sites or homes situated in an area in which they were now considered a minority had no guarantee of public security. In my view, without freedom of movement in Brčko the rest of our heavy agenda would atrophy. Freedom of movement was sine qua non to restoring civil order. Unless people came to accept their fundamental right to move about freely, they would resist returning to their homes. And until they returned to their homes in significant numbers, the prospects for holding free and fair elections would be up in the air; and with the elections would go prospects for the return of legitimate multiethnic government. So a great deal depended on our ability to restore freedom of movement. What follows are particular milestones in this endeavor that I either witnessed or facilitated during my tenure as supervisor.

TESTING RIPENESS: MAY DAY 1997

As the end of April 1997 approached, word came that a large delegation of Bosniaks from Sarajevo and Tuzla, led by Zlatko Lagumdzija, leader of the avowedly multiethnic Social Democratic Party of Bosnia and Herzegovina (*Socijaldemokratska Partija Bosne i Hercegovine*, or SDP), would arrive at Camp McGovern on May 1—May Day in the former Yugoslavia—in two buses and several private cars to cross the IEBL for a call on me in Brčko *grad*. The purpose of the visit was transparent. The Bosniaks wanted to probe whether I would rise to the occasion and approve the caravan for entry into the RS, as well as protect it from harm.

On hearing of the SDP plan, SFOR strongly advised me *not* to permit the delegation to enter the Brčko area of supervision. Since the previous evening we had allowed the RS police to turn back another bus from the Federation, I judged that were I to say "No" a second time in as many days it would be taken as a sign that we were not taking our mission to restore freedom of movement seriously. So, after informing Deputy High Representative Michael Steiner of my plans and receiving his support, I overruled SFOR's concerns and allowed the two buses—but not the dozen or so private vehicles trailing behind—to come in. The time consumed in coming to a decision that morning delayed the actual arrival of the buses to our office. And because of that delay, two SFOR buses that had been scheduled to carry several dozen soldiers to Hungary for "rest and recuperation" rolled north out of McGovern about ten minutes in advance of the SDP buses. As luck would have it, these SFOR buses bore the brunt of an ambush by a group of young Serb males who had been lying in wait to stone the Federation buses. The driver of one of the SFOR buses was hit in the head by a flying stone. He was, ironically, a Serb employee of SFOR. In the ensuing confusion, the thugs scattered and the two buses carrying the SDP delegation came slowly up the road several minutes after the SFOR buses had passed and emerged unscathed.

When the buses rolled into the small square on which our building was located, I invited Lagumdzjia and four of his lieutenants up to my office explaining that our discussion had to be brief because we feared further violence. In this I was not disappointed, because ten minutes into our meeting a guard poked his head in to say an angry crowd was gathering around the buses below. With this, I cut short the meeting—during which Lagumdzjia and his colleagues had been pressing me on a laundry list of demands—and encouraged my visitors to depart without delay. They, and seventy others in their party who had disembarked for cold refreshments in our reception hall, began reboarding the buses to the jeers and taunts of several hundred Serbs who had materialized, as if on signal, from neighboring houses, shops, and streets. Although the Brčko police force had been pre-alerted to the visit and were on scene, they stood passively by under the eyes of several dozen UN/IPTF monitors, making only desultory moves to control the mob.

Photo 3.1.   Treating the Injured—May Day Incident, 1997 (Photograph by Ian McLeod)

To avoid sending the buses back down the same heavily potholed road on which they had come in and risking a second ambush, we directed them to leave by the main road headed west out of town along Route Texas. As the buses began laboriously to pull away from our headquarters a Serb bus clumsily sought to block their passage. The all-Serb Brčko police performed abysmally in clearing the way for the two buses and, in fact, as they proceeded with UN/IPTF police vehicles escorting them fore and aft, and an SFOR helicopter hovering directly overhead, platoons of thugs darted out from between buildings pelting the buses with rocks. By the time the procession turned west on Route Texas most of the buses' windows had been broken as the passengers hunched down, heads between their legs. The harassment continued for another six kilometers to the intersection with the north-south Arizona Road. The buses reached the IEBL at the "Arizona Market" and passed south and back into the Federation portion of the Brčko *opština* where SFOR medics were standing by to treat the wounded. Miraculously, none of the passengers was seriously injured, although Lagumdzija was cut on the face and seven or eight others suffered minor bruises. The two buses, however, were so badly damaged as to be no longer serviceable.

I think it safe to say that had the decision been SFOR's to permit the SDP buses to enter into the Serb-dominated area of the Brčko *opština* that day, it would not have happened—perhaps later, but not on that day. At least two delegations of officers, one from McGovern and the other, headed by a brigadier general from SFOR's headquarters in Tuzla, came to see me that morning conveying the common message that to permit the buses to move north would be to needlessly and dangerously provoke the Serbs. It fact, were it up to the Serbs, the visit would not have happened, then or in the future.

As I reflected later on the day's events, several thoughts ran together in my mind. First, this was the first major test of my resolve in Brčko and I needed to meet it. In addition to those who opposed the buses coming in, there were the Bosniaks—and, watching from the side, the Croats—who wanted to put the new supervisor to the test. It was, after all, a peaceful delegation seeking only to drive a few kilometers down a public road and back. Second, the First Award stipulated the restoration of freedom of movement in the Brčko area as a primary objective of the arbitral process. "When," I asked the SFOR general sent to dissuade me from making a rash decision, "am I to get about addressing freedom of movement?" Conceding there were risks, I told the general we had to start somewhere. Finally, an unintended but important consequence of the gamble I took that afternoon—and, make no mistake, it was a gamble pure and simple—was to establish experiential baselines for violence in the community, police performance, and not incidentally my own tolerance for risk. All of these considerations went through my mind in the aftermath of this touch-and-go incident, of which I expected there to be many more.

I took away several important lessons from that afternoon's brush with tragedy. First, the Brčko police would need in the future to present, well in advance of such demonstrations and challenges to public order, a security plan for approval by the UN/IPTF, SFOR, and my office so that everyone, including me, would know what to expect.[4] Second, the unarmed UN/IPTF had definite limits on its power to restore order when matters either became, or threatened to become, out of hand. In fact, this event drove home the message far better than words that the DPA really did intend for indigenous police forces to provide local security in Bosnia. That being the case, it was now incumbent upon us—the supervisor, the UN/IPTF commander, and our staffs—to cooperate to the fullest in transforming the current Brčko all-Serb police force of more than five hundred ill-trained, ill-equipped, ex-wartime regular and paramilitary fighters into a stripped-down and multiethnic force of trained and qualified professional policemen (and later, women) capable of modern policing. The third lesson had to do with the reaction of local Serb hard-liners to a modest SFOR show of force, such as helicopters hovering over a civilian disturbance. Basically, those dark figures behind the bus stoning, calculating that SFOR would not intervene to stop the mayhem, had put out the word for local toughs and thugs brought in from adjoining towns to attack the buses with impunity. And it worked just as the dark figures had planned. It was clear to me that unless this dynamic were somehow interrupted our goose would surely, in time, be cooked. Finally, I learned many eyes were upon us as we began to translate the supervisor's authority and responsibilities from words on a piece of paper to a functioning operational reality.

While we knew that shadowy figures in the local power structure had directed, even hired, other locals to attack the buses, it was less than a month since we had begun our work and we did not know precisely the identity of the string pullers. I argued against going on a witch hunt, which I thought would be counterproductive and leave us with egg on our collective face, and reasoned instead that we absorb the hit and learn from it so we could prevent similar events from happening again. In any case, not even local Serb hard-liners, if we had been able to identify and expose them, would have had the final say. For that, you only had to go to the village of Pale, where Karadžić held court. But to take that step, of course, would be to pose larger risks to public order in the RS. Eventually, the matter petered out of its own weight.

There was an upside to the gamble as well. Ian McLeod observed that the Federation side saw me as having a royal flush—ten through ace all in the same suit—when in fact my hand was full of twos, fives, sevens, and nines and none in the same suit. Furthermore, various elements of the SFOR high command, in particular, visited Brčko in the wake of the event with the message, "We want to do all we can to help you in your huge task. Tell us what you need and we'll do everything we can to help." For me, this solidified the early beginnings of a very positive relationship with SFOR.

THE BRIDGE OVER THE SAVA RIVER

Early on in the struggle to unlock freedom of movement we received a welcome boost from an unexpected quarter. In late May 1997, the Department of State called to inquire whether a visit to Brčko by Secretary Madeleine Albright would be useful. We considered the pros and cons and an e-mail was tapped out to State flashing a green light for the visit. Secretary Albright's helicopter touched down on Camp McGovern's helipad on June 1. After mingling among the nearly eight hundred soldiers of the U.S. SFOR battalion, part of the U.S. Army's First Infantry Division—the "Big Red One," the secretary joined me for the ride north into Brčko *grad* on Route Kiwi. Because of heavy wartime damage to houses along the road, and to the roadbed itself, it took us nearly twenty minutes to traverse that short distance, which permitted me to brief her on the status of our efforts and to respond to her questions. It was obvious Secretary Albright clearly understood what was at stake and had complicated her schedule to make room for this side trip to Brčko. For my part, her presence was vastly reassuring in its own right and a welcome sign of future support within the U.S. government. By the time our cavalcade rolled into the center of town a small crowd had gathered to greet her.

Standing with her back to the war-scarred bridge that stretched for half a mile across the Sava River, Secretary Albright spoke to the watchful, subdued throng with warm words for those who were cooperating with Dayton and harsh words for those engaged in obstruction and delay. She further made a surprise announcement—the bridge was now open to civilian traffic! Within minutes the ceremony was over and, amidst cameras and a few shouted questions from (mostly Western) reporters, she reentered the limousine and back we went down the potholed road to her waiting helicopters. Fifteen minutes later, she and her party were but specks in the sky headed south to Sarajevo. Hers was a small gesture, perhaps, but one that had large implications for freedom of movement in Brčko.

I must admit that had it been left to me to come up with a proposal to open the bridge to civilian traffic, both wheeled and foot, I believe valuable months would have passed. Principally, my staff and I were uncertain how the intensely apprehensive Serb residents of Brčko would react to such an

Photo 3.2. Bridge over the Sava River, 1996 (Photograph by Alejandro Francisco)

announcement. We visualized one scenario, for example, in which the Serb populace might take the bridge's opening as an invitation to Croatians to infiltrate the town from the back door. Plus SFOR had a proprietary hold on the span, guarding entrances at both ends. This would have yielded only slowly, if at all, to lesser authority figures. In one stroke, Madeleine Albright moved the agenda off dead center and into the realm of possibility. For me, the object lesson came down to the simple realization that a civilian administrator in my position should invariably leap at the opportunity afforded by a high-ranking visitor to make a bold move—a sweeping gesture—that would use the moment to break through on issues heretofore blocked by hard-line obstructionists or clogged by inertia. I would recommend to future implementers to look upon such visits as opportunities for change rather than as burdens on you and your staff. Use their momentum much as ancient hunters used the energy generated by a slingshot to throw stones farther, faster, and more accurately than they could by arm alone. Such energy can accelerate the achievement of objectives that might otherwise languish in either indecision (your own) or obstruction (your adversaries). This holds particularly true during the early phases of a peace operation when the attention of participating governments keenly is fastened on ways to help you overcome the obstacles before you.

That said, things did not transform overnight. In fact, the day after the secretary's visit we began to tackle the details wherein the devil resided. I asked Gennadiy Shabannikov to chair a task force to open the bridge. The big question was whether a civilian automobile without an SFOR pass would be able to cross without hassle at either, or both, ends? Border authorities on both sides of the river had had no experience regulating international border crossings; since before the breakup of Yugoslavia the Sava River had been an internal, not an international, waterway. In order to travel in the Balkans region, all automobiles would have to be driven by someone holding a passport, a visa, a green international insurance card, his or her driver's license, and a valid registration document for the car. Very few people in the Brčko *grad*—in fact virtually none—would possess a passport because in order to obtain one they would have had to cross into the Federation and travel to Sarajevo. The RS did not issue passports! So without a valid passport and a rather expensive green insurance card, the possibilities for travel of people in Brčko across the bridge were nil. For Croatians living across the river in the village of Gunja, there would be little incentive to travel south because there was nothing to buy in Brčko. So the only real possibility for unofficial cross-bridge transit would be that of an international traveler—someone out of Vienna let us say—who was driving by road to Sarajevo. Or truck drivers, who in fact would be able to save thousands of deutschmarks (DEM) in duty fees by crossing at Brčko rather than the only alternative river-crossing point nearby—the expensive, time-consuming, and bribe-ridden ferry some twenty kilometers upstream in the Croat pocket of Orašje.

Ironically, our friends in the State Department, who early the next morning began calling us hourly to learn how many cars had crossed the bridge, either failed or did not want to understand these mundane issues, or that the community had been caught flat-footed by the secretary's announcement on a Sunday and we had little time to alert the local authorities so they could issue instructions to their minions in the field. It was one of those times when a little forewarning and planning on the part of policymakers could have facilitated a smoother transition. I spoke to the Serb deputy mayor first thing that Monday morning and made it explicitly clear that the bridge had to be opened without further delay. And, by some miracle, we were able to report by the end of the day that some thirteen automobiles had lined up on the Croatian side to cross the bridge from north to south. Of the thirteen, however, seven chose not to pay the exorbitant forty-five-DEM fee the RS police on the bridge were levying and instead turned back. But six cars did go through, which meant there was, in fact, freedom of movement and the bridge could technically be considered to be in operation! We quickly sent off a report to OHR-Sarajevo that would be communicated to the American Embassy and, through the embassy, to Washington. Although a host of complications still lay before us, we considered the mission accomplished for the moment. It took several days of cajoling and coaxing local officialdom and the people themselves to accept that the announcement was genuine. Then, near the third week in August, SFOR removed not only the barbed wire and the machine-gun emplacement from in front of the bridge, but also its M-1 tank that had for nearly a year barred access to all but SFOR official vehicles. Once that happened, not only did the bridge take on the appearance of a normal border crossing but Croat villagers from the other side of the Sava began, tentatively at first and then with increasing boldness, to walk cautiously across the bridge to a natural break at the end of the sidewalk from where they could wave at their Serb friends from before the war. For their part, the Serbs also stood back some fifty feet behind a barrier defined mostly by fear. One evening after work, I went down and stood quietly off to the side watching this remarkable human drama unfold as friends hailed friends they had not seen in over five years, tears streaming down cheeks on both sides—Serbs happy to see Croats, and Croats happy to see Serbs. At moments like this, which came only too rarely, I found myself thinking how blessed I was to be in my job and—given enough time, patience, and humility—how certain we could be of eventual success. It was the Albright initiative that had played a pivotal role in moving this entire process along.

CHECKPOINTS

No discussion of freedom of movement would be complete without mention of police checkpoints and the necessity to remove these ubiquitous impediments to ease travel on the roads. As I mentioned in the prior chapter, it was commonplace in Soviet and Eastern European countries, including former Yugoslavia, for police to perform their duties by setting up static points along the roads and highways, where they could randomly pull over automobiles to inspect documents and the vehicle's contents, to ask questions, and to solicit petty, and not-so-petty, bribes. The checkpoint was simply the standout feature of police practice.

Thankfully, Carl Bildt's request at Vienna for additional international civilian police officers to facilitate implementation of the First Award was responded to in kind by the UN Security Council. On March 31, 1997, resolution 1103 authorized an increase in the strength of the UN/IPTF by 186 police and 11 civilian personnel. Donald Grady, the local UN/IPTF commander, raised with me in our first days working together his desire to mount an intensive campaign to shut down police checkpoints and, in line with a larger program of reforms, to get the police moving around in the Brčko area of supervision. I wholeheartedly endorsed Grady's ideas and gave him the green light, subject to frequent review, to go after checkpoints as he saw fit. Now, I do not wish to imply here that I was in any way the architect of the UN/IPTF's anti-checkpoint policy. On the contrary, policing was an area in which I needed close guidance from the professionals. I had not in my Foreign Service career ever had to coordinate with internal police organizations abroad, much less take a direct hand in their operations. That said, it was important for Grady and the UN/IPTF contingent to know they had the supervisor's backing as they pressed forward in their campaign.

In those early days after the war, no Bosnian Serb would dare travel directly between the eastern and western "saddlebags" of the RS—for example, to cross Federation territory in order to save time driving from, say, Pale to Banja Luka. Instead they transited Brčko. This was not lost on the Pale regime. Tight control over Brčko's police was considered a highly effective means of controlling Brčko's populace—as well as a means of keeping sharp tabs on persons entering or transiting the RS portion of the Posavina Corridor, which by that time experienced nascent tension between hard-line eastern and less hard-line Serb elements coalescing around RS president Biljana Plavšić (1996–1997) in Banja Luka.[5] The local police commander, one Andrija Bjelosević, was a veteran of the war and by all accounts a practiced survivor capable of working on either side of the fence depending on the direction of the political wind. Thus surveillance methods were considered indispensable by the local power brokers, and the decision taken in Sarajevo in April 1997 to eradicate checkpoints throughout Bosnia was met with stiff opposition.

On May 12, I was present in Banja Luka when Bildt, SRSG Eide, UN/ IPTF Commissioner Manfred Seitner, and other top-level members of the international community met with Plavšić and several RS ministers, two of whom—Prime Minister Gojko Klicković (1996–1998) and Minister of the Interior Dragan Kijać—were over from Pale, to discuss checkpoint policy. Early into the formal discussion, Klicković, who appeared to be inebriated, began loudly to declaim against Bildt's opening remarks and flatly stated that, in effect, not only would there no longer be freedom of movement but it would be even further restricted in several RS areas. At this, the high representative asked Klicković whether he was threatening him. Turning to Plavšić, Bildt told her that this was a "very, very serious matter." Throughout Klicković's outburst, she had been tapping her pen on the tabletop—*tat tat tat tat tat*—trying to calm her prime minister down. Realizing, however, that he would not be slowed down, she let him go until he virtually ran out of gas. Plavšić then sharply rebuked Klicković, who, after grumbling in his cups, agreed not only to stop talking but apologized to Bildt as well. For the rest of the meeting the prime minister sat silently exchanging glances with Kijać, a tall man of about forty-five years, who resembled a snake with a sneer on its face. When the discussion turned to our policy of reining in police checkpoints, Kijać reacted viscerally. He let everyone, including Plavšić, know that Pale had no intention of giving up this powerful instrument of control.

Indeed, a month later, an SFOR patrol came upon an unauthorized checkpoint on a road off the main highway just outside of Brčko *grad*. The approved procedure for taking one down involved a four-Humvee patrol approaching the site in a nonmenacing manner, with two Humvees driving beyond the RS policemen and their vehicle forming the checkpoint, and stopping. The following two Humvees would pull in behind, thus straddling the checkpoint. At that point, two soldiers would dismount from one of the Humvees to query the organizers as to the authorization for their presence. If the police could not produce UN/IPTF-approved paperwork, the checkpoint would be dismantled under the watchful eye of SFOR. This is where things could, and did, get sticky.

When the Serb policemen were challenged in accordance with the foregoing rules of engagement, their commander refused to cooperate and instructed his men not to surrender their weapons. In a desperate maneuver to evade being apprehended by the SFOR patrol, the senior policeman tried to run away but was taken down and handcuffed with plastic wrist restraints. Only later did we learn that Dragan Kijać had issued orders from Pale to the effect that Brčko police officers were under no circumstances to give up their sidearms, even if challenged by UN/IPTF or SFOR. Indeed, they were instructed to defend them with their lives. Thus, the reaction of the checkpoint commander was fully in keeping with his superior's order. Had it not been for admirable restraint shown by the SFOR patrol leader, we could have had a nasty incident on our hands involving the wounding or, worse, killing of a Serb policeman. Such an occurrence would surely have sparked a riot in the town, with consequences that would have reached far beyond the confines of the Brčko *opština*. As it was, Pale immediately labeled the forcible handcuffing of the Serb police commander and his subsequent overnight incarceration by SFOR to be a gross violation of the man's human rights. For several days Pale pounded on this drum, but the fact the fellow was quickly released, unharmed, back to his police unit took the sting out of the SDS campaign to vilify the international community. In retrospect, we surmised that Kijać's intention all along had been to put his policemen at risk in order to stimulate an incident that would lead to a massive civil disturbance orchestrated, as always, from Pale.

Sheer persistence on the part of the UN/IPTF working in close concert with SFOR brought about the decline and eventual demise of the checkpoint mentality on the part of the Brčko police department. The area of supervision was soon declared free of checkpoints by about July 1997: an essential step toward restoring freedom of movement on the roads.

LICENSE PLATES

The most significant breakthrough for freedom of movement, however, came from Sarajevo and the simple but brilliant insight of a UN/IPTF civilian political officer from New Zealand. Faced with the insidious problem of factional license plates for vehicles—the Serbs with their cross and four "Cs,"[6] the Bosniaks with their fleur de lis,[7] and the Croats with their red and white chessboard—there seemed no way out of the dilemma. Not even a nationwide license tag would do the trick because of the two—Latin and Cyrillic—writing systems. Then there was the complication of colors. It seemed that each of the three ethnic communities had reason to object to most of the colors in the physical spectrum of light. For example, the Serbs and Croats would never accept green or any of its shades for use on a license plate since green is the color of Islam. The Bosniaks and the Serbs would object to the use of red because it signified the hated Croat *Ustaša*

Photo 3.3.   Private Vehicle License Plate, Republic of Bosnia and Herzegovina, 1998 Series (Photograph from the author's collection)

fascist organization that was active during World War II. The Croats and the Bosniaks would react to any color the Serbs used in their flag or in their national symbols. So there we were.

Then along came this New Zealander who cleverly noted that whereas both writing systems had thirty letters, eleven had the same physical appearance—even if some were pronounced differently. These common letters were A, B, E, J, K, M, H, O, P, C, and T. He proposed that these letters, used in combination with numbers printed in a simple black-on-white background, could become an acceptable formula for a national vehicle license tag. The general concept was adopted and after a brief interlude while the UN and OHR worked out the details, plans were quickly made to introduce the new tags to the nation. Finally, on February 2, 1998, the new standard vehicle tag was formally unveiled. As was to be expected, hard-line leaders of all three ethnic groups—especially Serb and Croat leaders—initially greeted the new tag with suspicion, seeing in its adoption a weakening of control mechanisms over the movements of their own followers. But, eventually, the sheer common sense of the new licensing scheme, coupled with the promise of freer travel on the highways, overcame the objections of even these dinosaurs; and the tags went into effect.

CONCLUSION

Thus through a series of actions and ideas, we were able slowly, ever so slowly, to begin to shape and nurture a semblance of freedom of movement in the area of supervision. The advent of the new license tags, on top of the elimination of checkpoints and the gradual but steady improvement in the Brčko police force away from its wartime, mono-ethnic (Serb) base toward a more disciplined, less exclusive organization, led to a painfully slow, but nonetheless observable, reduction in tension along the IEBL and in the road approaches to the town. We began to receive fewer requests from local Bosniak MZ leaders south of the line to be escorted, one on one, into town to conduct their business, or to visit my office. Gradually, they began to hazard the three-mile drive on Route Kiwi from the IEBL on their own in their automobiles. Notably, however, this growing sense of personal safety did not extend to Bosniak or Croat national figures, who would always ask me or members of my staff to travel south of the IEBL to meet with them at the Camp McGovern or Arizona Road crossing points.

Chapter Four

Refugee and IDP Returns

While conducting meetings in Sarajevo in anticipation of my supervisory role, I determined that the return of refugees and internally displaced persons (IDPs) to their homes in Brčko would be my ultimate priority. Annex 7 of the Dayton Accords had declared that all refugees and displaced persons had the right to return to their homes of origin, and that fulfillment of this entitlement would be a critical step toward bringing peace to the country. Families were not to be separated, nor compelled to remain in or move to dangerous or insecure locations. The parties to the conflict were not to interfere with the returnees' choice of destination and, further, were called on to provide assistance and facilitate voluntary return in a *peaceful, orderly, and phased manner* [emphasis added]. The First Award emphasized this point as well; I was tasked to oversee the phased and orderly return of Brčko's former residents to their homes of origin and to restore and allocate housing as necessary to accommodate old and new residents.

In the early 1990s, I had the honor of serving as U.S. ambassador concurrently to three small island nations in the South Pacific—Papua New Guinea (PNG), the Solomon Islands, and the Republic of Vanuatu. From 1990–1993, I resided in PNG's capital, Port Moresby, and I traveled extensively among the three Melanesian nations, whose combined population was approximately 4.5 million, comparable to that of prewar Bosnia. Apart from population size, I also saw other similarities between these disparate parts of the world. For one thing, PNG was, and still is, widely perceived as a wild and primitive place where over a thousand clans share an area the size of California. The total number of different languages spoken by the clans, exclusive of dialects, is 832 at latest count.[1] In fact, I found the people of PNG and the Solomon Islands, in particular, to be among the more isolated peoples on earth. The combined effect of inhospitable—though outwardly beautiful—lands and the ethnic complexity of their peoples served to keep PNG and, to a lesser extent, the other two island nations off the world's main trade routes. At the same time, however, these very factors have worked to keep PNG, in particular, alive in the imagination of anthropologists as one of the last frontiers of humankind. Much the same can be said, although on a different scale and with different emphases, about the Balkans at least so far as "civilized" Europe is concerned—many peoples (clans), many tongues, ancient traditions, and forbidding topography. The latter attribute is a particularly defining feature of both regions. Each is endowed with high mountains punctuated by deep valleys and non-navigable rivers that flow in unhelpful directions. Topography, therefore, can lead to isolation among the groups who inhabit it, and with the isolation comes an almost mystical attachment to land—land fought over and passed down from generation to generation, land that has seen, at least in the imagination of its denizens, rivers of blood expended in its defense. Such forbidding countryside fosters inward thinking among its inhabitants and a suspicion of outsiders that can effectively blunt dialogue not only with one's neighbors but with the world at large too. It was, however, this very primacy of land as a factor uppermost in peoples' thinking that struck me as most telling in comparing the two societies who knew next to nothing of the other's existence.

It is difficult for those of us involved in foreign affairs—civilian or military, official or private—fully to comprehend this mystical attachment to land. Many international workers in peace operations profess to understand why it is crucial for peace to give highest priority to the return of refugees and displaced persons to their homes. Indeed, most peace implementers work tirelessly to bring this about. But since they themselves spend large portions of their lives living away from home, they may not in many cases truly grasp how vitally important it is for a man and his family to be in their own home on both equitable and psychological grounds. For many international peace implementers, whose lives do not revolve around home and hearth, frequent moves from one place to another are taken in stride. Further, in developed countries there is always an established market for real estate that allows one to change homes with relative ease. Not so in the Balkans. In Bosnia, as in PNG, land means more, much more, than simple real estate to be bought and sold as circumstances in a person's life change. Land for traditional peoples, of which few international peace implementers count themselves as members, is a part of one's existential footprint on this earth, mixed with the very blood of one's ancestors and the cradle of one's family back to the fourth generation and beyond. Thus, to drive a person from his or her land in these societies is to deprive that person of a vital link to the past and to toss into the wind all plans for the future. To tamper with another's land in such traditional settings is to invite certain retaliation—if not immediately then later, perhaps years later, but certain it will be.

To illustrate this point, let me fast-forward to a warm Saturday afternoon in the summer of 1998 when, on an impulse, I decided to leave the office and take a leisurely drive through an outlying local community to mingle with some of the people who had actually begun to return to their prewar homes. As we pulled into the damaged community just to the south of town, I alighted from my vehicle and began to stroll down the dusty road. I soon came upon an elderly man standing in front of a bombed-out structure that I took to be his house. He was leaning over a pot suspended from an iron tripod above a small fire. When he saw me approaching, the fellow stood up, waved, and came toward me smiling broadly. He took off his cap and exclaimed, "*Hvala Vam!*" (Thank you!) I asked why he was thanking me, since we had never met. He replied that he knew very well who I was, having seen me on TV several times. The man said he simply wanted to thank me for approving his application to return with his family to their prewar plot of land. He pulled a folded piece of paper from his pocket and spread it out. Sure enough, there was my signature attesting to the fact that some months earlier I had OK'd the man's request to return to his land. (In fact, I had personally signed hundreds of such documents.)

Pointing to the pile of rubble that once was his home, I asked when he intended to start rebuilding. The man said his son, who owned the adjoining piece of property with a similarly damaged house on it, would be arriving in a few days and the two of them together would begin the process of clearing the rubble in preparation for building anew. Then the fellow told me how for four long years he and his family had been forced to live away from Brčko in cramped conditions more suitable for animals than men. He said during all that time he had experienced shortness of breath and painful discomfort in his chest. But just two days ago he had returned to Brčko and to his land. The moment he stepped onto his property, he told me for the first time in four years he had been able to take a deep breath without pain. He was breathing normally now, and for that, too, he thanked me sincerely. I complimented the gentleman—a Bosniak—for having had the courage to return. Without knowing it, he had made my day.

Thus, while still in Sarajevo, I had an intuitive sense that in the early and vigorous activation of the returns process lay the fundamental key to success of the DPA in the long run. But effectuating returns in Brčko would depend on my ability, in collaboration with SFOR and UN/IPTF, to establish a sense of security—a feeling among the populace that stability and calm were returning, slowly but inevitably, to the region. We would not—indeed, could not—persuade people to return to their homes at the point of a gun. Such an approach was clearly out of the question. Although I needed time to sort through the evolving structures and procedures the international community was experimenting with to stimulate the process of return, I was gratified to learn that work on a returns program for Brčko was already well in train and involved some of the more experienced international legal and refugee experts to be found in this field. I was, of course, willingly swept into this vortex the day after I arrived in Sarajevo. I quickly found myself haggling over concepts, phrases, and words I had heard all my professional life, but rarely had to confront with such operational immediacy. The intense serious-ness with which my newfound colleagues were approaching this drafting task brought home to me more forcefully than words ever could just how crucial to the success of the returns process throughout all of Bosnia was our getting this first-of-a-kind returns procedure to Brčko right. By the time my helicop-ter lifted off I had an approved text on the returns process tucked safely away in my briefcase, ready for launching on a date and time of my choosing.

Despite its socialist past under Yugoslav president Josip Broz Tito's (1946–1980) strong-arm leadership, the concept of land ownership—either individually, or by exercising the right to reside in socially owned property—remained firmly embedded in the psyche of Bosnia's four million inhabitants. Local property records, for example, had been largely protected during the Bosnian war even where they might cast a dim light on the actions of Serbs, both those from Serbia proper and Serbs indigenous to BiH, who had either destroyed the dwelling units of Brčko's former non-Serb residents, or chose to live in them. In those few instances where local property records had been tampered with, photostatic copies from before the war were kept on record in the Office for Geodesy and Property in Sarajevo. So the documentary basis on which a viable returns process would of necessity be grounded was, objectively speaking, already in place. How to access these records to insure their fair application to the problem at hand was, of course, a separate ques-tion. Fortunately, the drafters of Annex 7 of the DPA had the wisdom and forethought to establish a Commission on Real Property Claims (CRPC) that had as its primary mission to receive and decide any claims for real property in BiH where the claimant did not now enjoy possession of that property. The CRPC had a central role in validating and clearing for onward processing property claims that would become the fodder for the Brčko returns process.

As with all agencies and commissions established under Dayton, the CRPC depended on the international community for funding. Predictably, this fund-ing came in a less than reliable flow, which had partly to do with the fact that the term "real estate" and the role of the CRPC were not well understood by PIC member states. At least that was my perception viewing matters from the side. But without a robust CRPC performing its function and meeting regularly to render its decisions on individual property claims, the process of return of families to their homes of origin would become hopelessly bogged down. In fact, it was precisely because of this concern that I approached former U.S. ambassador Brunson McKinley, who chaired the Commission, with a request that property claims for Brčko be placed on a fast track within the CRPC so that we would have an initial pipeline full of at least validated property claims. When it was pointed out that the claims process called for official approval of each claim by the Commission assembled in formal session, McKinley and I, along with the CRPC's energetic executive director in Sarajevo, Bernie Siegel, worked out a plan to clear claims to Brčko on a prima facie basis—subject to reversal should contrary evidence emerge during the Commission's formal review process. This eminently sensible adjustment to CRPC procedures enabled us to start moving on our returns program.

BRČKO STRATEGY FOR RETURNS

As mentioned earlier, at the start of the war, Serb forces had effectively cleansed all non-Serb residents from both the Brčko *grad* and a large horseshoe swath of the *opština* to the south and west of town. Several theories have been advanced as to why the houses of central Brčko escaped the manic wave of destruction that engulfed the suburbs. One theory had it that the Serb wartime power structure of Brčko had struck a deal with their Croatian counterparts in Gunja, the town located on the opposite bank of the Sava River, not to shell each other's town center.[2] Another theory had it that Bosnian Serb leader Radovan Karadžić and his colleagues wanted Brčko's central residential zone spared so they could pack the town with Serbs and thus send out a clear message to the other communities never to attempt to return. A sub-theorem of the latter was simply that a town packed with Serbs would confront the international community with an insoluble problem, thus confounding its efforts to restore Brčko *grad* to its prewar ethnic configuration. None of these theories are mutually exclusive. Each can help to explain why the city was spared; for our planning purposes, however, the idea that the Serb wartime leadership had concocted this tactic to frustrate endeavors by the international community to restore properties to their original, non-Serb owners was the more compelling and its operational significance would be felt over time.

Thus, the concern uppermost in Serb minds as they were about to be forced to endure the imposition of an outside supervisor, who would henceforth play a major role in ordering their lives to conform with the terms of the DPA, was how this unwelcome intruder and his staff would affect their housing. As noted in the last chapter, there were two types of Serbs in the area of supervision, those who had been born in Brčko and those who had not. The newcomers occupied a good 80 percent of the *grad* and, like most honorable people everywhere, were keenly aware, although they would never voice it, that they were occupying houses and apartments belonging to someone else. Someday they knew they would have to leave those houses and go somewhere else—but where? Their own homes, too, were either occupied or destroyed elsewhere in BiH. Because neither they nor anyone else, including this new supervisor, could provide an answer to that question, they were living on a knife's edge and, unable to voice their fears, masked them in anger and hate for the "Other." Recognizing the core of the matter, in my maiden speech on the steps of my office to the Serb residents of Brčko, I pledged not to evict any family into the street if its members had nowhere else to go. This simple statement (which I reiterated often in coming weeks and months) did more, I was later told by a Serb politician, to calm nerves in the Brčko community than all the other points in my speech combined.[3]

Our first step was to call on the three mayors to explain to them the carefully drawn Procedure for Return that had been so painstakingly constructed in Sarajevo (see appendix). Because of sensitivities still raw from the war, each ethnic community insisted that formal documents be translated in their own variation of the nearly common local language—Serb, Croat, and Bosanski, as the Bosniaks called their branch of the language. I then arranged for three overhead projectors to be brought into my office where we invited the mayors for a simultaneous line-by-line explanation of the procedure, a process that took three hours. The next day—April 24, 1997—I published the procedure and entered it into force. With this step now in place, we began carefully preparing the ground for actual returns.

We first created a balanced and transparent Return Commission for Brčko, comprised of the three mayors (or their designated representatives) and supporting technical experts, with me, as supervisor, in the chair.[4] The purpose of the Commission was to receive and act upon applications for return whose bona fides had already been preliminarily established by the CRPC. The Return Commission met for the first time at my office on June 6, and weekly thereafter, until the pipeline began to fill up with names of aspiring Bosniak and Croat returnees. I made clear from the outset that decisions of the Return Commission were sufficient to establish a legal basis for return; any further processing on the part of Brčko's all-Serb wartime municipal government was therefore wholly unnecessary and certain to be pernicious in its intent.

Since in mid-1997 the idea of a *large* movement of returnees from south to north was out of the question for the foreseeable future, I was attentive to the advice and guidance of my staff, principally Anna Nylander, who brought her extensive experience with the UNHCR to bear on the problem. Pursuant to Annex 1(A) of Dayton, NATO's Implementation Force (IFOR) had demarcated the boundary in late 1995–early 1996 between the federation and the RS. A strip of land two kilometers wide on either side of the IEBL—a total of four kilometers—became known as the Zone of Separation (ZOS) and was controlled by IFOR's successor—SFOR—during my tenure. Our thoughts were to begin slowly filling in communities inside the ZOS to the south along the IEBL, where houses were either totally destroyed or heavily damaged. We believed international military control of the ZOS as mandated in the DPA would make Bosniaks and Croats feel more secure returning to local communities situated within its borders.[5] We would probe gently, first in the ZOS and then later across its border two kilometers north of the IEBL, as we proceeded tentatively to facilitate returns in a "peaceful, phased, and orderly" fashion.[6] Since I had the final authority to control the process, we built in to our planning the necessity for calibrating the rate of return to the amount of turbulence and Serb resistance the flow stimulated as we moved steadily north to the city limits and, eventually, into the *grad* itself. We carefully studied the prewar demographics of the Brčko area and did a quick calculation that by focusing only on destroyed and vacant housing in and just to the north of the ZOS we could, if all went reasonably well, facilitate the return of several hundred families, nearly all of them Bosniak. Returning families would be bundled together by their prewar neighborhoods so they could provide a measure of security to each other. Under no circumstance would we authorize the return of single families, or even two or three together, to areas where they would be isolated and thus vulnerable to Serb nighttime attacks.

Later, as we began to test the waters for serious return north of the ZOS, Nylander, Ian McLeod, Gennadiy Shabannikov, and Matthew Reece began to press on me, individually and as a group, the need for an overall strategic concept to guide us as we moved into uncharted, dangerous territory. After discussions lasting many days, staged as much to educate me to the realities we faced as anything else, we agreed broadly on a set of principles. First, we would concentrate our efforts on returning families to destroyed and unoccupied houses in local communities located farthest south and west from the *grad* itself. We would, in other words, work our way in from the outermost reaches of the area of supervision slowly converging on the town over a period of months, not weeks. No sudden thrusts, no unexpected moves, or surprises—all relevant decisions would be telegraphed to the parties from the open deliberations of the Brčko Return Commission.

Second, where we encountered resistance, we might consider pausing to assess the situation, but would not stop the process. Setbacks would be

Photo 4.1.   Knocked-Out Tank in the Zone of Separation, 1997 (Photograph by Ian McLeod)

viewed as setbacks only, not defeats. While steady pressure would be applied to the returns process, it would be calibrated in order to wear down
the opposition rather than to stimulate turbulence, although realistically the
latter could not always be avoided. As we facilitated return of families, local-
community-by-local-community, moving ever closer to the *grad*, we would
purposefully avoid those areas where the Serbs were most entrenched in favor
of filling empty neighborhoods with returnees so long as the stock of unoccupied and destroyed housing held out. Progress would be measured house-
by-house, settlement-by-settlement, as we plucked first the low-hanging fruit
and left the harder nuts to crack until the end. It was necessary, too, that we
prevail upon the Bosniak and Croat returnees to behave themselves so as not
to bait or rile the Serbs unduly.

Third, we would make every effort to ensure those who actually returned
would be looked after insofar as their minimum security and welfare needs
were concerned. Reece cautioned that a series of bad experiences, real or perceived, among returnees could easily scare off others and result in a *reverse
flow*, thus putting our entire return program at risk. We needed to be alert to
Serb provocations aimed at intimidating and frightening (or worse) Bosniak
and Croat returnees and, at the same time, to find ways of neutralizing such
orchestrated affronts so they would fail in their purpose.

Finally, I came early to the realization, after tough encounters with angry Serb residents, that we would need to be as, or more, attentive to their security and welfare concerns as to those of the Bosniak and Croat returnees. In the beginning, not everyone on my staff agreed with my evolving argument that a large number, perhaps the majority, of Serbs living in Brčko had had little or nothing to do with the atrocities committed there in 1992 against non-Serbs. As noted previously, the majority of Serbs residing in Brčko in 1997 had been driven there from other parts of Bosnia in the latter years of the war, some even after the signing of the DPA. These people, I argued, were just as much war victims as were the Bosniaks and Croats into whose dwelling units RS politicians had jammed them. True, these displaced Serbs were highly excitable and few held kind thoughts toward either the non-Serb returnees or the international community. That said, they too had basic human rights that needed to be protected. I proposed to protect those rights even when such a policy aroused a certain animosity among more than a few internationals who chose to see all Serbs as provokers of war and committers of atrocity. In practical terms, this came down to a long-running and hotly contested argument about what to do with the Serbs once it came time to contemplate evicting them from dwelling units they were illegally occupying in the *grad*. Who would pay for their relocation? Where would they go? How could we manage the eviction process so as to avoid sparking communal unrest and violence?

IDENTITY CARDS

Lawyers in OHR-Sarajevo had advised me that I would need to urgently address the question of internal identity documents in Brčko, since it posed a looming obstacle to freedom of movement and returns. Citizens of nations under the former Communist regimes of the Soviet Union and Eastern Europe had long been required by their governments to carry internal identity documents on their persons at all times and certainly when traveling. Thus, the RS, like the Federation, had a distinctive identity document about half the size of a standard passport, which carried the holder's photo, printed name, date and place of birth, as well as his or her current address. On the external cover of the RS version appeared the symbol of Serb unity fundamental to its people's nationalism—the Christian cross with the Cyrillic letter "C" interspersed four times between the arms. Needless to say, this symbol of Serb chauvinism was hated and feared among non-Serbs. In Bosnia at that time, however, if you were stopped by police and did not have the relevant ID on your person things could go badly for you, especially in the RS. Thus, it was indeed crucial that we look into this issue before launching our program for returns.

As mentioned earlier, when I first met Miodrag Pajić, acting as Serb mayor in the area north of the IEBL, he seemed full of reasonableness and one who was outwardly ready to cooperate with the supervisory regime. Mijo Anić, mayor of the Croat region of the *opština* known as Ravne-Brčko, gave us the impression that the Croats would let the more numerous Serbs and Bosniaks duke things out while they quietly slid back into their villages to the west of the *grad*. Munib Jusufović, Bosniak mayor of the region known as Rahić-Brčko, let us know the Bosniaks would hang tough until the Final Award was rendered. Jusufović made clear from the outset that he would never submit his people to RS laws and regulations. From April through September 1997, both Bosniak and Serb actions with respect to ID documents—each in their own way and for different reasons—stymied the initial return of persons to their prewar homes.

For some days following our arrival, McLeod, Shabannikov, and I discussed with Jusufović and his senior advisors, most notably Mirsad Djapo, local representative of politician Zlatko Lagumdzjia's SDP, prospects for the return of Bosniak families to their homes north of the IEBL. Given the sensitivity of this delicate issue, we had encouraged Jusufović and his staff to maintain a dignified public stance so that we could make quiet progress on obstacles as they arose. The question of the necessity for persons returning from the Federation to their former homes now in the RS portion of Brčko to carry RS identity documents immediately reared its head. Jusufović's message to me was clear—he would never countenance the carrying of Serb identification cards by Bosniak returnees! I gently but firmly explained that it was not in my power to change the provisions of the First Award, which was, incidentally, binding on all parties. The award clearly stated that until the political status of Brčko was decided, the laws of the two entities would continue to hold sway in their respective portions of the divided *opština*. Thus, since the process of return needed to get underway before Brčko's political status was likely to be determined, it would be necessary for Bosniaks and Croats returning to the Serb-controlled area to accept RS identity documents. Hearing this, the mayor angrily erupted, declaring that were he to bow to my ruling on this matter he would be "sending (his) people to their deaths!" I tried to reason with Jusufović, first, by noting that my office, backed by the UN/IPTF and SFOR, would be totally in charge of the returns process from beginning to end and, second, by vowing that we would never knowingly put anyone's life in jeopardy. Jusufović's was a false concern, I said, and added that if we wanted to catch the planting season, we needed to come to an understanding on this important issue without delay. Jusufović would not be mollified; he stated that if need be he would resign as mayor of Rahić-Brčko to prove his point. And in late April he did indeed resign, only to return to office in early May 1997.

It must be underscored here that the Bosniak leadership, locally and in Sarajevo, was motivated mainly by an understandable collective reaction to the injustice of having its people first driven from Brčko by force and now having to face the prospect of a long, interminable wait to return to their homes. On grounds of simple equity, but for tactical political reasons as well, they were eager to define my power in the widest and most sweeping terms. They chose to see the supervisor's role as equivalent to that of a proconsul in the Roman Empire, someone with the authority to simply set aside by fiat the laws of RS as they applied within the Brčko *opština*. Thus, the Bosniak leadership perceived no need for their people to accept identification cards issued by the RS in anticipation of the moment when their people might finally begin moving north across the IEBL to reclaim their homes. Indeed, Federation president Ejup Ganić strongly urged OHR-Sarajevo to issue its own identification cards to returning Bosniaks instead of insisting they accept RS ID cards. "This is very, very serious," he told me during a tense meeting in his office in Sarajevo.

I consulted with Michael Steiner, who suggested we seek a compromise solution, such as putting a stamp on the RS identity cards in Brčko that would state the area north of the IEBL was under international supervision. Such a statement would imply, without explicitly saying so, that RS jurisdiction over the area was superseded by the power of the supervisor who could be relied upon to protect the ID cardholder against RS misuse of authority in Brčko. As we began to wordsmith such a statement, I continued meeting with local officials who would contribute, knowingly or unknowingly, to the approach we would ultimately settle on in facilitating returns and ensuring freedom of movement. The chief of police in Rahić-Brčko, Mirsad Haseljić, was a Muslim educated at the University of Belgrade—ironically, a classmate of Andrija Bjelosević, the current chief of police in the Serb sector of the Brčko *opština*. In our first conversation, he fueled my fears that until the international community was seen to be apprehending and delivering to The Hague indicted war criminals, especially Radovan Karadžić and General Ratko Mladić, little progress in implementing major aspects of the Dayton process, especially returns or freedom of movement, could be expected. The Serb leadership opposed the idea of Steiner's stamp outright, because it tampered with an official document. Our solution to the Serb rejoinder was to devise an outer jacket, a sort of plastic sleeve, into which the RS ID card could be slipped, thus covering up the hated Serb symbol of unity. We crafted the following message to be printed in the local languages on the sleeve: "Valid for the period of the Interim International Supervision of Dayton implementation in the Brčko area until the final decision of the Arbitral Tribunal for the Brčko Area."

During this period, Jusufović took issue with me in exceptionally sharp and critical comments in the press, flying in the face of the informal understanding I thought we had reached to maintain a generally dignified public stance as we continued to search for a formula that would permit Bosniaks to begin moving back to their homes. When we presented our plastic-sleeve formula to him on May 27, after a brief discussion, he rejected it out of hand. With a show of raw emotion, he said I could have no idea about the suffering Serbs visited upon Muslims during the war. While he, like other displaced Bosniaks, longed to return to his home, he neither could nor would ever accept the RS ID card. He had told us that before and thought we understood; but clearly we had not, because what we had produced to meet his concerns was nothing. Jusufović vowed he would no longer work with me on this issue.

Resistance on the Bosniak side was ironically matched by outright obstruction on the Serb side. But we needed to move forward so we announced June 11 as the date to initiate the returns process in Brčko. At the first meeting of the Return Commission, we placed the village of Stari Rasadnik on the list for Muslim returns.[7] The big concern here was whether the RS would arrange to issue identity cards to returnees *on the day of and in the village of return* as called for in the Procedure for Return. Surprisingly, Police Chief Bjelosević actually attended a preparatory meeting on June 10 and sounded less negative about the possibility of ID issuance. At the time, though, I was wary, believing he had probably figured out, as had his bosses in the hard-line Serb capital Pale, that there would not in fact be that many Bosniaks to actually return, so that after making a pro forma attempt to comply, they could then say "Well, you didn't have anybody here, so we performed as we promised on the first day. You're on your own from now on."

On the first day of return Bjelosević delegated the on-scene policing responsibility to his deputy, Milorad Marić, who immediately began to stall saying, variously, that he did not have the authority to do the things UN/IPTF and SFOR were asking him to do, and in any case he had not been briefed. After putting the question directly to Bjelosević, who confirmed that his deputy had been provided instructions, we concluded that Marić—a Karadžić protégé under Interior Minister Kijać's thumb—had lied to us. Even worse, several Serb DP families had moved back into the Stari Rasadnik area over the preceding three days in direct violation of the word I had put out that such returns were unlawful. The Serbs were simply flat out against the returns process and over the next several months they would throw every trick in the book at us. For example, they would ask for building permits on the part of Bosniak returnees we had approved, while under the agreed Procedure for Return reconstruction was included as a basic right. Serb officials would spread rumors and disinformation about the dangers of returning to the ZOS.

Mixed-marriage couples would be quietly evicted from their homes—and the vacated residences filled with radicalized Serb DPs. Bjelosević would routinely fail to attend police meetings, stating they were beneath his level, while Marić maintained he was too low on the totem pole to have authority. RS police would allow Serb DPs to protest Bosniak returns and would even join in on the demonstrations. Mayor Pajić failed to attend Return Commission meetings and at one point RS president Plavšić wrote me to protest the proceedings, claiming that twenty-eight cases had been approved without legal claim to the properties in question. On a higher level, Banja Luka, although the legitimate RS authority at the time, was powerless; and powerful Pale was illegitimate.

In mid-June even Mayor Anić of Ravne-Brčko added to our difficulties by (untypically) siding with his Bosniak counterpart in declaring the Croats also would not accept the RS ID card, thereby effectively canceling returns to Ulice or Vuksić Gornje for the time being. In order to surmount these proliferating roadblocks, I decided to go over the politicians' heads in a series of radio "fireside chats" to speak to the populace directly. I also stepped up meeting with people in groups as well as granting interviews to the media. A month later, our fourth Return Commission was able to approve some fifty-six families—all Bosniak—to come back to MZs Stari Rasadnik, Brod, and Omerbegovača. That was progress to be sure, but there were still no physical returns on the ground. Ironically, on a visit to Sarajevo on July 17, I received a telephone call from an aide to Alija Izetbegović, the Bosniak member of Bosnia's tri-partite presidency (1996–2000), who said his boss wished to see me on short notice. This gave me the opportunity I needed to clarify at the highest level of Bosniak leadership the issues we were facing that were impeding returns to the Brčko area of supervision.

On July 20, U.S. ambassador to the UN Bill Richardson visited to remind me, in case I had forgotten, of how crucially important was a peaceful solution to the Brčko stalemate to U.S. policy in the Balkans. In the course of our conversation, I told Richardson about the ID-card issue. The next day in Sarajevo, as I was about to be ushered in to Izetbegović's office for a second visit, I was surprised to see Richardson and special envoy Bob Gelbard bustling out. On seeing me, Richardson cried, "We solved your [ID card] problem for you. He'll do it in three or four days. It's all fixed!" Then he and his entourage hurried on. Typical, I recall thinking to myself: Drones lay the groundwork and politicians swoop in to claim the credit!

In the room with Izetbegović was Bosnia's ambassador to the UN, Mohammad "Mo" Sacirbey, and the president's senior advisor, Mirza Hajrić. In spite of Richardson's boast that he had solved our problem, Izetbegović had several questions for me, the most important of which seemed to be, "Will this step, if I approve of it, in any way affect the outcome of the arbitration process?" In other words, would the very acceptance by Bosniak returnees of the RS ID card somehow legitimize the RS claim to the Posavina Corridor? Would it weaken in any way the Federation's argument for control of the Brčko *opština*? Like a thunderclap the realization came to me that Izetbegović's advisors, including Ganić, had not explained to him in clear terms the exact nature of what I was trying to do to get the Bosniak returns process moving in Brčko. They had exaggerated the scope and reach of my insistence on prospective returnees' accepting the necessity, under the First Award, of living within the laws of the entities—in this case, the laws of the RS—until a final decision regarding the political status of Brčko had been made. Thus, since all residents of the RS were required under entity law to be in possession of an internal ID card, new arrivals to the entity would fall under this requirement as well. I told Izetbegović that a simple reading of the First Award would confirm my interpretation of the supervisor's mandate. My intention from the beginning had been to make it possible for Bosniaks to return to their homes of origin in Brčko as quickly as possible, especially since the season for planting was quickly passing. I assured Izetbegović the ID-card issue had no wider significance than that. He responded with a look of surprise, saying this was the first time he had grasped what the ID-card question was all about. Izetbegović asked whether I would be prepared to put into writing my assurance that the arbitral decision would in no way be influenced by returnees' accepting RS ID cards. I said he would have a signed letter by the end of the day containing my assurance that acceptance of the ID card and our laminated overlay would not in any way prejudice the outcome of the final decision regarding Brčko's political status. With that, the deal was done.

Izetbegović said in two or three days he would come out in favor of Bosniaks accepting the RS ID card along with OHR's laminated insert encased in a plastic pouch. He assured me at the same time that Serb displaced persons would in turn be welcomed back into the Federation, particularly into Sarajevo. He urged me to do what I could to arrange contact between cantonal representatives in Sarajevo and the Serb DPs in Brčko *grad* to help smooth the way for the latter's return. Although this appeal was little more than window dressing on Izetbegović's part, especially in light of the intense fear and hatred still sitting upon the land, I nonetheless considered the forty minutes spent with him that morning among the more productive moments of my then three months in Bosnia.

This brush with the Bosniak wartime leader served as a useful vignette for future reference. For starters, it brought the lesson home forcefully to me that when matters of high policy were at stake I should not tarry long trying to sort out, or overcome, obstructionist tactics at the local and regional—or, as the military would say, at the tactical and operational—levels. Although the principle of subsidiarity[8] should be generally adhered to in foreign as well as domestic settings, its application can be overdone, especially where lower-level functionaries are unable to act on their own, whatever their lofty titles or positions. Although more effective with Bosniaks, who generally supported the Dayton peace process, than with Serbs and Croats, who in differing degrees did not, I nonetheless decided from that moment on I would raise matters sooner than later to the highest levels. True to his word, on July 25, Izetbegović went on Federation TV accompanied by ten other Bosniak party representatives to declare his acquiescence with the supervisor's requirement that returnees to Brčko should accept the RS entity's ID card. From that point on, it was Serb obstruction alone that prevented returns.

On August 11, I called on Miodrag Pajić and pressed him regarding the RS ID card and my plans to come out with a supervisory order the following day should it not be resolved. The mayor became visibly anxious over what I had to say, asserting that I was about to do what Ganić had wanted all along—for the supervisor simply to take responsibility for ID-card issuance out of the hands of Serb authorities and assume it himself. Viewed from his perspective, of course, Pajić was absolutely right. By my forcing the issue, the Serbs could indeed interpret my actions as taking the side of the Federation when, in fact, I was simply trying to break the logjam so the returns process could begin in earnest. The upshot was a lot of scurrying around on the RS side, with many phone calls back and forth to Pale.

At Gennadiy Shabannikov's urging, the Russian ambassador in Sarajevo went to see the Serb member of the tri-partite presidency, Momčilo Krajišnik (1996–1998), on the same day I was calling on Pajić, with the same message. If the Russian failed, I was determined to issue my order and institute the new proposal by the beginning of the following week. Further delay would risk stimulating the latent lawlessness among increasingly impatient Bosniaks along the IEBL. At the same time, I had to resist the Federation game of wanting to push the IEBL all the way to the top of the ZOS line. So, as would often happen, circumstances had driven me, as civilian administrator, to decision point. Unlike our military brethren, we civilians were rarely able to "shape the battlefield" to our ideal liking. That said, my staff and I were keenly aware of the absolute necessity of keeping in front of our problems and not losing the initiative to the obstructionists in Pale. Basically, either we kept our balance—and the initiative—in the face of Serb obstruction, or they would ensnare us in a cycle of reacting to their games.

Since Krajišnik was unmoved by the Russian ambassador's appeal, and having heard nothing from Pajić, I issued on August 12 an "Order on Identity

Cards for Returnees to Brčko." The gist of the order was that returnees to the RS-controlled portion of the Brčko municipality needed to possess a valid identity card in order to be assured of the same rights and obligations as all other residents of that part of the municipality. Since RS authorities had thus far refused to comply with my instruction that they issue identity cards *on the day of and in the village of return* for persons from the Federation who were duly approved for return to their homes in Brčko, Federation identity cards under OHR plastic covers with laminated inserts would henceforth be accepted as valid cards so long as my order remained in force—until I was satisfied Serb authorities in Brčko were fully complying with my instructions that they issue the requisite RS identity cards to returning Bosniaks and Croats. A second order notified the mayors of Rahić-Brčko and Ravne-Brčko that they were to make plans seven days in advance so that my office would be informed when and where people were returning. A third order simply directed the Serb chief of police to attend the weekly chief of police meetings with his neighboring Croat and Bosniak counterparts.

On the afternoon of August 13, we had word from Pajić saying RS prime minister Klicković had directed him to convey the message that the dam had broken and that the RS government would permit the issuance of ID cards in the village of return on the day of return, starting the following Monday, August 18. Matthew Reece then called to say Klicković wanted to come to Brčko to see me on Friday or Saturday, so apparently Pajić's message was not definitive. The prime minister used the next two days to blast me in the Serb press with statements about how I was favoring the "other side." Klicković was quoted as saying the RS would never bow to pressure from outside. On August 18, the day on which ID issuance was to begin, I went on television in Banja Luka where I was asked about a letter just released by Klicković in which he said Serb authorities in Brčko would *not* issue the RS ID card on the day of and in the village of return—instead they would only issue the card after a twenty-four-hour processing period. Caught off guard in front of the cameras, I responded by saying that if Klicković had indeed signed such a letter then I rejected it out of hand. Later in Brčko, when the RS deputy minister of the interior came to my office, I gave him the same message.

So we continued to prepare to issue the little white card in a laminated pouch on which we had worked so long to kick-start the returns process. Two weeks later I finally met with Klicković in my office and he agreed at long last to the issuance of the RS ID cards. At the time, I was concerned because in essence those loyal to Pale were asking me (and the international community) to recognize and deal first with them. Only then would they cooperate. But this procedure, if followed, would undercut Plavšić's authority as RS president. I remember thinking to myself that we should take what we could get from Pale and then return to dealing with her camp. Future peace implementers may have to face similar dilemmas created wherever split governments prevail.

The RS police began to issue ID cards to Bosniaks and Croats on September 26, 1997. It was a clear, sunny day. Wheeled conveyances of all sizes and shapes, including SFOR convoys on patrol, were, as usual, sending up clouds of dust as they moved along the unpaved and potholed Route Kiwi. Ian McLeod, who was observing the process, recounted to me later that he caught sight of a matronly woman of about sixty emerging from a canvas-covered police lean-to, holding in her hand a newly stamped RS identity card. As the woman came into the sunlight, a female Serb journalist named Ljerka approached, pad and pencil in hand. Ljerka, a young woman in her thirties, was known for her strident nationalist and anti-Muslim views.[9] She bluntly asked the Bosniak woman if she understood the full import of what she had just done by accepting the RS ID card. Did the woman realize, Ljerka went on disparagingly, that in so doing she had just given up her rights to a pension under Federation law and would from now on be dependent on the Republika Srpska for all her rights and privileges?[10] The Bosniak woman, without missing a beat, replied, "I don't care. I'm home, that's all that matters!"

Time and again in coming weeks, other courageous men and women returning to their homes, families in tow, would echo this woman's gritty resolve in returning to a municipality—laden with malice—where they would be in the minority. Simply to observe people stepping forward and exposing themselves to such danger was humbling to those of us charged with facilitating their safe return. I was particularly aware of my responsibility to work hand in glove with SFOR and the UN/IPTF to create safe and secure conditions for return so that returnees would not be placed in harm's way. But how to create those conditions became the burning question. A cardinal element in that mix of elusive ingredients was the overarching need to establish a modern, trained, and multiethnic police force. Until that key element was in place, we could hardly expect Bosniaks and Croats to venture back in large numbers into a jurisdiction whose police force was comprised of loutish, ill-trained Serbs, most of whom moved overnight from fighting the war to policing Brčko's streets, in the same purple uniforms.

Realistically, we could not expect to be physically present at all times and in every local community to observe families slowly and in groups trickling back to their destroyed or damaged homes. And SFOR, for its part, had a mandate to protect lives only when people were in immediate danger: a mandate that did not extend to the protection of property per se. The problem was that returning families had no way of protecting their daytime reconstruction efforts from marauding Serb thugs who could roam at night through the unlit countryside virtually at will. Our (SFOR's and my) partial solution to that yawning disconnect was randomly—and at the margins—to adjust the routes of Camp McGovern's wheeled patrols as they made their way into and out of town. Instead of driving straight into town, for example, the patrols would meander on a random schedule through the devastated neighborhoods on the outskirts of Brčko. SFOR soldiers would not dismount from their Humvees nor did they expose themselves more than they would normally do while patrolling streets of the town. This simple maneuver was intended to put Serb thugs lurking in the darkness on notice that they would probably not be able to do their dirty work and escape unnoticed. At the same time, the very sight of SFOR patrols rumbling through neighborhoods would provide a measure of reassurance to the Bosniak and Croat returnees. In order for this to work, however, it was vital that I cultivate and maintain a close, continuing relationship with Camp McGovern's battalion commanders and their higher-ups in Tuzla. To me, it was essential that the matter could be decided informally at the local level where it made eminent sense to all parties. As a civilian administrator, I sensed that if my idea had always to be broached at levels higher up in the military chain—say at SFOR headquarters or, heaven forbid, in the Pentagon, where the opinion of army lawyers would be sought—the random patrols might never have been authorized, and even if they eventually were, it would not be in the time frame I needed them.

Photo 4.2.   Destroyed Homes in Rijeke, 1998 (Photograph by Ian McLeod)

BIOLOGICAL BLOCKERS

The Pale crowd, correctly assuming that non-Serb prewar residents of Brčko would eventually try (with or without the aid of the international community) to return to their homes, decided, as part of its overall defensive strategy, to erect a barrier to returns along the upper boundary of the ZOS, two kilometers north of the IEBL. This "barrier" took the form of some forty destroyed Bosniak houses lined up along an east-west axis centered on Route Kiwi— roughly twenty houses stretching out to the east and twenty to the west of the road. The RS government simply requisitioned these houses, renovated them, ran in special electricity lines, recharged their water wells, and installed homeless Bosnian Serb families in them—over a hundred persons in all. Imagine the sight from the air—a nearly straight line of reconstructed houses with red tile roofs standing out against a bleak expanse of destruction that stretched for kilometers in all directions. The local Serb authorities under the thumb of Pale never offered an explanation for why, of all the structures that needed to be reconstructed in the municipality, these few were chosen in the MZ Stari Rasadnik. But their purpose was clearly to pose a dilemma for non-Serb IDPs contemplating returning to their homes or to the facilitators of the returns process: Either confront the Serb occupants of the houses with an eviction order and risk bringing down the wrath of Serbs throughout the *opština* or accept their presence as a fait accompli and avoid returning to that area altogether. Once again, I needed to remind myself that the Serb occupants of the houses, "biological blockers" as Anna Nylander liked to call them, were little more than pawns in a much, much larger game. So our response to the gauntlet Pale had thrown down had both a strategic and a human component.

In the early 1960s, while in uniform, I taught naval history at the U.S. Naval Academy in Annapolis, Maryland. With World War II still fresh in the nation's memory, several lectures were devoted to American naval strategy around the globe. In the Pacific theater, Admiral Chester Nimitz and General Douglas MacArthur faced the awesome challenge of defeating a heavily fortified enemy on islands stretching from Micronesia to the Japanese main island. By controlling these island approaches to their homeland, the Japanese planned to stop the inevitable American counteroffensive in its tracks and, in those cases where the Americans were able to break through, to interdict their supply lines. U.S. commanders shrank from the prospect of huge losses in lives and materiel that dislodging the Japanese from the Marshalls, Gilberts, Carolines, Marianas, and Micronesian island chains (as they were then called) would entail. So a strategy was settled upon to engage the Japanese on only a selected number of strategic islands, skipping over and leaving others to wither on the vine, thus keeping losses to a minimum while neutralizing Japan's seaward defenses. As bloody battles on, for example, Tarawa and Iwo Jima proved, island-hopping was a brilliant countermaneuver to the Japanese strategy.

Too much detail, perhaps, but the foregoing account contains the seeds of my own approach to the "biological-blocking line" of Serb-occupied houses along the ZOS boundary. Rather than react as the RS leaders hoped I would— by putting pressure on the forty Serb families to leave the houses, if need be by force—I proposed that we simply bypass the blockers for the time being and begin resettling Bosniaks in front, on the side, and behind them. In time, this stratagem resulted in totally surrounding the Serb residents of Stari Rasadnik (see map 4.1) with Bosniak returnees. Before we had a chance to pat ourselves on the back about how cleverly we had neutralized the biological blockers, however, came the realization that now we had a corollary problem of how to protect these Serb families who, like so many others in Brčko *grad*, were simply being used as pawns in Pale's game of obstruction.

If anything, this story testifies more to the bankruptcy of Pale's strategy than to the cleverness of our response to it. In any case, it was not long before a delegation of six angry Serb men paid a call on me to loudly decry the dangerous situation in which I had placed them and their families. How

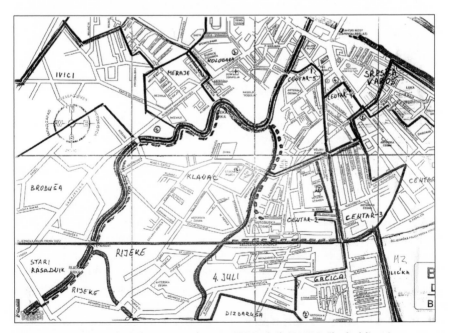

Map 4.1. Local Communities Surrounding Stari Rasadnik (OHR-Brčko holdings)

could they live in safety, surrounded as they now were by the enemy? Irate and frightened, they said it was my responsibility to extend the supervisor's mantle of protection over them. At the same time, they wanted assurances I would not evict them and their families from the houses in which they were living. When each of the six had had his say, I reminded my callers that it was not my office that had illegally installed them in other people's houses, a wrongful act in which they had apparently acquiesced. Nonetheless, I pledged to do all in my power to keep their families safe in these circumstances. Repeating the promise I had made to the crowd on my first day, I told them flatly that I would not evict them so long as they had nowhere else to go. They could relax on that score for the time being, but, I added, it was clear they could not live in other people's homes forever.

Since my visitors were in a belligerent mood, I thought it useful to recall the words of Radovan Karadžić, their wartime leader, who reportedly had declared that Serbs would eat grass before they would let Bosniaks and Croats return to their homes in the RS. I urged them to reflect for a moment on Karadžić's words, since they had indeed been put into a position of figuratively eating grass while Bosniaks were returning all around them. At the same time, did they really think their leader, Karadžić, would ever eat grass? No, I said, he would likely dine each day on *kolbasa* (sausage), pastries, and *šljivovica*. My visitors said little as they took their leave. Later, I chided myself for having treated these worried men so roughly. They were, after all, between a rock and a hard place and had no one besides me to turn to for help. Certainly Pale had neither the intention nor the means to assist them now. The biological blockers soon became, in a twist of irony, special wards of my office as Bosniak landowners continued to return not only to Stari Rasadnik but to MZ communities to the north and west of it at a slow but steady pace.

As happens in life, we found in our "solution" to the biological-blocker problem in Stari Rasadnik the germs of an opportunity, albeit born of necessity, for bold change. This potentially explosive situation called for tight coordination between SFOR, UN/IPTF, humanitarian NGOs, and my office. Indeed, Stari Rasadnik quickly became a lead topic on the agenda of our weekly joint meeting between the heads of all agencies and NGOs in Brčko. Through a process of brainstorming between official and nongovernmental civilians and our military partners—experienced hands as well as newcomers, experts as well as neophytes—some innovative ideas began to flow on how best to insure a peaceful return process to the wider community. I have already spoken of the informal arrangement we struck with SFOR to run its random patrols through local communities as they made their way from Camp McGovern to the *grad* so it was easy to include Stari Rasadnik in that mix of MZs. In fact, the single-lane, heavily rutted road into and out of the community ran alongside the line of biological-blocker houses. The SFOR battalion commander, LTC Jim Greer, came up with an additional idea. He proposed positioning two Conex containers side by side at the intersection of Stari Rasadnik's two main roadways. These large, self-enclosed metal containers are similar to those transported by flatbed tractor-trailers on land and cargo ships at sea. Conex containers, however, are fitted with a door and several windows. The U.S. Army uses Conex containers to set up temporary base camps, housing for officers, and for other special purposes. Greer suggested that the location would serve as a gathering place where representatives of the two ethnic groups could meet either at the behest or under the supervision of the international community: a place to hash out and, perhaps in time, resolve differences. The Conexes would become a sort of community center where international agencies could disseminate information directly to the people of Stari Rasadnik.

We quickly agreed to the SFOR proposal and within days two Conex containers were in place, guarded by a soldier with an officer in charge. Predictably, the residents at first ignored the structures, showing no desire whatsoever to palaver across ethnic lines. A few weeks later, however, I received an invitation from an SFOR major to speak before a group of women he was convening at the Conex center the following morning. The major said he had invited a dozen or so Serb and Bosniak women to sit down for a get-acquainted session and thought it would be a good opportunity for me to bring in the civilian perspective. I readily agreed. When I arrived the next morning, the women were sitting quietly—ten Serbs on one side of a long narrow table and ten Bosniaks on the other. All were mothers, several with babies and little children in tow. The major, speaking through his interpreter, expressed the hope that this would be the first of many such gatherings designed to build bridges between the two communities. He then introduced me and, building on the major's words, I told the women that SFOR and my office were working closely together on ways to improve their difficult situation. Uppermost in our minds was the imperative to do all we could to provide for the safety and security of them and their families. We were keenly aware of the fear and uncertainty they lived in day after day. In convening this meeting, we hoped to encourage them to open up to each other so that problems they faced in common—lack of drinking water, electricity, medical services—could be openly aired. We wanted to know directly from them what was on their minds. We were there to listen, not to talk. As I squeezed into a vacant seat, I could not help but notice a few women had tears streaming silently down their faces. With that, the major, an experienced facilitator, swung into action. Before long, a few women began, at first tentatively, to speak up and, sure enough, basic human needs were foremost on their minds.

Although I had to leave after thirty minutes, it was clear to me that this face-to-face dialogue, which by then had drawn several other women into the discussion, was full of promise and long overdue.

In the coming weeks, SFOR and members of the NGO community sponsored several meetings—not only with and between the women of Stari Rasadnik, but with the men also. Truth be told, the men were not so easy to bring together and, at first, the Bosniaks and Serbs insisted on convening in separate Conexes. But gradually the hostility among the two sets of males began to relax ever so slightly although there were strict boundaries to how far and fast that process might proceed. For example, one day while escorting a congressional delegation to Stari Rasadnik, I approached a Serb male standing on the steps of a Muslim house. I asked the fellow how long had he lived there. "Two years," he replied. "At some point," I said, "the owner will return and you may be asked to move to alternate quarters. What will you do then?" "I will go into town and kill the person who made that decision," the man replied, dead serious, as he mounted the steps, entered the house, and closed the door behind him.

As autumn waned and with winter coming on, SFOR outfitted the Conex containers with generators for light and heat. In the spring, so impressed was UNHCR's collaborative regional director, Santiago Romero-Perez, with our

Photo 4.3.   Stari Rasadnik Conex Containers, 1998 (Photograph by Ian McLeod)

Conex experiment that he cornered me with an architectural design he had commissioned for a small building of about three hundred square meters (five hundred square feet) to replace the Conex containers and henceforth serve as Stari Rasadnik's permanent community center. Romero-Perez proposed to replicate the structure's basic design elsewhere where returns were beginning to take place throughout my area of supervision, including in the Croat local communities some ten kilometers to the west. In a matter of weeks, UNHCR had contracted its modal design out to Catholic Relief Services, which quickly engaged a local construction firm to put the building up. Plans soon were made to install a telephone—a pipe dream in those days, but a great idea nonetheless. Further, Major General Larry Ellis, Commander of MND-North in Tuzla, sent his chief engineer to see what might be done about drilling a well for water in front of the new community center. At last, we were beginning to make real progress in moving the returns process along.

Upon reflection, I have difficulty understanding why I did not myself come up with such an obvious and commonsensical idea as the setting up of a community center—a gathering spot—in the midst of a combustible neighborhood where once friendly people had become hostile to each other. As I observe elsewhere in these pages, it took me awhile to recognize what social psychologists—or any astute politician—would have quickly perceived from the outset: The intensity of violence, anger, and threats that our returns program could provoke if poorly coordinated was in direct proportion to the prevailing level of fear in the community. In the Brčko area of supervision, I came to see it was primarily fear among Serbs that was at the root of most of our problems. It slowly dawned on me that if we could learn to look beyond the outrage of the moment and find a way of addressing this underlying fear, we might in time be able to tamp down the more violent manifestations of Serb anger and paranoia in a community that felt itself, not without justification, under siege. One way to do that, of course, would be to facilitate meetings between antagonistic groups not only at the top but also at the grassroots level. And what better device to facilitate such encounters than a "community center" strategically installed (as with SFOR's Conexes) or constructed (as with Romero-Perez's more permanent structures) in tense locations like Stari Rasadnik?

Looking back, our decision to go around rather than through the line of Serb-occupied Bosniak houses along the northern boundary of the ZOS had a salutary effect that went well beyond the tactical advantage of avoiding what could have been—and, if Pale had had its way, most certainly would have been—a violent confrontation. Although we could not foresee the benefits that would eventually flow from our shying away from violence in Stari Rasadnik, they began to emerge within a few weeks. Let me take a moment to enumerate the advantages, in rough chronological order, that accrued to us in the wake of this decision.

First, Stari Rasadnik quickly became a focal point of our concern for common safety at a point where Serbs and Bosniaks were forced to live side by side without a social buffer. Put differently, our need to seriously confront and manage the combustible reality we had, in a narrow sense, chosen to create by throwing the two ethnic groups together so early in the process came into sharp focus. Thus, an unintended consequence of our tactic in Stari Rasadnik was to jump-start our process of managing points of potential conflict at the local, or retail, level. Stari Rasadnik became a laboratory for the bigger effort looming ahead when we would begin facilitating returns in the *grad* itself.

Second, because of its immediate relevance for all international actors with offices in Brčko, we were at pains to include every agency in our planning process for the Stari Rasadnik effort. This inclusive approach elicited a spirit of cooperation among agencies that brought out the best in all of us. Ideas came to the fore, resources were shared, and synergy reigned as we all came together to keep the lid on and move the returns process forward.

Third, although it took time for this to sink in with me, Serbs in Brčko *grad* were watching how we dealt with the biological blockers for signs of how we might treat them when the time came. As we worked out some of the kinks between returnees and resident Serbs in Stari Rasadnik, the news would spread to other MZs where returns were about to take place. While I do not wish to read more significance into events in Stari Rasadnik than the facts will bear, nonetheless they did have a certain demonstration effect for the entire returns process.

Finally, Stari Rasadnik quickly became the go-to site for introducing visiting politicians, military flag officers, and international civil servants to the realities involved in bringing the destroyed villages around Brčko back to life. Inevitably, when such visitors dismounted from their vehicles—first, onto a muddy, rock-strewn clearance in front of the Conex containers and then, in time, onto less muddy and less rock-strewn ground as the permanent community center came into being—a small crowd would gather, providing easy conversation partners from whom our visitors could hear it straight from the horse's mouth. Nor was I unmindful of the fact that a Bosniak woman, who had returned to Stari Rasadnik with her war-widowed daughter and infant granddaughter, was eking out an existence in her dynamited house just opposite the community center. Whenever we escorted a delegation of outsiders past this woman's house, she would burst out of her door, fling her arms around whatever neck seemed most convenient, all the while shedding copious tears and effusively thanking the supervisor and his staff for all they had done for her and her family. We called her the "weeping woman." Without fail, once she had vented her tears, she would invite the delegation to come inside her little house to see the baby, which normally softened the hardest of hearts. Among U.S. senators to visit Stari Rasadnik over time were John Warner (R-VA), Kay Bailey Hutchison (R-TX), James Inhofe (R-OK), and Joseph Biden (D-DE). Visitors from the House included, most prominently, Newt Gingrich (R-GA), Dick Gephardt (D-MO), John Murtha (D-PA), and Bob Livingston (R-LA).

I am confident that these positive developments would not have happened had we chosen to demand that the Serb families either vacate the Bosniak houses in which they were living or agree to double up with the Bosniak owners. Beyond serious doubt, that approach, at a minimum, would have inflamed the Serb families and their confederates in the *grad*, providing an opening for Pale to jump in and add to the turbulence. Not incidentally, my promise not to evict Serbs from dwelling units in which they were living if they had nowhere else to go would have been rendered hollow. It would have been a disaster from which the fledgling returns process might never have recovered. Instead, within a year, Stari Rasadnik had gained a reputation as the first spot in Bosnia where two ethnic groups were again living in, albeit tentative and fearful, proximity to one another. In fact, the Serb leader of the biological-blocker families and his Bosniak counterpart in Stari Rasadnik soon established a rapport sufficient to their becoming reliable discussion partners with whom we and refugee agencies were able, with reasonable confidence, to interact.

In devoting so many pages to the Stari Rasadnik saga, I am in danger of implying that that single community consumed all or most of our energies as the returns process got seriously underway. Such was decidedly not the case. We were also hard at work in other outlying local communities, laying the groundwork for return at the same time this story was unfolding. From our earliest days, we recognized that returns could not begin until we had cata- logued all of the thousands of damaged and destroyed houses in the Brčko area of supervision under a marking scheme we in the supervisor's office controlled. Working closely with the CRPC and relying on prewar property records on file at the municipal office, a CIMIC team methodically—and intrepidly—walked the length and breadth of the area of supervision record- ing, photographing, and marking every house and apartment. I say intrepidly, because we all feared the Serbs, after destroying the houses, might have either booby-trapped the rubble itself or laid mines nearby to discourage the owners from ever coming back. As this ticklish work went forward, so too did our efforts to coordinate at weekly meetings of the Return Commission the pace and destination of returns in order to minimize their exposure to danger. Even in Stari Rasadnik—or perhaps especially in Stari Rasadnik, since it lay north of the ZOS and thus represented an early thrust into RS-controlled territory— houses reconstructed during daylight hours would come under surreptitious attack when darkness fell: roofs destroyed by grenades, newly erected walls knocked down by satchel charges, and construction materials stolen. Not every night, nor even every other night, but often enough to keep us all on edge. To give an idea of the hair-trigger tensions in the area of supervision, one day a rumor raced through the *grad* that armed Bosniaks were marching up Route Kiwi toward the town. Ian McLeod and Matthew Reece rushed to the scene only to find several dozen Bosniak returnees with shovels, pitchforks, hoes, and other long-handled implements over their shoulders as they headed up the road to their homesteads. With a Serb crowd gathering to challenge the Bosniak advance, McLeod and Reece persuaded the returnees to lower their tools and disperse to their individual plots of land without delay: crisis defused, but symptomatic of the local mood.

KLANAC

This next story serves as an example of the advantage of being on offense rather than defense, of having an active rather than a static program, when engaging in post-conflict peace implementation. We encountered stiff opposition, uncommon even by Brčko standards, among Serb residents of Klanac, a nearby MZ sitting athwart the main north-south road into Brčko *grad* (see map 4.1). Before the war, Muslim families had resided there peacefully in some seven hundred freestanding houses. Although the Serbs inflicted significant damage during the April–May 1992 period, I imagine that since Klanac was close by, the Muslims in their terror may have hastily abandoned their homes, thus sparing Serbian paramilitary forces the trouble of having to destroy every house as they did in communities farther away from the *grad* where the residents put up more resistance.[11] As our returns program progressed, we began approving families for return to MZs farther north of the ZOS. With each passing day, the necessity to deal with mounting Serb resistance and paranoia bore down upon us.

Each Return Commission decision to approve more returnees moving north of the ZOS was preceded by meticulous preparation and hard debate. The "peaceful, phased, and orderly" mantra was paramount. Nice words, but when it came to Klanac there was no getting around the fact that the Serb DP families squatting in some five hundred of the MZ's seven hundred houses[12] were in no mood to let even a small number of Bosniak families return to rebuild uninhabited homes. The Serbs in Klanac were clearly dug in for what was shaping up to be a major test of our returns strategy—a very, very hard nut to crack.

Beginning in June 1998, our returns program had evolved to the point that Klanac now hove into view as an imminent venue for return. The Serbs living there certainly understood this and began openly to interfere with our house-marking teams. On June 23, a crowd of some fifty Serbs screaming epithets turned back our house markers. The same day an unfortunate Bosniak with the Federation fleur-de-lis on his license plate was struck in the face and his car stoned as he tried to back out of the mob. Things were not going well. I convened a strategy session to consider our course of action. After considering the options, we decided to hold the city government responsible for the mob action, which, according to an inside source, had been orchestrated from on high. All eyes now shifted to Klanac as the final testing ground of our returns program to the suburban MZs surrounding the *grad*. Munib Jusufović, whose homestead as it happened was in Klanac, told me he had money to reconstruct six hundred houses there and elsewhere and pressed for stronger action.

To compress a long, violence-studded story into a few paragraphs, it took a full year of steady, unrelenting pressure to bring Klanac into the fold of MZs that would accept Bosniak returnees. The community leader, a die-hard Serb given to bombastic threats, was a master at keeping his enclave on edge. So we settled on a strategy of wearing him down. The late William Quayle, our able, resourceful, and stubborn returns officer, more than once had to repeatedly interpose himself—in the presence of a (by then) multiethnic police contingent—between angry Serb squatters and exploratory parties of returnees to keep Klanac from going over the edge. During this time, Ganić sent me letters protesting my permitting Serb mobs to threaten Bosniak families who had waited six long years to return to their land. I pointed out to the Serb mayor, Borko Reljić,[13] that Ganić's letters were a clear signal that the Federation was busy building a record of noncompliance against the Serbs over Klanac to be used against them at the next arbitral hearing in Vienna.

By condemning Serb threats of violence in Klanac in media statements and by proceeding steadily to authorize the return of Bosniak families to bombed-out houses in adjacent MZs, we maintained relentless pressure on the Klanac Serb leader to bow to the inevitable. Gradually, although it was difficult to calibrate, Serb defenses began to crumble. At the same time, we began to criticize Federation leaders, both national and local, for failing to create an atmosphere in which displaced Serb families were encouraged to return to their homes of origin in the Federation, especially in Sarajevo whence the plurality of Brčko's displaced Serbs came. Returns were a two-way street, I reminded Ganić, and the Brčko returns process could not be accelerated until the Federation's leadership, too, got into the game.

Willie Quayle later advised me that the Klanac Serbs felt they had nowhere to go and therefore had nothing to lose by engaging in physical obstruction and confrontation. This was a fundamentally different situation from what we had encountered in the other MZs. We decided to bring together the local leadership from both sides. Willie told them, "You are both DPs. You have been f***ed by your own politicians. Neither of you is responsible for the situation the other finds himself in. No one is helping either of you. You both want your own homes. Now tell us what the differences are between you and what you want?" Stripping out the acrimony from the ensuing debate, the Serb position boiled down to this: If they could be given plots of land, the Bosniaks could then return to their original homes.

Accordingly, following my establishment of the Brčko District in March 2000, we devised a delicately balanced plan that involved offering the Klanac Serbs plots of land elsewhere inside the Brčko *opština* in exchange for their willingness to vacate the Bosniak houses they were occupying. We knew this plan was bound to stir up controversy among human rights groups, who would attack it on grounds of equity. Their argument ran like this: By awarding plots of formerly state-owned land to Serb DPs, we would in effect be rewarding Serbs for ethnic cleansing. To get around this valid objection, I decided to offer equal plots of land to *all three ethnic groups*. With that, Serb resistance truly began to crack. Literally within days of our offer, as Willie Quayle suggested to the Serb leader that a small number of houses be cleared initially, the Serb leader asked, "Why only a small number? We have the agreement, let's get on with the whole of the job!" With that remarkable—and unexpected—concession, the issue of Klanac went away. Michael Doyle, then of Princeton University, visited in June 2000 (just days after my departure) and took note of the Klanac agreement in an article he published later:

The other part of the credit belongs to the courage and common sense of the Klanac residents, both Bosniak original and Serb current. Manipulated for years by their hard-line DP organizations and the ethnic political parties that relied on them for cheap votes, both groups of DPs stood up for themselves and stretched a hand across the ethnic divide when they saw a way to live together safely. Taking advantage of an offer from Supervisor Farrand, the Serbs agreed to vacate the Bosniak houses they occupied in return for free and secure land plots elsewhere in the District. When the DP leadership organizations balked at this sensible compromise and the new local District Assembly hesitated to pass enabling legislation, the current Serb and prospective Bosniak residents threatened to organize a multi-ethnic demonstration. (This surely would have been Bosnia's first.) The Assembly voted wisely and Klanac is now at peace. (Doyle 2000, par. 7)

Willie Quayle was pleased to observe that what had become in effect a joint Serb-Bosniak leadership dealt firmly with subsequent instances of inter-ethnic confrontation. He reported one example of the Serb leadership evicting a Serb DP from the Bosniak house he occupied for causing trouble; and two instances where Bosniak returnees were banned from their own MZ by the Bosniak leadership for the same reason: causing interethnic tension.

By applying relentless, steady pressure on the Serbs while exploring alternative paths to endless confrontation, the Klanac debacle was brought under control. After months of flirting with near disaster, the tipping point was finally reached whereby former antagonists decided to put aside their differences and cooperate for the common good. As I write this down, I still find myself nearly as perplexed as I had been during Klanac's darkest days in thinking about how the conflict would eventually end. One thing seems clear—in the end the fellow on defense has fewer cards to play than does the fellow on offense. The trick for you, the civilian peace implementer, is to recognize this simple axiom while you are in the throes of wrestling with the problem and, in spite of your doubts, to persevere. You may take a smidgeon of comfort from the thought that your antagonist faces a greater challenge holding his people together than you do yours.

CONCLUSION

Klanac was our first return incursion into the *grad* itself. Although ground-work for returns to the *grad* had been laid during my tenure, the final results would come only after I departed Brčko. I conclude this chapter on returns with two comments. The first relates to the importance of understanding the shades of gray—the subtle differences—in your environment and using this knowledge to your advantage.

I previously mentioned the makeup of the different Serb groups residing in my area of supervision. All along, as we began to fill unoccupied houses in such MZ communities as Broduša, Ivići, and Dizdaruša, moving closer and closer to the *grad*, we were systematically—and ineffectually—ob-structed by the newly elected Serb mayor Borko Reljić. Like his predeces-sor, Miodrag Pajić, Reljić was a *Brčak* who presumably wanted the best for his town, which, he rightly perceived, would benefit from a level of coop-eration with the supervisor and his partner agencies. As SDS politicians, however, both men were under incessant pressure from Pale—including threats to themselves and their families—to toe the hard line in confounding the supervisor's mandate wherever possible. Understanding this game, we played the crease whenever we could by, for example, appealing to the better instincts of the two men. However, they perceived the carrots we were able to dangle, at least in the beginning, as uncertain and ephemeral—no match for the sticks Pale brandished that they (rightly) judged certain to be wielded if Pale were crossed. This psychology of fear held true for the Serb population of Brčko as a whole.

But slowly, slowly, chinks in the Serb armor began to appear. Taken together, these chinks gave us the first clues as to how we might go about returning Bosniaks and Bosnian Croats to their occupied houses and apartments in the *grad*. First, the Serb DPs (Outsider Serbs), who constituted roughly 80 percent of the population, had no particular affection for Brčko, and were in turn roundly disliked by the indigenous *Brčaci*. Second, during the years 1993–1994, after ethnic cleansing had left its indelible mark, several *Brčaci* helped themselves through party connections to choice Muslim and Croat dwelling units left vacant by the forced departure of their owners. Some of these poachers, in fact, were not satisfied by taking possession of only one dwelling unit, but helped themselves to two and, in a few instances, to three houses or apartments. As we began to pick at the edges of this scab, we were dismayed to learn just how widespread was the multiple-occupancy practice. In fact, its very magnitude gave us ample room for driving a wedge between the different elements of the Serb population of Brčko. It turned out, for instance, that the Outsider Serbs were fully aware of the double-occupancy phenomenon that worked almost exclusively to the benefit of the *Brčaci*. Although no Serb resident of whatever stripe could be expected to express this view in public, we were privately encouraged to go after "multiple occupants" as the first step in the eviction process. So far as I was concerned, this would be an easy, backdoor way to introduce the idea of evictions—that were bound to come, in any case—to a community that was, at least on the surface, terrified at the very mention of the word.

After long discussion, my staff agreed that as a first step I should begin (in mid-1998) flagging our concern over multiple occupancy during press and media interviews. Predictably, no one came forward to declare themselves violators of the rule against double occupancy. At the same time, however, no one reacted vociferously to my announcements, and they passed without creating a fuss, which tended to confirm our underlying thesis: Multiple occupants had no sympathy in the broader Serb community. Thus, we gave ourselves a yellow caution light to proceed with a limited eviction program focused first on removing persons from second and third dwelling units. Absent an understanding of the various shades of gray among Serbs in Brčko, we would not have been able to implement this extremely touchy final phase of the returns process as early as we did.

My second comment has to do with the civilian administrator's perception of his own work, as against the perceptions of others, especially those who were bent on obstructing and frustrating the peace process. These actors will of necessity loom large in the administrator's mind and will occasionally block out his ability to accurately assess his daily progress. As the administrator proceeds openly, impartially, and in compliance with the peace agreement, he may find it hard to step outside himself from time to time and reflect on the possibility that his actions, over time, may have gained the begrudging (though unspoken) "trust" of his antagonists. Put differently, the administrator may have become so used to viewing things through the optic of the "fight" that he fails to catch small changes in his opponent's behavior and thus underestimates the progress he is making. In other words, he may in fact be succeeding even as he judges, perhaps with a whiff of paranoia, that he is failing.

Toward the end of my tenure, the "easy" return cases—evicting those Serbs in the *grad* who had commandeered two, and sometimes three, dwelling units and who had no supporters even among fellow Serbs—had sharply diminished in number. We now had to turn our attention to Serbs living in one dwelling unit only: the hard-nut cases for which we had long been bracing ourselves. Working closely with the Brčko District government, especially the police, we probed one or two houses first and were pleasantly surprised when the Serb families put up only mild resistance before agreeing to vacate. Breathing a sigh of relief, I nonetheless kept a weather eye out as the process inched along, preparing myself for a reverse in fortunes.

I did not have long to wait.

One sunlit morning, as the Brčko police, closely monitored by a UN/IPTF contingent, approached a Serb-occupied house near the railroad tracks, the man of the house let it be known that neither he nor his family would vacate the premises without a fight. A crowd of Serbs quickly materialized and within minutes the mood grew ugly—shouts and taunts and loud expressions of support for the Serb family inside. The police commander on scene approached Bill Thomas, a battle-hardened member of my staff from the U.K., and asked whether he could have more time—twenty-four hours—to work through this difficulty. Bill immediately informed his chief-of-staff, Tim Yates, who came to me straightaway.

As the first real test of our strategy for the *grad*, I knew instinctively that were we to mishandle this one, the fragile mood of cautious, if resentful, Serb acceptance of our step-by-step approach to the return of non-Serbs could vanish in a heartbeat. We would then be in real trouble, including the possibility of violence in the streets. I asked Tim whether he and Bill thought a twenty-four-hour delay in the eviction process was reasonable: In other words, did they trust the police to turn the situation around overnight so that a peaceful outcome could be assured? Tim replied that, while there could be no assurances, we had little choice but to give the police more time since the immediate objective was to get the crowd to disperse quietly. It was a tight call, but I agreed the police needed more time to resolve the standoff. After the commander informed the family they could stay another day, the crowd seemed mollified and to our great relief faded away. Nor did the crowd reappear the next morning when the police arrived early to speak to the head of household, who quietly agreed that he and his family would leave the house without raising a ruckus. We dodged a bullet, and we knew it.

In looking back, I recognize that perhaps because I was so close to the issue, I failed to credit the fact that over many, many months we had established a solid track record of proceeding fairly, if resolutely, in facilitating the return of non-Serbs to their homes in the Brčko *opština*. Our willingness to talk, explain, persuade—with words, not physical force—had not been lost on the Serbs, who had come grudgingly to acknowledge our impartiality and concern for the safety and welfare of *all* the people—Bosniak, Croat, *and* Serb. Although I failed to see this clearly at the time, our good reputation stood us in good stead as we proceeded with returns into the town center.

Chapter Five

Democratic Governance and Multiethnic Administration

The wonder is not how well the bear dances; the wonder is the bear dances at all.

—Old Russian (?) Proverb

It is hard to make the people take a share in government; it is even harder to provide them with the experience and to inspire them with the feelings they need to govern well. The will of a democracy is changeable, its agents rough, its law imperfect. I grant that. But if it is true that there will soon be nothing intermediate between the sway of democracy and the yoke of a single man, should we not rather steer toward the former than voluntarily submit to the latter? And if we must finally reach a state of complete equality, is it not better to let ourselves be leveled down by freedom than by a despot?

—Alexis de Tocqueville (2000, 315)

The DPA called on the OSCE to prepare, organize, and monitor elections throughout BiH. The First Award subsequently charged the supervisor to work with that body and other like-minded international organizations to ensure that free and fair local elections were conducted in Brčko before the end of the international supervision and, following such elections, to issue such regulations and orders deemed appropriate to enhance democratic government and multiethnic administration of the Brčko *grad*. Now in an all-perfect world, you might be able to conceive of disparate groups of people—who until recently had been busily raping, torturing, and killing each other—laying down arms, setting aside their anger, and entering into rational dialogue with one another. In such an ideal world, the notion that democratic elections

administered by outsiders could rapidly improve the lives of former combat-
ants, both military and civilian, might even have some tenuous validity. For
several months after my arrival in Brčko, however, I failed to encounter a
single person or group of persons sufficiently recovered from the dehuman-
izing effect of war that they could be expected to participate unemotionally
in elections: voting for their economic self-interest, rather than blindly for
their ethnic brethren. With Serbs shouting such epithets as, "We will never
live with the Turks again!" or "Brčko is Serb and will remain Serb forever!"
and Bosniaks and Croats grumbling, "Death to the killers of women and
children!" the reader will not quibble when I say it was difficult to get a
civilized interethnic debate started on any topic, never mind on such warm
and fuzzy issues as public services, health care, school bonds, and parks and
playgrounds. In fact, because of latent tensions, I found it well-nigh impossible at that particular point in time to conceive of an electoral process that
would do more than simply validate the current underlying demographic mix.
The fact was that people were simply too fearful, too bruised, too traumatized
by war to do other than vote for members of their own ethnic tribe—and this
without taking into account the exquisite pressure their factional leaders were
exerting on them not to break ranks. At that early stage, as rational actors, the
denizens of Brčko could be forgiven for concluding that voting for their own
kind *was* in their self-interest.

In any case, organizers of the elections were faced with a mountain of
historical baggage to overcome. For two generations, elections in Eastern European countries during the Cold War had been thoroughly rigged affairs with
thoroughly predictable outcomes. Central committees of Communist parties
in countries throughout the region—Czechoslovakia, Poland, and Bulgaria,
for instance—simply picked slates of candidates and ensured through total
control of the electoral process that these slates were "elected." The same
dynamic, if it can be called a dynamic, held true in near-Communist Yugoslavia. Thus, I would contend that the word "elections" conjured up meanings in
the Balkan mind far different from the meanings intended by OSCE election
organizers. In fact, by pushing so hard and so early for elections as a means
of force-feeding democracy into the Bosnian equation, the international community became in effect the *demandeur*, thus investing in the electoral process itself a value akin to that of a bargaining chip that could be exploited by
the three ethnic factions in different ways. In other words, the notion that the
mere conduct of elections was a conspicuous, even vital, element in the international community's peace plan gave—albeit unintentionally—the three
ethnic groups a lever that each could use to advance its agenda.

In retrospect, therefore, to hold early elections in BiH—an objective the
international community vigorously pursued—was to ask a great deal of the

indigenous Serbs, Croats, and Bosniaks. The OSCE clearly desired that prospective voters, hammered by war and barely coping with their lives, would not only absorb the somewhat arcane mechanics of registration and balloting, but have the popular wisdom to vote for moderation as well. On the latter point alone, questions like these must have roiled the minds of potential voters from all three groups: What is a moderate anyway? Who looked out for any but their own ethnic clan during the war? Why should a Bosniak, say, vote for a Croat or, heaven forbid, a Serb party slate? Why should a Croat or a Serb cast a ballot for a Bosniak? What was the percentage? Finally, "Why," as a Serb put it to me, "should anyone vote for a party that's not in power, since only parties that are in power can do anything for you?"[1]

This chapter will detail how democratic governance and a multiethnic administration were introduced to post-conflict Brčko. Focus is given to the role of elections and then to the development of institutions. While the executive and legislative branches will be covered below, the reformation of the judiciary and police force will be discussed in the next chapter on rule of law.

1997 MUNICIPAL ELECTIONS

The OSCE had conducted national elections on September 14, 1996, in accordance with the timetable set out in the DPA, and approximately 2.4 million people cast their votes. Municipal elections, which had been postponed three times by the time I arrived in BiH, were scheduled for mid-September 1997 and I chose to ride with that timing for Brčko. Whatever else elections might fail to achieve, they would at least provide us with a rough idea of what Brčko's underlying demographics would look like once freedom of movement had been restored and our returns program was fully up and running. Since the last official census in BiH had been conducted in 1991, before Yugoslavia fell completely apart, it would not be possible—or even desirable, as I came to realize—to conduct another census so soon after the war.[2] From a purely practical viewpoint, who would organize and pay for the census; and just as importantly, who could be trusted to do the count? Moreover, from a larger perspective, the last thing we needed just then was precision in population numbers. An element of inexactitude in Brčko's postwar demographics was no bad thing, since hard numbers in the wrong hands—and they were *all*, to varying degrees, wrong hands—would only ensure more communal flare-ups. A certain degree of ambiguity in this area, therefore, suited my purposes just fine.[3]

That said, we would need *some* objective, numerical basis on which to carry out the supervisor's mandate to enhance democratic government and multiethnic administration in Brčko. An election count meshing the number of those who registered to vote with the number who actually voted (including absentee ballots) would provide an objective basis—rough to be sure, but objective nonetheless—from which we could calculate the ethnic percentages we would need in the delicate task of forming a multiethnic government. That, to me, was the heart of the matter. While I had virtually no illusions that elections would establish an immediate basis for democracy in Brčko, I felt certain they would give us a launching pad for the heavy lifting that would follow: forming a multiethnic government in all its complexity.

OSCE's Approach to the Elections

OSCE had experienced a number of problems in conducting the September 1996 general elections. Its Provisional Election Commission (PEC), therefore, adopted new rules and regulations on January 28, 1997, that stipulated that all potential voters had to reregister for the upcoming municipal election. The latest plan defined all persons who had either resided in a particular locale (in my case Brčko) in 1991—thus, before the war—or who could show proof of continuous residence in that locale before August 1996 as eligible to register to vote. Persons wishing to vote had to register in person and be positively identified before their names would be added to the roll. Documentary proof took the form of a residency receipt or a DP card issued by the local municipality on or before July 31, 1996. Preparation of physical facilities and procedures to register potential voters in Brčko, and the registration process itself, occupied a significant amount of our time, energy, and coordination during the spring and summer of 1997.

Although the wording of the First Award was clear in stating that the supervisor and OSCE would work together when the time came for municipal elections in Brčko, the devil, as always, was lurking in the details. It helped that Ambassador Bob Frowick and I had known each other for years. But his responsibilities as head of OSCE extended over all of BiH and his large staff was understandably interested in maintaining a standard set of rules and procedures to guide the electoral process throughout the country. Inevitably, with the same tensions persisting in Brčko that had led to the city's emergence as Dayton's Achilles' heel, my staff and I needed to pay inordinately close attention to OSCE election preparations within the prewar *opština*. Nowhere in BiH, so far as we could tell, were all three ethnic groups in such close proximity to one another as in the Brčko area of supervision.

On April 16, barely a week after my arrival in Brčko, I became aware through conversation with Frowick's Canadian deputy, Jerry Robinson, that OSCE wanted me unilaterally to declare exactly what were the geographic limits of my area of supervision—as though, in other words, it was separate from OHR's. OSCE seemed puzzled, even bedeviled, by the presiding arbitrator Roberts Owen's liberal use of the term "relevant area" in the award. I sat down at my computer late that night and with Ian McLeod's help tapped out a message to Carl Bildt in which I spelled out OSCE's concerns and noted that I had no desire to be split apart from OHR in any way. I laid out my own understanding, based on a close reading of the award, of the geographic reach of my authority. I emphasized to Bildt the IEBL was a fact of life in Brčko and I could not alter it however I defined my job. A crisp e-mail reply awaited me the next morning in which the first high representative confirmed my understanding of the situation.

Frowick came to Brčko on April 27 with a retinue of about ten people. He wanted to share with me his plan to split the Brčko *opština* into four local election commissions, two north and two south of the IEBL. The Bosniak and Croat enclaves to the south—Rahić-Brčko and Ravne-Brčko, respectively—would each have their own local election commission (LEC). Since I had difficulty understanding the need for his proposal, I questioned whether it was wise to become more rather than less complicated as we approached this sensitive exercise in democracy. As regarded the IEBL and my ability to affect its location—to move it north so that the Federation would have access to territory still claimed by RS—to make it easier to administer elections, I informed Frowick not only was the line a construct of Dayton, but it was also the very heart of the matter under arbitration. It was therefore beyond my power to move the IEBL—that was a matter for the Arbitral Tribunal to decide. As he was leaving, Frowick seemed to waver a bit on his plan. Another consideration that occurred to me after the OSCE group's departure was that a complicated election procedure for Brčko could also adversely affect our program of returns, which—although it had yet to be formerly launched—had been painstakingly crafted weeks before.

In early May, I learned from Bildt that Frowick had visited Owen in Washington, D.C., to try to get a firm fix on what the latter had meant by using the term "relevant area." At the time, I thought it wrong for either local parties or international players in the Brčko enigma to attempt to consult directly with members of the Brčko Tribunal for interpretations of the award. As I saw it, the presiding arbitrator had created a useful mechanism for dealing with the issue and he should now retire from active involvement and let those charged with implementing the mechanism—like me—do their work. My concern, frankly, was that unless the tribunal kept its distance from the process, the parties would try to manipulate its members—essentially Owen—in ways that would tend to confuse the task of implementation on the ground. That was almost surely an unfair assessment of the presiding arbitrator; but I did not know him well at that point and therefore approached the question with a skeptical eye. In any case, it was clear that OSCE's Frowick was on edge concerning how to conduct elections in the hybrid atmosphere of Brčko.[4]

On May 2, 1997, OSCE announced ninety-three parties would be submitting candidates for the September elections. Forty-three of these were new. Three days later, it opened 420 offices throughout BiH to register voters through June 16. Out-of-country registration was scheduled May 5 through June 7. An agreement, however, still had not been formulated for Brčko and our registration offices remained closed. On May 8, Frowick held a press conference detailing the arrangements the PEC had agreed upon to address reregistration in Brčko. As chair, he had taken the decision that municipal elections would go forward in the Brčko area, and that an electoral district for those elections would be established in that area of the prewar *opština* which was under Serb control north of the IEBL. On the Federation side, however, de facto governing arrangements in Rahić-Brčko and Ravne-Brčko created a split in the municipality. Therefore, standard application of PEC rules and regulations prohibited the body from proceeding with elections in the area south of the IEBL. In practical terms, this latter decision meant that only DPs originally from the area north of the IEBL and now residing south of the line would be able to register and vote. Carl Bildt, present at the press conference, welcomed and supported Frowick's decision as the logical conclusion of the First Award, and as a means to facilitate the supervisor's work over the upcoming months and year. The OSCE reiterated on May 14 that elections would proceed in Brčko in this manner. Brčko's registration centers began opening five days later. Finally, in late May, Frowick announced OSCE would be reorganizing its presence in Brčko to meet what it had been called upon to do under the award. Rather than a single field office, an OSCE "Brčko Center" would be established with a strengthened staff and would report directly to the head office in Sarajevo.

The Serb Approach to Elections

The Serbs, typically, decided to approach the electoral process with jabs, feints, deception, and fraud. Knowing they had no choice but to comply when the supervisor decided to hold elections, they made all the right outward noises as they prepared to subvert the electoral process in any way they could. Almost from the moment the process of voter registration began, reports of fraud started trickling in. At first, we tended to downplay these reports on the grounds that local registrars were inexperienced and OSCE monitors, only recently arrived, were similarly fresh to their jobs. In any case, we allayed our initial concerns by acknowledging realistically that a certain amount of fraud was to be expected—it also had occurred during the 1991 elections. Nonetheless, OSCE's Brčko leadership, Jesse Bunch and Marc Bender, sat down with Ian McLeod and me in the early days of registration to agree on a common approach to the incidence of fraud. At first, we agreed to increase our vigilance by bucking up the OSCE monitors. Later, however, as reports grew on incidents of fraud buttressed by credible evidence of flagrant violation of rules, we would decide with OSCE headquarters' approval to close down the four voter registration offices and start again from scratch.

Bunch and Bender drafted a report, based on close observation of the registration process, cataloguing the dirty games the Serbs were playing. In addition to issuing phony residence documents making it possible for Serb DPs to vote in Brčko rather than in their prewar municipality, literally hundreds of people had been bussed in from neighboring Serbia to swell the ranks of potential voters. OSCE monitors caught local Serb registrars redhanded as they accepted spanking new identity cards presented by people who were supposed to have had such cards in their possession for over a year. Described earlier in discussions over freedom of movement and returns, these ID cards consisted of laminated cardboard, folded at the center, with a facial photograph of the bearer, and the usual identifying data. In normal use over a year, however, these ID documents would have become worn, smudged, and, in the case of males, contoured to the bearer's pocket. Within the space of two or three days, however, OSCE monitors watched as potential voters presented ID cards so stiff and new they refused when laid flat to stay folded, but would snap open of their own accord. Even more outlandish, serial numbers appearing in the ID cards of, say, a dozen voter registrants would track perfectly in order as their holders moved through the registration line. For example, number 451 would be followed by 452, and then 453, and so on. Then, to add insult to injury (or farce), the identifying facial photographs would show bearers dressed in the same jackets, shirts, dresses, and blouses that they were wearing as they stood before the registrars. The photographs, in other words, had been taken the same day. As to the validity of addresses shown on the ID cards, our harried team of OSCE monitors was not able, given the crush of over four hundred registrants per station per day, to go out in the neighborhoods and verify the location of each alleged address. It would have been a nice trick in any case, since the Serbs had destroyed most houses in the Brčko area of supervision and either obliterated or changed the names of streets in a manner that made them unrecognizable to outsiders.

One day I dropped in on a voter-registration center to observe the interview process firsthand. An American monitor, a prosecutor from the West Coast of the United States, was shadowing the interview of a woman who was clearly lying about the period of time she had lived in Brčko. The monitor showed me the woman's ID card. It looked to be brand-new and without a scratch, showing a date of issuance of more than a year earlier. As the OSCE monitor intervened with the local registrar to turn the woman down, she told me this had been but one of dozens of similar cases that day. We both reflected on how badly the Serbs, by these crude, sophomoric tactics, were hurting their own cause. By ham-handedly seeking to turn the registration process to their advantage, they were exposing themselves to charges of fraud that would come back to haunt them. It was too bad, we mused naïvely, that the Serbs could not simply go along with the rules, letting the chips fall where they may. The stakes, however, were too high—not only for the Serbs, but for the others as well. It was foolish of me to forget even for a moment that they all were still in a war mentality. The organized violence may have subsided, but the war raged on in the hearts and minds of the people. At the risk of repeating myself, for the Serb, Bosniak, and Croat residents of Brčko, past and future, "democratic" elections held a meaning far different from the one ascribed to them by their well-intentioned international organizers.

The Bosniak Approach to Elections

The Bosniaks pursued a strategy different from that of the Serbs to skew the outcome of the electoral process in their favor. Rather than enter freely into the first stage—voter registration—they sought in every way they knew to persuade the supervisor to assure an "equitable" result by guaranteeing *beforehand* that the elections would restore the prewar demography of Brčko. The Bosniaks would emerge on top, with the Croats and Serbs falling in somewhere behind. Failing that precooked outcome, the Bosniaks were prepared to consider a backup, post-election formula that would distribute power equally among the three ethnic groups. Two intense conversations I had with Federation president, Ejup Ganić, will give a flavor of the Bosniak approach.

On May 14, 1997, Ganić drove north from Sarajevo to meet me in the Bosniak village of Brka, just south of the IEBL. Surrounded by advisors and hangers-on, he opened by complaining it had been difficult to be in touch with me. I said that, as he well knew, when it came to matters concerning Brčko, OHR-Sarajevo preferred to interface with politicians at the national level, leaving it to me to deal with officials at the regional level. Ganić launched into a lengthy peroration on how he thought the elections should be conducted so that Brčko would end up with a multiethnic administration. Basically, he saw two options. The first was to base the elections on the 1991 census. That is, the supervisor would exercise his powers in advance of the actual balloting simply to restore the ratios then existing among the ethnic groups, with the Bosniaks restored to a 45 percent plurality throughout the *opština*. The second option was to distribute offices in the municipal administration, including the police, courts, and seats in the assembly (*skupština*), in accordance with a power-sharing formula of one-third to each faction. It became clear from his presentation that Ganić had been assigned the task of ensuring the Serbs would not retain control of Brčko either after the elections or, indeed, after the final arbitral award. Basically, the Bosniaks hoped to achieve through deft manipulation of the supervisor and his powers what they had been unable to achieve either during the war, or at Dayton, or through the arbitral process to that point. Both of Ganić's options depended upon the use of my supervisory powers to fix the outcome of the elections in advance. And neither option foresaw a *role* for the electoral process. Ganić concluded his opening presentation with a statement, which I took to be a threat, to the effect that unless I assented to one of his two options, the Bosniaks would refuse to register to vote. They would boycott.

I told Ganić I found his plan of action rather remarkable in light of the well-publicized fact that persons who refused to register would not be permitted to vote in the municipal elections. Thus, should the Bosniaks choose not to register, the whole thing could be decided quickly. For unless they registered, they could not vote; and by not voting they would imperil their chances for orderly participation in the Brčko government. After that, whatever strategy the Bosniaks settled upon to reclaim their political and property rights in the Brčko area of supervision would matter little. The meeting ended on that inconclusive note.

Despite my best efforts that day to clarify the dire consequences of his—and Bosniak tri-partite president Alija Izetbegović's—decision to prohibit their ethnic brethren from registering to vote, Ganić continued to play the boycott card. Bob Frowick and I had confirmed our intention to go ahead with elections in the Brčko area of supervision and, as the days rolled by, I became more and more anxious about the Federation's blindness to the indispensable role the registration process played in democratic elections. Coupled with Serb shenanigans, it was clear that the parties to Dayton had yet to emerge from their near-Communist mindset nurtured in a Yugoslavia where, since 1945, elections as engines of change meant little. I found my estimation of Ganić either dropping, because he was a fool, or rising, because he was pursuing some extremely clever strategy. Since I could not, for the life of me, figure out what that strategy might be, I inclined toward my first estimation. At about the same time, however, we became aware of fissures opening between Ganić on the national level and Brčko's Bosniak mayor, Munib Jusufović, on the local level, with the latter beginning to question the wisdom of a strategy prohibiting Bosniaks from registering to vote. Then we learned that Carl Bildt and his principal deputy, Michael Steiner, would be relinquishing their positions in Sarajevo. The departure of these two men meant we would be losing their sure policy touch just as elections were looming over Brčko and throughout BiH. In view of these contradictory developments, we redoubled our energies in order not to lose momentum in what was rapidly shaping up to be a critical juncture.

In discussing freedom of movement, I had mentioned the importance of the civilian administrator taking advantage of targets of opportunity, such as high-level visitors, whenever necessary to increase pressure on local recalcitrants. On May 20, Russian deputy foreign minister Igor Ivanov surprised us with a side visit to Brčko on his way from Moscow to Sarajevo. Although Gennadiy Shabannikov had long suggested the utility of such a visit as a way of bucking up the Serbs, as well as the election process, we had not counted on its happening. After we spoke briefly in my office, Ivanov repaired to my tiny apartment where he met with each of Brčko's three mayors one-on-one for nearly two hours. He was firm in his message that they all should comply with Dayton not only in letter but also in spirit. Later, Ivanov suggested that I issue a statement guaranteeing that the principle of multiethnic government would emerge from the elections. I assured him that was my intent and obligation. Nonetheless, I later spoke with Carl Bildt by phone and he assured me he would reiterate to Ivanov when the latter arrived in Sarajevo that Brčko would indeed have a multiethnic administration following the elections. He agreed that Ivanov's idea that I issue a public statement to that effect to tamp down Bosniak and Croat fears was excellent and I undertook to draft and make public such a statement. The Russian deputy minister's visit was a highly useful reminder, too, that Brčko was of concern to all PIC powers and was not an American, or even Western, problem alone. Beyond doubt, Ivanov's message fell on attentive ears among the Serbs and might have had a salutary effect on the Bosniak position as well. In any case, the visit could not have been more timely or welcome.

Seeking alternative ways to bring pressure on Ganić, we decided to up the ante by educating Bosniak officials in neighboring regions to the folly of this position. We needed them to understand how damaging it would be *for them* were their people not to register to vote. On May 25, Ian McLeod and I paid a call on the energetic mayor of Tuzla, Selim Beslagić, to press our case. The mayor met us in the Tuzla Hotel where we sat down over supper with his deputy, governor of Tuzla Canton Sead Jamakosmanović, two other high-level politicians, and Beslagić's wife. For more than two hours, we discussed the Federation's decision not to support the registration process. Ian and I made impassioned pleas to persuade them to at least agree to *register* to vote in order to save for their people the *right* to vote. Because of his long association with the Bosniak hierarchy in Tuzla, Ian's words carried special meaning. Also, Santiago Romero-Perez of UNHCR had joined our party and sat alongside me, giving me invaluable pointers on how to deal with the issue as the discussion intensified.

At some point during the long meal, I flatly stated to our Bosniak hosts that we were not their enemies, but their friends. In encouraging them to encourage their own people to register to vote, we were trying to save them from themselves. Drawing on his close knowledge of the election process, Ian launched into a masterful presentation, at the end of which, and without warning, the ice finally broke. It was as though someone had hit them with a heavy stick. After a moment of exchanged glances and mumbled conversation, the mayor caved and said, "Fine," they agreed! They would encourage their people to register. To us the significance of this went far beyond Tuzla. We knew word of Beslagić's decision would spread quickly to Sarajevo and put pressure on the center to come around as well. A day and night well spent.

On May 27, Ganić came again with his advisors to Brka where we met as before in the pink municipal building that housed Jusufović's office. It was clear that the Bosniak leader was exceedingly worried about how registration was going among the Serbs. Without saying it in so many words, Ganić conveyed the Federation's overriding concern that we were too naïve to detect Serb fraud. As regarded the Bosniaks continuing to boycott the registration process, he trotted out the same tired list of objections and demands that he had served up two weeks earlier. As I listened to him my patience wore thin. When he finished speaking, I leaned forward in my chair, pounded my hand on the table, and asked in a loud voice whether he knew what he was playing with here. Did he really intend to make the awful mistake of not allowing his people, both in the Federation and outside BiH, to register to vote in Brčko? Did he really want to put at risk the entire election, the purpose of which was to give all parties a place at the table? Were these his intentions? If they were, I said, and if the Federation persisted in its foolish boycott, I could guarantee one thing: the Serbs would win the election. At that, the room, including Ganić and me, fell silent. After a polite interval, I rose from my seat and my party and I took our leave.

Later that week, Bosniaks began registering to vote in the Brčko area of supervision. Since they were starting so late, we gave them another week to complete the process. In view of Serb transgressions, however, this was not a major concession on our part. In fact, after we had shut down Serb registration in order to tighten procedures and beef up the number of OSCE monitors, both major ethnic groups were about on a par with each other coming into the final stretch. Now it was the Croats that began giving us fits.

The Croat Approach to Elections

The Croat community emerged from the war as the smallest of the three ethnic enclaves in the Brčko *opština*. The ferocity with which Serbian paramilitary forces bore down on Brčko in April–May 1992 was aimed not only at Muslims—although they certainly took the brunt of the attack—but also at Croats, whose settlements were located generally to the west of the *grad* itself. From many conversations with leaders and residents of Ravne-Brčko; Croats in diaspora in Croatia, especially near Slavonski Brod, and in Zagreb itself; and Vinko Cardinal Puljić, the Roman Catholic prelate in Sarajevo, I pieced together the following picture of Croat life in prewar Brčko. First, the Croats were, for whatever reason, generally better off than their Muslim and Serb neighbors. They lived in farming communities nourished by the rich, loamy soil of the bottomland that extended for several kilometers south (and north) of the Sava River. The tiny Brka River also flowed north through Ravne-Brčko to the Sava and frequently overflowed its banks in the spring, further enriching the soil. Second, the Croats tended to be better educated, especially in technical sciences, and members of their community were often found in top executive positions in the twenty-odd manufacturing and agricultural-processing factories in Brčko. Third, the Croats tended to live in large houses set back from the road on expansive plots of land. Each Croat village had a Roman Catholic church and school that together served as focal points of community life. Although intermarriage between Croats and members of other ethnic groups was not unheard of, given the Catholic Church's strictures against intermarrying, the Croats generally stuck together in tight family units. Finally, unlike their hard-bitten and hard-line brethren in the mountainous regions of western BiH inland from the Dalmatian coast—north and south of the contested city of Mostar—the Posavina Croats were considered, like the fertile soil they lived on, to be of somewhat softer demeanor, a bit less confrontational, a tad more pragmatic. No saints, surely, the Croats often played a useful swing role in the Brčko drama even as they kept a low profile while the Serbs and Bosniaks clashed over freedom of movement and the right of return. That said, the Croatian Democratic Union (*Hrvatska Demokratska Zajednica*, or HDZ), the hard-line Croat party, still held sway over Croats in Ravne-Brčko just as it did over Croat settlements scattered across BiH. And the party line—laid down by Croatia's then president Franjo Tudjman (1990–1999) and his cronies in Zagreb and then transmitted to Bosnia's Croats through HDZ's Bosnian headquarters in Mostar—was that the elections in BiH were to be boycotted. Although the Bosniaks also threatened to use the same tactic unless their demands to guarantee the electoral outcome in advance were met, the Croats had no interest in deals. The HDZ hoped utterly to undermine the elections—to wreck them—by their nonparticipation. Or so it appeared to me from the vantage point of Brčko. While the registration process in Ravne-Brčko did not shut down altogether, local response to it was anemic at best with a resulting poor turnout at the polls and a corresponding reduction in Croat representation in the multiethnic administration we were able to cobble together after the votes were counted.

Registration, Appeals, and Elections

In post-conflict situations, an international civilian decision maker may have to take purposeful actions to surmount resistance to his or her agenda. On June 11, 1997, acting on the advice of OSCE's local director, Jesse Bunch, Frowick and I agreed jointly that the registration process in the RS portion of the area of supervision had become so flawed as to necessitate pulling the plug on it and starting over. My OSCE counterpart had by then largely overcome his apprehension about the anomalies Brčko presented for the election. He acknowledged my co-responsibility for the "free and fair" aspect of the process and had come to see the damage that could be done BiH-wide by allowing Serb fraud in Brčko to stand unchallenged. So we summarily closed down the registration process for a week to straighten matters out and to send a clear message. Luckily, we still had time to do it. The following day OSCE announced the voter-registration deadline would be extended in light of the fraud. The president and secretary of the LEC, and the presidents at each of the four voter-registration centers, in Brčko *grad* were replaced. In the meantime, we explored other ways we could punish the Serbs if they continued playing games. A sampling of potential sanctions included: knocking candidates for office off the top of party lists (slates); decertifying a party (which, in the case of the SDS, would frankly be playing with fire); and levying a series of fines on all SDS party members responsible for this charade. I reflected again on the wonderful mindset that infected the Balkans. In one breath they agree to cooperate, but in the next breath do all they can to undermine your best efforts to help them solve their own problems. Adding salt to the wound, they blame you when you stumble in the attempt.

On June 16, OSCE sent word that voter registration in Brčko would open again the following week in six, not four, centers with one-on-one monitoring. Another thirty-eight monitors would be added to the fourteen we already had to bring our total to *over fifty monitors*. Great news! The next few days were abuzz with internal talk about the elections and the need to reform the police force. One evening I invited several senior staff to my tiny apartment for some food and to watch the first tape of the BBC documentary *Yugoslavia: Death of a Nation*. It was useful to remind ourselves how the madness with which we were dealing got its start in the fevered, ambition-driven mind of Slobodan Milošević. As I was about to turn in that evening, a knock came on the door. OSCE's Christopher Wren, son of the *New York Times* reporter, handed me a report (confidential, from Jesse Bunch and Mark Bender of OSCE) recounting the latest abuses the RS was visiting upon the voter-registration process. Looking beyond its depressing aspects, I saw in the report an opportunity to strike names of the more repugnant hard-liners from the SDS list of candidates, an act that would benefit more moderate candidates—thin gruel, indeed, given the tight relationship to Pale of every candidate on the SDS list. But, in the circumstances, we found it marginally more productive to deal with intelligent subjects of Pale than with its more blockheaded, thuggish confederates. Reregistration of qualified Brčko voters began a second time on June 18 and ended July 12.

On July 15, an angry crowd of about 125 people gathered in front of my office to complain about the hard rules we had imposed on voter registration. Members of the orchestrated protest were particularly vocal about their distrust of the OSCE appeals process to adjudicate disputed cases. I used the occasion to phone Frowick to express my own concern that prospective appeals would be dealt with honestly, since we could not both preach democracy and at the same time fail to process rightful appeals in a proper way. I had become aware of a rumor circulating among OSCE's international adjudicators in Brčko that OSCE-Sarajevo might simply shred upwards of thirty-five hundred appeals likely to be filed from our municipality. While I acknowledged the vast majority of such appeals would be bogus, I needed to make the point with Frowick that the manner in which we proceeded on these appeals would be under close scrutiny by the Serbs and others. What I really hoped we might pluck from Serb manipulation of the electoral process would be the removal of particularly objectionable candidates from the rolls. The man I most wanted to knock off the list was the ultra hard-line Serb, Deputy Mayor Radoslav Bogičević.

One week later, the Election Appeals Sub-Commission (EASC) issued a ruling with regard to 3,688 individual appeals to register to vote in the Brčko *opština*. It also considered allegations of irregularities during the reregistration period. Each appeal was reviewed and it was determined that 181 would be allowed to register in Brčko. However, 3,270 persons were denied registration because they did not have valid documentation—once again the only documentation sufficient to allow an individual to vote in their current municipality was a resident receipt or a DP card issued by the appropriate municipal authority on or before July 31, 1996. Such persons were, though, able to register to vote in the municipality where they resided in 1991. The remaining 237 appeals raised questions of citizenship and were referred to the Citizenship Verification Sub-Commission for determination.

The EASC further found that the SDS, local police, and municipal authorities actively participated in the creation and the dissemination of invalid documentation needed by DPs to register in Brčko. The body noted the local police failed to cooperate with OSCE efforts to verify the residency of DPs seeking to register in Brčko; maintained a register of 1,104 names, none of which could be verified as being residents in Brčko; and provided registration applicants with backdated documents or listed addresses, which upon inspection, reflected either destroyed or uninhabitable properties. It was determined that the Brčko Red Cross Center, run by the local authorities, was conditioning humanitarian assistance upon proof of registration and that there had been at least two announcements in the local media suggesting that residents who did not register were "traitors" and would suffer unspecified negative repercussions. One such announcement was made by the president of the LEC on June 22, 1997. The EASC found no mitigating evidence that the police, municipal authorities, or SDS took any action to recall the invalid documents they distributed for the first registration period. Further, the EASC was satisfied that OSCE personnel successfully identified and isolated invalid documentation during the reregistration period. The body ruled that the SDS, as the ruling party in Brčko, should take responsibility for the irregularities that occurred and struck the first, second, and third candidates off the SDS party list. The LEC president was fined one month's salary for his June television statement. The Serbs responded by throwing a hand grenade outside my residence and making bomb threats against OSCE's Brčko office.

The stakes continued to rise in the face of the Plavšić-Pale split. The dissolved National Assembly of the RS, representing hard-line SDS interests, called for a boycott of the municipal elections. On August 26, OSCE representatives began talks with FRY president Slobodan Milošević to gain support for the upcoming ballot. The following day Frowick rejected the old National Assembly's proposal to postpone local elections. August 27 further witnessed a contest over control of police headquarters in several key RS towns, including Brčko, and the outbreak of a citywide riot in Brčko *grad* the next day. OSCE lost four days of valuable preparation time in the wake of that incident. In early September high-level officials continued to meet in Belgrade and Zagreb to break the SDS/HDZ boycotts. On September 10, we saw six hundred Serbs hold a rally in the *grad*, ironically to protest not getting paid four hundred DEM for attending a previous rally in Plavšić-controlled Banja Luka. September 10 also brought news of an agreement in which the

SDS leadership agreed to participate in the OSCE-supervised election—now but three days off. As concerned Brčko, Frowick gave the benefit of the doubt to some 259 registration appeals that had been delivered to the Citizenship Verification Sub-Commission. Also added to Brčko's rolls were some 2,285 registrations originating from the Dom Kultura voter registration center in the *grad*, the largest registration center there, during the second registration attempt. These names were added to correct a date error on a memo forwarding valid numbers of registration documents to OSCE's Sarajevo headquarters in July.[5] Although similar in number, and despite the Serb leadership's attempt to portray them as such, these were *not* the same people who had their appeals rejected by the EASC on July 21. The Croat HDZ boycott was not lifted until midafternoon on the first day of polling.

On September 11, we learned that LEC president Teodor Gavrić had informed OSCE that he had not carried out the necessary preparations to conduct the election in Brčko arguing that he had not expected them to move forward! Whether born of procrastination or obstruction, this meant our OSCE counterparts had to redouble their efforts to see that activities, such

Photo 5.1. View of Brčko Bridge/Customs Area, 1997, Scene of Riot on August 28, 1997 (Photograph from the author's collection)

as preparation of polling stations and recruitment and training of staff, were completed on time. Brčko's Serb mayor Pajić also advised OSCE that there were serious irregularities in the registration of Bosniak and Croat voters. He alleged that 186 individuals were originally from the area south of the IEBL; 92 had registered twice; 493 were not registered in the ID issue book; 540 on the final voters list had incomplete data associated with their names; and another 2,308 on the final voters list were not present on the 1991 census. We found it interesting that the total was similar to the number of Serb citizens whose appeals to register in Brčko had been rejected by the EASC. OSCE-Brčko duly passed the complaint along to the PEC.

Our concerns regarding Brčko's precarious position grew steadily in the days leading up to the elections. The need to minimize security threats both to the September 13–14 voters themselves and to the polling stations where OSCE poll-watchers and election administrators would be gathered consumed our thinking. Coordination of security planning among local elements of SFOR, UN/IPTF, OSCE, and my office was intense. We all accepted the likelihood of turbulence. We readied ourselves by planning proportional and coordinated responses to whatever occurred. We had to be on our best form and prepared to speak with one voice. Interagency squabbling at this point could be disastrous. At one point, I traveled to Sarajevo expressly to appear before the PIC Steering Board and brief them orally on our election preparations. In my presentation, I was openly pessimistic about the dicey security atmosphere in Brčko. In particular, we had those 3,270 Serbs whose fraudulent applications to register had been thrown out. Fair or not, such a large number of Serbs excluded from the electoral rolls heightened the pre-election climate of threat in the area of supervision. Put bluntly, we expected riots during the elections. I cautioned the steering board that were the Serbs to lose their majority position in the election, we should brace for yet another violent backlash.

OSCE later estimated that approximately 2.5 million persons had registered for the municipal elections, of which some 87 percent participated in the actual September 13–14 vote. Irregularities were observed more in the Federation locales of Drvar and Žepča than in Brčko, or even in the contested city of Mostar. In Brčko, we experienced blatant attempts by the Serbs to manipulate the elections process. In one polling station on the first day, they provided Brčko ballot papers to current Brčko residents who were registered to vote for their 1991 municipality. Once discovered, we took immediate measures to correct the problems—all ballots cast were sealed and placed under OSCE control along with the polling station records, and all voters told to report back the following day to recast their ballots. But there was also an issue with the number of people voting versus those present on our lists. For instance, at the Krepsić polling station we discovered that the final voters list was substantially smaller than the preliminary one—only 180 names were listed, whereas we had expected about 900. Voters were arriving with valid registration receipts, and therefore eligible to cast a ballot, which caused a commotion. OSCE's Jesse Bunch and Mark Bender met with Gavrić and Pajić and they agreed that the only option for these persons would be to vote by "tendered" ballot. Others who brought registration receipts from the first (canceled) Brčko registration were also processed in this manner. The tendered ballot was placed in a sealed envelope with the person's details written on the outside. These envelopes were to be sent to the counting center in Sarajevo where the information would be checked against the computer database, and if the details were validated the ballot would be counted.

Added to these jarring blows—some admittedly self-inflicted—to Serb electoral prospects was the post-election OSCE announcement that all ballots would be physically counted in Sarajevo. With Serb howls of outrage ringing in my ears, I suggested to OSCE that we make an exception to the rules so that Brčko's ballots could be counted in Brčko. In light of all the other negative blows they had absorbed, the Serbs wanted local ballots physically tallied in Brčko to insure the accuracy of the count. Serb paranoia zoomed off the charts at the prospect of ballot boxes being removed to Sarajevo where Bosniaks and Croats could gain access to them.

Once again, I remonstrated with the OSCE high command, this time with Frowick's deputy, German ambassador Richard Ellerkman. After consulting with his staff, he called back to say it would not be possible to make an exception to OSCE rules for ballot counting in a location other than Sarajevo. "Brčko," Ellerkman said, "would simply have to bow to that long established rule." I asked whether the ballot-counting rule was grounded in a high policy decision or was merely technical in nature. Again conferring with his staff whose voices were audible in the background, Ellerkman replied that technical considerations underlay the rule. I said in that case it should be possible, given the high stakes in Brčko, to find a way around the technicalities.[6] On the advice of his chief election advisor, Frowick's deputy remained adamant—there could be no exception to ballot-counting rules for Brčko. At that point I realized it would take a dramatic move to budge this issue off center.

In the early evening of September 14, I convened an emergency meeting of our own election experts, including Ian and Gennadiy, and invited OSCE's Bunch and Bender, by then trusted members of our policy family, to sit in. We quickly agreed that to ignore the admittedly overblown fears of local Serbs concerning the physical removal of ballot boxes to Sarajevo would be foolhardy and put at risk the entire electoral enterprise in Brčko. Accordingly, I asked our SFOR liaison officer to ram through an emergency request for a helicopter to take me and a small party to Sarajevo that very evening. At the same time, I placed an urgent phone call to Frowick's office to inform them we would be arriving at Ilidža, the suburb of Sarajevo where SFOR headquarters was located, later that evening. I needed to meet with him immediately to hash out this issue. I reminded his aide of our joint responsibility for conducting elections in Brčko and made it clear that Frowick himself should attend the meeting.

Although we made the flight over Bosnia's mountainous midsection in forty minutes, it was midnight before we touched down on Ilidža's helipad. Normally, SFOR was wary about sending its helicopters aloft at night, but the Tuzla Main commander understood the gravity of the situation and readily made one available for my use.[7] Once on the ground, we were whisked to a large military briefing room.

As we settled in around the horseshoe-shaped table, I could tell Frowick was peeved at having been called out at such an ungodly hour. Quickly taking the floor, he let me know that he considered the meeting highly unusual and of questionable necessity. I waited patiently until he finished venting his pique before reminding him that in view of Brčko's importance to the Dayton peace process in BiH and of our joint responsibilities under the award for conducting fair and open elections in Brčko, I felt fully justified in demanding the late-hour meeting. While I regretted that he and his party had to traverse Sarajevo late at night, my party and I had to cross the mountains in the dark by helicopter. The need for an emergency meeting between the two of us could have been avoided had our staffs been able to reach an acceptable compromise on technical election rules earlier in the day. In any case, we both had jobs to do and I suggested, in the interest of time, that we get down to business. At that, Frowick relaxed, smiled, and asked me to summarize the problem at hand.

A vigorous forty-five-minute exchange involving "technical" and "political" people on both sides of the table ensued. In the end, however, we agreed on a solution that I felt confident would help to defuse Serb paranoia on the issue of ballot counting and forestall further violence in Brčko. This involved the tedious photocopying of ballots so that when the originals were sent to Sarajevo for counting, copies of those originals would remain under lock and key in Brčko as a check against Serb fears of tampering by Bosniaks and Croats. The actual details of our agreement, though, are not as important as the fact we were able to reach consensus on the need to treat ballots from Brčko with extra care and sensitivity.

Back in Brčko the next morning, I received a phone call from the State Department in which Bill Montgomery thanked me for having taken the bull by the horns with Frowick and the OSCE. Somehow word of our midnight sojourn had gotten back and he wanted me to know the Department agreed with my course of action. "That's what we pay you for!" Montgomery said.

DETERMINING RATIOS FOR POWER SHARING

When the dust had settled and final OSCE election tallies were complete, we faced the challenge of sorting through the registration lists and voter rolls to determine a workable and defensible method of determining the ethnic mix to guide us in introducing Brčko's multiethnic governing institutions. Immersing ourselves in the election results, which involved a physical eyes-on combing of both registration and voting rolls to cull out Serb-sounding, Bosniak-sounding, and Croat-sounding names, we came to the moment of truth. Civilian decision makers and their staffs in peace operations rarely have the luxury of gaming various options before they must decide. Unlike most modern military contingents that routinely train with live exercises and intensive war games prior to deployment, the civilian side of the equation rarely engages in such training opportunities where differing courses of action may be tested against one another in a risk-free setting. More often, civilian peace implementers will find themselves deciding among available options live and on the spot. No rehearsals, no second chances—just weigh the options, debate the alternatives, and decide. And if ever the timeworn adage "not to decide, is to decide" has operational relevance, it is in the civilian decision-making process during peace operations. In our case, the question boiled down to a simple reckoning of how to allocate power between Brčko's once and future ethnic groups in a manner that would be seen as just and workable. Now that the elections were over, we no longer had the options of either delaying or not deciding at all. This was showtime.

The question became: What data or combination of data would we agree on to use in measuring the size of each ethnic group—registration numbers or voting numbers? Should we favor one over the other, or perhaps amalgamate the two into a common set of figures? We still did not have, after all, the sort of definitive precision in numbers that a fresh census would have provided. Nor could we be sure, because of delayed Bosniak acceptance of the need to register and the concomitant Croat boycott, that these numbers came close to an accurate reflection of the current demographic mix in the Brčko area of supervision. But, on the other hand, these were the only numbers we had—the only numbers that could reasonably be ascribed to have an objective base—however flawed and ambiguous that base might be.

Another question had to be urgently sorted out: How and in what manner would we introduce our findings into the life of the community? After days of internal discussion capped by a long evening with UN Civil Affairs officer Salman Ahmed, I decided simply to amalgamate the registration and actual polling statistics to serve as the definitive, if necessarily imprecise, criteria from which ethnic percentages could be derived. These combined criteria would guide us in our maiden attempt to form multiethnic and, in time, democratic government institutions for Brčko. After many hours of careful checking and counterchecking, the percentages emerged as follows: Serbs (52.2 percent), Bosniaks (39.1 percent), and Croats (8.7 percent).

At the same time, the ratios generated from our amalgamated data for each of the three ethnic groups had an inherently destabilizing implication for the next step in our post-election process. Taking each ethnic group in turn, let me explain what I mean. First, although the Serbs' 52.2 percent margin gave them a clear, if narrow, majority, it nonetheless represented a sharp reduction from the notional and estimated—but palpably real— figure of 97 percent de facto Serb presence in the area north of the IEBL. Even though Serbs had comprised barely 21 percent of the Brčko *opština's* prewar population, we feared that the war-induced facts on the ground would skew their judgment since the election results would require them to swallow a more than 40 percent drop in their actual hold on power, how- ever illegitimate the means they had used to attain it. In relying solely on registration and voter numbers to award the Serbs an electoral edge of 52.2 percent, moreover, I could expect to be second-guessed by members of the international community and sharply criticized by the Bosniaks and Croats for failing to seize the moment to put the Serbs forcefully back in their pre- war place. Their margin of victory of some 13 percentage points over the second-place Bosniaks would be, I was certain, attacked as an odious and highly suspect outcome that reeked of manipulation.

Although I did not perceive this clearly at the time, the fact that the Serbs merely huffed and puffed rather than took to the streets when I announced their electoral showing of 52.2 percent not only had significance for the future of the *opština*, but for the Dayton process as well. Pale was almost certainly ready to react, probably violently, to a Serb electoral margin be- low 50 percent. It is a safe bet that when the Serb number came in above 50 percent, the Pale crowd was caught off guard and forced to reassess their options. Basically, they may have seen an opening to gain their objectives by begrudgingly accepting the results of the election and then using their narrow but real advantage to frustrate and confound the establishment of multiethnic, democratic institutions in Brčko. Following this line of rea- soning, Karadžić and company could be expected to insure that the SDS candidate for mayor was a political neophyte wholly subservient to the party's leadership. Pale's game was to stymie, if possible and without undue turbulence, the supervisor on his own turf. This is easy to see looking back, but not so clear at the time.

Although the content of the Final Award—or even the fact that there would *be* a Final Award—could not have been known at the time, the 1997 election results helped lay the foundation for a further refinement and definition of the goal of multiethnic government in Brčko. As I saw it, the Serbs, by accepting a sharp diminution in their de facto majority position in the area of supervision inadvertently revealed their strategic vulnerability and weakness. In effect, therefore, those elections planted the seeds for a further reduction in Serb power when the time came to refine the degree of multiethnicity in government institutions under the 1999 Final Award. Although months would pass before I grasped fully the impact of all that had transpired, this process conformed nicely to our "step-by-step" method of proceeding. Let the Serbs get used to a sharp reduction in their authority de jure for a year or so, and then bring them below the 50 percent margin to attenuate their political influence over the community. And that is exactly how events played out in real life.

The Bosniaks were not at all happy with an electoral showing of 39.1 percent, especially since they had held a plurality position of 45 percent throughout the *opština* as a whole before the war, and a solid majority position of 54 percent in the *grad* proper. They were, therefore, the first to cry foul and to enlist outside observers in their cause. But we were able to deflect their complaints simply by referring to the egregiously long time it took for Bosniak leaders like Ejup Ganić to give up their senseless threats of boycott and come around to the necessity of registering and voting in order to protect Federation interests in Brčko. The time lost in such futile maneuvering had come to cost them dearly in getting out the vote, especially absentee ballots to the diaspora in Western Europe and further abroad.

Finally, Mijo Anić, the moderate HDZ mayor of Ravne-Brčko, was visibly upset by the low figure of 8.7 percent for the Croats—roughly one-third of the prewar demographic. While I had certain empathy for his position, I was compelled to point to a concerted Croat campaign emanating from hard-line HDZ headquarters in Mostar and beyond to boycott the elections entirely. That some Croats residing in Ravne-Brčko, as well as many in the Croat diaspora, had had the good sense not to heed the call to boycott the election process spoke well for the relatively moderate state of mind among Croats living in the Posavina Corridor. Anić himself had expended a great deal of time and energy traveling out to Germany, Austria, and Switzerland, among other countries, seeking to persuade Croat refugees from Brčko to vote in the municipal elections. Nonetheless, it was important that we proceed on the basis of hard numbers—as hard as such imprecise data could be—in order to reduce the element of arbitrariness to within acceptable limits. I told the Croat mayor that I, too, would have preferred a higher showing, but we were where we were and would have to go forward on that basis. While I could not speak for them, I believed Anić and his core advisors knew well of what I spoke and reluctantly accepted that their weak showing was of their own doing. The sad result of all this was that it served to discourage for the next two years or more both Croats in diaspora and their displaced brethren from returning to their empty MZs in the area of supervision north of the IEBL.

CONVERTING NUMBERS TO REALITY

It was now time to apply the electoral results to each of the three branches of government—legislative, executive, and judicial—so that within a relatively short period of time the people of Brčko would see that elections had real consequences—some good, some less so—for their lives. This process posed one of the larger challenges the supervisor's office would face during my tenure. Although our approach to each of the governmental branches differed in every detail, the underlying necessity to bring together under one roof, figuratively speaking, three disparate ethno-religious factions who, until recently, had been engaged in open, active warfare against each other remained the fundamental principle. Ian McLeod, with his unsurpassed knowledge of local party structures and the workings of the Bosnian electoral system, undertook to oversee the initial restructuring of the municipal administration—the *Skupština* and the Executive Board—using the 52.2—39.1—8.7 percent election-generated ratios. Gennadiy Shabannikov, who held a degree in international law, agreed to take the judiciary under his wing and to shake out and replace dead wood from the top down. Meanwhile, I asked Matthew Reece, assisted by Karen Decker, Salman Ahmed, newly arrived OSCE head Edward Joseph, and others, to work closely with Don Grady of the UN/IPTF in overseeing the ongoing process of police integration. Each of these formidable undertakings consumed hours and hours in direct discussion with local actors, individually and in groups, and in every conceivable setting—from dark, smoke-filled rooms to official confrontations over green-covered tables. At one point during this intensive period, I recall remarking that for every hour we spent engaged directly with the parties, another two hours was taken up in strategizing among ourselves to insure coherence in our overall message and thinking.

Reconstituting and Transforming Brčko's Governing Institutions, 1997

As early as the summer of 1997—and well before the elections—my staff and I first began conceptualizing what multiethnic administration might look like in Brčko. The First Award noted the supervisor was responsible to take such measures as required in order to "enhance democratic government and a multi-ethnic administration." The March 1997 Vienna Conference clarified that the police were included in this process. We decided that the existing municipal structure already in place in that portion of the Brčko *opština* north of the IEBL should serve as the basis—the starting point—for establishing a multiethnic administration. The existing structure was defined and governed by the May 31, 1994, "Law on Territorial Organization and Local Self-Government for Republika Srpska." Article 20 of that law outlined municipal administration functions, as follows:

> The Municipality, through its bodies, in accordance with the law shall:
> 1. Adopt the program of the development of the activities in its competence, urbanization plan, budget and final account;
> 2. Regulate and secure the development and realization of the communal activities;
> 3. Regulate and secure the use of the communal construction sites and business facilities;
> 4. Take care of the construction, maintaining and using of the local roads and streets of significance for the municipality;
> 5. Take care of satisfying certain needs of the citizens in the area of: culture, education, health and social care, social protection of the children, physical culture, public information, craftsmanship, tourism and restaurants, protection and the advancement of the environment and in the other areas of direct interest for the citizens;
> 6. Plan the tasks and undertake measures in case of the elementary and other dangers in the municipality and create conditions for their removal;
> 7. Execute the tasks and other regulations and general acts of the Republic [RS] whose execution was transferred to the municipality, secure the application of the regulations and other general acts of the municipality;
> 8. Secure legal aid to the citizens for execution of their rights;
> 9. Establish bodies, organizations and serve for the needs of the municipality and regulate their organization and operation;
> 10. Conduct other activities defined by the constitution and the law, as well as by the municipal statute.

To suit our purposes, we believed the municipal structure should be defined as broadly as possible, to include the legislative, executive, judicial, social services, police, and other branches of municipal government. The fifty-six seats in the *Skupština* should be allocated strictly according to the results of the municipal elections, based on proportional representation for each political party. The legislative process should be amended to provide safeguards for ethnic minorities on issues of "vital interest." We judged that this could be accomplished through requiring a two-thirds majority—rather than a simple majority. The remaining branches of government, including the police, should be constituted according to the ethnic breakdown of the 1997 voters list.

Working from Party Lists

The task we faced in multiethnicizing Brčko's municipal administration was complicated by the necessity to work from preordained party "lists," rather than having the latitude to select candidates from a wider pool of talent. We had permitted ourselves—for lack of time—to go along with the "closed list" system, which had long been in use in Yugoslavia. It is important to note that political party affiliation *within* ethnic groups is a consideration the civilian peace implementer must take into account in devising a plan for introducing, or reintroducing, multiethnic pluralism into an indigenous governmental structure. That said, I would argue party affiliation is secondary to the overriding strategic goal, which is to restore ethno-religious diversity where it had been weakened or destroyed by conflict. That is the primary strategic objective. Whereas a mixture of political parties *within* each ethnic faction is a laudable—even valuable—aim, it should not be permitted to interfere with the fundamental object of the exercise—multiethnicity. Variety among political parties is, in other words, a secondary objective or goal, subordinate to the main proposition. Why is this so? Well, in the beginning stages of a post-conflict peace operation, party affiliation within disparate ethnic groups will mean little when the chips are down. When one community feels under pressure from "the Others"—which effectively means all the time—its members will put aside their shallow political differences and vote unfailingly as an ethnic bloc against the other groupings. So it will not much matter in the early stages how politically diversified the groups are within themselves. What will matter more is that a group has enough weight in *gross* numbers to protect its broad interests. The nuances of party affiliation within the group can come later. In the beginning, you will need to keep your eye steadfastly on instilling pluralism of the first, most basic, order—multiethnicity in cardinal, not pastel, colors.

Let me cite an example of how this reasoning affected my own decision making in Brčko following the 1997 elections. As the final vote was being counted down in Sarajevo, my colleagues and I became increasingly worried the Serbs would not do well enough to retain electoral control over the Brčko area of supervision. Why should this have mattered to us? Weren't the Serbs, after all, the bad guys? Why take such a counterintuitive position, which would surely appear as our taking sides with the Serbs? In reply, let me say that while we certainly had no desire to see the Serbs retain anything like the

97 percent control of the territory north of the IEBL—indeed, we wished to see their controlling majority sharply reduced—we fervently hoped the Serb parties, taken together, would retain control because their numbers were simply greater on the ground. At the time, the Serb electorate in Brčko was comprised primarily of members of Karadžić's hard-line SDS party, Vojislav Šešelj's even harder line SRS, and the Socialist Party of Republika Srpska (*Socialisticka Partija Republike Srpske*, SPRS), a remnant of Yugoslavia's prewar Communist Party under the presumed and lingering influence of Slobodan Milošević's Socialist Party of Serbia (*Socialisticka Partija Srbije*, SPS) in Belgrade. The simple fact was that an outcome other than the Serbs retaining control would be untenable. Remember, the process of return for non-Serbs to the area of supervision had yet to get underway in meaningful numbers. Thus, multiethnicity had yet physically to emerge on the ground. Imagine our trying to install a Bosniak or, less likely, a Croat as mayor of Brčko! How could that have realistically been done in the absence of free-dom of movement or, in the same context, significant numbers of Bosniaks or Croats living north of the IEBL? The answer: It could not have been done.

So, like it or not, we found ourselves quietly praying for the Serbs to win a small—not large—majority in the elections so they could continue to run Brčko for a while longer. Word began to reach us during the vote count, how-ever, that the outcome between the Serb vote and the combined Bosniak and Croat count was going to be very, very close—even too close to call. At one point we found ourselves staring at the possibility that the *Skupština* would be split: twenty-eight Serbs versus twenty-eight non-Serbs. Such an outcome would have led to stasis, requiring me to intervene constantly in the legisla-tive process to break deadlocks with supervisory orders of one sort or another. It was thus with a deep sigh of relief that I welcomed the midnight arrival of an exhausted representative from the OSCE in Sarajevo who carried a sealed envelope from Bob Frowick with the election results for Brčko. Lo and be-hold, the Serbs had eked out a small but comfortable absolute majority over the combined non-Serb vote count: thirty Serb against twenty-six non-Serb votes divided between three parties on either side. The dominant party on the Serb side was, of course, the SDS with seventeen votes. The dominant party on the Bosniak/Croat side was a coalition led by the SDA; the SDA got nine votes and the coalition as a whole got sixteen. The HDZ, the Croat party, got three votes only. This result effectively broke the logjam so that we did not have to face hostility all around.

Lest I appear wholly dismissive of the importance of political parties—even in the early stages of a peace operation, I offer the following example about the Croat enclave of Ravne-Brčko. Six or seven months after the September 1997 elections, in which he ran and won as a member of the hard-line Croat HDZ party, Mayor Mijo Anić had an opportunity to leave the HDZ and join a less rigid, more moderate political camp. At the time of the elections, the HDZ had been the only party effectively representing the Croats. In August 1998, however, Krešimir Zubak, a former wartime general in the Croatian Defence Council (*Hrvatsko Vijeće Obrane*, HVO), formed a moderate Croat party to counter the unyielding nationalist face of the HDZ. Concerned with securing a future for all Croats in BiH, the new party was named the New Croat Initiative (*Nova Hrvatska Inicijativa*, NHI). Anić was invited to join the NHI, and he did.

As noted elsewhere in these pages, Croats in the Posavina Corridor had built a reputation for political moderation, especially when compared to their Croat brethren living further south and west among the craggy mountains along the Dalmatian Coast. So it came as no surprise when we learned that Anić, his deputy, Mato Jurišić, and most of the people in Ravne-Brčko had made the switch from HDZ to NHI. In fact, we were delighted when we heard the news because it moved the Croats within the Brčko *opština* toward the center where we hoped all Brčko's political leaders would eventually migrate. Not surprisingly, however, news of the defection was greeted with outrage at HDZ party headquarters in Mostar (Bosnia) and Zagreb (Croatia). Within a short time, Anić began to feel the heat from the hard-line high command as they dispatched functionaries to Ravne-Brčko to harass and intimidate him and his small community.

One day in midsummer, Anić came to my office in some consternation to report that a Croatian army officer and several soldiers dressed in civilian clothes, but carrying sidearms, had shown up in Ravne-Brčko from Zagreb. While the Croatian officer was threatening Anić in his office, the mayor alleged the Croatian soldiers slouched around the municipal grounds intimidating employees and passersby. Incensed by Anić's report, I immediately phoned Bill Montgomery, who was by then U.S. ambassador to Croatia, and told him I would be coming up to Zagreb to request the American Embassy's assistance in confronting the Croatian Ministry of Defense (MoD) about this alleged gross intervention in the affairs of another state. When I arrived a day or two later, Montgomery agreed to send his defense attaché to the Croatian MoD to present the facts, as we knew them, and demand an explanation. The attaché returned in a couple of hours with a predictable report that the Croatian MoD denied such a thing had ever happened. Never mind, the point had been made—Anić never had to complain again about such open and blatant harassment from Croatia.

Back in Brčko, I issued a brief supervisory order on July 13, 1998, prohibiting the dismissal of elected or appointed officials from their municipal offices on the grounds they had freely exercised their democratic right to change political parties, or to sever party affiliation altogether. Although triggered by circumstances in Ravne-Brčko, we carefully worded the order so it would have broad application in the wider political context of the Brčko area of supervision as well. A leading HDZ figure from the Federation, Franjo Čančarević, backed by his regional boss in Tuzla, Ivo Andrić-Lužanski, three months later brushed my supervisory order aside and on October 27 engineered a municipal council vote in Ravne-Brčko to oust Anić and his deputy Jurišić from office. The HDZ charged that the mandates of both men had expired and, furthermore, they were corrupt and had abused their offices.[8] The hard-liners further argued the mayor and his deputy had forfeited their right to office by changing their party membership while in office, precisely the position my supervisory order was issued to combat. In convening the municipal council, the HDZ leaders also dismissed a recent ruling by Federation Minister of Justice Mato Tadić, a Croat with rumored leanings toward the NHI, holding that as an anomalous—even artificial—jurisdiction created during the heat of the war, Ravne-Brčko should remain in its current form until the arbitral decision on Brčko's status. Tadić further ruled that Ravne-Brčko's councilors should in the meantime come only from *within* the boundaries of the prewar *opština*. Thus, in Tadić's view, outsiders like Čančarević and Andrić-Lužanski had no standing to convene the Ravne-Brčko Council. The HDZ leadership, of course, dismissed Tadić's ruling as bearing no official weight. The ball was back in my court.

Faced with a decision, I raised this contretemps with OHR–Sarajevo, initially with a young and, as it turned out, headstrong Canadian political advisor to High Representative Westendorp. I reminded her that my July supervisory order, which had been cleared with OHR's legal division, upheld the right of officeholders to change party affiliation while in office without forfeiting their elected position. I cautioned that should the HDZ continue to ignore the order and, by extension, the supervisor's authority in its war of intimidation against Ravne-Brčko, it would be incumbent on the High Representative to come down hard on the HDZ's top leadership in Sarajevo, if necessary, by removing one or two of them from office. Well, this was all too much for the young Canadian political advisor, who let me know I was way, way off base in suggesting that a local dustup of this nature should ever rise to the national level. She then treated me to a schoolboy lecture on the need to maintain perspective and not to lose sight of the "big picture." With that, I went around and over her to fashion a coordinated response to the HDZ challenge to my authority with more seasoned hands. Result: a letter from High Representative Westendorp—who quickly saw the larger import of what was happening in Ravne-Brčko—to the HDZ's national leader, Ante Jelavić, went out the next day. The upshot was that not only did my order set policy for the Brčko area of supervision—it later was relied upon by Brčko's Serb mayor,

Borko Reljić, when he felt the need to switch parties while in office, from the hard-line SDS to the less hard-line Serb Democratic Party-Serb Country (*Srpska Demokratska Stranka–Srpskih Zemalja*, SDS–SZ)—but it eventually wormed its way into OHR policy for all of Bosnia.[9] The point to be made here is that differences between political parties steadily take on added significance as the peace operation matures. In the beginning phases, however, as I have said, such party differences take a backseat to the need to develop a reasonably objective, if necessarily crude, basis for multiethnicity.

Implementing the Orders on Multiethnic Administration

The OSCE pressed for swift formation of local councils and assemblies following the September 1997 elections. Accordingly, the PEC certified Brčko's election results on October 9; the following day I issued an "Order on Multi-Ethnic Administration in the RS Municipality of Brčko" that stated:

1. The Municipal Assembly of Brčko shall have a President, a Vice President and a Secretary. All three shall be of different nationalities.
2. Decisions of the Assembly will be taken by a simple majority. Decisions on issues of vital national interest shall require a qualified majority, including approval of at least half of the Assembly Members of each national group represented with a minimum of 5 percent of the Assembly seats.
3. The President of the Executive Board (the Mayor) shall have two deputies (Vice Presidents). The President and the Vice Presidents shall all three be of different nationalities.
4. The President of the Executive Board shall represent the Municipality of Brčko and shall administer its Municipal Administration. He/she will be assisted in his/her duties by the two Vice Presidents.
5. The President and Vice President of the Executive Board shall ensure that the staff composition of the municipal administration as well as that of those public services which are financed by the municipality shall reflect the composition of the population of the RS Municipality of Brčko, based on the voters registry and as reflected by the results of the municipal elections of September 13 and 14.
6. Finally, no referendum shall be called during the period of supervision in Brčko.

November and December were spent wrangling with local political leaders on both the legislative and executive fronts—as they were extensively intertwined.

One of Ian McLeod's first tasks was to arrange for the proper swearing-in of members of the *Skupština*, which he accomplished on November 10, 1997. It was truly an unforgettable experience for all of us to sit and watch members of the three ethnic groups struggle with their emotions as they raised their hands to take the common oath. On the same day, Ian pushed the newly sworn *Skupština* members to elect a president. They were unable to do this on the first pass, since we had stipulated that the new president would be a Bosniak. The Serbs, not unexpectedly, proved themselves constitutionally unable to vote for someone outside their ethnic group. So the first session ended in stalemate. Sensing we were at a crossroads where we must not be seen to waver, Ian advised me that we needed to reconvene the *Skupština* within a day—two at the most—and, once convened, to keep it in session until the issue of the presidency was resolved. I agreed with Ian's perception that this was a defining moment of my supervision.

On November 12, we reconvened the Assembly and kept it in session from two in the afternoon until late in the evening when an election was finally and successfully held. In a lengthy strategy session the previous evening, we tried to think through every angle of what might take place when the *Skupština* sat again, hoping against hope we were getting it right. (See "Potential Pitfalls" memo in this chapter as an example of the kind of skull work we put into preparing for such events. This particular memo was hashed out by Karen Decker, Matthew Reece, and the UN's Salman Ahmed.) But, as was often the way of it at such critical junctures, the Serbs threw another curveball at us. This time it had to do with electing the chief of police. The Serbs directly challenged me by voting in Teodor Gavrić, who had been the LEC president when we suspended voter registration because of blatant fraud in which he had undoubtedly participated. They also elected a Bosniak and Croat as Gavrić's two deputies. Finally, the Assembly members put forward their candidacy for the presidency of the *Skupština*. Foolishly, I thought they might bow to the inevitable and put in a Croat as part of an obvious compromise. Wrong. The Serbs again caught me off guard when they once more challenged me head-on by voting in a Serb. So I rose, walked to the podium, and declared their election of a Serb to be in violation of the municipal statute and of my supervisory order on multiethnic administration. I therefore declared the "winner," a Serb, to be vice president of the *Skupština*, and the man receiving the next highest number of votes, Mirsad Djapo, a Bosniak, to be president. Djapo was not well liked among the Serbs—in fact, he was roundly disliked—so I knew this arrangement would test our resolve. It was important to show, however, that rules mattered. That said, we took as a harbinger of things to come the fact that the Serbs had stubbornly refused to vote for other than their own kind twice in a row. They seemed incapable of adopting a strategy in which the concept of compromise played any role whatsoever. And this, a full eight months after my helicopter had first set down on Brčko's soccer field!

With respect to the Executive Board, November 12, 1997, was also a significant day. Predictably, the SDS high command had packed the top of its lists for the Brčko *opština* with obedient hacks and thugs who would do the party's bidding. Because we were unanimous in our view that the SDS was behind most if not all obstruction we had encountered during the registration process, we had warmly welcomed the EASC's July ruling that recommended the top three names be struck from the SDS list. As it worked out, the fourth name on the list was that of Miodrag Pajić, the appointed mayor with whom we had developed a reasonable, if minimally effective, working relationship for half a year. Weak though he was, Pajić at least had a glint of intelligence and moderation in the way he initially approached the issues—until, of course, Pale crudely overruled him from afar.

In our haste to tinker with the party list, I momentarily forgot—or perhaps never knew—that in keeping with our policy of working with the existing system to the extent we were able, the selection of Brčko's next mayor was not ours to make: That choice would fall to the *Skupština*. True, we could knock people off the top of the SDS list and thus reduce the body's options, but the decision as to which SDS party member would take over the mayoral seat was in the hands of the Assembly, not mine. By the time this reality sunk in, it was clear the SDS leadership in Pale had decided to push Mayor Pajić aside and insert a new face—one more tightly tied, if that were possible—to Pale's policy direction. Thus, we were about to witness not only the departure of Pajić but also the *Skupština*'s voting in of one Borko Reljić, a local banker whom we did not know and with whom we had had no prior dealings. We braced for the worst.

Textbox 5.1. Potential Pitfalls during Assembly Session

1. **Nominations Commission argues over how many candidates can be put forward:**
   Answer: As many as they wish, but there should only be five ballots:
      President of Assembly;
      President of Executive Board (Mayor);
      Serb Chief of Police;
      Bosniak Deputy Chief of Police;
      Croat Deputy Chief of Police.
   Suggestion: OSCE makes this point immediately to Commission at 12:00.
2. **RS parties counterpropose to just hold vote for Executive Board and/ or Police, but not the President of Assembly position.**
   Suggestion: Do not accept this—it is a can of worms. Then follow para. 3.

3. **One or more of RS parties decide the above is unacceptable and threaten to walk out:**
   Suggestion: OSCE hints that if there is enough for a quorum (i.e., at least one RS party), the Assembly can go forward with the vote (bluff only).
   If bluff doesn't work, then point out potential sanctions available under OSCE/ERIC [Elections Results Implementing Committee] rules.
   If that doesn't work, RWF points out noncompliance.
   Bottom line: Don't give in to such tactics. No legitimacy.

4. **There is disagreement on the order of voting:**
   Suggestion: Allow the Assembly to vote on it. It is a concession to the RS parties, who will want a simultaneous vote, but it is a legitimate concession, because there is precedent for all votes taking place at the same time.
   If Fed parties threaten boycott, as per para. 3 above.

5. **A simultaneous secret vote leads to Serbs winning President of Assembly and Executive Board:**
   Suggestion: OSCE informs parties of procedures should this happen, beforehand.
   Suggest: Serb parties to choose which post they want. (The position they give up goes to second leading candidate of different nationality.)

6. **RS parties vote in Croat for President of Assembly; Bosniaks threaten boycott:**
   Suggestion: OSCE/OHR back the decision if the Croats accept position, despite the fact that Bosniaks may threaten to boycott;
   If Croats do not want position, they are allowed to resign and candidate with next highest number of votes gets the position;
   Recast of ballots required to ensure Croat in position of Secretary or Deputy President of Assembly.

7. **Any one of three Police candidates does not get two-thirds majority:**
   Suggestion: No problem, then the Supervisor will appoint them.
   Maybe concede another vote, provided it is with the consent of all parties, and takes place later in the day, or the next day. No later.
   If that doesn't work, inform parties that criteria for appointment will be announced very shortly.

END RESULT: Votes are held for all five positions or specific parties are identified for being obstructive. Apply punitive measures, in a graduated fashion, according to sanctions provided by ERIC, and as a last resort, noncompliance issued by Supervisor, if necessary. Sanctions/noncompliances should remain in effect until the candidates take office.

At a hastily arranged banquet in the Revena Hotel downtown—the rumored site of uncounted Serb atrocities during the war—Reljić was openly jubilant as he presided over a huge table laden with food and drink around which were gathered two dozen of his SDS (and SRS) cronies in the wake of his election. Protocol and good sense demanded that I show my face as the new mayor's honored guest. Later, as I was departing these, for me, forced festivities, Ian McLeod beckoned to me from across the hotel lobby. He had just come from a restaurant on the city square where ousted mayor Pajić—along with his lovely pharmacist wife and a few members of his outgoing executive board—was licking his wounds in a private room. Ian thought it important for me to drop in and give Pajić a few words of encouragement before calling it a night. I readily agreed and we followed Ian's car to the restaurant where Pajić was holed up. Not wholly to my surprise, the former mayor was well into his cups when I arrived and was openly bemoaning his loss of office and, most intriguing, how badly he had been dealt with by his own party. He was "happy" to see me. Through tears and slurred speech, Pajić gave me to know he felt closer to the supervisor's office than to his own party. It was not a thoroughly lucid moment, of course, but he was sober enough to let me know what I had only suspected before—there were serious divisions in the SDS organization. This was a highly useful piece of information to have confirmed.

The same day, Serb Radio Brčko broadcast a public statement issued by the Association of War Veterans and other hard-line organizations that listed names of elected councilors of the Brčko *Skupština* and called for their arrest as war criminals. I viewed this action as yet another direct attempt by elements of the SDS to undermine the implementation of the peace process and referred the matter to the EASC and the Media Experts Commission for action.

In the meantime, we had settled on the need for nine departments in the Executive Board to be divided up ethnically as follows: five Serbs, three Bosniaks, and one Croat. This was the only way we could distribute the small number of executive positions using the ratios generated by the elections: 52.2, 39.1, and 8.7. When you work with ratios, the smaller the number of units you have to distribute, the lumpier the distribution becomes. We could not, for example, have distributed four positions to the Serbs, three to the Bosniaks, and two to the Croats without overturning the electoral Serb majority.

We also thought it important for me to issue an "Addendum to My Order on Multi-Ethnic Administration" on November 15, containing the following provisions:

1. The President of the Executive Board (Mayor) and the Vice Presidents shall ensure that the staff composition of the municipal administration of Brčko as well as that of those public services which are financed by the municipality shall reflect the composition of the population of the RS Municipality of Brčko, based on the voters registry and as reflected by the results of the municipal elections of September 13 and 14, 1997. This proportion shall be 52.2 percent Serb, 39.1 percent Bosniak, and 8.7 percent Croat. This proportion shall be applied, in the first phase, to the Executive Board and within its Departments.
2. The President and Vice Presidents shall submit to the Supervisor a comprehensive staffing plan within thirty days of their election; this election now being confirmed as completed on November 13, 1997. Such staffing plan is to be implemented by December 31, 1997.
3. The Supervisor is, in accordance with provision VII.I.B.(1) of the Arbitration Award, the final authority for all issues related to the implementation of the multi-ethnic administration.

Two weeks later, following another of our internal strategy sessions in which we debated a wide range of issues having to do with the practical aspects of multiethnic administration, I tempted myself with the thought that by keeping the pressure on—through municipal elections, police restructuring, supervisory orders, all of these things—we were beginning to put Pale on its back foot. From where I sat, Karadžić and his colleagues seemed to be wavering just a little under the onslaught of all this. Wishful thinking, perhaps, but the overt indicators certainly pointed in that direction.

A week later, however, my euphoric feelings proved fleeting and premature. Mladen Bosić, a young SDS heavy, took to the radio to denounce my two supervisory orders on multiethnic administration and the judiciary as falling outside my authority and therefore to be ignored. The Croats also refused to respond to a convening call by *Skupština* president Djapo, arguing like Jesuits that the first assembly session had never been formally closed because the last agenda item had somehow not been properly disposed. On December 6, I sent a letter underscoring Djapo's position, but it did not yield the desired result. Two days later, Radio Brčko quoted Bosić stating: "Pajić will be the one to call the next Assembly session as the Assembly President's election was irregular and so the session is still a continuation of the first." Pajić dutifully sent out notices the next day for councilors to report to the *Skupština*'s continuation session on December 15. The session was short-lived, however, since those Serbs in attendance recognized that OHR/OSCE had not acknowledged the meeting. Further, the Federation delegates were not present, and three Serb councilors were absent—thus no quorum existed.

The Serbs were further experiencing difficulties creating the staffing plan for the Executive Board. In early December, in contravention to my November 15 order, Reljić proposed the body should consist of the mayor, his two deputies, and two additional secretaries. He and his Serb colleagues argued this complied with Article 78 of the municipal statute which stated: "The Executive Board shall consist of a President, two vice-Presidents, and other members, as *decided by the Assembly*." The secretary positions were to be filled by Serbs and maintain administrative function over five departments, whose heads and those of some ten divisions would be filled by what he considered "professionals." Thus fifteen government officials in Brčko's executive branch would be subject to our percentages. Reljić told Ian McLeod that the secretary posts would go to the SRS and SPRS, and in a rare moment of unguarded candor, that Pale had instructed him to hold to a multiethnic administration that reflected the actual 97 to 3 percent ethnic balance in Brčko north of the IEBL!

Ian informed Reljić and the Serbs that this would be unacceptable. This staffing scheme, if allowed, would enable the Serbs to hold complete political control in Brčko should they choose to block out the two non-Serb deputy mayors. It was further a showstopper for the Bosniak side. From a percentages position, we had been leaning toward a seven-member Executive Board—four Serbs, two Bosniaks, and one Croat. At Ian's urging, I met with Reljić on December 13. Two days later the mayor presented us with two variants of the staffing plan for the Executive Board and its departments. The first was the fifteen-member model under negotiation for the past two weeks. The second, Reljić said, was extremely unpopular with the Serb parties and he had had a difficult task getting it on the table. Reljić proposed an eleven-member Executive Board, consisting of the mayor, two deputy mayors, and four secretaries. Each secretary would be in charge of two or three departments. One would be a Bosniak. The heads of department would therefore be arranged among six Serbs, four Bosniaks, and one Croat—with the designation of actual incumbents to be decided by the parties. Reljić's proposal reduced the Bosniaks from 39.1 to 33 percent, versus the Serbs at 55 (vice 52.2) percent, and the Croats at 11 (vice 8.7) percent. The 125 posts within the departments then would be distributed according to the required ethnic proportions. When we briefed the Bosniak and Croat deputy mayors on what the new mayor was proposing they offered no immediate views. Ian argued that although we had a plan that neither side really desired, it was workable within our criteria for multiethnic administration. It was, moreover, along the lines of what we would have imposed by supervisory order had no agreement been forthcoming. The four secretariats would be organized as follows:

1. Secretary for Agriculture, Waterpower Engineering, Forestry, Reconstruction and Development
   a. Department for Agriculture, Waterpower Engineering, and Forestry
   b. Department for Reconstruction and Development
2. Secretary for Economics
   a. Department for Economics
   b. Department for Private Economy
   c. Department for Inspection Services, for Market and Prices
3. Secretary for Urbanism, Town Planning, and Housing and Public Utility Services
   a. Department for Urbanism
   b. Department for Town Planning
   c. Department for Housing and Public Utility Services
4. Secretary for Budget and Finances, General Administration and Social Activities
   a. Department for Budget and Finances
   b. Department for General Administration and Social Activities
   c. Department for Social Security

For his part, Reljić made no effort to meet with his deputies—or to provide office space for them in the municipal building. Time was running out for us to meet the December 31 deadline, so on December 26, I issued a letter to all Serb councilors warning them that they would be found noncompliant if they continued to prevent the *Skupština* from meeting. I further advised Reljić of the likelihood that he would be held responsible and noncompliant should he not have the Executive Board in place, along with an agreed ethnic breakdown of the department heads, a list of nominations for these posts, and a detailed plan for implementation. Ian met with Bosić, Pajić, and two members of the RS Commission for the Arbitration, leaving them in no doubt that while there could be no repeat of the election, we were open to considering some compromise in the procedure of a future assembly. We were willing to concede that, since the last assembly had ended in some confusion, a "final" session of the constituent assembly could be called by Pajić to finish the agenda. Once in session, the former mayor would ask the supervisor to "confirm" to all councilors that the previous elections were in accordance with my supervisory orders. This confirmatory statement would be accepted by the delegates and the next assembly would be announced to follow immediately, after a short recess, under the stewardship of the *Skupština*'s new leaders. Ian, Gennadiy, and I met with Bosić, Pajić, and Reljić the next day to further refine the plan. I made it as clear as I could that we would accept no more games. Ian told me later that all three Serb politicians seemed intent on getting the process moving again.

The local OSCE team backed up this plan by meeting in parallel with the heads of political parties represented in the *Skupština* on December 27. Our office informed the parties of the agreed procedure, which was accepted by all. The group then crafted an agenda that would be formally issued to all councilors as part of Djapo's invitation to join the second assembly. Ian was pleasantly surprised when the Serbs seemed well prepared and constructive in their approach. He had an inkling some direction from a higher level in the RS had come down on Brčko's Serbs to achieve sufficient agreement to get beyond the December 31 deadline without serious noncompliance.

The December 30 meeting of the *Skupština* would also be responsible for accepting the plan for the Executive Board and the election of its additional members. Ian pointed out to the councilors that while the compromise plan was acceptable to me, it could still be the subject of a supervisory order should further problems arise. Reljić and his deputies met December 28 to fine-tune the plan for presentation before the Assembly.

Accordingly, December 30 saw a successful handover of the presidency to the Bosniak, Mirsad Djapo. I rose briefly to declare to the assembled delegates that Djapo was their new president and promptly sat down. Djapo was flanked by his Serb vice president, Bogdan Savija, and his (visibly bored) Croat secretary, Mato Jurišić. A seven-member, rather than the proposed nine-member, Executive Board was also voted into being—four, two, and one. In truth, with regard to the latter element, my staff and I had come around strongly to favor the smaller number for the Executive Board as being more workable and efficient.

Ensuring Participation and Overcoming Crises

By the end of January 1998, I was able to report to the PIC Steering Board in Brussels that Brčko was the sole municipality in the RS to have a Bosniak president of its legislature. Moreover, it was the only RS municipality to have a Croat and Bosniak vice president of its executive board. Further, Brčko was the only municipal administration in the RS that had non-Serbs serving in five out of eleven executive department-head positions and where departmental staffs would also in short order reflect an electorally validated ethnic ratio. I reminded the PIC members assembled that it was one thing to declare a multiethnic government had been founded, but it would be quite another to help guide it through its growing pains and ensure multiethnic decision-making was finally (and successfully) taking place. Our experience with the Executive Board serves as an important case to illustrate this point.

We encountered many and varied difficulties over the next year. One centered on the relationships among Mayor Reljić and his two deputies, Mirsad

Islamović (Bosniak) and Ivan Krndelj (Croat). The disturbing (and, at one level, maddening) reality at the time was that the Serbs, with their thin but absolute majority in all branches of government, embarked on a process of blocking and obstructing non-Serb initiatives at every turn. There was total antipathy within the Serb community to any idea of bringing non-Serb actors back into the Brčko governing circle. No Serb, not one, in my recollection, ever willingly embraced the idea of a non-Serb working on his or her staff. This applied with particular force to the actions of Mayor Borko Reljić, who proved to be a thoroughly loyal soldier in Pale's shadowy political army. As with his predecessor, Reljić would smile and pretend to be responsive to my concerns one day and turn completely around the next day, after having dutifully reported up the SDS chain of command and being summarily told to reverse his position with me. When the pressure from both sides threatened to overwhelm him—which happened frequently—the mayor would simply disappear from the scene for a week or so. We would learn sometime later that Reljić had slipped away to "take the waters" in one of Serbia's many hot mineral springs in order to calm his nerves.

Simple things such as copying one another on correspondence plagued Reljić and his two non-Serb deputies. On October 11, I advised Reljić in writing that I would no longer accept correspondence from his office, or from other members of the Executive Board, unless it had been clearly copied to his deputies. I pointedly urged the mayor to establish a policy in the municipality's protocol office whereby incoming and outgoing correspondence would be logged, retained, and made available to the public and press to ensure transparency. Despite my admonishments, however, the Serbs would continue at the weekly and monthly meetings of the various branches of government openly to resist any non-Serb idea or legislative suggestion, often with a sneer or in a crudely dismissive manner. With such an incompetent as Reljić in the Brčko municipality's top seat, I was forced to resort to the supervisory order more than I frankly wanted.

Reljić routinely made policy without either consulting his deputies or attaining their consent. For instance, he was very much interested in creating an association of RS municipalities and towns. The Brčko municipal statute, however, made clear that any initiative of this nature would have to be put before the *Skupština* for scrutiny. In a session held July 27, the legislature looked at Reljić's proposal and rejected it. On October 22, the mayor brushed aside the *Skupština*'s rejection and pushed ahead with his plan to constitute the association in Brčko, appoint himself as its president, and bring Brčko Municipality into the umbrella organization. Failing to gain the deputy-mayors' consent placed him in contempt of the municipal statute. I advised him by letter on November 9 to place the issue on the Executive Board's agenda for debate, as well as at the next session of the municipal assembly. Six days later, I found him noncompliant with the DPA. As of December, this still had not been resolved.

There was a real and growing frustration among the elected Bosniak and Croat members of the Executive Board—and *Skupština*—who were justifiably outraged by the Serbs excluding them from meaningful participation in the government. For instance, Reljić consistently disallowed items suggested by the deputy mayors for inclusion in the Executive Board agenda. On November 10, I convened Reljić, Islamović, and Krndelj in my office to thrash out this matter. I directed them to amend the Executive Board's rules of procedure, as follows:

1. Invitations for the Executive Board sessions were to be delivered to its members and copied to the supervisor's office *five* days in advance. Nonparticipation by a board member had to be substantiated in writing to us within twenty-four hours of the Executive Board session.
2. All items suggested by the mayor and/or his two deputies had to be included in the agenda for its session of the Executive Board. The agenda would then be cosigned by the three and submitted to the other board members and the supervisor's office with all relevant supporting documents at least *three* days in advance.

Unfortunately, while the Bosniaks and Croats regularly brought their concerns to our attention, and we just as regularly leaned on the Serbs to be more open and receptive to their views, the facts were it was never enough and the non-Serb members of government began to boycott meetings, which led to even greater stasis in the governing process.

Filling job vacancies proved to be another challenge. In fact, it was several months before we were able to work through the painful necessity of moving Serbs out of jobs in various branches of government so that non-Serbs could be moved in. It would be hard to exaggerate the sensitivity of this issue. Basically, we were asking the mayor to let people go in a labor environment in which there were absolutely no alternative employment possibilities of any kind. None! A terrible situation in any circumstance, it was particularly wrenching in Brčko's tense political environment. So delicate was this maneuver that I found it necessary to visit Madame Plavšić in Banja Luka in early January 1998 to explain to her what we had in mind and alert her to the real possibility of a Serb backlash. She reacted predictably, declaring the move "horrible" for the Serbs in Brčko and one that was wide open to political manipulation by the other ethnic groups. After much reassurance, she reluctantly agreed, however, to provide some RS support to laid-off Serbs in Brčko for a brief period while we sought to make other arrangements for them—admittedly a stopgap measure, but exceedingly helpful to me at the time.

My October 10 and November 15, 1997, orders stipulated that the Executive Board and its departments be fully multiethnic, according to the specified ethnic proportions, by December 31, 1997. It was not until February 2, 1998, however, that Mayor Reljić issued a Comprehensive Staffing Plan for the departments of the Executive Board. In typical fashion, the plan's implementation—and therefore the fulfillment of multiethnicity in executive governing institutions—was still not fully in place as we moved into the spring. The mayor had advised Ian McLeod that he could go as far as placement of the department heads, but he would be unable to reorganize the remainder of the department staffs. We countered that the reorganization must be completed by May 1 or Reljić would be found noncompliant with my 1997 orders, with all the attendant ramifications having consequences for Serbs in this time of arbitration. On April 17, Ian directed Reljić to provide specific job descriptions of each of the Executive Board secretaries and their heads of departments. In part, we wished to ensure that government officials in charge of specific issues were qualified in their function and appropriate to their position. The next day, Ian maintained pressure on Reljić for the full staffing plan of all public services—other than the Executive Board and its departments—financed by the municipal budget.

On July 1, the mayor finally issued a proclamation laying off fifteen municipal workers of Serb nationality. At the same time, Reljić noted that thirty-five workers of Bosniak and Croat ethnicity had begun work on June 6, and that the new municipal administration had been expanded in size to 154 employees. Within that total number, sixty-six workers were to be of non-Serb ethnicity. Ten days later, another seven Serb employees were laid off.

At the beginning of September, Ian strongly recommended to the Executive Board that it restructure itself to incorporate two more departmental secretaries—Public Works and Budget and Finance: the former to be headed by a Serb, and the latter, a Bosniak. We judged this necessary to improve the performance of the government. At the time, 80 percent of the budget and 50 percent of municipal employees were effectively controlled by a particularly hard-line SDS politician, Nikola Ristić, secretary for Budget and Finances, General Administration and Social Activities. In creating the two new secretarial positions, we reduced Ristić's power and generated a more equitable distribution of power and responsibility, bringing us closer to our ethnic power-sharing percentages. The Executive Board adopted the plan on September 29, and the Assembly, on October

6. Creating the new slots and actually filling them were horses of a different color, especially since the Serbs, true to form, began actively to resist complying with the instruction to restructure. The non-Serb deputy mayors, too, began boycotting their work in mid-October, although the government continued to limp along without their participation. The Serbs and Bosniaks/Croats stepped up their public attacks on one another. Ian tied these actions and reactions to a number of circumstances. First, there was division between the Serb political parties as the SDS continued to rely on obstructionist policies and tactics. Mayor Reljić's overbearing management style also contributed to the unhealthy atmosphere. Second, there was an air of uncertainty generated by the recent September 12–13 elections in the RS and the increased violence in Kosovo. Finally, the Bosniaks and Croats viewed disengaging from the multiethnic administration as a tactic to embarrass the Serb majority.

On October 26, I wrote to all seven Executive Board members in response to the cries of some that the restructuring would alter the balance between political parties in the municipal administration. This was a persistent complaint as the weaker parties within each ethnic faction continually looked to me to strengthen their positions within their respective groups. I reminded the Executive Board that the balance that I, as supervisor, was committed to maintaining was that among ethnic groups broadly understood, not among political parties *within* those groups; in other words, how each ethnic group divided positions among its affiliated political parties was up to the parties themselves to resolve in an open and democratic manner. The supervisor and, by extension, OHR, had no responsibility to ensure that an individual political party's representation remained proportional to the 1997 election results. In a democracy, the strength of one political party relative to another (or others) will wax and wane between elections. I thus put the monkey back on each ethnic group's leadership to resolve the issue. I reminded the mayor and his Executive Board that first among his and their official duties as members of the government was an inescapable obligation to serve the municipality's interests in a professional way without regard to ethnic affiliation. A bit Pollyannaish, perhaps, but I considered it a necessary point to make in the context of the times.

Friction, however, continued to mount with the result that the Executive Board's activities eventually ground to a halt in November 1998. On November 2, we called in the heads of the local SDS, SRS, and SPRS parties and laid a twenty-four-hour deadline on them to select a Serb candidate for the secretary of Public Works. The following day, only the SRS and SPRS returned with separate candidates. On November 11, I called in the Executive Board and Assembly officials and gave them five days to come up with a solution to the crisis over the election of two new secretaries. On November 13, the Assembly held an extraordinary session to address the matter. Mayor Reljić, with the support of the SDS and SRS parties, put forward three separate SDS candidates for the position of Secretary of Public Works. This maneuver backed the SPRS and the Bosniak/Croat parties into a corner: They would appear to be obstructing the process if they voted against all the candidates. Having been carefully briefed on the matter by Ian, I made a short appearance in the Assembly and placed all the Serb candidates on the table at once. None received the required majority of votes, but Djordje Dragičević (SPRS) and Mustafa Nuković, the sole candidate put forward by the Bosniak/Croat parties to head the Secretariat of Budget and Finance, received the relative majority. On November 16, I issued a "Second Addendum to the Order on Multi-Ethnic Administration in the RS Municipality of Brčko" appointing the two in the wake of the Assembly's failure to do so. The Executive Board was restructured, with approximate number of employees shown in parentheses, as follows:

1. Mayor Borko Reljić (Serb)
2. Deputy Mayor Ivan Krndelj (Croat) and Deputy Mayor Mirsad Islamović (Bosniak)
3. Department for Expert Services to the Executive Board (8)—Danica Pejovic (Serb)
4. Secretariat for Public Works (13)—Djordje Dragičević (Serb)
a. Department for Public Works (12)—Vinko Marjanović (Croat)
5. Secretariat for Agriculture, Waterpower Engineering and Forestry (18)—Sulejman Kusturica (Bosniak)
   a. Department for Agriculture and Forestry (10)—Savo Ostojić (Serb)
   b. Department for Waterpower Engineering and Development (6–8)—Slavko Milić (Serb)
6. Secretariat for Economy and Development (19)—Siniša Kisić (Serb)
   a. Department for the Economy (8)—Stojan Mičajković (Serb)
   b. Department for Development (10)—Saud Burić (Bosniak)
7. Secretariat for Urbanism, Construction Inspection, Environmental Planning, and Ecology (23)—Luka Bodiroga (Serb)
   a. Department for Urbanism and Construction Inspection (17)—Olivera Dragutinović (Serb)
   b. Department for Environmental Planning and Ecology (5)—Rifet Mujanović (Bosniak)
8. Secretariat for Budget and Finance (21)—Mustafa Nuković (Bosniak)
   a. Department for Budget and Finance (16)—Nebojša Zarić (Serb)
   b. Department for Computer Services (4)—Gelib Busuladžić (Bosniak)

9. Secretariat for Social Activities and General Administration (70)—Nikola Ristić (Serb)
   a. Department for Social Activities (10)—Izet Banda (Bosniak)
   b. Department for General Administration (59)—Luka Purić (Serb)

Forming the Brčko District Government

As previously noted, on March 5, 1999, Presiding Arbitrator Roberts Owen issued the Final Award for Brčko, concluding the area should not be governed by the Federation or RS, but rather established as a unified, multiethnic "district" of Bosnia and Herzegovina. A core principle of the Final Award was consolidation of the three, mostly ethnically based parallel governmental institutions present in the then split Brčko municipality. New or reorganized institutions that would form the backbone of the neutral Brčko District were to be put into place by December 31, 1999, or shortly thereafter.

After more than a year coping, barely, with a contentious and nearly unworkable municipal administration, as well as a legislature similarly cobbled together in conformity with the 52.2—39.1—8.7 election ratio percentages, we welcomed the opportunity to correct the weaknesses and worst excesses of the dysfunctional government in the spring of 2000. I must admit, though, this bumpy period of dysfunction—as frustrating and maddening as at times it seemed to be—was actually serving a most useful purpose, although its virtues were hidden from us at the time. To begin with, the very fact that we had been able to corral all three parties under one roof and begin the long process of socialization—resocialization, really, since most of those involved in government had been friends and acquaintances before the war—was a significant achievement. I recall a couple of years later reading a report about that period in which the author, an outsider, declared in print that the multiethnic government of Brčko was a "sham." From a strictly literal point of view, the writer had a point, of course. Multiethnicity, as a fully flowering and functioning ideal, had certainly not been achieved in Brčko by late 1999/early 2000. As part of a gradual step-by-step process of political development, however, the time spent with the Serbs in control (if only by a 52.2 percent voting margin), and thus able to block Bosniak and Croat initiatives, was far from wasted. Nor was it a sham, for progress was indeed being made despite the imbalance. In fact, a certain grudging respect between some members of the other factions began to emerge—not many, but a few. I was struck in this connection by the occasional displays of genuine statesmanship and political maturity of several members of the municipal government and legislature. You could discern the infrequent, but real, breaking down of acid hostility as the *Skupština* met, month on month, in the same long, low-ceilinged room to consider courses of action to meet the municipality's yawning needs. Not that the councilors had much in the way of tangible resources—in fact they had none—to do anything about reconstructing the town. But in the very act of sparring with one another and learning to air differences without always trading insults, in a chamber where certain rules of conduct were expected, was in itself part of the social-rehabilitation process. I do not wish by these few words to mislead the reader into thinking that our initial experience with multiethnic governance in Brčko was anything but a time of extremely hesitant steps along a road strewn with obstacles, violence, and intimidation. At the same time, however, it was a time of learning not only for me and the brave members of my accomplished team, but also for the main antagonists themselves. We all (they and us), each in our own halting way, learned a lot that year.[10] In fact, had we not navigated that hard year together, we would have been in no position to advance to a higher, more meaningful level of multiethnicity after the Final Award was handed down in March 1999 and we were then charged with establishing the Brčko District government.

I have mentioned earlier that the civilian peace implementer should take advantage of outside opportunities as and when they present themselves. In early 2000 the OSCE promulgated guidelines that stipulated municipal assemblies throughout BiH should be comprised of between twenty-eight and thirty-one members. Having struggled for over a year with an unwieldy and unproductive fifty-six-member body, we eagerly looked forward to slimming the legislature down to nearly half that size! On March 18, 2000, Sophie Lagueny and my political advisor, Mike Austin, sat down with me to go over a plan I had asked them to draw up for selecting and installing members of a twenty-nine-person *Skupština*. Each of us was keenly aware that this was a golden opportunity to transform the way the new district would be governed.

Let me briefly outline the sort of considerations involved here. By fixing the figure of twenty-nine for the membership of the Brčko District *Skupština*, we were staying within the OSCE guidelines. Many on my staff, however, had been pushing for a much more radical reduction in size for the body. They argued we should bring the Assembly down to the twelve- to fifteen-member range to improve its agility, responsiveness, and accountability. While I acknowledged the merits of their argument, I nonetheless judged we needed to avoid administering undue shocks to the system. We also needed to preserve within the *Skupština* institutional space in which to accommodate a diverse range of political and gender representatives drawn from each ethnic grouping. The Serbs, whose representatives would drop into the single digits even if I held their ratio at 52.2 percent, were of particular concern. Finally, the lower the number of members, the more difficult it would be to apportion participation among ethnic groups in meaningful ways. You cannot parcel out human beings by precise percentages. The Croats, for example, had only three representatives in the fifty-six-member *Skupština*. Were we again to apply the 8.7 percent ratio to, say, a twelve-person assembly, the Croat participation would drop to 1.04 persons—or to one person, for a net loss in absolute numbers of two. Such a result would do nothing to improve, and in fact would severely damage, prospects for encouraging Croat return to Brčko, one of our fundamental reasons for existence. To avoid such unhelpful outcomes, we needed the added flexibility—or "headroom"—that the figure of twenty-nine representatives afforded us.

With their political antennae crackling, the leaders of the various ethnic groups, as well as party heads within each group, began by various means to let me know of their minimal demands. The Serb hierarchy warned through Mike Austin that I had better keep them above the 50 percent mark if I did not want trouble. Through Ejup Ganić, representing the Party of Democratic Action (*Stranka Demokratske Akcije*, SDA) interests, and local heads of the SDP and the Party for Bosnia and Herzegovina (*Stranka za Bosnu i Herce-govinu*, SBiH), the Bosniaks came on hard (once again) for a return to the 1991 *opština*-wide census count of 45 percent, up six points from the 39.1 percent they had been living with since 1997. And the Croats made a strong pitch to be restored to the 1991 census figure of 26 percent, up 17 points from the paltry 8.7 percent they, by their own misstep, had been forced to swallow as a result of boycotting the 1997 elections. The successful Croatian businessman Tomislav Antunović, himself Brčko-born, came to see me on March 20, 2000, accompanied by Mijo Anić, to plead for higher numbers. I simply listened and made no substantive comment.

It is worth tarrying for a moment to explore the inner dynamics of our solution, which had been born, after all, of necessity and best intentions. One easy way to capture the key points of a wide-ranging discussion among many participants is simply to mark them down on butcher-block paper. Because we were dealing with three ethnic groups, we routinely used colored pens to differentiate among names and data: blue for Serb, green for Bosniak, and red for Croat. This simple, some might say childish, device helped us (mainly me) keep our thoughts straight. Facts that would be easy to forget in the jumble of oral give-and-take were jotted down for quick reference. Just as important, these marked-up sheets could be put aside and reviewed later to avoid needless repetition. In this connection, my able special assistant, David Greenberg, was a whiz at condensing long debates to their essence.

Before jumping to the results of our skull work, let me confess that at no time during my time in Brčko did I feel the responsibility of my job weighing down more heavily as when we were sorting through candidates for the Brčko District's government. All we had been working for three years to achieve—freedom of movement, a program of return, democratic institutions, rule of law, and so on—was on the line as we grappled with the complexity of forming a district government nearly from scratch. Especially sobering, since elections were not in the offing, was the likelihood that the government I installed would wield authority over the new district for at least two years. In fact, I was so concerned about this that in later announcing the composition of the new government I made clear that the appointments were interim only, and elections would be held at some future point to either change or validate those appointed to office. Although I kept the timing to myself, it was my intention, had I remained as supervisor, to hold elections within two years—or by March 2002. So the responsibility for "getting it right" weighed heavily on us all.

At the time, I could think of no other situation where it fell to a single person to name and install the members of a government in a municipality inhabited by thousands of people. It was good I had no choice in the matter for had I lingered long over such thoughts I might easily have frozen in my tracks. By the time this momentous decision rolled around, however, we had all been exposed to living under the umbrella of the supervisor's authority and felt comfortable, if that term can ever apply in times of uncertainty and stress, with the process of deciding large issues and moving on. Tacked on my office wall was a quote attributed to Winston Churchill: "Let our advance worrying become advance thinking and planning." And that is what we tried, in the main, to do—analyze, decide, act, and let our worries take a backseat. In fact, as I have said, we had little choice.

Whatever apportionment we settled on, I was determined that no single ethnic group would emerge in a position unilaterally either to legislate or to block legislation without seeking support from one or both of the other factions. I also was determined to restore to the Croats some balance in their anemic share of power so their representation in the interim *Skupština* would reflect more closely the historic Croat presence in the *opština*. But it was clear these conditions could only be met if we cut each faction back from its so-called minimum demands. If that meant angering each one of them, then so be it—better to disappoint them all more or less equally, than to favor one over the other two, or two over one. The latter course, we knew, would lead only to turbulence and, possibly, to violence. Nor could I be sure the path we had chosen would avoid such consequences, but the odds seemed favorable.

Several desiderata informed us in our deliberations about the composition of the new *Skupština*. First, to the degree possible, we wanted to replace dead wood with new, younger faces. Second, we hoped to appoint more women, especially those with useful qualifications or who showed particular promise as community leaders. Third, we intended to raise the overall level of education in the legislature by appointing more persons with university degrees, including lawyers, physicians, teachers, and the like. Fourth, we kept uppermost in our minds the need to strike a fair balance between hard-line and less hard-line political parties in each ethnic group so that as wide a range of political tendencies as possible could be brought under the *Skupština*'s tent. In keeping with this broad strategy, we crunched numbers, compared notes on political figures, assessed their strengths and weaknesses, and tried out one idea after another as we sought to thread the multiethnic needle. Finally, after several days of intense internal debate, we came up with thirteen Serbs (44.8 percent), eleven Bosniaks (37.9 percent), and five Croats (17.2 percent), to equal a total of 99.9 percent.

Also of critical note were our decisions to distribute power within each group's delegation by fragmenting party blocs. For example, we fragmented the Serbs by giving the obstructionist SDS party only five slots and arraying eight members from rival Serb parties against them. For beginners, we ruled out the ultranationalist SRS party entirely, thus depriving the SDS of its natural ally on the right. And we dropped the SPRS, the Bosnian offshoot of Milošević's SPS, the former Communist Party in Tito's time, down to only two. There was no love lost between the SDS and the SPRS. We were bent on mixing it up as much as we intelligently could to keep the process fluid, transparent, and open. We gave one position to the Serbian People's League (*Srpski Narodni Savez RS*, SNS), founded by Biljana Plavšić, and reserved five positions for "Others" in the Serb community. As regarded the Bosniaks, our task was made a bit simpler by the fact that actual divisions had emerged in that community since the war. To Izetbegović's hard-line SDA we assigned three slots; to Haris Silajdžić's SBiH we gave three slots as well. And to two smaller, splinter parties within the Bosniak camp we gave one representative each: the Liberal Party, and the Civic Democratic Party (*Gradjanska Demokratska Stranka BiH*, GDS). Taken together, these four Bosniak parties were loosely referred to around the country as "the coalition." The one Federation party I have not accounted for in the above tabulation was Lagumdzjia's SDP—not a part of the coalition. In touting the party's commitment to multiethnicity, Lagumdzjia freely pointed to a handful of its members who were, at least nominally, Serb and Croat. Well entrenched in Rahić-Brčko south of the IEBL, the SDP unwittingly provided us with a useful safety valve for thickening the ethnic diversity of the interim *Skupština*. Table 5.1 summarizes our calculations by ethnic group and party.

Three dynamics were at play as my civilian advisors and I sat down to appoint a municipal assembly that took into account not only ethnicity, but also party differences within ethnic groups. First, the Serb majority of 52.2 percent under the previously appointed government was reduced in the new

Table 5.1. Brčko District Interim Assembly by Ethnic Group and Political Party

Group	Party	Number	Percent	Total Percent
Bosnian Serb				
	SDS	5	17.2	
	SPRS	2	6.9	
	SNS	1	3.4	
	Others	5	17.2	
Sub-Total		13		44.8[a]
Bosniak				
	SBiH[b]	3	10.3	
	SDA[b]	3	10.3	
	Liberal[b]	1	3.4	
	GDS[b]	1	3.4	
	SDP[c]	3	10.3	
Sub-Total		11		37.9[a]
Bosnian Croat				
	HDZ	2	6.9	
	NHI	3	10.3	
Sub-Total		5		17.2
Total		29	99.6[a]	99.9

[a] Difference due to rounding.
[b] Member of Coalition (Bosniak).
[c] Lagumdzija's SDP-claimed multiethnic membership.

scheme to a plurality of 44.8 percent, roughly half the de facto Serb presence in the pre-district area of supervision. The Bosniak representation was reduced from 39.1 percent to 37.9 percent, a loss of nearly two percentage points. The reduction made room for an increase in Croat representation from 8.7 percent to 17.2 percent, or 8.5 percentage points. This was roughly double the Croat share under the 1997 election-based government, though still eight percentage points shy of their 1991 census number, to which the Croats had demanded I restore them on equity grounds in the appointive process.

My not-so-hidden agenda here was, as stated earlier, to emerge with a more balanced *Skupština*, one that reflected current realities on the ground and at the same time insured that no single ethnic group could legislate without the cooperation of one or both of the other groups. The fact that this led to sharp disappointment, even anger, within all three groups—the Serbs because we dropped them below 50 percent for the first time in three years, the Bosniaks and Croats because we refused to restore either of them to their prewar census numbers as both were demanding on grounds of equity—was no bad thing. Judges in divorce cases, it is said, recognize that when both parties to a marital breakup are more or less equally unhappy with the final decree, the court has probably struck the right balance. As it happened, each of the three ethnic groups was indeed unhappy, but none more so than the Bosniaks, who considered their slight percentage drop totally unacceptable. But, in fact, they had contributed to this result by introducing into the mix three candidates from the SDP, a party that, its leaders proudly proclaimed, was "multiethnic"—with one member of each ethnic group included in the party's slate. Thus, by categorizing the SDP three as "independents," we in effect inflated the Serb and Croat components by one each, which concurrently reduced the Bosniak subtotal by two councilor slots. An added dividend accrued to the process when we learned that the Croat member of the SDP contingent was a woman, a fact that meshed nicely with my intent to introduce more women into the *Skupština*. So, the SDP had, certainly unwittingly and possibly with good intentions, contributed to a result they later regretted.

As regarded differentiation within each group by political party, the following observations, without going into great detail, seem relevant. First, regarding the Serb delegation, although I chose to include the SDS party in the mix (against the strong wishes of several observers, most notably the American Embassy in Sarajevo, which wanted to declare the SDS illegal), I held their representation at five councilors only. Given that I had long since read the SRS[11] out of Brčko politics some months earlier, the five SDS councilors were therefore denied support from hard-liners on their right and outnumbered by the eight other Serb delegates. This was not to say, however, that I thought the SPRS, SNS, and other Serb parties harbored delegates who were truly moderate in the Western sense. I did not. But in the unsettled world of Final Award Brčko, which was still in the process of working toward the more stable state of a neutral district as called for in the Final Award, even minor gradations among Serb hard-liners provided me, as civilian administrator, with opportunities to exploit.

As regarded the Croats, Anić's earlier decision to leave the nationalist HDZ and throw in his lot with Zubak's NHI opened the door for moderating the Croat contingent in the reconstituted *Skupština*. Thus, I chose to appoint three NHI to two HDZ councilors, for a total of five Croat members (not counting the Croat female in the SDP delegation) in the twenty-nine-member body. In selecting the individual members of that delegation, however, I was forced to make a fateful choice. I had long heard muted criticisms of Mijo Anić's leadership from within the Ravne-Brčko community, most stemming from the fact that he had sat out the war in Zagreb. Although you had always to be suspicious of whatever you heard from one member of a group about someone else in the same group, the evidence that Anic ran Ravne-Brčko with a heavy, autocratic hand had steadily mounted over the years that I knew him. He was, so far as I could tell, far from universally loved by his constituents—respected perhaps, but not loved. Nor did his questionable involvement with the notorious Arizona Market commend him to me as a candidate for high office in the new district. So I decided to drop his name from consideration not only for the *Skupština* but also for a high executive position in the administration. This was one of the harder decisions I had to make in order to accommodate our agenda for enhancing democracy by, among other things, introducing new faces in all branches of government and ensuring that women were better represented than ever before.[12]

Three other decisions had been or were being made in parallel to that involving the *Skupština*. Taken in their totality, these were critical to persuading residents of the new Brčko District to accept our social engineering of their government and, ultimately, their lives, without excessive unrest. From my perspective, of course, the institutional changes we were making were entirely benign and in the best interests of all peoples of the neutral district—Bosniaks, Serbs, and Croats.[13] But "benign," like beauty, is in the eye of the beholder. So I was not surprised—disappointed, but not surprised—when our careful balancing act was challenged to a greater or lesser degree by all three antagonists. In the tactical sense, it was an outcome I had actually hoped for; on the strategic level, however, I will admit to some frustration over either the inability or unwillingness of the parties to see that what we were trying to do was in their best long-term interests. Call me naïve.

On March 31, 2000, I announced the composition of the interim *Skupština*. Shortly thereafter, a leading Bosniak figure in the local SDP, Zekerijah Osmić, came to see me in my office, declaring his party leadership's unhappiness with the number of Bosniaks included in the reconstituted Assembly. It was imperative that I reapportion the councilors by adding one, preferably two, persons to the Bosniak wing. Osmić, a jeweler, whose shop in Rahić-Brčko survived the war intact, was a relatively prosperous man used to getting his own way. I listened attentively to his lament, noting how he was dropping all reference to multiethnicity when he spoke of the SDP—the more he spoke, the more the SDP came across as a Bosniak party pure and simple. Partly because of that background and partly because of the hours we had spent in crafting our fragile solution to the vexing *Skupština* question, I was hardly in a frame of mind to tinker with an admittedly imperfect, but nonetheless perfectly workable, outcome from our labors. And the fact I had named Mirsad Djapo to be speaker of the Interim Assembly confirmed in me the intent to stand firm. By awarding this crucial post to the SDP, I felt

I had no need to make further concessions either to the SDP as a party or to the Bosniaks as a whole. When Osmić finally wound down, I thanked him for sharing his thoughts with me. I then said, politely but firmly, that I had no intention to change the announced lineup of the interim body. It would remain as it was. Osmić, a physically imposing man, rose from his chair and angrily took his leave.

The consequences of my refusing Osmić's demand—that is, adding one more Bosniak to the *Skupština* at the expense of the Croats and, to a lesser extent, the Serbs—were not long in coming. A smear campaign was orchestrated by a group of well-off Muslim doctors, lawyers, academics, and other professional people originally from Brčko but living in Tuzla since the war, who formed an association called *POVRATAK* (Return) that painted me as an incompetent, rudderless do-nothing. The campaign reared its head mostly in newspaper and magazine broadsides denigrating my stewardship of the Brčko arbitral process. The irony was that most of these people considered themselves entitled to return to Brčko in positions of high authority because of their advanced levels of education. For example, they wanted their houses in Brčko *grad* returned to them without a reciprocal commitment on their part to reoccupy those houses. In other words, the members of *POVRATAK* wanted to remain in Tuzla until it was "safe" to reenter Brčko on their terms. In effect, then, they would have *two* places to live in a land where many families were doubled or even tripled up in a single house. The intent of their campaign, however, was clear—they wanted to punish me for not granting them a plurality in the interim district *Skupština*.

Then the Bosniaks delivered their final blow. A major article appeared in the Sarajevo weekly magazine *Slobodno* in which I was accused of fathering the child of a "Serbian woman from Belgrade." The substance of that false accusation made clear that the Serbian woman in question was none other than my trusted interpreter, Tamara Radenković, who was young enough to be my granddaughter. The sheer callousness and enormity of such a charge— which, by its nature, cannot be rebutted—took the wind not only out of my sails, but, more important, out of the sails of a devoted employee and friend. And that was not all. The article also named others on the Brčko staff that were romantically involved with members of the local community. Although inundated with myriad matters that had to be addressed in installing the neutral district government, I needed to decide whether I should respond to the *Slobodno* article with a letter to the editor or simply let it pass. Monserrat Radigales, my press spokesperson, argued it was absolutely essential that I respond in writing to the charges. My legal advisors, on the other hand, urged me to ignore the piece and not dignify it with a reply. That would have been an acceptable course of action so long as I was the only person hurt by the slander. But such was not the case. Others who had been unflinchingly loyal to me through tough times were also being dragged into it. So, in the end, I came down on the side of responding, persuaded that my silence would hurt not only Radenković, but also another young person on my staff who was identified by name and accused of having an intimate relationship with a local Serb woman.[14] I felt I owed it to both persons, whom I respected and admired, to send a letter to the *Slobodno* editor demanding a public retraction of the outrageous slurs against me and members of my staff.

Civilian crisis managers can expect to be separated from their families for long periods of time while administering complex contingencies in dangerous venues like BiH, Kosovo, East Timor, Afghanistan, or Iraq. That being the case, one must be ready for the sort of unpleasantness I experienced at the hands of the Bosniak SDP party as I ended my tour in Brčko. Rare are the cases, especially in the early stages of a peace intervention when chaos either exists or threatens, in which families will be authorized to accompany principals into the conflict zone. Even in the unlikely event the living environment was reasonably safe, the crushing, around-the-clock demands of the job would argue for leaving the family behind. Thus, the civilian implementer is almost certain to be living singly and, thus, will be left wide open to personal attacks on his or her behavior and character whenever a local faction gets it in its collective head to strike. If I learned anything at all from this experience, it is that I should have anticipated the smear campaign from the very moment Zekerijah Osmić left my office.[15]

THE DISTRICT MANAGEMENT TEAM

If there was an aspect of our mission that deserves special attention, it is the marvelous contribution made to civilian institution building by a team of professional city managers that the U.S. Agency for International Development (USAID) recruited in the United States and offered to the Brčko supervisor's office as an invaluable resource of practical advice and repository of time-tested expertise on how to run a city (or municipality). The District Management Team (DMT), as we called it, was the brainchild of USAID's director, Craig Buck, and one of his deputies, William Yeager. In a capsule, the DMT's mission was to move directly into the offices of the municipal government in Brčko and sit—a better term, perhaps, would be "babysit"—alongside department heads to inject directly into their daily decision making the principles of modern bureaucratic management with heavy emphasis on accountability and transparency. These latter two concepts were totally foreign to the thinking of local politicians and civil servants not only in Brčko but, I would hazard a guess, throughout the Balkans. In contrast, it needs to be said that virtually all large towns and small cities in America are managed day-to-day by a cadre of professional city managers who spend their careers moving from place to place working for elected mayors and city councils running towns and cities under management contracts.[16]

Under the arrangement we worked out with USAID, the latter would pay expenses for the members of the DMT to live and work in Brčko, as well as provide them with technical support. For policy direction, however, they were instructed to look to me and to my staff for guidance and coordination. It was a sign of the professional maturity and operational competence of the five members of the DMT team that we were able to work harmoniously under this arrangement and avoid major conflicts of interest. Team leader Terrence O'Neil impressed us all with his calm, no-nonsense demeanor and his penchant for observing and nudging rather than preaching and pushing in the mayor's office downtown.

Beginning its work in October 1999, the DMT helped us to design a legal, organizational, and personnel framework in anticipation of the formation of the Brčko District on March 8, 2000. In Brčko's three ethnically based local governments, some sixty-five agencies had sprung up after the war willy-nilly and without an overarching plan for economizing on services or eliminating wasteful overlap in budgets and civil responsibilities. Working with our office, the DMT and the newly appointed Brčko District executive departments consolidated these into a dozen departments, one district assembly, and an independent district judiciary. Over thirty-five hundred employees were interviewed for the twenty-five hundred full-time positions envisioned by the new framework. Later, the DMT helped the Brčko District government transparently to construct, enact, and implement its 2001 budget. The DMT remained in Brčko through 2002, some two years after my departure.[17]

CONCLUSION

It is a safe assumption to say that the difficulties we experienced conducting elections and establishing multiethnic governing institutions in Brčko among the Serbs, Bosniaks, and Croats will hold equally true for other civilian administrators dealing with fractioned ethno-religious communities, such as, for example, Shiite and Sunni Muslims, Kurds, Chaldeans, Christians, Afghan tribal groups, and so on. In my view, the holding of early elections, in an environment in which the former warring peoples will quickly see that voting for their own kind *is* in their self-interest, is neither the most positive nor pressing exercise in democracy. At the risk of repeating myself, I viewed the September 1997 municipal elections primarily as a means for generating numbers from which I could derive the demographic basis on which to form multiethnic government as envisioned in the First Award. For me, the important thing was to make certain the elections went forward in a timely manner so I could meet the arbitration tribunal's year-end deadline established for enhancing democratic government. Thus, I was not so much concerned about how each political party, qua party, fared within each ethnic group as I was about the total count of voters (and registrants) from each ethnic group taken as a whole. In other words, I was driven by the need for practical, deliverable outcomes, instead of philosophical purity of process. Pragmatism over idealism is perhaps another way of putting it. In the early phases of a postwar crisis, practical results that move the situation, however haltingly, along the spectrum from chaos to order—or a semblance of order—are important to achieve. Movement in the right direction, rather than perfection in execution, is the operative goal.

I stress again my conviction that political parties will certainly play a growing role as the peace operation matures. I do not deny for a moment that hard-line nationalist parties will add to an administrator's plate of problems and should be taken down a peg or two whenever possible. The facts were, however, that party affiliation would matter little when it came to voting. For instance, the representatives of the much-despised parties of Karadžić (SDS), Šešelj (SRS), and Milošević (SPRS) would all vote together as a "Serb" bloc. One can expect from the post-conflict parties, as was true with the Serbs, that one community will use their slim majority to block and stymie legislative initiatives put forward by the others. In our case, regrettable as that phenomenon was, it was far preferable as we made our first sally into postwar governance to having a totally unworkable Bosniak or Croat majority in place. All parties, the Serbs especially, needed time to get used to the idea of working with and within an elected *Skupština*. At the same time, the more moderate, middle-of-the-road parties had to be nurtured and encouraged. In and of itself, this outcome was enough for the moment—quite enough, in fact. My only point is: These transformations cannot be achieved overnight. They are secondary to the more immediate, and therefore primary, objective of achieving a workable degree of multiethnicity in local government structures.

Finally, the civilian implementer should ensure clear timelines are established for the parties and then apply steady pressure to see they are adhered to. Close monitoring—as we did for the Executive Board meetings and *Skupština* sessions—is imperative. Unless you multiethnicize well down into the ranks, members of each ethnic faction will frustrate and obstruct everything their bosses (of other ethnic factions) give them to do. You must not be party to this dynamic. If the parties are clearly not compliant, you must immediately call them on it. You may, however, be flexible in deciding to accept what you have gained as *sufficient* so long as the process can be seen as moving forward. Finally, never forget that local officials will almost surely be getting their orders from above, as were Reljić and Islamović in Brčko. Should the obstruction reach such a point—which only you can determine— that all forward progress comes to a halt, or worse, goes into reverse, you will need to bring pressure on the local bad actors from above in their own organization. This will involve, as in my case, requesting your own "center" to intervene with the national leaderships of the relevant factions to bring a halt to local obstruction. Ian McLeod calls it "activating your top cover."

Chapter Six

Rule of Law

The overarching necessity for legal order should not be relegated to just another in a long list of priorities, but placed at the top of the agenda from the first day. Imposing the rule of law, or a close approximation of it, is at once the most important and most difficult task to achieve in the confused period following the cessation of armed conflict. But, difficult or not, its realization must be pursued from the first days of a peace operation if progress toward legal (and judicial) reform is to be made within an acceptable time frame.

—Author's remarks before the annual meeting of the American Society for International Law, Washington, D.C., April 6, 2001

The first days of a post-conflict intervention are chaotic. Not only is the indigenous population frightened and disoriented, but the outside interveners, military and civilian, are struggling to gain their footing—first, by neutralizing the lingering remnants of war and, second, by establishing communication with, and authority over, the populace. From sad experience, I know how easy it is for civilian administrators—humans all—to focus on the noisy problems that demand immediate attention and push the seemingly less pressing, less clamorous issues to the back burner. In the urgency of sorting out a myriad of operational issues, it is only natural for peace implementers to concentrate their initial energies on fixing what has been destroyed *physically*—electricity grids, water and sewer mains, hospitals, bridges, schools, and houses—rather than what has been torn apart *institutionally*. We all have a knee-jerk tendency to favor the quick, short-term result over a more lasting outcome, especially when that outcome requires long-term operational planning.[1]

The highest aspiration, the bounden duty, of a peace mission should be to leave behind a nation capable of standing on its own feet politically and economically under the *rule of law* at peace with itself and its neighbors. Such a happy outcome once achieved would permit an orderly exit of all or most military forces from the host country. As one of the two-star commanders of Eagle Base at Tuzla said to me one day: "In a very real sense, then, civilian implementation of the peace plan *is* the military exit strategy!" I could not have said it better. Thus, it is incumbent upon the civilian administrator to look beyond the tumult of the moment and begin the process of planning for the truly vital task of implanting the rule of law in all its many faces: a modern police force, a basic statute (constitution), a revived legal profession, an independent court system, and a humane penal regime. A robust information campaign to educate the populace to the new dispensation will also be a key element in this planning.

In the absence of such enabling documents as the Brčko Arbitral Awards, however, critics from both the domestic conflict zone and the international community will expect civilian administrators to explain and justify their plan—a frustrating position to be in, especially where the rule of law has completely collapsed under the weight of war. In such circumstances, administrators will be far better served adopting a practice of proceeding step-by-step under an agreed policy instrument, whether it is a formal peace agreement (like the DPA), a United Nations resolution, or a series of binding awards handed down by a legal entity like the Brčko Arbitral Tribunal. Any one of these sorts of formal documents would lend authenticity to the peace operation and provide civilian administrators with legal and moral legitimacy in moving to implement the peace plan. And nowhere will such legitimacy matter more than at the point when the process of imposing (or reimposing) the rule of law on a shattered society begins.

As I soon learned, establishing the institutions and instruments of modern law in an environment where essentially one man or one party had been in the saddle for decades was like building a wilderness road—you knew where you wanted to go, but had only a dim idea how to get there. The immediate objective in bringing the rule of law to bear, therefore, must first be to establish civil order. Nothing new here but, to accomplish that, you will need a professionally trained police, either drawn from the host-nation population or brought in from outside. As a practical matter, you will be best served by combining elements of both, as was done in BiH with hundreds of unarmed UN/IPTF policemen and policewomen collocated as trainers and monitors of indigenous police forces around the country.

You then need a democratically elected or, if elections are not yet in the offing, an appointed (interim) lawmaking body, empowered under a basic statute (or written constitution) to enact laws under your watchful eye. Next in theory, but simultaneous in practice, comes the task of reforming the court system as an independent arm of government both to dispense justice and to serve as a check on laws enacted by the legislative arm of government. Given the pervasive climate of fear prevailing in all these situations, it will be well-nigh impossible to identify qualified and willing persons to sit as impartial judges in criminal and civil cases until tensions have to a considerable extent abated. Beyond these challenges will be the necessity of somehow persuading outside donors to make funds available for upgrading and expanding the penal system: prisons, jails, and wardens. I say "somehow persuading" because in my experience most donor agencies do not take penal systems into account when drawing up their budgets for funding development projects. "We don't do jails!" was the refrain I repeatedly encountered among donor agencies. Since there were no jails of any account in the Brčko area of supervision, we (the UN/IPTF and I) were forced to make arrangements with municipalities in the neighboring entities—Bijeljina in the RS and Tuzla in the Federation—to hold Serbs and Muslims apprehended for breaking the law. Additionally, we looked to the Federation to find a suitable site for incarcerating persons arrested in the Croat enclave of Ravne-Brčko. Hardly an ideal solution to an issue of immense importance and, frankly, it was one I did not fully resolve during my tenure as supervisor.

Concomitantly, of course, will be the requirement to strengthen and modernize the legal profession itself. This process may well involve a thorough revamp of the way individuals are educated and certified, as well as an extensive housecleaning to rid the profession of older, corrupted members who may be unable, unwilling, or both, to break with the past. The objective will be to refresh and renew the legal profession's obligation to uphold the law and to empower its members to serve as bulwarks against the law's arbitrary misapplication. Such a tall order, realistically speaking, can only be achieved over several years of patient, persistent effort. That said, steady and early progress in this crucial area will nonetheless be an essential element in the overall fulfillment of the peace mission.

This chapter will focus on three issues. The first issue concerns my use of the supervisory order as a means of imposing the rule of law. The discussion will then turn to the creation of a multiethnic police force and judiciary for the area under supervision—a continuation of the previous discussion of multiethnic administration reform. Finally, I will examine the process we used in the drafting of the basic statute for the Brčko District and in the closely related work of the Brčko Law Revision Commission (BLRC).

INITIAL REGULATION IN BRČKO: SUPERVISORY ORDERS

During my three-plus years in Brčko, I issued over two dozen supervisory orders. Each of these focused on a specific issue or family of issues. Taken as a whole these orders addressed the broad spectrum of matters related to the governance of a war-shattered community whose surviving inhabitants were basically left without an equitably functioning system of law. The issues addressed in these supervisory orders ranged from establishing a program for former residents to return to their homes, restructuring the local police force, and collecting customs fees at the Brčko bridge, to installing a housing commission for the adjudication of property rights, and so on. A complete list of my supervisory orders by subject and date may be found in the appendix.

In light of the extraordinarily wide authority the First Award bestowed on the supervisor, I approached the decision to issue each order with caution and circumspection. As my guide, I adopted certain principles. The first of these principles was reliance on the "peaceful, orderly, and phased" formula originally derived from DPA language as my operating mantra, with an occasional changing in the order of the words. This recipe served as a useful brake on any tendency I might have had to overreact to the emotions of the moment. I found that when tempers flared or violence threatened from one quarter or another, the value of repeating these three words while taking a deep breath was not to be underestimated. Indeed, they soon became integral to my approach to problem solving across the board. Rendered in the local languages as *"miran, metodičan, i postepen,"* I committed this trilogy to memory and liberally sprinkled it in public statements and at official meetings. After all, who could disagree—except, perhaps, the Bosniaks who were continually pressing me to move faster, ever faster against the Serbs—with such a sensible way of proceeding? With so many eyes watching my every move, I decided to function in as open and transparent a manner as possible, avoiding sudden stops and starts—all in keeping with the operating mantra. So often did I repeat the three words and a related expression, *"korak po korak"* (step-by-step), that regulars at our press conferences would not infrequently mouth the words along with me.

In practical terms, we subjected each draft supervisory order to an internal decision tree to guard against egregious error, mindful always of the physician's rule: "At a minimum, do no harm." I also wanted to be satisfied that there was no other way to deal with the matter at hand than to issue a written order. If no alternative course of action could be found, then we needed thoroughly to explore the potential for downside consequences if we went ahead with the order. In fact, as I have mentioned several times, from day one

I was under pressure from the Bosniaks to exercise my powers in one grand sweep of the hand to restore the Brčko area of supervision to its antebellum state—where Bosniaks had been the largest ethnic plurality. No warm-up, no break-in period—"just do it and do it now"—was the message the Bosniaks conveyed to me at every opportunity. I decided early in the game, however, that only a fool would wade in wielding such authority like a shillelagh. I routinely took counsel with a circle of advisors outside of OHR—including representatives of the international organization (IO) and NGO communities, and relevant others—putting such questions to them as: "What is *wrong* with this draft order?" "Will it achieve our intended aim?" "Is there another way to accomplish the same end?" We adopted a firm rule from the start to circulate each draft order through OHR-Sarajevo's legal and political divisions for comment. They would then critique our draft order, seeking comments from other relevant OHR offices, and finally passing it back to Brčko with editorial or substantive changes. In those halcyon days before the Final Award, a generally cooperative atmosphere had prevailed at OHR headquarters in Sarajevo regarding Brčko; the head of OHR's legal division—Johan von LaMoen, an experienced international lawyer from Holland—and I had an easy personal rapport that went a long way toward enabling our offices to stay closely in tune with the common Dayton agenda. I can recall but very few instances in which I disagreed with Sarajevo's suggested changes to our draft orders. Von LaMoen's suggestions virtually always improved our original texts and where we differed we were able to find compromise language without difficulty. Only when I was fully satisfied that we had covered the waterfront of potential consequences would I sign and send out an order.

It is fair to say that the supervisory orders went a long way toward restoring a sense of order in and direction to the life of the *grad*. Taken as a whole, the orders became a skeletal substitute for the rule of law, serving as a bridge between the state of postwar lawlessness—or near lawlessness, since the laws of RS, such as they were, continued loosely to apply in the area of supervision—and the arrival of the BLRC in late 1999. Even during the several months while the BLRC was gearing up for the task of revising, harmonizing, and enacting new laws, we continued to rely on the supervisory order to regulate the area of supervision and to clamp down insofar as possible on obstructionist and criminal activity. Below is one particularly relevant supervisory order—having to do with the establishment of the multiethnic police force—to serve as an example of how we used this instrument in achieving DPA and arbitral-award objectives.

No sooner would I issue a supervisory order than certain international organizations would question whether it was legitimate for me to instill democracy—its institutions and practices—by fiat. These organizations included,

Textbox 6.1. Brčko Arbitral Tribunal for Dispute over the Inter-Entity Boundary in Brčko Area

Order on Multi-Ethnic Police in the RS Municipality of Brčko

As the Supervisor for Brčko, I herein issue the following Order in accordance with my authority under the Award on the Interim International Supervision in the Brčko Area of 14 February 1997:

Article VII.I.B(3) of the Award stipulates that the Supervisor should coordinate with UN/IPTF to provide services with the objective to ensure that the relevant authorities will undertake normal democratic policing functions and services for the protection of all citizens of Bosnia and Herzegovina within the relevant area. Article VII.I.B(5) of the Award stipulates that the Supervisor should issue such regulations and orders as may be appropriate to enhance democratic government and a multi-ethnic administration in Brčko. The Chairman's Conclusions of the Brčko Implementation Conference of 7 March 1997 and the Sintra Political Declaration of the Steering Board Ministerial Conference of 30 May 1997 specify that the installation in the area of a new multi-ethnic administration, including the police, shall be based on the municipal elections scheduled for 13 and 14 September 1997, including the composition of the voters registry.

In accordance with these decisions, a multi-ethnic police shall be established in the RS Municipality of Brčko by 31 December 1997. The establishment of this police force will be guided by the following principles and provisions:

1. Welcoming the proposal of the Republika Srpska authorities, the police force within the Supervision area shall commence restructuring on 23–24 October 1997, in accordance with the "Principles of Police Restructuring in the Republika Srpska, dated 16 September 1997." The arrangements described in paragraphs 2, 3 and 4 below, however, recognize the special circumstances pertaining to the Supervision area.

2. The Supervisor, in consultation with UN/IPTF, shall specify the total number of police that may operate within the Supervision area, bearing in mind that this Order and the restructuring process shall apply to all personnel operating within the Supervision area who carry out police functions, or who have law enforcement powers, irrespective of whether they are called police, in accordance with paragraph 4 of the "Principles of Police Restructuring in the Republika Srpska" of 16 September 1997. Special Police forces, subject to controls imposed by SFOR in accordance with Annex 1A of the GFAP and COMSFOR supplemental instructions to Special Police, dated 15 August 1997, shall cease to be based within the Supervision area, and to operate therein, as of 31 December 1997, unless authorized to do so on

a case-by-case basis by SFOR. Furthermore, Reservist Police shall cease to function in the Supervision area as of the date of issuance of this Order.

3. The Police Chief of the Brčko Municipality shall have two Deputy Police Chiefs. All three police officials shall be of different nationalities. The Police Chief shall be chosen from among the nationality which has the greatest number of citizens physically residing within the Supervision area. The Police Chief and his/her Deputies shall be elected by a two-thirds majority of the total number of councillors in the Municipal Assembly, in its constituent session no later than 30 days after the technical certification of the municipal elections of 13 and 14 September 1997. If the Municipal Assembly fails to elect the Police Chief and his/her Deputies within the given timeframe, the Supervisor shall, after consultation with UN/IPTF, make the appointments.

4. The composition of the police force, as defined in paragraph 2 above, shall reflect the composition of the population based on the voters registry and as reflected in the results of the municipal elections of 13 and 14 September 1997. The Supervisor shall inform the parties of the exact proportion which is to form the basis for the composition of the multi-ethnic police in Brčko in due course. For this purpose, the Police Chief and his/her Deputies, shall elaborate, in cooperation with and the consent of UN/IPTF, a staffing plan for the Brčko police force, including detailed job descriptions for the Police Chief and his/her Deputies, and submit it to the Supervisor no later than 30 days after their appointment. If the Police Chief and his/her Deputies are unable to elaborate a staffing plan, then the Supervisor, after consultation with UN/IPTF, shall do so.

5. UN/IPTF shall complete the certification of police personnel in the Supervision area no later than 31 December 1997. All police personnel, as defined in paragraph 2 above, who have not been certified shall be considered as unauthorized police and shall be dealt with by SFOR according to its mandate. The Supervisor, in consultation with UN/IPTF, shall monitor and evaluate the restructuring of the police in the Supervision area and report accordingly to the Brčko Arbitral Tribunal on its effectiveness and progress.

6. With immediate effect, the Brčko police should undertake the necessary measures to accommodate UN/IPTF in the Brčko police stations. By 23 October, the Brčko police shall accommodate UN/IPTF in the Brčko police stations in accordance with the UN/IPTF co-location plan.

Noncompliance with this Order shall constitute a major breach of the Parties' obligations under the Arbitral Award.

Robert W. Farrand, Supervisor for Brčko

variously, the OSCE, NGOs, think tanks like the International Crisis Group, and even OHR-Sarajevo's human rights division. All became, at one point or another, cool to the supervisory process. I could count on one OSCE human rights officer in Brčko to complain whenever I promulgated an order that he deemed Draconian, wrongheaded, or worse. From this fellow's perspective, I tended to be too hard, too callous, too indifferent toward local sensitivities—sensitivities to which he, of course, was uniquely attuned. Although I never conducted a survey to find out, I am confident that this OSCE officer's views were broadly reflective of opinions the wider human rights community came to hold about me. These negative views tended to coalesce around the idea that many actions taken by expatriate decision makers (like me, but not only me) to restore order and a semblance of institutional government in their areas of responsibility ran contrary to democratic principles. Why? As I understood my critics, their overriding concern was that such actions were decided unilaterally rather than emerging from a process of public debate. The fact that an international supervisory regime had been legally installed in Brčko by an Arbitral Tribunal sanctioned by the DPA in response to the stubborn refusal of the three ethnic parties to cooperate—never mind to engage in rational, multisided debate—on even the smallest disputed matters seemed not to faze the moral certitude of this highly critical quarter.

As for me, I came quickly—and surprisingly easily—to the view that if you wish to plant the seeds of democracy in soil where they had rarely, if ever, been sown before, you sometimes needed to take the bull by the horns and impose your solution much as parents do with squabbling children. That is a precarious analogy, but few parents discipline their children with other than the aim of making them better persons. All parents administer discipline precisely because they want their children to grow up strong and with a healthy regard for themselves and others. Just as parents who want their children to succeed in life must do, civilian administrators must search for effective ways to bring together and, eventually, to reconcile—under a democratic framework *adapted to local custom and tradition*—factions that were bitterly antagonistic a short while ago. Under such extreme circumstances, the niceties of a fully matured democratic process may have to be temporarily suspended while you soften the ground for the later introduction of such procedural and institutional refinements. And this paternalistic approach takes on even greater significance when you are operating, as I was, under deadline.

This is not to say, of course, that the iron fist is the only way to get things done. As Andrew Joscelyne, a retired colonel with the British Army who succeeded Ian McLeod as deputy supervisor, said to me one cold day in January 2000: "Although you *can* govern by diktat, you don't want to!" Precisely. But in extreme circumstances where parties to the dispute, whatever its nature, are flatly opposed to rationally discussing their differences in the presence of the hated "Other," a strong outside hand will be necessary *and proper* to impose commonsense rules as a prelude to the long-term, and hugely demanding, process of introducing democracy in light of local custom on the combustible state of affairs.

CREATING A MULTIETHNIC POLICE FORCE IN BRČKO

Before describing the process we used in establishing a multiethnic police force in Brčko, the reader needs a little background information. First, we must clarify the mission of UN/IPTF in BiH. One of its major responsibilities was to support planning by the conflicted parties for the reduction (in numbers), restructuring, and training of their police forces. On April 26, 1996, the UN/IPTF reached an agreement with Federation officials over a timeline for police reorganization. A month later, UN/IPTF commissioner Peter FitzGerald issued formal guidance on downsizing Federation (Bosniak and Croat) uniformed police from a total of some twenty thousand to a maximum of eleven thousand. A parallel agreement would not be reached with the RS until September 16, 1997, following the sharp split between the RS political leadership in Pale and Banja Luka. Both entities eventually agreed to adhere to a UN/IPTF statement of internationally accepted principles for democratic policing, associated operational standards, and a new code of conduct for police officers.

Second, we need to describe the state of the Brčko police force in April 1997, a year after the UN/IPTF agreement with the Federation. Actually, to dignify the motley collection of nearly five hundred irregular and ex-paramilitary Serb fighters by calling it a police force would be to insult professional police services everywhere. This ragtag collection of insolent thugs clad in purple wartime camouflage fatigues and berets, slouching through Brčko's streets and roads, was a far cry from a democratic police force. Their uniforms carried no official badges, identification numbers, or photographs of the wearer. Although a few may have been policemen before the war and therefore had a modicum of professional training and experience, their policing skills had clearly atrophied. The great majority were merely posing as policemen and were nothing more than armed civilians whose sole function was to intimidate the local populace, protect the SDS party leadership, and create a menacing climate that would discourage non-Serbs from returning to their homes. As mentioned previously, their standard policing tactic was to set up roadside checkpoints and, from these positions, harass, fine, or even detain members of other ethnic communities for simply having, for example, the temerity to want to visit family gravesites. Non-Serbs had no rights what-soever when it came to public security in the Brčko area of supervision.

In the chapter on freedom of movement I illustrated the Brčko police's egregiously poor planning for the visit of SDP party leader Zlatko Lagum-dzija on May Day and their failure to control mob activity throughout the area of supervision north of the IEBL. Such shoddy planning was mirrored in police behavior at the time throughout the RS, where police would even be seen joining in demonstrations. The divorce between Pale and Banja Luka during the summer of 1997 further increased tensions as control over police stations featured prominently in both factions' ability to control population centers in the eastern and western saddlebags of the RS. As the narrowest point between the two RS territories, Brčko and its police station took on unprecedented importance in this intra-Serb power struggle, which reached its climax on August 28, 1997.

On that morning, UN/IPTF had been scheduled to conduct weapons stor-age site inspections throughout BiH, including at the Brčko police station. Totally unrelated to this routine operation, during the week before there had been reports of an increase in the number of Serb males bussing into the *grad*. Unknown to me or to UN/IPTF commander Don Grady, the local RS chief of police, Andrija Bjelosević, and a few of his deputies had been in talks with Biljana Plavšić (and perhaps with SFOR) concerning the need to physically defend the police station against infiltrations from Pale. SFOR made known later that it had become aware the previous day (August 27) that civilian police were moving about Brčko with long-barreled weapons and that con-frontations between the different police factions seemed likely. Accordingly, the American SFOR commander deployed troops from Camp McGovern to downtown Brčko in the early morning hours of August 28 as a precaution. The SFOR movements triggered hard-line Serbs to call out their supporters in the middle of the night.

I had poured myself into bed down the hall from my office just after mid-night.[2] An hour or so later, I was awakened by the wail of a siren—a sound I had not heard before in Brčko.[3] Half asleep, I concluded there must be a fire and rolled back over. Some minutes later, however, I awoke again to the siren's wail. This time I sat up and tried to make out through the pitch blackness what was going on. The sound of feet, many feet, running past on the street below, snapped me to attention. Poking my head out of the open window—the August night was hot and muggy—I discerned the shapes of men, women, and boys furtively moving through the dark in the direction of the town center.

Throwing on my trousers, I hurried to the office to fire up our generator-powered computer. My overriding concern was to get the word out to Sarajevo and beyond that trouble was brewing in Brčko. Since we had no telephone communications across the IEBL, I could not call OHR-Sarajevo directly. Because of the still quirky nature of Internet connectivity, complicated by the chance positioning of the construction crane in Brussels, my only course of action was to send e-mails in the blind hope that someone would come to the office early, open their computer and alert the high representative. Luckily, that morning the radio beam and the connection with OHR-Sarajevo went through. Labeling my first transmission "SITREP #1" (Situation Report), I tapped out a brief summary of what I had seen, noting that violence was in the making.

Earlier we had reported to OHR-Sarajevo that we had observed instances in recent days of open hostility between the Pale and Banja Luka Serb factions. There was little doubt in my mind that the drama unfolding on the streets below was a manifestation of those tensions, but since I had no means of communicating either with members of my staff, scattered in dwelling places around town, or with the UN/IPTF commander, I could not confirm these suspicions. Only a lone member of my personal security detail was in the building and he could not, for obvious reasons, leave the premises to reconnoiter. Transmitting in the blind, I informed OHR-Sarajevo I would send out a SITREP every fifteen to twenty minutes until we made contact.

Using a short-range walkie-talkie to rouse my senior advisors, McLeod, Shabannikov, and a handful of others, I instructed my security guard to try to get the message out to other staff members to stay put in their apartments until we knew more. My worry was our staffers might be set upon by the swelling crowds if they were to step into the streets. Ian McLeod, as was his wont, immediately found his way in to the office, as did several others, despite my admonishments.

As the darkness slowly began to give way to light in the eastern sky, it became perfectly clear that something big was underway. The *grad* was in turmoil with muffled sounds of explosions reverberating from downtown. There followed a thirty-hour period of high tension. The young Serb males who had been bussed in—my staff called them "rent-a-thugs"—darted about with local hotheads destroying property throughout town. A standoff occurred at the Sava River bridge between SFOR troops—some in Bradley fighting machines—and Serbs hurling projectiles, including Molotov cocktails. Another took place at the local police station where the crowd surrounded the two downtown buildings, surging this way and that under the direction of hard-line elements—the phony furniture maker, Boško Maričić, key among them—pulling strings from behind the scenes. Mobs pelted stones and sticks at UN/IPTF facilities, resulting in injuries to monitors, and leaving more than forty vehicles destroyed and the UN/IPTF "superstation" at the western edge of town on Route Kiwi heavily damaged.

Since our headquarters was located a kilometer south of the town center, we were effectively at the fringe of the confrontation. From sketchy reports that began trickling in, however, we figured it would be but a matter of time before the mob turned our way. In fact by late morning it had done just that: smashing our office windows, overturning and torching UN/IPTF vehicles parked in front of our building, and committing general mayhem. So here, in a remarkable twist of irony, you had the all-powerful supervisor and his staff holed up in their indefensible headquarters building with little protection against even minor assaults, not to mention a full-scale mob action, bereft of communications, and relying on a six-man personal security detail whose writ was narrowly defined by contract. What a pickle!

My principal concern remained how to get the word out to Sarajevo and the wider world about what was unfolding in Brčko. Proceeding, as I had learned over years in the diplomatic service, to notify first the civilian side of the house—in this case, OHR-Sarajevo—to our predicament, I forgot momentarily that SFOR, surely in the middle of the fray by now, would have its own secure channels of communication with Sarajevo, Brussels, and Washington. Thus, the word was almost certainly getting out, it just was not getting out from me. So I continued in my effort to raise OHR headquarters in Sarajevo by whatever means I could. As time passed it dawned on me with an upwelling of frustration that OHR—this hybrid, multinational organization—had made no workable provision to stay abreast 24/7 of breaking events. Specifically, OHR had neither foreseen the need for an around-the-clock operations center nor for a special-duty officer designated on a rotating basis to be available at all hours. In any case, I sent about a dozen or so SITREPs before OHR-Sarajevo responded, informing me they were already seeking the assistance of the RS government in Banja Luka in restoring order not only to Brčko, but to Banja Luka and Bijeljina as well.

The UN/IPTF contingent, of course, was quickly roused from their scattered sleeping quarters around town. Following Commander Grady's operations plan, UN/IPTF officers began to assemble at predesignated points. As it happened, UN/IPTF headquarters were still collocated on the ground floor of the supervisor's building. Only later did Don Grady and I come to the conclusion that collocation, which seemed a good idea at the time, turned out to be a hindrance rather than a help to our joint operations. Rather than bolstering our mutual security, it actually weakened it by physically separating the UN/IPTF commander from his troops—his operational core—at the Route Kiwi superstation. But that was an issue we would sort out later.

As dawn broke on August 28, Grady, with typical presence of mind, tried on foot to reach the office of Chief Bjelosević, located in a high-rise building some three hundred meters away from the Brčko police station, which had become ground zero for the morning's violent confrontations. It later emerged that a certain trigger for the uprising lay in the unannounced movement of SFOR troops from Camp McGovern to the *grad* with the objective of laying concertina wire around the police station. One version had it that, alerted to SFOR's action, the hard-line Serb leaders called out the people, who quickly converged on the center of the *grad*, surrounding and ironically catching SFOR troops in their own net. Since there had been no communication between my office and either the local SFOR commander or his superiors in Tuzla and Sarajevo, I had no advance inkling of this. Our LNO had left his station in my office by early evening on the 27th to return to Camp McGovern for the night. He spent the next day locked down—or "behind the wire," as the army likes to say—at the camp.

Carrying this line of reasoning a step further, it must also have been the case that the high representative was kept in the dark regarding SFOR plans to intervene on the side of Banja Luka in its struggle with Pale. Had the SFOR commander made his intentions known to the high representative, I am confident that he would have notified me in a timely way of the impending action. This is an aspect of the incident that I have yet to fully understand. What is incontrovertibly true, though, is that in the chaotic flow of events that day a sizeable contingent of international civilian peace implementers were separated not only from their own friendly police force, but also from their presumptive military protectors. Given the evident intent of the Pale government to push the issue—as the Serbs could be counted to do in such matters—to the point of no return, such a confrontation as occurred in Brčko on that day might well have been inevitable. That said, it is at least worth raising the question of whether some advance notification might not have improved the margin of safety for international actors all around. My answer to that question is unequivocal: It certainly would have. I am of the view that SFOR's decision to move in the way it did had more than a little to do with its institutional and deep-seated distrust of civilians to keep a secret, even civilians of your own stripe and kind. To be fair and speaking generally, they have a point but, I would like to think, not in this particular case with a fellow American, working in the same area, for the same objective.

To repeat, SFOR's nighttime action ostensibly to protect the Brčko police headquarters from a takeover by Pale came as a complete surprise to me. Only in coming weeks did facts begin to dribble out that made it possible for me and my staff to piece together what had actually happened that day. Whatever the true explanation, my sense then and now was and is that SFOR never came fully clean with either OHR-Sarajevo or me about the August 28 incident. In any case, the experience left me wary about the safety of my office and staff, and of SFOR, my military partner. But rather than engage in fruitless recriminations I determined to embark on a concerted effort to strengthen my relations with all levels of the SFOR command. What was necessary, it seemed to me, was to persuade SFOR that in the Brčko supervisor they had a person—and an organization—they could trust. Tall order, but I had to try.

When the violence subsided, we were fortunately able to look around and realize that, blessedly, there had been no reports of loss of life in the melee. After the UN made the decision to evacuate, they were able to safely remove about fifty of their personnel; and SFOR assisted in the evacuation of another forty. Although half a dozen SFOR troopers had been injured during the riots, one seriously, the force had come through remarkably unscathed. While many injuries among local (and outside) rioters had been anecdotally reported, we could get no firm fix on how many and how widespread were these injuries. No one on our staff had been hurt or injured. For all the turmoil, it appeared as though we were going to be able to clean up the city, repair the international community's damaged buildings and property, and get back to work relatively soon. That was, at least, my firm intent.

Momčilo Krajišnik, the Serb member of the Bosnian tri-partite presidency, would later congratulate the crowd on Pale Radio: "I hope that you will repeat this feat a hundred times if we find ourselves in danger because we have the right to defend ourselves." In contrast, his Bosniak counterpart, Alija Izetbegović, believed Plavšić was gaining the upper hand in what he called a critical phase for the Dayton agreement. It was Ian McLeod who in the end put things in perspective for me when he compared the events of August 28 with "a quiet night in Northern Ireland."

On the positive side, several weeks later I had a chance conversation with Don Grady's executive assistant, Angela Maddox, who in normal life was a police officer from Texas. She shared with me some intriguing anecdotes that UN/IPTF monitors had related to her concerning the withdrawal from and return to Brčko. Most had to do with local Serb landlords who quartered the monitors in their homes and apartments throughout the *grad*. For instance, several monitors reported to Maddox that virtually all landlords had greeted them upon return with open arms—several with tears of joy. During the height of the mob activity, landlords and their immediate neighbors actually came to the defense of trapped UN/IPTF monitors. One Serb male landlord reportedly grabbed a gun and went outside to confront several thugs intent on destroying his tenant's parked vehicle and actually succeeded in driving them off, thus saving the vehicle. One elderly, female landlord armed with a gun did the same, but was less successful. The thugs drove her back inside her house before torching her tenant's vehicle. According to Maddox, many landlords expressed sorrow and outrage to their UN/IPTF tenants over what had taken place on August 28, attributing the violence to "outsiders." They apologized repeatedly for the actions of a "trouble-making few."[4]

Finally, a month later I had a conversation with SFOR commander general Erik Shinseki during his farewell visit to Brčko. He told me that, in his view, the Pale crowd had given it their "best shot" on August 28 and had failed. So far as Shinseki was concerned, Pale's power over all of BiH had been in decline ever since. Looking at it solely from a military perspective, I could not help but agree with the general's broad assessment; though given my experiences with the Serb power structure in the RS, I chose to remain on guard.

Returning to our topic at hand, faced with such an anomalous and divisive set of circumstances as existed in Brčko in the spring/summer of 1997, Commander Don Grady immediately set about the task of identifying each and every member of the local police force to separate wheat from chaff. In this process, Grady hoped to determine who were genuine policemen and who were merely armed civilians pretending to be police. For this task, the UN had put at his command an extraordinarily large—in comparison to other sectors in BiH—contingent of UN/IPTF monitors assigned to Brčko—initially 258 very quickly rising to 315—representing some thirty-six countries. This robust contingent was a critical factor in enabling Grady relatively quickly to make his presence felt in conveying the unmistakable message that a wholesale police restructuring was in the works. During this pivotal moment, he was also fortunate to have the advice and counsel of Salman Ahmed.

I have mentioned that my staff and I first began conceptualizing in the summer of 1997 what multiethnic administration might look like in Brčko, drawing on the March 1997 Vienna Conference declaration that the police were included in this transformational process. We determined then that several steps had to be taken to move the issue forward. First, I should issue a supervisory order directing the RS police to comply with UN/IPTF-guided restructuring to unblock the impasse that existed between RS factions over control of the police. Second, the critical establishment of a multiethnic police force should take place concurrently with restructuring—all candidates from the three ethno-religious communities should undergo the same certification process for entry into the Brčko police force. Finally, the police force should be constituted according to the ethnic breakdown of the 1997 voters list.

In late September 1997, around the time of the elections, Don Grady came to me with a disarmingly simple question: "When do you want the Brčko police force made multiethnic?" Caught off guard, I paused a long moment before replying. Knowing so little about all that would be involved in such an undertaking, I had yet to formulate in my own mind even the barest outlines of a strategy on how to proceed toward this overriding objective. "By the end of the year?" pressed Grady. "You could do it by the end of the year?" I asked. "If that's when you want it done, I can do it," he said. "Then do it by December 31," I declared, feeling in charge again.

Over the course of the next three months, Don Grady and I conversed every other day about strategy and tactics. Looking back, after being in Brčko for three years and after UNMIBH had quietly—without notifying me—whittled back our UN/IPTF contingent from 313 monitors to roughly half that number; and after I had the rare privilege of working with seven UN/IPTF commanders who came after Don Grady and two UN Civil Affairs officers serving as political advisors who came after Salman Ahmed, I came to understand how blessed I was to have such a well-meshed and cohesive team as Grady, Ahmed, and their able UN staffs working on my side in those early days.

On October 13, I issued an "Order on Multi-Ethnic Police in the RS Municipality of Brčko." In briefest terms, several timelines had to be met:

- October 23: The process of restructuring the RS local police was to begin, including certification, background checks, and publication of names in the local newspapers; UN/IPTF monitors were also to be collocated with the local police in the three Brčko police stations.
- November 8: The *Skupština* was to elect a chief of police and two deputies.
- Thirty days later: The staffing plan for the new police force (including ethnic composition) was to be drafted with the consent of UN/IPTF and submitted to the supervisor for approval.
- December 31: The multiethnic police force was to be in place.

Grady and his team oversaw the complete overhaul and downsizing of the municipal police force, interviewing and evaluating some six hundred individuals who applied for the positions. He brought in experts on psychological testing to conduct written examinations and oral interviews with candidates to determine which ones had the requisite qualities to become policemen. Grady's team measured and fitted the successful candidates for modern, New York–style police uniforms complete with badges on which their identification numbers and full-face photos were displayed. They also initiated a program to standardize the sidearms the police would be carrying. Finally, Grady pressed the UN headquarters in Sarajevo for handheld radios so police on patrol would be able to communicate with headquarters and with each other easily. On January 3, 1998, thanks to the Japanese government, two dozen new squad cars were delivered to the Brčko police along with several computers so that the long process of modernizing the manner in which vital police information was stored and manipulated could get underway.

Given Brčko's tinderbox atmosphere, we agreed that the ratio of police to the population should be markedly higher than in a normal peaceful community. The number we came up with was 230 policemen divided into three ethnic components based on the ratios that emerged from the registration/ election results: 120 Serbs, 90 Bosniaks, and 20 Croats. This decision was memorialized in my November 10 "Addendum to Order on Multi-Ethnic Police in the RS Municipality of Brčko of October 13, 1997." Under this scheme, with minor adjustments for scheduling anomalies, all two-man foot patrols would henceforward be bi-ethnic—one Serb policeman, accompanied by either a Bosniak or Croat patrol partner and a UN/IPTF monitor. No two-man foot patrol would be comprised of just one ethnic group. The test would be to implement such a dramatic change without sparking a violent Serb backlash.

On the morning of December 29, 1997, to help launch the program I addressed the entire restructured force assembled in our large common hall. Standing before this room full of tough, unsmiling men, my unspoken thoughts were: first, what a marvel it was to realize we were actually at a decision point on the multiethnic police and, second, I was plagued with grave doubts that we could actually make this work. What, I wondered, could I possibly say to this crowd of grim-faced men that would make a difference in their outlook? Knowing that most of those present had never seen the supervisor before, I decided to keep my words solemn and appropriate to the occasion. Any attempt at levity or humor, I sensed, would not be well received and would, in all likelihood, backfire on me. So, with Don Grady standing by my side in full uniform, I began by congratulating the crowded room for having survived the rigorous selection process. I said the policeman's role in keeping order in my area of supervision could hardly be exaggerated. Although we did not know one another, I intended to place my trust in them as trained professionals. I pledged my support to them in their difficult and dangerous work. I did not sugarcoat what lay ahead for them, but let them know how much the people of the town would be looking to them for a sense of security, of order, of fairness. As I finished my remarks and turned to go, I was caught completely off guard by the applause that washed over the room. Although I kept walking, you could have knocked me over with a feather! We were launched!

After a hiatus of nearly six years, multiethnicity was alive again in the Brčko police department. Lest the reader think all went swimmingly, however, within the first ten days of operation roughly 10 percent of the newly restructured force—about twenty-eight policemen in all—resigned. Not surprisingly, most were either Bosniak or Croat. But as we braced for more losses—indeed, I feared a hemorrhage—the initial outflow slowed and then stopped altogether. Although instinctively we knew we were far from home free, we permitted ourselves a collective sigh of relief.

Police Chief Teodor Gavrić (Serb) and Deputy Chiefs Mirsad Haseljić (Bosniak) and Pero Androšević (Croat) presided over an organization that included border police, uniformed police, traffic police, criminal police, and support and administrative personnel. Field deployment progressed in stages. First, substations were opened within the villages of return, originally Stari Rasadnik, Dizdaruša, and Ulice, to ensure twenty-four-hour police coverage of those exposed local communities. Other low-risk areas, such as the Sava River bridge and the periphery of routes Arizona, Kansas, Kiwi, and the Lončari Junction, were also assigned multiethnic police patrols. The police were directed to patrol on foot or in vehicles to ensure the safety and security of the citizens residing in their area of responsibility, and were closely monitored by UN/IPTF. Gradually, the teams moved closer in to the *grad*. Multiethnic teams of investigators conducted criminal investigations. In fact, in early January 1998 the Federation media praised the police for the manner in which they handled their first joint operation—an investigation of a robbery in the ZOS.

The long, slow process of breaking down wartime hostilities and starting down the treacherous road to occupational bonding among the police began. I was to learn over coming months something that professional policemen everywhere know, and that is it does not take long for natural cohesion and internal loyalty, which are hallmarks of a well-organized and trained police force, to assert themselves, even in an ethnically divided community. Simply put, policemen, whose jobs are inherently dangerous, tend to look out for one another and come to one another's aid when the chips are down. This phenomenon, of course, was not felt immediately in Brčko, as the resignation of twenty-eight non-Serb policemen testifies. But in time, subtly and without fanfare, an inward sense of professional pride and unity began to emerge.

To demonstrate this change, I shall highlight the actions of the police during the NATO bombing campaign over Serbia and Kosovo in April 1999. At the time, local Serb parties, egged on by hard-liners in Pale and Belgrade, began to organize weekly demonstrations to support their Serbian cousins. At first the demonstrations drew only a few hundred people, but gradually they grew in size and aggressiveness and began peaceably marching through the streets. One day, the marchers turned toward OHR headquarters where my staff and I were holed up, shouting, waving their fists, and throwing rocks and eggs as they came. As it was later recounted by the UN/IPTF commander, Brčko's police, on alert since early morning, formed a phalanx a hundred meters from the entrance to our building and prepared to meet the mob as it approached. In the ensuing melee, jeering Serb hotheads began to probe the police line of interlocked arms for weaknesses. Recognizing a Bosniak policeman on the line the hotheads suddenly turned their ire on him. Without hesitation, his two Serb colleagues—one on the left and one on the right—pushed the Bosniak to the rear and locked their arms in front of him to prevent a break in the line.

Photo 6.1.   Bill Farrand and UN/IPTF Commander Donald Grady, 1997 (Photograph from the author's collection)

The spectacle of two Serb policemen protecting one of their Bosniak brethren would have been unthinkable only months earlier.

CREATING THE BRČKO DISTRICT POLICE FORCE

While much progress had been made in multiethnic policing, at the time of the March 1999 Final Award and August 1999 Annex three separate police services still operated in the territory of the prewar Brčko *opština*—the multi-ethnic police force north of the IEBL and the Bosniak and Croat police forces south of the line. All had to be integrated into a unified Brčko District Law Enforcement Agency. Each operated under principles and procedures left over from the former authoritarian regime, with rigid chains of command and little flexibility or discretion on the part of officers. Furthermore, the services were shot through with political patronage and party affiliation. None had made much progress in terms of adopting contemporary professional polic-ing management methods or procedures. None had actively embraced the community policing philosophy that is accepted practice throughout Europe and North America, even though its principles had been broadly adopted by entity and ministerial authorities. Consequently, police officers did not act on their own initiative, but would wait for explicit written instructions from their superiors, who, in turn, feared assuming responsibility until orders from the Ministry of Interior and their political bosses were issued. Additionally, the skill level of the police needed upgrading across the board. We sought and received funding to train senior and middle-management police command staff in contemporary leadership techniques, supervisory practices, concepts of delegation, and methods of motivating employees. The goal was to break out of the authoritarian mold that all services had come to accept, and to reverse the political patronage that had come to dominate discipline and promotion. We wanted to develop and implement a comprehensive performance evaluation and promotion system and train senior and middle-management police command staff to implement the system. We wished to take senior and middle-management staff to European police departments of comparable size for two to three weeks of intensive training in police management. Further, we wanted to train patrol officers in community policing philosophy and techniques; to train border police, traffic police, criminal investigators, and internal-affairs investigators in modern methods; and to train and equip forensic technicians.

All three police services had obsolete information systems. Accurate records were nonexistent. There was virtually no computerized record keeping. Report writing by police officers was haphazard, incomplete, and inadequate to meet the needs of a modern law-enforcement agency. Important data on criminal activities could not be gathered from police records. Even if measurable, reliable, and accurate crime statistics were available, none of the departments had the expertise or equipment to analyze the data for planning or operational purposes. None of the departments had the capability to generate an annual budget, let alone control expenses. We sought and received funds to design and implement a computerized police information-management system and train police officers to use the system; design and implement new police reporting forms and train police officers to use the forms; design and set up a criminal-analysis department and train police officers in criminal analysis; train senior and middle management to plan operations based upon data produced by the criminal-analysis department; design and implement a budgetary process; and establish a budget department.

The most significant task before me during this tight period involved the selection of a district police chief and his deputies, a thorny matter in the best of times. In a post-conflict peace intervention, the selection of an *effective* police chief takes on overriding importance in the process of establishing order in your battered area of responsibility. Every eye will be on that key appointment, since it has far more relevance for law and order in the short run than does, say, reforming the court system, which everyone knows will take time to get right. Simply put, installing a well-led police force will, for good or for ill, have a greater immediate impact on the lives of all residents in the community and their sense of well-being than any other lone factor in the peace operation.

In approaching the selection of a police chief, I had to weigh the likely practical outcome of our choices against certain equitable and moral dimensions. Let me clarify what I mean here. While in equity terms alone, it would have been "mete and just," to use the Biblical phrase, to appoint either a Bosniak or a Croat to the chief of police position, we also needed to address the practical question of whether a non-Serb could, under the circumstances, effectively police a jurisdiction where Serbs still, de facto, overwhelmingly dominated the landscape. What you might gain in terms of moral rectitude you could very well lose in terms of effective law and order in the community.[5] Thus, to a considerable degree, my decision would have to deal with this tension between morality and practicality. Time to go back to fundamentals, to my mandate, which, as I understood it, was to reconcile, not punish—to defuse tensions in the Posavina Corridor, not to cause a spark that could reignite the war. We needed carefully to consider whether Serb thugs and criminals were more likely to defer to a Serb-led multiethnic police force, at least in the more mundane matters of public order like neighborly disputes, and family squabbles; or whether they would challenge all authority, especially a police force led by a non-Serb. Could we, in other words, risk placing a Bosniak in charge of the police?[6] Everyone with whom I took counsel—Eric Scheye, political advisor to UN/IPTF; the UN/IPTF commander himself; and Mike Austin, my political advisor—concurred that, as inequitable as the Bosniaks and Croats may have perceived our line of thinking to be, we needed to bow to reality and nominate an experienced, qualified Serb for the job, since no one, especially not the growing number of Bosniak returnees, would benefit from a return to open violence in Brčko's streets.

The trick, therefore, was to identify a comparatively moderate and levelheaded Serb to fill the job and then sandwich him between two strong, professionally qualified Bosniak and Croat deputies. Several advisors argued that the search for a "moderate and levelheaded" Serb would be a fool's quest and a contradiction of terms—"oxymoronic" was the word often used. But, as I saw it, we had no choice but to move in that direction. So I asked Scheye and Austin separately to identify a Serb candidate (or candidates) with solid prewar experience in police work who would fit the description we had settled on. I told them I would personally interview each candidate they put forward. Within ten days, Scheye had flushed out three or four names from his extensive contacts in the police community and Austin had developed several other names in quiet conversation with his Serb contacts in government and on the street.

As the messy process of screening candidates went forward, we were made painfully aware of just how flawed our ability was to verify "facts"—facts of any kind—about each candidate. This impinged heavily on our ability to make sound judgments—like looking through a glass darkly, only worse. If ever there was a time when the three factions had their ears keenly pricked, it was during those days as we sat around my conference table peering over the names of potential chiefs of police searching for someone who would have the capacity to lead a 230-person tri-ethnic police service in BiH's potentially most combustible precinct. Control of the Brčko District police apparatus would be, in the eyes of most local observers, the crown jewel in the new interim government. Scheye and Austin, joined by chief of staff Tim Yates and political officer Sophie Lagueny, were devoutly aware of the need to get this one right.

As days passed and the time neared for decision, one name began to emerge from the pack as a Serb who had genuine prewar police experience and a wartime record remarkably free of allegations of human rights violations. The latter in particular was an encouraging sign, since allegations of atrocities committed against non-Serbs during the war tended to dog any adult Serb male involved in the conflict. The name was Duško Kokanović. Having met by then with two or three other candidates, I was eager to meet this fellow, who seemed, frankly, too good to be true. A man of lean build in his late forties/early fifties, Kokanović had dark hair with flecks of gray and a chiseled face. I recall being struck by his outwardly calm and steady demeanor in what must have been for him a stressful moment. After we had conversed for half an hour on a range of topics having generally to do with police work, Kokanović offered a flat statement: "No one in his right mind would be caught sitting at this table with you discussing the possibility of becoming chief of police of the Brčko District!" This seemingly spontaneous assertion went far toward softening my doubts as to his candidacy. What reasonable person could disagree with him? Certainly not I. We were putting him in a tight spot, no question. Kokanović's words alongside his wartime record persuaded us, finally, that we should offer him the job. After mulling our offer for a few days, he agreed to take it despite his misgivings.

Now it was time to choose Kokanović's two deputies, who, of necessity, would be a Bosniak and a Croat in that order. Back in November 1997, the *Skupština* had named Mirsad Haseljić and Pero Androšević as Teodor Gavrić's deputy chiefs for the police force operating north of the IEBL. Both men had shown courage and fortitude as they braved the trip into the *grad* each day along the semi-protected Route Kiwi and reported to work in an organization still dominated by Serbs. Having been favorably impressed with their performance over a significant period of time, it seemed logical to continue with the two as Kokanović's deputies in the new Brčko District police force. My thinking—heavily influenced by Scheye, Austin, Yates, and Lagueny—was that these two veteran cops, working more or less in tandem, could, if left in place, exert a balancing influence on Kokanović and on each other as he settled in. Haseljić had a reputation as a strong, capable manager who indulged in an occasional flash of temper. Androšević was acknowledged to be an excellent planner with a quiet, unflappable demeanor that commanded the respect of his men. Civilian administrators should continually remind themselves of a simple truth—easily understood and casually ignored—that, as important as are organization charts in planning for the post-conflict reconstruction of institutions, of infinitely greater importance are the caliber of people you choose to fill the boxes on those charts. Although the Brčko public came to know the names of Kokanović and Haseljić, it was the self-effacing Androšević, who in his quiet way contributed most in its early days to the integrity and cohesion of the district's tri-ethnic police force through his ability to mediate—particularly operational issues—between the two.

On January 20, 2000, I issued a "Supervisory Order on the Establishment of the Brčko District Police Service and the Appointment of the Chief and Deputy Chiefs of Brčko." Kokanović, Haseljić, and Androšević were thus formally named to their positions for an interim period of eight months. Until the district government was established, they were to report directly to me and operate under the instructions my office issued in consultation with UNMIBH.

RECONSTITUTING AND TRANSFORMING THE JUDICIARY

We clearly perceived in 1997 the pressing need to reform and re-staff Brčko's discredited Serb-controlled court system. Gennadiy Shabannikov, my Russian deputy, came to me one day and offered to take on the task of vetting the fifteen sitting members of Brčko's three-tiered court system (as it was then constituted) with a view toward removing unqualified judges and retaining some of the better ones. An educated *advokat* (as lawyers were called in Russia) with a specialty in international law, Gennadiy was eager to shake up the court system by weeding out deadwood and placing a number of qualified non-Serbs on the bench. One day in the fall, he and I paid a call on the Serb chief judge in his run-down quarters on the second floor of a commercial building downtown. What we found was a court under the total control of Bosnian Serb judges, compromised politically, and barely functioning. The court was, to use the mildest applicable term, dysfunctional. Years of war had reduced the judicial system to shambles. The court's physical facilities were woefully inadequate and the small staff—clerks, orderlies, and bailiffs—that administered the courtrooms were to the outside eye listless and poorly managed.

As it was with the Executive Board, *Skupština*, and police, so it would be with the courts. Each judicial position, which in a perfect world should be free of political influence, had to be drawn into Brčko's tri-ethnic demographic equation. In other words, the courts were to be comprised of judges who, as a body, reflected the ethnic (and, to a lesser extent, religious) spectrum in the community just as did councilors in the *Skupština*, and members of the interim executive branch—the mayor and his department heads. The chief judge, of course, would of necessity belong to one or another of the ethno-religious groups, thus his or her ethnicity would figure in the overall demographic balance among and between governmental branches. While we took little pleasure in working with these demographic ratios, the time for safely putting such considerations aside was still a long way off. So, we plowed forward doing the best we could with the facts and figures we had in hand, however imperfect they might be.

With his characteristic thoroughness, Gennadiy launched into a careful process of interviewing whatever judicial talent, including those already sitting on the courts, he could identify in the community. He exhaustively vetted each of the dozen or so current Serb judges in Brčko, all of whom, as mentioned, had been compromised politically. Gennadiy weeded out those with the weakest record and settled on the few remaining names for my approval as possible interim candidates for Brčko judgeships. He then turned his attention to the Bosniak and Croat communities south of the IEBL—Rahić-Brčko and Ravne-Brčko, respectively—to ferret out names of potential non-Serb jurists whom we might consider appointing to the courts once the September 13–14 municipal elections were behind us.

Here again, we ran into the same issue of not being able to discover enough about the Bosniak and Croat candidates (that either came forward or, far more likely, were put forward by their respective political leaders) for judgeships to enable us to form solid opinions concerning their suitability for service. Since we were under time pressure, however, Gennadiy had to make do with the lists of candidates before him, subjecting them to the same vetting process he used with the sitting Serb judges. Eventually, a fairly useful pool of non-Serb names began to emerge. At long last, we were drawing near to the point of making our first stab at forming a multiethnic judiciary in Brčko.

On October 10, 1997, I promulgated a supervisory "Order on Judiciary in the RS Municipality of Brčko," which laid out the provisions and principles on which the composition of the judicial bodies of Brčko would be based. Stripped to its essentials, the order had this to say:

- The Basic Court would have a president and vice president of different "nationalities" (not the best word, perhaps, but in the context of the times it was a widely understood and accepted term).
- The president of RS, Madame Plavšić (in Banja Luka), in consultation with the RS prime minister, Klicković (in Pale), and the supervisor, would appoint the president and vice president of the court within thirty days after certification of the September municipal elections.
- The composition of the court would reflect the composition of the population of the RS Municipality of Brčko, based on the voters registry and as reflected by the results of the municipal elections.
- The president and vice president of the court were to devise a staffing plan for the court to be implemented by December 31, 1997. The RS president was also to have appointed other judges to the court by that date.
- Brčko was to have a public prosecutor and a deputy public prosecutor of differing nationalities, as well as a Magistrates' Court comprised of three judges, again, of differing nationalities.

The order declared that if the RS president failed to appoint and/or confirm these various officials within the given time frame, *the supervisor would make the necessary appointments.*

A Judiciary Working Group (JWG) was set up to serve as a forum in which to discuss issues related to the order's implementation. Headed by my office, over time the JWG's membership would include members of the international community, as well as judicial officials from Brčko and the Federation. The JWG was also charged with developing a longer-term, comprehensive model for restructuring the judiciary to consist of such considerations as: strengthening the working conditions of judges, magistrates, and prosecutors; and modernizing their training, security, and salaries. On the operational level, the JWG would improve access to law texts, automate offices, renovate the court building, and expand public-information activities, including court monitoring and public access to free legal aid. An ambitious program to be sure, but we needed to get the courts up and running as fast as we could.

The challenges we faced in multiethnicizing the Brčko judicial system were interlocked in ways that would dog our every step. For starters, our friends in Pale had no desire to see an effective judiciary functioning in Brčko. Pale's idea of justice was a judiciary totally subservient to its political designs. This, of course, meant the courts would either shy away from any matter that touched on politics or give it predictably tender treatment. Then there was the aforementioned paucity of qualified jurists to draw from. Pale would continue to exert pressure on the Serb officials, whether by manipulating paychecks or by threatening personal security. The RS National Assembly would, of course, continue to pass new laws while existing laws remained on the books. Similarly, the appeals process would remain unchanged. Added to our woes was the halting pace of IDP and refugee return, which meant we did not yet have a truly fertile source of non-Serb judges to draw on. Then there was the issue of a huge gap between salaries paid to judges in RS, as compared with the much higher salaries paid in the Federation. As with all other public sectors, the ratio was roughly one to six: a judge in the Federation would earn twelve hundred KM (convertible marks) to a judge's salary of two hundred KM in the RS. And, we believed, Bosniaks and Croats would likely make decisions in accordance with BiH law, applying RS law only if it was not in contravention of the constitution of BiH. Finally, overarching all these serious matters was the enormous fear factor, which was part and parcel of a judge's agreeing to sit on a court that would try cases in which members of the other ethnic groups were involved. Again, the fear factor intrudes on planning.

We in "the West" often take for granted the role of judges in society. We tend to see judges in their black robes as living in a special world all their own—a safe and secure world in which they go about their business behind the scenes, quietly, and free of danger. But judges by virtue of their station are regularly required to decide the fate of others—a fact that can arouse negative passions in those who come before the court. If that truth holds in our relatively ordered and democratic societies—and it does—how much greater would the fear factor be in the minds of judges in a place like Brčko when asked to decide the fate of persons of other ethnic factions, particularly ranking political figures? Elsewhere in these pages I assert that instilling the rule of law in a broken society like Brčko is at once the most necessary and the most difficult of tasks standing before the international peace implementer. In making that statement, I had firmly in mind the severe difficulty we encountered in identifying, locating, and appointing persons of sufficient education, mental stability, and integrity—not to mention simple courage—to perform as judges on Brčko's courts. As proof of this, I need only point to the skittishness of higher authority figures in both RS and the Federation to engage with me in overcoming the obstacles to setting up a judiciary in Brčko.

Since my initial area of supervision still fell under RS law, we were obliged to draw in the RS entity government in our plans for revamping Brčko's courts. On October 17, armed with the results of Gennadiy's inquiries into candidates' credentials and judicial experience, we traveled to Banja Luka to propose to Madame Plavšić a consolidated list of names for her approval and action in appointing judges to sit on Brčko's courts. The president, however, failed to act on this list of names and allowed the November 8 deadline set down in my supervisory order of October 10 for appointing a president and vice president of the Brčko Basic Court to pass without taking action of any kind—neither accepting nor rejecting our list of candidates. She simply sat on the list of names. I should not have been surprised by Plavšić's ducking of this issue or by her reluctance to lend her name, or the name of her office, to the prescription we laid on her for fixing Brčko's courts. For one thing, despite her generally positive—or, better said, less openly negative (in comparison to Pale's)—approach to my role in Brčko, Madame Plavšić certainly did not share my sense of urgency in restoring multiethnic justice to that municipality. The war's end was still too close, suspicions still too high, the international community (especially the supervisor of Brčko) still too untested for her to jump immediately on board with our plan. In her defense, let it be said that my supervisory order was asking a lot. For starters, she was to consult with RS prime minister Gojko Klicković, the unsavory SDS thug who operated out of Pale under the thumb of Radovan Karadžić. On the few occasions I found myself in his presence, he was either drunk or talking inappropriately (and loudly) out of turn in Plavšić's presence. Then there was the not inconsiderable issue of asking the RS president to sign off on a list of candidates that included non-Serb names. Had she agreed to lend her name to such a list, she would have been roundly attacked by hard-liners, not only in Pale, but in her own political camp as well.

Why did I not foresee these fatal impediments before coming to Plavšić in the first place? In point of fact, I think I did, at least on one level. Subconsciously, I knew the idea of asking Plavšić to help us out by signing off on our list of proposed candidates for the court was a long shot—something akin to pulling an inside straight. But what choice did I have? We were committed to our strategy of always keeping local Brčko authorities up front in the decision-making process wherever and whenever possible. This was simply an extension of that settled (and correct) strategy, albeit on a higher level. A second consideration had to do with our policy of transparency in coming to important decisions. In other words, by taking the optional—but in hindsight necessary—step of presenting our program openly to Plavšić, we were proofing ourselves against RS criticism that we acted in an underhanded way. In any case, the trip to Banja Luka cost us nothing except time and we were still some two months from our December 31, 1997, deadline. The time invested would have been wisely spent if Plavšić had decided to come on board. And,

even if she did not, we were buying credibility and trust—two valuable commodities in a sea of suspicion and fear.

In any event, Plavšić failed to cooperate. She simply fell silent and declined
to respond to my letters and phone calls reminding her of the deadline in my
supervisory order. Realizing that the ball was back in my court—a court that,
in truth, it had never left—Gennadiy and I proceeded to implement Plan B,
which was to draw up a follow-on supervisory order naming judges to the new
court system. Accordingly, on December 5, I issued an "Addendum to the
Order on Judiciary in the RS Municipality of Brčko," appointing four judges—
two Serbs, one Bosniak, and one Croat—to the Basic and Magistrates' Courts:

Basic Court:
Dragan Mihajlović (Serb) for president of the Basic Court; and
Jozo Andjić (Croat) for vice president of the Basic Court.

Magistrates' Court:
Milenko Mihajlović (Serb) for president of the Magistrates' Court; and
Safet Pizović (Bosniak) for judge in the Magistrates' Court.

Irfan Selimović (Bosniak) was named the public prosecutor and Slavo Lakić
(Serb) deputy prosecutor. I reserved the right to appoint a third judge to the
Magistrates' Court in the "near future." Since all of the appointed judges/
prosecutors were male, we hoped to find a qualified female, preferably a
Croat, for the Magistrates' Court—not an easy bill to fill, given the slow
rate of Croat returns. Thanks to Gennadiy's assiduous searching, however,
there surfaced a Croat woman with prewar judicial experience. Her name
was Adela Božić. The issue was, however, that Božić's house in Brčko *grad*
had been heavily damaged and needed extensive repairs before she would
agree to serve. Given the absolute priority we attached to a functioning
judicial system, Gennadiy intervened directly with those responsible for
habitat restoration to bring the Božić house up to minimum UNHCR living
standards[7] as quickly as possible.

Under my order, the court officers were mandated to take up their positions immediately, at least on paper. We had several practical issues still to
overcome. Nonetheless, and at long last, we had taken a major step in filling
the last gaping hole left in Brčko's government by the war—a dysfunctional
judiciary. We were under no illusions, though, that our solution was other
than interim. It was imperative that a democratically elected judiciary would
one day displace our appointed court. But ours was a good start and, in any
case, all we could achieve at that moment in time. A more fully elaborated
court with duly elected—*or, rather, duly appointed by a duly elected* admin-

istration—court officers would have to await the final decision of the arbitral tribunal as to Brčko's permanent status.

On December 31, I issued my "Second Addendum to the Order on Judiciary in the RS Municipality of Brčko," naming the following individuals to judicial positions based on a staffing plan developed in coordination with the president and the vice president of the Basic Court:

Basic Court:
Slobodan Zobenica, president of the Basic Court;
Ilinka Gavrić, judge of the Basic Court;
Zijad Kadrić, judge of the Basic Court;
Spomenka Kondić, judge of the Basic Court;
Mirjana Mrdjen, judge of the Basic Court;
Zekerijah Mujkanović, judge of the Basic Court;
Srdjan Nedić, judge of the Basic Court;
Mara Perić, judge of the Basic Court;
Stevan Sofić, judge of the Basic Court; and
Milorad Zivlak, judge of the Basic Court.

The third and fourth Bosniak judges for the Basic Court were to be appointed in the near future. We further named Adela Božić judge of the Magistrates' Court. The judicial officers were to take up their appointments and carry out their offices immediately. As a consequence of these appointments, four Serb judges had to be released from their work in Brčko, but the RS Ministry of Justice found new positions for them in nearby Bijeljina.

All appointed judges were in their offices and began their duties on February 2, 1998. At the time the Supplemental Award was issued in March 1998, the third and fourth Bosniak posts in the Basic Court remained unfilled. We made several requests of the governor of the Tuzla-Podrina Canton to provide qualified judges to fill those vacant positions. Finally, on May 4, two names were put forth. The JWG interviewed Abdulaziz Dizdarević and Amir Morankić and found they satisfied the criteria we had established for Brčko judges—professionalism, a clean career record, and nonparty affiliation. The RS Ministry of Justice was apprised of their approval two days later; and on June 16, the RS National Assembly appointed the two judges to the Basic Court in Brčko at the ministry's request. *Thus, by June 16, 1998, we had achieved full multiethnicization of Brčko's judiciary—some fourteen months after our arrival in April the previous year.*

Our attention next turned to support staff. We had three objectives in mind: first, to provide the judges with a professional staff; second, to employ as many qualified returnees as possible; and third, to avoid laying off as many

Serb employees as we could. We asked the heads of judicial bodies to prepare individual staffing plans. The JWG adopted two of those plans: one for the Basic Court and prosecutor's office on April 15, and one for the Magistrates' Court three weeks later. We were relieved to learn that there were sufficient vacancies in the plans, so that no Serb layoffs would be required. That was the good news. The bad news was that hiring non-Serbs proved more difficult. Once again, sharp salary differences between the two entities made the prospect of working in Brčko unattractive. Further, and more worrying, we were unable immediately to identify persons among Bosniak and Croat returnees who had the requisite qualifications and skills to fill positions on the judiciary's support staffs.

The prosecutor's office required the least number of support employees. Prior to the staffing plan's adoption, three Serbs and one Croat served in the office. We hired one Bosniak and considered its staff fully multiethnic according to the 1997 ratios on July 1. It took another six months, however, to hire three Bosniaks for the Magistrates' Court in order to complement the existing six Serbs and one Croat. Staffing within the Basic Court would remain only partially implemented through the issuing of the Final Award in March 1999. The staffing plan called for fifty support staff: twenty-six Serbs, eighteen Bosniaks, five Croats, and one "Other." Lack of qualified personnel, low salaries, and the unstable political atmosphere in the RS triggered by events in Kosovo and the rise of Serb hard-liners such as Nikola Poplasen, left us shy five Serbs, fourteen Bosniaks, and one Croat.

The key problems that continued to hinder the effective functioning of the new judiciary remained largely practical in nature. There was a lack of funds for heating and a legal library, and the need for office space and reconstruction of the court building. During the summer of 1998, the NGO Catholic Relief Services undertook a major task of replacing and glazing broken windows as well as repairing the central heating system at the courthouse. We donated six computers and put on a computer course for twenty-five employees. And in December 1998, the European Union donated three vehicles, twenty-five computers, a copy machine, and furniture in response to my call for assistance.

Brčko's demilitarization, called for under the 1999 Final Award, also helped promote the multiethnic judiciary. General Eric Shinseki, Commander of SFOR, assigned his deputy, British Lt. Gen. Sir Hew Pike, to work closely and directly with me on the process of demilitarizing the territory of the prewar Brčko *opština*. Thanks in large part to Pike's penchant for tight, efficient planning, he and I hammered out a clear strategy with operational timelines for executing this enormous undertaking. We agreed up front on a division of labor—I would work the demilitarization process through the political leaders of all three factions, while General Pike would deal face-to-face with the military commanders of the Army of Bosnia and Herzegovina (*Armije Bosne i Hercegovine*, ABiH), Army of Republika Srpska (*Vojska Republike Srpske*, VRS), and the HVO. What was most refreshing about working with Hew Pike was his breezy informality and common sense. He traveled frequently to Brčko to hammer out details with me so as to hasten along the decision-making process. He never stood on protocol, nor did I. We simply had a task to accomplish and, in crisp British style, we got on with it. The result: Brčko was successfully demilitarized a full three months before the new district was formally announced in March 2000—surely, a unique milestone in the *opština*'s history, as well as in that of BiH.

Among the fruits of the demilitarization were three large military compounds left vacant by departing VRS units: the centrally located headquarters compound with two large barracks and numerous administrative buildings; a sprawling maintenance compound for heavy military vehicles located inside, but at the edge of, the *grad*; and a weapons storage facility ten kilometers to the west of town. This huge facility came with massive bunkers set in the ground amidst a large stand of trees that stretched from the main road nearly to the banks of the Sava River some two kilometers away. As supervisor, I let it be known that I would be carefully watching over and determining the disposition of these spacious grounds with their several large buildings. Needless to say, the very existence of these windfall parcels of unassigned land attracted wide interest. For instance, no sooner had the last elements of the VRS departed from their former headquarters compound in the heart of Brčko *grad* than I began to receive strong hints from the office of Jacques Paul Klein, SRSG in Sarajevo, that this prime location should become the site for a nationwide police academy. The SRSG's argument ran that Brčko, as a neutral district, would be an ideal venue for an all-BiH police training center, since to locate such an academy in one of the entities would immediately raise the other entity's ire. Moreover, to install such a prestigious educational and training institution for police in the heart of the Brčko *grad* would send a strong signal to criminal elements to keep their hands off the new district. With the military gone, such a dramatic infusion of police presence would help stabilize the new district and brand it as a bastion of law and order in BiH, or so the argument went.

To broach this proposal formally with me, Klein sent UN CIVPOL advisor Robert Gravelle in to see me. I listened politely to Gravelle's pitch and told him I would think about it, which I did because, frankly, Klein's argument was not without merit. Realistically, however, my own staff and I were already deep into an in-house debate to determine the optimal use of the VRS headquarters compound. Both Ilias Chatzis, head of our legal-affairs division, and Michael Karnavas, executive director of the BLRC, were strongly of the opinion that Brčko's decrepit and overcrowded court building should be re-housed in the renovated barracks buildings. Ever since Gennadiy Shaban-nikov had undertaken the task of vetting and interviewing judges for Brčko's Basic and Magistrates' Courts, we had been scratching our heads about how to expand and centralize the physical space available to house the judiciary. So it came down to two questions: first, need; and second, the image we hoped to project. At this point, I sat down and wrote Klein a letter suggesting that he consider locating his police academy on the vast grounds of the former weapons storage facility to the west of town. I wrote that a police academy would logically require a small-arms firing range, which would be better accommodated outside the city proper. In response to my letter, Klein sent deputy SRSG Julian Hartson, a senior UN civil servant from New Zealand, and a passel of UN experts to Brčko to inspect the weapons storage facility. Predictably, they found the site unsuitable for a UN police academy and made one last pitch for the downtown location. Pressed to decide, I had no choice but to inform my visitors that the former VRS headquarters downtown would be occupied by the new district's judiciary and not by the UN's proposed po-lice academy. The image of law and order, I said, would be as well or better projected by a modern court complex as it would by a police training facility. At the same time, I regretted the UN's rejection of my proposed alternative site for the police academy. Hartson was not at all happy with my reply. We parted on that note.

A few weeks later the Department of State sought my advice as to what Secretary of State Albright might include in her kit bag when she arrived in Brčko for the formal inauguration of the new district on March 8, 2000. I said she should emphasize U.S. support for the rule of law in Brčko and, to under-score that, be prepared to pledge funds sufficient to underwrite the renovation of two former VRS barracks buildings to house the district's judiciary. This idea hit pay dirt with the Secretary, and today, thanks to a million-dollar con-tribution from U.S. taxpayers, Brčko is graced with two modern court build-ings replete with spacious courtrooms, well-equipped chambers for judges, and attractive waiting rooms for the public.

CREATING A BASIC STATUTE FOR BRČKO:
THE WORK OF THE BRČKO LAW REVISION COMMISSION

Presiding arbitrator Roberts Owen wrote into the Annex to the Final Award, promulgated in August 1999, a highly innovative and, or so it seemed to me, precedent-setting directive requiring the supervisor to establish a multiethnic

Photo 6.2.   Brčko Judiciary Building, 2005 (Photograph by Allison Frendak-Blume)

commission to harmonize the laws of the two entities for uniform application in the new district. The exact wording in paragraph 5 of the Annex follows:

> The Supervisor shall establish and appoint a Law Revision Commission with responsibility for proposing new laws or modification of existing laws so as to produce an appropriately uniform system of laws through the District. The Commission shall be chaired by an international jurist and include representatives of both Entities. The Commission's recommendations will be submitted to the Assembly for approval and thereafter be subject to approval of the Supervisor. If the Assembly fails to act, the Supervisor may determine the disposition of the Commission's recommendations after consulting with appropriate BiH and Entity officials.

The BLRC was empowered to draft new legislation where necessary in order to bring laws in the new Brčko District into line with modern legal standards. I instructed the commission to view its mandate as an unprecedented opportunity to bring all applicable laws of both entities currently operating within the geographic boundaries of the now expanded area of supervision under a microscope with an eye to ridding them of ethnically discriminatory clauses, anachronistic legalisms, and "old think" (Communist) precepts wherever such barriers to right legal thinking—and to justice—were encountered. I frankly did not think the new district could long survive if the Final Award's call for an "appropriately uniform system of laws" was reduced to little more than tinkering with legal Band-Aids in order to effect a papier-mâché harmonization of entity laws. As I read the tribunal's intent, we needed a corpus of law rooted in the European tradition, since BiH's destiny lay solidly in Europe; but we also needed progressive, forward-looking laws of the sort being adopted by other formerly Communist Eastern European states, which were making the transition from single-party, top-down government to democracy. As I saw it then, and continue to see it today, here was a once-in-a-lifetime chance to break with the past and show a way to the future not only for Brčko, but also for BiH.

The key to progress, however, was to move smartly forward so as not to lose the momentum the Final Award had imparted. As a first step, I approached my friend Bob Barry, then head of the OSCE Mission in BiH, to see whether he would agree to release Finn Lynghjem, a well-respected international jurist from Norway, who was at the time serving as head of OSCE's EASC. In the tense period following the 1997 elections, Lynghjem had impressed me with his flinty integrity in addressing electoral disputes that were erupting all over BiH. Given his international stature and in-country experience, I thought the judge would be ideal to head the BLRC. Since the EASC was marking time between elections, Barry graciously agreed to release Judge Lynghjem for the Brčko position.

The BLRC was staffed by qualified legal and juridical representatives from BiH—one from each of the three ethnic communities—as well as a revolving staff of American lawyers skilled in legal drafting. One of those American lawyers, Michael Karnavas, having worked under Finn Lynghjem in Cambodia a few years earlier, responded enthusiastically to the judge's invitation to join him in Brčko. He would take over a few months later as Lynghjem was unexpectedly called back to Norway.

As regarded initial funding, the U.S. government undertook to support the BLRC with a million-dollar grant. The BLRC secretariat was comprised of national and international lawyers supported by a highly skilled team of interpreters and translators. In order to provide these newcomers with a common, contiguous work area, we reconfigured half of an entire floor of the supervisor's building to accommodate BLRC offices. I considered it vitally important that the BLRC be collocated with my staff rather than housed separately somewhere across town. Given the immensity of the BLRC chairman's mandate, I knew he would require policy guidance, especially in the early stages, so I wanted his office physically nearby, especially since it was my habit to drop in unannounced on colleagues' offices for quick updates on their work programs. I found that an invaluable way to keep on top of the issues we were grappling with daily and I wanted to extend that practice to the BLRC operation as well.

In any case, since it was my job to "establish and appoint," I took it as my prerogative to set the limits of the BLRC's work, and I chose to set them wide. I encouraged the BLRC chairman to seize the moment and, as Karnavas would later note, go for "maximum reform rather than choosing and adopting whole-cloth laws from the RS or the Federation and simply inserting 'the Brčko District'" on them (2001, 11). Initially, the BLRC staff formed working groups by subject, which, proving unworkable, were later disbanded. Embarking on a thorough examination of laws then on the entities' books, the BLRC let its eye roam over legislation being adopted in other formerly Eastern European countries—countries also in the process of democratizing their systems. The staff similarly combed relevant legislation in advanced Western European countries, as well as in the United States, for what they had to offer. It quickly became clear that significant portions of both entities' laws were in need of major overhaul and revision.

The BRLC incorporated such democratic principles into its strategy for crafting legal reform as the separation of powers among the three branches of government; mechanisms to enforce transparency, accountability, and uniformity in public services; and the independence of the judiciary. The Commission was keenly aware from the outset that whatever laws and procedures emerged from the harmonization process had to be in full accord with legal standards of the European Union. BiH was, after all, headed toward eventual membership in that prominent institution.

Karnavas (2001, 12–14) employed a practical, step-by-step approach in preparing draft laws for presentation to the *Skupština*—whether those laws were to be harmonized, modified, revised, or drawn up from scratch. The process went something like this: First, on any given legal question or topic, the BLRC staff would thoroughly review applicable laws of both entities. Second, they would subject those laws to comprehensive legal research, either comparing or contrasting such laws to each other to determine which of them were most amenable to adaptation and/or adoption as district law. Third, the staff member charged with drafting a particular law would prepare a short memorandum for discussion with their staff colleagues. Fourth, following an often spirited staff discussion, the lead staffer would prepare a working draft of the law for review by BRLC lawyers. Fifth, once the draft law had the blessing of Chairman Karnavas, it would be sent down to the OHR legal division in Sarajevo for further discussion and review. Often the discussion draft would also be shared with other relevant international agencies, such as the OSCE, UN/IPTF, et al. If necessary, an intensive working session would be convened in Sarajevo to address points raised by these agencies and to iron out differences. Agreed-upon revisions would be incorporated into a final draft, which would then be explained to members of the Brčko government and heads of political parties. Following a discussion session with the BLRC commissioners, the draft law would then be formally submitted to the *Skupština*.

The *Skupština*, in turn, distributed the draft law to all its councilors and, in particular, to the Legislative Committee and to the mayor's experts. A first reading of the law would be conducted in session. Following the first reading, councilors and the mayor would then propose amendments to the Legislative Committee. BLRC chairman Karnavas and his lawyers would attend a session of the Legislative Committee to discuss any and all proposed amendments. The committee would then present its opinion of the draft law to the *Skupština*. Following a second reading of the draft law before the assembled councilors, a vote would be held on amendments. The process would continue until there was a final vote on the draft law. As supervisor, I would then approve the final legal text adopted by the *Skupština* and the law would be submitted for publication in the Official Gazette of the Brčko District of BiH. Eight days after publication, the law would take effect.

So that, in a nutshell, is how it was done. The reader will note that even though this process involved considerable top-down pressure in order to keep the legislation moving along, we were at great pains to include Bosniaks, Serbs, and Croats in the deliberations leading up to the final decisions. Critics may with some justification point out that this exercise in lawmaking would not meet the standards of a smoothly running democracy. True, but keep in mind we had less than a year under the Final Award to bring about a harmonization of entity laws for application in the soon-to-become Brčko District. Then, too, the incontrovertible fact remained that left to themselves, the three ethnic factions were wholly incapable of making a democratic legislative process work without outside expert advice and counsel.

Despite my near-total ignorance of legal theory as it related to the creation of a uniform body of law from the ground up, I sought to impress on Michael Karnavas my urgent desire to see commercial, contract, and property law placed at the top of the BLRC's drafting agenda. I viewed instilling the rule of law primarily in pragmatic terms: as a means of smoothing the way for *early outside direct investment* in the Brčko area of supervision. I was therefore eager that laws relevant to investment—especially laws on contracts and property—would be enacted quickly so we could begin attracting foreign investors to Brčko. To my mind, it was that simple. After listening politely to my entreaties, Karnavas said that while he shared my eagerness to improve the investment climate quickly, a great deal of legislative groundwork had to be laid before the BLRC could get down to drafting specific laws like those I had in mind. For example, he said legislation in overarching areas like executive authority, police, and the judiciary logically had to precede consideration of laws on property, commerce, and contracts. Karnavas's instructive and fascinating mini-lectures on the philosophy and hierarchy of law were, for me, the beginning of an intense, if scattershot, education on a facet of governance I had until then taken largely for granted and only vaguely comprehended. I have no doubt that he viewed my inexpert interventions with great humor, but if he did he never showed it. In any case, I gave him to know that in the end it was his call. Who was I to throw my weight around in such an exacting and intricate arena?

The first priority in establishing the Brčko District of Bosnia and Herzegovina was to construct the legal basis for the district by writing a new district statute and consolidating the overall legal framework. Work on installing a two-tiered judiciary proceeded in parallel with these developments. In the process of becoming educated on the district's need for a foundational statute (or covenant, as it was sometimes called), I found myself swirling about in the esoteric world of constitutional law. In that world, as this layman came to understand it, the corpus of law in its entirety is revealed as a hierarchical edifice built on a foundational law—known variously as a constitution, charter, covenant, or basic statute—from and on which workaday laws flow and depend for their legitimacy. A fundamental principle of government is that *no polity can function without a foundational law*. Given its unique status, the new Brčko District would also require such a basic statute as the trunk from which other laws could sprout—and gain their legitimacy—in the normal legislative process. The courts, in exercising their oversight function, would judge these lesser laws against precepts embedded in the fundamental law.

I entrusted to Ilias Chatzis, the Greek attorney who headed my small legal staff, and Goran Duka, his able Bosnian Serb deputy, the sensitive task of drafting the basic statute in close consultation with Michael Karnavas's BLRC and with OHR-Sarajevo's legal division. Both lawyers jumped at the opportunity to have a hand in shaping and instilling the rule of law in the new district. Except for establishing a few basic ground rules—like, for example, ruling at the outset against any mention of ethnic quotas of any kind in the basic statute and insisting that the statute clearly reflect the one-step process by which the two entities delegated their authority under the Final Award to the new district—I let Chatzis and his colleagues go at it. With assistance from Karnavas and the BLRC, in relatively short order they gave birth to the first draft of the Basic Statute of the District of Bosnia and Herzegovina.

Having first assisted our legal team in creating the district statute, the BLRC turned its full attention to the core task before it. Karnavas (2001, 14) recommended a phased strategy for prioritizing its work. First the BLRC would draft or harmonize laws having to do with executive authority, *Skupština* rules and procedures, police operations, and administrative procedure. It would then embark on an overhaul of all laws relating to the judiciary. Third, and finally, laws related to commerce, property, contracts, and social issues would be addressed. The last two of these drafting phases overlapped with the preceding phase; in other words, while drafting went forward on the judiciary, laws drafted in the first category would be proceeding on their own track toward enactment and implementation. Under Michael Karnavas's able but stern leadership, the process ground forward day in and day out.

In fulfilling its primary mandate, the BLRC staff, after refining the process described above, oversaw the enactment into law of some forty statutes, only a few of which were in place before I departed Brčko in May 2000. Before launching into a discussion of the BLRC's strategy for prioritizing its work program, let me say one more word about the significance of the step-by-step process for drafting and harmonizing laws. Quite apart from its value as an innovative tool in the attainment of a lofty and difficult objective, hidden in the acceptance of the step-by-step process by all affected parties was a not-so-subtle victory over the centripetal forces of hatred and fear that had for so long torn at Brčko's social fabric. The very fact that legal experts—practicing lawyers and professors of law—from all three groups were able to come together in an (admittedly fragile) atmosphere of professional tolerance and tacitly accept the discipline of compromise inherent in the step-by-step process was a small miracle in itself. If there is a lesson here, it is perhaps this: Part of the value of a procedural approach to problem solving is as much for the cooperation it tends to elicit from participants as it is for the practical outcomes it may (or may not) produce. People, even former enemies, that are formally tasked to find solutions to common problems under imposed or mutually agreed ground rules may occasionally—and largely unintentionally—forget themselves. In a lucky moment of rare grace, they may actually focus on the issue at hand rather than on each other.[8] Who would have thought just two years after the citywide violence of August 28, 1997, that representatives of the Serb, Bosniak, and Croat communities would agree to gather under one roof—and at not inconsiderable personal risk—to rewrite the laws of their community?

So significant was our draft statute, it actually broke new ground in international law and caught the attention of the prestigious Venice Commission in Europe. This esteemed group of constitutional scholars, jurists, and legal practitioners initially came together pro bono in the immediate aftermath of the Cold War to assist nations of the former Eastern Europe in crafting new constitutions as they made the transition from communism to democracy. The Commission would meet periodically, say, twice a year, in Venice, Italy, to discuss and critique draft constitutions and offer suggestions on how to bring them into line with modern democratic theory. Ilias had suggested that I touch base with the commission to inquire as to a critique of our work. The chairman, Justice of the Italian Supreme Court Antonio La Pergola, replied with an invitation to come to Venice and address the commission on Brčko's draft basic statute.

At the Commission's morning session attended by upwards of fifty persons, La Pergola warmly welcomed Ilias and me and said the body had found our work on the basic statute for Brčko exceptionally well conceived. I thanked the Commission for its careful review of our draft statute, a copy of which we had sent them weeks before, and assured the assembled experts that we would take seriously their suggested changes to the text. We left Venice with what we wanted—the good opinion of our basic statute by some of Europe's more prominent legal minds.

In my judgment, the BLRC method for revising and harmonizing laws should be carefully studied for possible application in other peace interventions, including Kosovo, Afghanistan, and Iraq. Although not widely perceived at the time, the new Brčko District in fact presented the international community with a fine opportunity to piggyback on the fruits of the work of the BLRC by using the district as a laboratory, a seedbed, for how to harmonize and revise entity laws across the whole of BiH. Here is how I saw it: The corpus of uniform law so painstakingly produced by the BLRC involved representatives of all three ethnic factions at every stage, including debate in Brčko's twenty-nine-member multiethnic *Skupština*. It was a treasure trove in microcosm of chewed over, sharply debated legislation, which, with appropriate modification, could be brought before the BiH parliament and, following procedures for accelerated consideration by that body, converted into laws for application nationwide. In short, I rather grandly (and naïvely) envisaged the BLRC process as a potential incubator of ethnically neutral, balanced law for the entire nation. For my idea to take hold, however, would have required me to spend a great deal of time in Sarajevo, marketing the idea within OHR and with other relevant international agencies. I considered that eminently doable once the harmonization/revision of laws project in Brčko began to produce tangible results; but it was not to be.

My time in Brčko, although I did not know it, was drawing rapidly to a close. Five months after my departure, the BLRC, in an extraordinarily short-sighted decision by the high representative, was shut down in October 2001 ostensibly on budgetary grounds, which, on close inspection, turned out to be specious.[9] I cannot help but surmise from this that the generally unhelpful mindset regarding Brčko, which was triggered by High Representative Westendorp's negative reaction to the Final Award, mentioned earlier in the chapter on supervisory authority, continued to hold sway in OHR long after my departure as supervisor.

In arguing for a wider application of the BLRC model for harmonizing and/or revising laws in other complicated settings, I am pleased to note mine was not the only voice that saw value in this approach. A year after arriving home, my spirits were lifted by a passage in the House of Representatives Report 107-142, *Foreign Operations, Export Financing, and Related Programs Appropriations Bill, 2002*, which devoted a paragraph to Brčko and the Final Award:

> The Committee believes that the terms and conditions specified in the Final Award of the Arbitral Tribunal overseeing the Brčko boundary dispute constitutes a package of innovative reforms that hold significant promise for rebuilding vital civil institutions. In particular, the Committee believes that the work of the Law Revision Commission to modify existing laws to produce a uniform and fair system of laws throughout the Brčko District should be seen as a model for making similar reforms in the broader region. The Committee believes the Secretary [of State] should use his offices to highlight the institution-building mechanisms developed by the Brčko Tribunal and urge that this be used as a model for making needed legal, judicial and penal, law enforcement, customs service, taxation, and financial management reforms in the Federation of Bosnia and Herzegovina and the Republika Srpska. (2001, par. 303)

In a related vein, none other than Lord Paddy Ashdown (2002–2006), Wolfgang Petritsch's successor as High Representative, had this to say about the rule of law in an October 28, 2002, *New York Times* article: "In Bosnia, we thought that democracy was the highest priority and we measured it by the number of elections we could organize. In hindsight, we should have put the establishment of rule of law first, for everything else depends on it: a functioning economy, a free and fair political system, the development of civil society, and public confidence in police and courts" (2002, par. 4).

CONCLUSION

My hope is that this exploration and explanation of the genesis of Brčko's modern history has conveyed the immense amount of thought and effort that went into setting up its multiethnic administration and development. As a microcosm of BiH, my staff and I believed Brčko could easily become the nursery, the seedbed (*rasadnik*) of sound, modern, democratic governance and set the pace for reform throughout the country. We were small, we were nimble, and we could make things happen under the innovative mantle of the Brčko Tribunal's Arbitration Awards. In particular, the BLRC's extraordinary task "to produce an appropriately uniform system of laws throughout the District" we saw as revolutionary—an open invitation, which as supervisor I warmly welcomed, to make a real difference by ridding the entities' legal systems of old Tito-style Communist thinking and replacing it with up-to-date laws, improved civil and criminal procedures, and a streamlined judicial system in a newly defined jurisdiction that could serve as a laboratory for legal and judicial reform throughout BiH. That, in any case, was our vision, born and incubated in a little city on the Sava River far from the center.

The reader may ask why, at certain points in these last two chapters, I went into such detail in describing the process, for example, by which we selected and then installed various officers for the courts, the police, the administration—first, in the initial Brčko area of supervision, and then, in the new Brčko District. I did so because, contrary to the popular saying "Don't sweat the small stuff," I firmly believe that in a post-conflict environment, with local passions and resentments still running at near fever pitch, the international administrator cannot afford *not* to sweat the small stuff. It is in the so-called "small stuff" that some of the more dangerous problems lurk. Process becomes the heart and soul of the peace program; unless process is perceived to be open, fair, and evenhanded, the enterprise will falter and, eventually, fail. The outside civilian administrator must ride herd on process at all levels if he or she is to be seen as unbiased and fair. In peace interventions, as elsewhere in public life, little things matter a great deal. So, get used to it.

Some thoughts with respect to the people one might work with in implementing peace reform: First, it is well to remember that the skills of conflict resolution need not always come from the outside; they can also, if rarely, be found among persons in the local community who are, as it were, staring you right in the face. Such persons, for example, Croat deputy police chief Pero Androšević, may not at first be easy to identify, but the effort to find them, given the stakes involved, is well worth making. Indigenous conflict resolvers can be of extraordinary value to the civilian administrator because they bring to the table an incomparably more textured understanding of the situation than an outsider can ever do. You must take care, of course, not to lavish attention on such brave souls for fear the hard-line obstructionists will come down on them and their families for cooperating with the international community and its mission of peace. This is always a danger; the benefit outweighs the risk, however, if you approach your decision with respect for the safety of the person in question and simple prudence in determining what you will ask of him or her.

Second, civilian peace implementers must try always to keep responsibility squarely on the backs of local government officials in implementing reform. More often than not, the local power structure will seek to avoid deciding sensitive issues and duck making hard choices, preferring to let you do it even as they rail against you for exercising your authority. When this happens, you may be left with little choice but to implement changes yourself—relying upon your best judgment and the advice of experts. In closing, I can state unequivocally that while our actions might have been far from perfect, there was no question in my mind that the Brčko Executive Board, *Skupština*, police, and courts all began to function on a much more rational and enduring basis due to our efforts.

Chapter Seven

Setting the Stage for Economic Revitalization

Few among those of us laboring to build peace in the Balkans took issue with the proposition that lasting, durable success would depend ultimately on revitalizing the devastated economies of the region. Civilians driven out of their homes and communities by war are reluctant to return in the absence of an active economy that calls for their labor. People who can see a better life ahead—which means, at a minimum, securing a paying job—will be less disposed to revenge and violence than to finding ways of adjusting to, putting aside, or somehow absorbing the tension and pain in their lives. Such people will hopefully be less inclined to heed the call of hard-liners in their midst to wreak revenge on the "Other," hard-liners who will willingly forsake the prospect of peace for renewed violence. The importance of breathing life back into moribund economies, therefore, must rank near the top of the international community's peace-building strategy in the Balkan region.

The First Arbitration Award fully recognized the vital role Brčko's economy would play in restoring peace to the municipality, using such language as: "Given the significance of economic revitalization (particularly in terms of easing ethnic and other tensions in the area)" and "Since revitalization of the Sava River port in Brčko is of paramount interest to both parties." The award charged the supervisor to assist international organizations with development and implementation of a targeted economic revitalization program, to guide efforts to attract public and private investment in the port facility, and to assemble a group of international customs monitors to work with Bosnian officials to establish efficient customs procedures and controls. The Supplemental Award further authorized and encouraged the supervisor to focus on reintegrating the economy in the area of supervision north of the IEBL with the economies of surrounding regions; creating a duty-free or special economic zone to stimulate the region's economy; establishing a privatization program for state-owned and socially owned enterprises; and reopening the Sava River port. Finally, the Annex to the Final Award empowered the supervisor to bring economic activity in the area of the so-called Arizona Market into full compliance with relevant tax laws.

To give some sense of the utter state of disrepair into which Brčko's economy had fallen, I offer my first impressions of the scene that greeted me on arrival. Even at this distance of time, I flounder for words to describe the utter devastation I beheld as our helicopter descended over the outskirts of Brčko *grad*—houses and buildings flattened, streets and roads pitted by mortar shells, outlying neighborhoods deserted, rubble everywhere. All seemed empty.

Despair and hopelessness hung like a fog in the air. Someone commented later—I think it was High Representative Bildt himself who was to preside over the arrival ceremony—on the utter silence that enveloped us once the helicopter's blades stopped whirring. No birds could be heard singing in the trees, no dogs barking in the distance. Silence. In the *grad* itself, economic life had screeched to a standstill except for a number of tiny kiosks selling

Photo 7.1. Destroyed Homes Outside Brčko *Grad*, 1997 (Photograph from the author's collection)

smuggled cigarettes and dimly lit restaurants serving forgettable food. People standing or walking along the streets as our convoys passed seemed quiet and subdued. The *grad* was shrouded in darkness once the sun went down since the electricity grid was basically out of commission; streetlights were out, a single bulb lit most dwelling units.

Unemployment, by conservative estimate, hovered somewhere north of 70 percent. The fact is, however, nobody really knew what the real unemployment figures were—neither in Brčko, nor anywhere in BiH. You did not need the sight of middle-aged men sitting around in dingy cafes all day, or of elderly women shuffling along the street with empty shopping bags, or of several young men in their late teens and early twenties in fancy leather jackets driving late-model BMW motorcycles to know something was gravely wrong with the job market. Row upon row of shuttered businesses and burnt-out factories said it all. The few jobs that did exist were connected either to the local government (and doled out by the Serb parties) or to the black market (for smuggled cigarettes, alcohol, chocolate, cosmetics, and other consumer luxuries).

In the years prior to 1992, Brčko was, by Balkan standards, a bustling hive of economic activity. The city had been an important transit area—the only locality in Bosnia where road, rail, and river routes converged to form a nexus for multimodal transport. The *opština* had some twenty-eight active factories, including the large Bimal oil-seed-processing plant (said to employ, at one time, close to eight hundred workers), the Bimeks meat-processing plant,[1] the Tesla automobile battery plant, the Interplet textile factory, the Izbor shoe factory (with perhaps five hundred employees), a large brick factory, and a number of smaller enterprises employing a score of workers or less. In April 1997, however, the Brčko port on the Sava River remained closed and both the road and rail bridges spanning the river had been rendered structurally unsafe by Serbian explosives. As noted in an earlier chapter, the free movement of people and goods throughout the *opština* was halted entirely.

Although we faced daunting obstacles to the tasks of restoring freedom of movement, returning refugees and displaced persons to their homes, presiding over free elections, and establishing multiethnic government institutions in Brčko, the job of resuscitating the municipality's economy was by far the most difficult task we encountered. It was not, in fact, a single task, but a complex series of tasks, a massive and complex process that involved all the other objectives being woven together, with top priority given to imposing the rule of law on an essentially lawless community. Donor funds were, of course, available in the beginning to help prime the pump, but such monies were far from adequate to the magnitude of the task, slow to be disbursed,

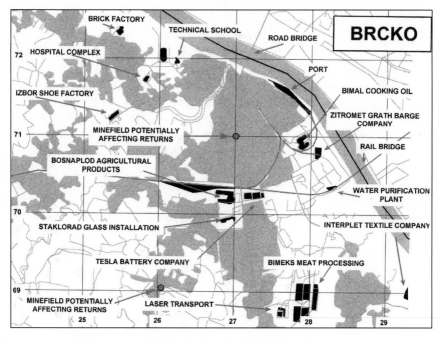

Map 7.1. Brčko's Prewar Industries (OHR-Brčko holdings)

and under constant threat of being withheld or funneled to other crisis zones as donors shifted their priorities.

This chapter focuses on our work to restart Brčko's "white"—as opposed to "black" or "gray"—economy. My staff and I viewed *outside direct investment* as the main benchmark by which success would be measured. Restarting the larger enterprises would simultaneously create honest jobs and reduce the huge pool of the unemployed and gray/black market employees. Despite all our good intentions, however, we were forced to face the cold fact that, with the legal system in need of total overhaul and the courts in disarray, it was far too early, in mid-1997, to mount a campaign aimed at persuading private investors in Western Europe and elsewhere to come to Brčko, or anywhere else in BiH for that matter, to test the investment climate. We accepted the hard reality that, before outsiders would even consider putting their money into Brčko, much more had to be done to stabilize the political and institutional environment. In fact, by the time I left in May 2000, much of this necessary institutional stabilization had begun to fall into place, in large part thanks to the issuance of the Final Award. Thus, as I reflect on my role in the revitalization of Brčko's ailing economy, I reluctantly conclude that it was largely to set the stage for a more concerted and comprehensive push on the economic front later on, by formulating an integrated plan for privatizing the government and socially owned factories: in other words, to lay the foundation upon which successive supervisors would seek to consolidate economic progress and gains made by my office during this period. It was always going to be a daunting task, one that would require time and careful planning, especially since there were stark differences between the way I planned to proceed and the way the Europeans in Sarajevo did.

In short, the OHR-Sarajevo plan was to privatize BiH's Tito-era production enterprises through a complicated system of vouchers that had previously been used—unsuccessfully—in other Eastern European countries in transition. The voucher system is based on an unrealistically determined "book value" of the company's assets in question, then dividing up that value in the form of vouchers to those who could prove that they had been workers in the establishment before the war. While the voucher system was intended to serve a laudable aim—giving the workers some nominal return for their role in helping to build and operate the factories that now lay inactive—it also had the unfortunate effect of allowing and even encouraging local power figures and war profiteers to manipulate and defraud these former employees. In other words, a war profiteer could easily drum up the money to buy out the vouchers from individual workers at much less than the official book value, and thus amass a larger or even controlling share of the company. Needless to say, this would represent a complete reversal of the aims of the voucher system. Therefore, I proposed a clearer approach to the privatization issue: Place the government and socially owned plants up for tender to arms-length bidders. Let the market decide what the plants were worth and sell them for whatever price they could command.

Although this approach may have appeared less directly generous to former factory workers than under the voucher system, in fact, we were seeking to safeguard their rights. Through foreign direct investment into the defunct industries, former state workers faced a better chance of regaining their old employment at the plants than had we left the field open to profiteers. In fact, I repeatedly stated, both inside my office and in public, that I would be willing to sell off these industries for one dollar each if the investor would commit to generating employment for hundreds of former factory hands within a year or so of restarting the plant.

I quickly realized that the battle over approaches to privatization would be ideological, especially since the French, who were in charge of OHR's economic section, could be counted on to resist any privatization program that did not explicitly or immediately favor the former state factory workers—never mind that the voucher approach was unlikely to produce a single job for them. My concept, on the other hand, would, or so I hoped, get those few plants and factories that were actually commercially viable up and running again relatively quickly and in a position to hire workers.[2]

Given that there were still many unresolved issues on the table and that prospective outside investors were still few and far between, I decided, with more than a little tinge of regret, that I would have to leave the heavy lifting of economic revitalization to my successors. As a career diplomat whose in-house specialty had been economic and commercial affairs, I had truly been looking forward to the invigorating challenge of converting a lifetime of observing and analyzing the economies of other nations into "real" life practice. Alas, it was not to be so. In short, it fell to my team to create the legal framework and conditions that would serve as a launch pad to Brčko's future economy, rather than launching it ourselves then and there. Here we will limit the discussion to how we found the means to best undertake our tasks, as well as a few words on the phenomenon known as the Arizona Market.

FINDING THE MEANS

By its very nature, the Brčko supervisory regime was, as the British would say, a "one-off" operation. In other words, there were few, if any, precedents to go by when it came to planning for civilian staffing, financial and technical resources, and the like. Be that as it may, civilian administrators in a multinational peace operation need to have a clear understanding from the very beginning as to sources of financial assistance available to them and how those sources may be accessed. The importance of tying resources tightly to the civilian decision-makers' wagon cannot be overemphasized. In my case, each of the three arbitral awards, taken either singly or together, laid out a set of broad objectives that could only be met if the resources, both human and financial, were sufficient to the task. While the three awards cited no specific figures, a careful reading of them leaves the reasonable reader with the impression that the size and accessibility of those resources could not and should not be left to chance or to the whims of individual donors who could quite easily dance around responsibility for rebuilding Brčko, shifting it from one to the other. Unfortunately, the logical conclusions one might draw from the awards did not always translate into logical action on the ground.

In my initial meetings at State, Bill Montgomery verbally assured me that I would have the full support of the Washington bureaucracy. To begin with, I would have direct access to and control of a revolving fund of over one million dollars ($1.4 million to be exact), for projects of my own choosing that would have a "quick impact" on the community. Given the frenetic pace with which I was hustled from meeting to meeting around Washington in the wintery spring of 1997, it was only natural, perhaps, that small details, such as putting verbal agreements into written form, slipped through the cracks.

The promised quick-impact fund never materialized during my entire thirty-eight months in Brčko. As I reconstruct the sequence of events, I am persuaded that Bill Montgomery had been sincere when he told me about the fund and that he had truly done his utmost to nail down the details with the State Department's office of Support for East European Democracies (SEED). The Department of State rarely engages in disbursing foreign-assistance funds directly; normally this function is left to professionals in USAID. However, since USAID's expertise was traditionally in the "third world" and not in the "second world"—as formerly Communist countries making the transition from centrally planned economies to market-oriented economies in the period following the Cold War were categorized—Congress passed the SEED Act of 1989, which gave State Department authority to de-cide the level and direction of aid to these countries. But even SEED money had to be processed through USAID, which had a framework in place to handle and account for such money flows.

In my admittedly limited experience, it seemed to me that once USAID be-came involved in the disbursement process, matters slowed to a near standstill. The necessity for checks and balances aside, the fact was that Brčko needed that money for emergency reconstruction and needed it now. Bureaucratic jug-gling served only to starve the area of much-needed resources and to cripple my office in its early efforts to revitalize the local economy. A distinct falling off of high-level pressure also meant that the informal, oral commitment on funds I had been given could now be easily dodged by second- and third-tier decision-makers in Washington, thus rendering later attempts on my part to formalize the pledge an exercise in futility. As always in the business of peace-keeping, problems with financial and technical assistance for one's program remain few so long as the people who originally recruited you remain in a position of authority. As new players enter the game, and old players depart, however, my experience is that the issue of funding becomes bogged down in a bureaucratic quagmire replete with blank stares and shaking heads—unless you have an airtight, written agreement, which, alas, I did not have.

In retrospect, my mistake was in not having insisted on a complete survey of assistance sources and potential pledges while I was still in Washington and, later, in Sarajevo, where a large number of donor branch offices were located. Always better to talk to a donor's headquarters first and get its broad commitment to your plan than to seek to persuade its field office people, who can always shrug their figurative shoulders and tie you up in endless delays, claiming lack of authority to make decisions on funding. And yet, the rushed nature of my briefings in the respective capitals left precious little time for in-depth meetings with donor institutions, had I even been nudged in their direction—which I was not. Furthermore, I was suffering under the illusion that the sense of overwhelming urgency and importance surrounding the Brčko endeavor was shared equally by all actors in the international community, and not only in the U.S. government. In other words, I assumed, rather naïvely, that when the time came to support the actions I would be taking in consonance with the arbitration awards, the international donor community would respond to my needs generously and expeditiously.

The reality differed sharply from my expectation. After an initial flurry of nonspecific offers of support, we were largely left to our own devices to persuade, cajole, and scrounge for funds to underpin our plans for restructuring the Brčko area of supervision and, eventually, to launch a "targeted economic-revitalization program."

FUNDING CHALLENGES

The extent of the physical destruction in Brčko was so vast that even an untrained eye could see that the cost of reconstructing homes alone would run to tens of millions of dollars. The UNHCR initially calculated that some twelve thousand houses and apartments were in need of major repair; but a separate damage survey conducted later by the engineering consultant firm the International Management Group lowered that figure to between nine and ten thousand destroyed or badly damaged dwelling units. For international donors, reconstructing houses for refugees and IDPs is one thing, but reconstructing the crippled factories and boarded-up businesses to which returnees would inevitably turn for jobs is quite another. In negotiating the shoals between returning displaced persons to their homes and providing a hopeful environment for their eventual employment, I learned quickly about the limits to international giving. As we struggled to coordinate efforts to repair Brčko's gutted infrastructure, I soon discovered that I had no control over the financial and technical resources needed to accomplish these objectives—not even close.

Donor governments may choose to deliver their aid either bilaterally through their own foreign-assistance arms—such as USAID, the UK's Department for International Development (DFID), or Germany's *Deutsche Gesellschaft für Technische Zusammenarbeit* (GTZ)—or multilaterally through international financial institutions (IFIs) like the World Bank, International Monetary Fund, or European Bank of Reconstruction and Development (EBRD), which also depend on donated public funds from member governments. My staff and I devoted a great deal of time to figuring out, first, how to tap into these sources of external assistance and, second, how to get beyond the donor mindset of "relief aid only" in the economic revitalization process. As I mentioned earlier on, we realized it was far too early for us to expect serious investment, either foreign or domestic, in Brčko's devastated production facilities. The time was not yet ripe for a robust inflow of investment capital, nor would it have been advisable at the time. That did not mean, however, that we held back from devising several stratagems to draw attention to Brčko and its need for infusions of financial and technical aid. The devastated infrastructure cried out for repair. We desperately needed to demonstrate tangible, if tentative, progress toward creating jobs for returnees. Without jobs, or at least the *hope* of jobs, we feared that many returnees, principally Bosniaks, would opt to stay put elsewhere, be it inside or outside BiH, rather than return first to the local communities surrounding Brčko *grad* and then, eventually, to the *grad* itself. But as I soon learned, the creation of jobs—even the creation of a single job, for that matter—is a very, very hard task to achieve.

At the risk of repetition, let me say that during my initial round of meetings in Washington and Sarajevo, the overwhelming sense of urgency surrounding the Brčko effort gave me to believe that all relevant actors in the international community shared equally in the view that bringing peace to Brčko was a top priority. This belief was reinforced over time as successive arbitration awards progressively vested the supervisor with increased authority, including taking steps to stimulate a targeted revitalization of the economy. Here again, though, little was done by way of educating the international donor community, either bilaterally or multilaterally, as to Brčko's unique legal and moral status. Despite the First Award's clear language instructing me to assist donor nations and agencies in crafting a targeted economic-revitalization program, no one with whom I had initially spoken among those donor agencies seemed familiar with that part of the First Award or, truth be said, with the award itself. Everyone had of course heard about Brčko and the fact that a civilian supervisor from the international community had been appointed to take control of the town in the hope of reducing the danger it posed for the Dayton peace process. Few donors with whom I spoke, including the USAID office in Sarajevo, were aware that the First Award *opened the door for me to make special demands on donors to help meet Brčko's most urgent needs.* I had assumed, incorrectly as it turns out, that all potential donors were fully on board and saw the First Award as a document that affected them also. Sadly, few, if any, of the IOs, NGOs, or IFIs had been educated to, or informed of, the need to view Brčko as a special case. This lack of donor buy-in played itself out in several ways.

My interlocutors nearly always cited timing as the main factor that tied their hands from helping. As an example, early on I paid a courtesy call on Rory O'Sullivan, the World Bank's man in Bosnia. During a pleasant conversation over Turkish coffee in which we were joined by the Bank's specialist for development projects, I matter-of-factly raised the deplorable state of Brčko's infrastructure—electricity grid, water mains, sewers, roads, etc.—and inquired how the World Bank might be able to assist in their repair. O'Sullivan responded that very little could be done in the 1997 calendar year nor, perhaps, even in 1998, because the Bank had just that week closed its budget cycle for 1998. Projects not included in the 1998 submission would have to await the following year's budget cycle. He regretted having to respond in a negative way; but he wanted to be factually clear about the circumstances he faced in helping me out in Brčko. I explained that had I known a year earlier of my impending assignment to Brčko I might then have been in a position to make a timely request for assistance from the World Bank, but as it happened, I had only learned of my assignment a few weeks earlier. Indeed, I continued, the very idea of an arbitration tribunal's imposing international supervision over Brčko was unknown a year ago. Surely there must be some way of bringing the might of the World Bank's assets to bear on the problem I faced. After all, Brčko was a special case and, as such, surely deserved a special, separate approach by donors. Brčko was a challenge for us all, and not just my office, given that it represented a microcosm of BiH as a whole and was thus a test case for all international actors. "Afraid not, not just now in any case," O'Sullivan replied.

I left the World Bank office that morning in a somber frame of mind. Nor would it be the first time a donor would tell me that my request had arrived at an awkward time—"off-cycle" insofar as their budgets were concerned—and that therefore little could be done to be responsive either in the short or medium term. More than once I was told that if only I had come knocking on their doors a year to eighteen months earlier, when the 1997 budgets were being drawn up, maybe then something could have been set aside for Brčko—*maybe*. As it was, there was nothing for Brčko in the current pipeline. Sorry!

Our efforts were also stymied by the intractability of donors' priorities at particular points in time. IFIs and NGOs alike were, understandably enough, unwilling to begin committing financial and human resources to the task of restarting plants and factories until BiH's basic humanitarian demands had been met. It was not that these agencies were insensitive to the need to get the divided nation's economy going again—on the contrary, economic development was at or near the top of every international donor's agenda—they simply judged that it was too early to start throwing money at Bosnia's moribund production facilities in the vain hope that they would somehow spring to life again. In this regard, they felt that we needed to accomplish much more by way of institution building (or rebuilding)—including, most importantly, institutions related to the rule of law and justice—before the process of revitalizing the economy could get seriously underway. And they were right.

I well recall trying to engage with Claude Ganz, a successful businessman and "Friend of Bill,"[3] who had been sent out by the White House ostensibly to oversee OHR's economic development efforts in BiH. I say "ostensibly" because whenever I approached Ganz for guidance in crafting a plan for Brčko's economy, he seemed chronically unable to respond in any meaningful way. He seemed to be, in fact, a bit out of his element in a collapsed socialist economy from which all the pillars of capitalism, the system with which he was intimately familiar, were glaringly absent. For example, Bosnia had no equity or bond markets, no commercial banks worthy of the name, and no laws upholding the sanctity of contracts. To top it all there was no class of managers versed in the fundamentals of corporate finance—in short, *no* "Wall Street" equivalents of any kind. *Nema nič* (nothing). To a man who had spent his life in a well-developed capitalist economy, the lack of these financial instruments and institutions must have been a rude shock, and our urgent focus on reanimating what were mostly blue-collar jobs must have seemed, to him, less than compelling.

In many ways, those few of us diplomats who had been exposed off and on to the command economies of the then Soviet Union and Eastern Europe[4] were in a better position to comprehend the depths to which BiH's economy had truly sunk and the drastic measures that would be needed to nurse it back to health than were the more technically competent business experts from the West. One thing we knew for sure, for example, was that men past a certain age—and, almost without exception, it was men rather than women who had managed Brčko's plants and factories before 1992—were thoroughly versed in, and ideologically committed to, the ways of Tito's semi-command economy. With few exceptions, such prewar managers were entrenched bureaucrats with Communist Party affiliations, who more often made business decisions based on directives from central government ministries than on the real movements of the market or the chill winds of international competition. Although Yugoslavia's economy, in comparison with the Stalinist economies of Eastern Europe (Bulgaria, the then Czechoslovakia, Poland, etc.), had been marginally more exposed to the rigors of international trade and competition, it still suffered greatly from the Yugoslav government's practice of artificially setting prices for selected commodities, goods, and services.

Thus, the economic planners and industrial managers from the prewar era with whom Claude Ganz came in contact were, to a man, wholly lacking in that essential attribute of capitalism: the spirit of entrepreneurship. Consequently, the production lines that these men once managed—before the war shut them down—had been technologically lagging behind the times even before the war began, and so poorly maintained during and since the conflict that even if a way could have been found to bring them online, the goods they were likely to have produced would never have competed on world markets. Added to these negatives, moreover, were credible rumors that the Serbs had systematically stripped machinery and tools from several of Brčko's factories and shipped them back to Serbia for installation in factories there. One example of this thievery may have been the Izbor shoe factory on the southwest edge of town. Once one of Yugoslavia's premier producers of leather shoes, this bustling enterprise had directly employed, according to local word of mouth, some five hundred employees. Assuming a family size of four—a conservative number given the traditionally large size of Muslim families—this would mean that the factory had provided direct economic support for at least two thousand people in Brčko. But in July 1998, when I walked through Izbor's burnt-out shell of a factory with ABC's *Nightline*, I found no machinery of any kind or description. The factory had been stripped from top to bottom. Since the Serbs had controlled the area from mid-1992 onwards, the finger of suspicion necessarily points to them as the culprits.

In late September 1997, I had a conversation with Claude Ganz just before he packed his bags for home, a frustrated man. As he had hinted earlier, the problem was that he had simply come to BiH too soon. In retrospect, Ganz said he should have delayed his coming a year or two to ensure that the relevant institutions were in place, most critically the laws on commercial enterprise, contracts, labor, public finance, and so on, that would support (and protect) outside investment in plant and equipment. In his words (paraphrased): "It's simply too early for me and the sort of expertise I bring to the table to make any serious difference at this stage." And he was dead right. In fact, his words stuck with me, taking on deeper meaning over time.

In other cases, we were informed that our project was simply not appropriate. Another incident evoked the same sort of frustration in me that Claude Ganz must have experienced, albeit on a larger scale. I was in my office late on a cold and drizzly evening when my secretary, Doris Hoffmann, poked her head in to say that an elderly gentleman, standing on the street outside, wished to see me. The fellow, tall and slightly stooped, was hatless in a long, tattered coat. Judging by his refined demeanor, however, I took him to be a professional man of some sort. He apologized for disturbing me and said he was a displaced Serb living with his wife in a high-rise apartment building that had been damaged during the war. Because the elevators did not work, the residents of the building, many of them elderly, had to walk up and down several flights of stairs to the street where they had been able to fill water buckets from a common spout in the courtyard. The other day, though, my caller said the pump supplying water to the common spout had broken down. He regretted coming directly to the supervisor with such a "minor" problem, but he feared that without a reliable source of water many older people in the apartment building would soon fall ill. The municipal authorities had been unresponsive to his requests for help. He wondered whether I would be willing to intervene with them to either repair the water pump or provide a new one. I assured my caller that I would look into the matter right away. He thanked me warmly and went away.

Discussing my visitor's problem with members of the staff, we agreed that finding a new water pump through the city's water authority was a nonstarter. So I asked our economic unit to identify a suitable international donor organization and, in my name, request funds from it for a new water pump to be installed urgently at the apartment building in question. One by one, every organization we approached, however, responded with a variation on the theme that projects like replacing a water pump were simply too small to be funded by their assistance programs. Such minor items as this would have had to be folded into a larger budgetary package, the deadlines on which had—once again—already passed. USAID, to be fair, directed us to the U.S. Army's headquarters at MND-North in Tuzla where the agency was underwriting a small—under fifty thousand dollars per project—Community Infrastructure Repair Project (CIRP) program. Quickly pursuing that avenue we learned that, predictably, MND-North had already committed its CIRP funds for the fiscal year. Once again, we were out of luck.

The upshot of this minor saga was that our hero, the supervisor, with all his wondrous powers, was not able to replace a simple water pump at a time and in a place where it was sorely needed. An inexpensive opportunity to gain some credibility among the elderly residents of Brčko simply slipped through the cracks. Several months later, I learned that persons unknown had eventually repaired the water pump. I never ran into my elderly visitor again and, frankly, I was just as happy that I didn't. But his initiative in coming directly to me with his problem taught me a valuable lesson: I learned to keep my expectations low when seeking assistance for small-bore emergency needs like broken water pumps. Sometime later I raised the water-pump case with USAID's mission director, Craig Buck, as an example of my need for the as yet unfulfilled promise of a "quick-impact" fund. Buck said that I should look upon MND-North's CIRP program as my quick-impact fund! An easy way to deflect my request, but the facts of the matter were that a succession of MND-North's commanders jealously guarded the CIRP program money as their own. We were occasionally able to suggest projects for funding under CIRP, but the final decision rested always within the military, where low-ranking officers did most of the planning.

In full recognition of the desire of military commanders to have at their disposal funds set aside for community development in their areas of operation, I find myself in strong disagreement with this policy when a civilian administrator shares the same space. In the latter circumstance, I am firmly of the belief that control over the disbursement of such funds should be transferred by law to the civilian administrator, where responsibility for economic development logically lies. Thus, CIRP funds would pass from military to civilian hands.

In late spring of 1997, not long after the water-pump incident, I was sitting with Brčko's Serb mayor, Miodrag Pajić, in the drafty municipal building, discussing issues and priorities. I asked Pajić if he had but one request to make of me, what that request would be. Without blinking an eye, the mayor replied, "Streetlights!" Here again, a simple, straightforward request that few could fault. Pajić said no one felt safe at night on the city's streets, which were only barely illuminated by the few lights from shops and restaurants. In the neighborhoods, homes and apartments were lit, if at all, by a single bulb. The city descended into near-total darkness as night fell. Without minimizing for a moment the technical obstacles that would have to be overcome in bringing the electricity grid back online, I wholeheartedly agreed with Pajić that municipal lighting would go a long way to dispelling fear. We placed streetlights, a no-brainer, at or near the top of our list for donor funding.

Once again, however, in a replay of the water-pump caper, donors came up with every kind of reason why our streetlight request was premature, not in the queue, too late for that year's budget, and so on. To spare the reader needless detail, I can report that a full two years passed after my conversation with Mayor Pajić before the first streetlamp shed its beam of light on the streets of Brčko. On that occasion, a local electrical crew simply showed up one day, without a word of notification to me, and began refurbishing broken lampposts along the street where our office stood—not in the heart of town, where they were needed more, but no matter. At long last, we had streetlights! Because the work was carried out with CIRP funds it became an MND-North (SFOR) project, but that was just fine with me.

Sometime later, one of Brčko's two dentists invited Ian and me to dinner. Our host told us that of all the contributions the international community had made to the betterment of life in Brčko, few matched that of installing lights along some of the city's streets. The dentist pointed to the streetlights as a tangible sign of our intention to improve life in the *grad* even as we were facilitating Bosniak and Croat returns to MZ communities at the edge of town. I took from his comment the frail thought that streetlights gave the Serbs a reason to believe there might, just might, be something in it for them after all—in other words, that we might not just be hell-bent on making their lives unbearably hard after all.

As a bittersweet endnote, the long-awaited quick-impact fund was finally activated in Brčko about a year after my departure; a former staff member of mine in the economic unit in charge of running the fund kept in contact with me and informed me that the major part of the funds actually went to installing street lighting in all remaining neighborhoods of Brčko *grad*. As I and the former Brčko mayor had predicted, the advent of light into these formerly dark neighborhoods had a dramatic effect on the sense of security enjoyed by ordinary citizens, and helped to make the area much safer. I say "bittersweet" because although the quick-impact fund certainly improved the quality of life for the citizens in Brčko, I cannot help but think that we could have brought about these basic gains had the fund been released to us sooner, when it was most desperately needed.

DONORS' DAY IN BRČKO

Faced with a refusal on the part of in-country bilateral donors, IOs, IFIs, and NGOs to commit funds to Brčko on what they saw as spur-of-the-moment initiatives, I decided to go over their heads to their country capitals in order to secure wider participation in a targeted economic-revitalization program for Brčko. In late summer of 1997, I invited high-ranking officials from several donor countries and agencies to spend a day in Brčko learning about our plans and priorities for the broken economy. My message was that we knew where we wanted to go and had a clear plan to get there. Our economic unit, ably headed by German diplomat Nicholas Graf von Lambsdorff,[5] distributed a paper that outlined major projects for funding and described our evolving strategy across the board. I had earlier sought Carl Bildt's informal thoughts on this mini donors' conference and he considered it a good idea. In any case, we were gratified when a majority of the officials we invited made the trek from capitals to faraway Brčko to engage in a daylong exchange of views. Although this unique event did not trigger an immediate flow of funds, it nonetheless had the salutary effect of softening resistance among in-country donor representatives, as participants returned to capitals and spread the word down the ranks. That was the upside. The downside was that the modest success of this mini-conference lulled me into believing that OHR-Sarajevo would continue to agree with our strategy for pursuing, in a highly targeted way, development funds for Brčko in the future. But such was not to be. Although we were given a fifteen-minute spot on the agenda of a huge donor conference held in Sintra, Portugal, in May 1997 (High Representative Bildt in the chair), our subsequent efforts to get the word out about Brčko's reconstruction needs at such gatherings never went smoothly thereafter: not in Brussels (1998), nor in Bonn (1999), nor, again, in Brussels (1999). In each case, I had to fight to keep Brčko on the agenda in the face of OHR-Sarajevo's "forgetfulness."

Despite these frictions, however, we were under fixed time constraints and had little choice but to move forward wherever we could. As we geared up for the final push to create[6] the Brčko District by the spring of 2000, though, our economic team—headed by the dedicated and innovative Jesse Bunch and ably supported by U.S. Army Civil Affairs officers Major Roland de Marcellus and Major Brooke Allen, as well as the talented Claire O'Riordan, who liaised closely with NGOs in Brčko—crafted a polished brochure that clearly and succinctly laid out the key projects in need of priority funding. Each project in our twenty-page brochure was presented in a technical format preferred by donors. Just minutes before I was to go on, Bunch and his colleagues fanned out around the huge hall, distributing the brochures to donor representatives. After my ten-minute pitch, during which I drew attention to the projects in the brochure, I noticed that many in our audience were actually perusing the handout. Maybe, just maybe, we had gotten something right!

THE ARIZONA MARKET

A potentially important factor in Brčko's economic recovery was the emergence of the Arizona Market (*Tržnica Arizona*), situated on the Donja Mahala–Orašje Road at the intersection of the IEBL separating the Federation from the RS. The catchy name "Arizona" derived from NATO's designation of the north-south highway as Route Arizona. The market was the brainchild of two U.S. Army officers serving with IFOR in 1996—COL Greg Fontenot, regimental commander at MND-North, and his subordinate, LTC Anthony Cucolo, battalion commander at Camp McGovern. Driven by a desire to rekindle low-level communications between the hostile factions whose nerves were still shattered, these two officers gambled that even sworn enemies would barter simple goods to meet basic needs if there was a venue where such transactions could take place in safety. Fontenot and Cucolo selected a small parcel of land in the ZOS just a hundred meters or so south of the IEBL, along the western side of Route Arizona. To provide site security, they parked an M-1 tank nearby and manned it around the clock. Makeshift lean-tos and tiny kiosks began springing up as local entrepreneurs warmed to the idea. By the time the Arbitral Tribunal handed down its First Award establishing the supervisory regime, the Arizona Market had been operating for nearly a year.

For several reasons, as the new civilian supervisor I had no influence over the pace and direction of the market's growth as it expanded south in a jumbled manner down Route Arizona. First, the actual territory on which the market was located—and on which it remains to this day—fell just outside my original area of supervision, a situation that persisted for the next two and a half years. Second, the systemic weakness of Brčko's institutions in 1997 and 1998, including its fledgling police force, would have totally precluded the municipality effectively regulating the market. Third, given all the other issues crowding our agenda, were we to have added regulation of the Arizona Market just then would, quite frankly, have stretched our capabilities to the breaking point. Our work program under the First Award was full to over-flowing and driven by a March 1998 deadline. Beyond being uncomfortably aware, therefore, of the market's existence on the periphery of "my" territory, I had neither the time nor the staff to reflect deeply on its long-run implications for Brčko's economy. My civilian counterparts in Sarajevo, moreover, were similarly disposed not to intervene at the market. Occasionally, I would express concern about the site to my OHR colleagues, but with all the issues they were confronting, they, like me, had little interest in adding the Arizona Market to their list.

As for the role of the U.S. Army, which, as the IFOR/SFOR standard-bearer in northeast BiH had (or should have had) primary jurisdiction over Arizona Market activities, especially in light of its role in establishing the market, times had changed. Gone were the days when the able Fontenot/Cucolo team had simply positioned a tank to protect the to-and-fro of the market's traffic. Both of these officers had been reassigned well before I arrived on the scene. Then, in September 1997, five months after my arrival, SFOR decided unilaterally that the Abrams tank could be safely withdrawn from its watch along Route Arizona. The good news was that SFOR now judged the security situation along this major artery to have improved to the point that the security gap left by the tank's withdrawal could be filled by routine SFOR patrols. The bad news was that the tank itself, having become a symbol of stability—and, in a certain sense, of (enforced) civility—may, by its withdrawal, have contributed to the freewheeling, Wild West atmosphere that came to symbolize the market. In any case, it did not take long for criminal elements to start moving in. Nonetheless, having created the market, SFOR now concluded it was timely and safe to pull back from its day-to-day monitoring of market activities, especially with an international civilian authority now on scene. That was, in any case, the answer I got when I inquired as to SFOR's reasons for deciding to pull the tank away. Had SFOR consulted with me on this matter beforehand, I would have educated them to the fact that the supervisor lacked direct authority over that portion of the prewar Brčko *opština* that the market occupied. What was done was done, however: water under the bridge. To be fair, it was perhaps inevitable that Bosnian Croat political and criminal elements would have eventually filled the power vacuum at the Arizona Market, no matter whether a tank was in place or not.

By early 1999, the market had grown from a handful of open-air lean-tos to several hundred enclosed stalls that no longer displayed only trinkets but rather a wide array of consumer goods—mostly from outside BiH—as well. The only natural inhibitor to the market's rate of growth was the general poverty pervading Brčko's countryside. Increasingly, goods for sale were being smuggled in from southeastern Europe via Croatia, and to a lesser extent from Serbia, across BiH's unregulated and porous borders. Added to the usual luxury items (cigarettes, alcohol, chocolate, cosmetics) was a stream of textiles, rugs, household appliances, TVs, electronic devices of every description, and the ubiquitous CDs and tape cassettes—all pirated, of course.

The Arizona Market's unchecked growth had several repercussions. Property rights, for example, were simply pushed aside as vendors rushed in to set up shop on tiny plots of rural farmland. Alongside the law of unintended consequences stands its corollary: No good deed goes unpunished. The good deed in question here—the opening of a tiny channel of communications between the Serb, Croat, and Bosniak communities—was in time "punished" by the hard feelings that arose between vendors and the prewar owners of the agricultural land on which the vendors had set up shop. In the postwar confusion, the market's organizers—IFOR, then SFOR—seemed to have simply turned a blind eye to property rights when they encouraged vendors to open stalls on land they neither owned nor rented. Given the prevailing mood of fear and intimidation, these seeds of discord were muted and awaited less menacing times before germinating into full-blown conflict. Another negative aspect—or punishment, if you will—concerned the total lack of public-health amenities at the market, including metered electricity, potable water, public sanitation, protection from the weather, and so on. As the market became ever more crowded, the public-health issue approached a crisis point.

Among those few international officials concerned about activities at the Arizona Market, speculation ran high that large transfers of cash were moving under cover of night from the market to Mostar, where the HDZ, the hard-line Croat party, had its BiH headquarters. Indeed, most of the prominent Croat operators at the Arizona Market belonged to a shadowy—and even harder line, if that were possible—offshoot of the HDZ, a veterans' group known by its initials *HVIDRA* (*Hrvatskih Vojnih Invalida Domovinskog Rata*, Croatian Homeland War Disabled Veterans Association). Unwittingly then, the originally benign market and postwar healing instrument known as the Arizona Market—and by association, the entire Brčko *opština*—almost certainly became a lucrative source of finance for the highly nationalist (and secessionist) community of Croats in southern BiH, a region they provocatively called *Herceg-Bosna*. Although this issue did not, for reasons noted, loom large in our initial strategizing over how to regulate the market, it should have been a strategic concern for OHR as a whole—as well as for all other international agencies headquartered in Sarajevo—in its dealings with Croat (and Croatian) obstructionists in Mostar.

By the time the Final Award came down in March 1999, perceptions about the market had sharpened dramatically. It had grown into an issue that could no longer be ignored. The Arizona Market's growing de facto importance to the economy of the region that was about to become the Brčko District made the need for a straightforward, transparent plan to bring its activities under legal control both obvious and urgent. More importantly, the annex to the Final Award, promulgated five months after the Final Award itself, gave the supervisor unambiguous authority to do just that. The annex stated that the supervisor had the authority "to bring economic activity in the area of 'the Arizona Market' into full compliance with relevant tax laws." Moreover, the annex expanded the area of supervision to encompass not only the narrow portion of the Posavina Corridor (between the IEBL and the Sava River) but also the entire territory of the prewar Brčko *opština*—a total area of some eight hundred square kilometers.

We could now take under serious study what measures to consider in regulating the unruly conglomeration of shops and kiosks that formed the core of the Arizona Market. The fact was that, each day the market remained free of regulation, Brčko lost out on revenue from property and sales taxes. Sometime later, Dr. Tarik Arapčić, president of Tuzla Canton, told me the estimated loss in tax revenues from the Arizona Market was one million DEM per month. The need to capture those lost tax revenues for the new district's treasury dominated our thinking and planning.

Nor were we alone in our analysis. During one of our weekly meetings, the Serb chief of police Kokanović, accompanied by his Bosniak and Croat deputies, Haseljić and Androševič, proposed that I authorize them to start planning for the imposition of law and order at the market. Ever alert to hidden agendas, I was nonetheless impressed (and a bit surprised) that all three policemen had come together in suggesting this course of action. They seemed to sense where we were heading and wanted to signal their full support up front. Remember, this was barely two years after my arrival in Brčko, a city that still held the potential to destabilize the entire Dayton peace process and, although a fast-receding possibility, to reignite the Bosnian war. We had certainly come a long way, I mused to myself. In any case, we considered the police proposal a sign that we might actually be able to bring the market under control with a minimum of fuss. Of particular note was Androševič's acceptance of the proposed planning. As a Croat, Androšević certainly under-stood the political and security risks of police action as well as, or better than, we did. While I applauded their initiative, I nonetheless thought it premature for the police to engage in detailed tactical planning until we ourselves had hammered out a comprehensive strategy. Later, I faulted myself for so hastily deciding against the police proposal. What harm would have been done had I given Chief Kokanović the green light to go ahead with quiet planning for an Arizona Market operation? Probably none. On the other hand, once set in motion, such planning might have tipped our hand to the market's organizers before we were fully ready. In any case, the willingness of Brčko's police to broach the issue with me on their own initiative renewed my resolve to raise the matter in Sarajevo without further delay. But before taking that step, we needed to come up with a bulletproof strategy for addressing the manifold issues swirling about the market.

Despite the Final Award's clear language empowering the supervisor to tax economic activity at the market, the situation on the ground was not con-ducive to my acting alone. The police commanders' initiative notwithstand-ing, Brčko's tri-ethnic police force, although growing in competence and cohesion, had yet to attain the degree of professionalism required to tackle a task of such magnitude. We would therefore need outside assistance. Given the market's ever-creeping encroachment on the adjacent land since its early days, and the degree to which criminals had penetrated its operations, includ-ing the opening of several bordellos, we concluded that the Brčko police would need, at the very least, UN/IPTF technical advice in drawing up their plan. The close collaboration of SFOR would also be required, especially if serious violence broke out when the police began to move in.

We promptly set about developing a strategy for our presentation in Sara-jevo. I was optimistic that so long as we had UN/IPTF, SFOR, and, of course, the high representative on our side, the task of imposing supervisory control at the market would be neither dangerous nor overly difficult—not nearly so difficult, say, as had been the process of returning non-Serb families to their homes. We therefore set out to develop a plan that would draw mainly on local police resources in achieving our objective without a lot of opposi-tion. Now that the necessary enabling language was in the annex to the Final Award, I felt confident about my authority to proceed. What, I asked myself, was there not to understand in the wording of the annex? Unfortunately, that little bubble of optimism was soon to be burst as the Arizona Market suddenly became a hot topic in Sarajevo, and ensnared in the center-versus-periphery dynamic described in chapter two.

I called in a small group of advisors led by Timothy Yates, my chief of staff, and put the Arizona Market issue on the table. I tasked the group with scrutinizing the market through a series of on-site visits and face-to-face interviews with a wide sampling of vendors. What we needed was a quick, clear-eyed assessment of market conditions, warts and all. The group fanned out, and within a few days, Yates produced a draft report accompanied by a preliminary plan for imposing supervisory authority over the market. I phoned the high representative's chief of staff, Ambassador Roger Short (UK), to ask that he put the Arizona Market on the agenda of the next meeting of the Inter-Agency Planning Group (IAPG) in Sarajevo.[7] Assuming the IAPG would approve our proposal, I began planning to present our findings and preliminary action plan to the Principals' Group for its blessing and support. Short agreed the issue was ripe for discussion at the highest level and put us down for an early November principals' meeting.

On November 1, Tim Yates, Darryl Veal, and I ventured down to Sarajevo. Veal, an American attorney on the BLRC staff, had drawn up a legal brief, including a fact sheet and slides, cogently outlining our rationale for reforming and regulating the Arizona Market in an orderly fashion. As expected, our preliminary outline was waved through the IAPG with only a few suggestions for change. This encouraged me greatly because, only days earlier, we had picked up on rumors that SRSG Klein, upon learning of our growing attention to the Arizona Market, was now pushing for a hard-line approach among his international colleagues. According to rumors, Klein was arguing for the market to be shut down completely—actually, to be bulldozed—and the land returned to agriculture! My own interpretation of this rumor, however, was that, even if true, Klein's argument would have been intended primarily for its shock effect to help polarize the looming debate, rather than a realistic prescription for action. I therefore decided not to react, simply taking note of the rumors, since I knew UNMIBH had neither the mandate nor the funds to act on its own insofar as the Arizona Market was concerned. In the unlikely event that the SRSG was serious about using bulldozers to flatten the market, he would need SFOR to do the heavy lifting. From my long association with SFOR, however, I was sure the military had no stomach for intervening at the market—especially not now that it fell under civilian authority, at least on paper. So I dismissed Klein's rumored intentions as bluff. After all, the UNMIBH representative at the lower-level IAPG meeting had made no allusion to his boss's desire to close down the market.

On November 1, with the IAPG review under our belt, we were invited to attend the principals' meeting to present our proposal. Our objective was to persuade the principals to sign onto a collaborative team effort, involving UN/IPTF, SFOR, and OHR, aimed at bringing the Arizona Market under control. Chief of Staff Short assured me that in view of the positive IAPG review, I could expect smooth sailing at the principals' meeting. Unfortunately, his was too rosy a view. A wave of opposition to our plan, of which Short was evidently unaware, had somehow built up between the dates of the IAPG and the principals' meetings. Two of the five principals—SRSG Klein, whose cooperation I needed, and head of OSCE Bob Barry, whose organization had no direct role as regarded the market—were openly skeptical, questioning whether the site was worth regulating at all. "Isn't the market doing more harm than good to the economy and fabric of life in the Brčko *opština?*" Klein asked, castigating my presentation as showing only the positive side of the Arizona Market, emphasizing its benefits and revenues, and ignoring its criminal aspects and costs. He lambasted the market as a cesspool of illegal trade in stolen cars, smuggled goods, and, horror of horrors, prostitution. (Even if true—a proposition I was not ready to concede—were these not precisely the conditions that regulation of the market would correct?) Barry chimed in, saying he had heard children, as well as women, were being bought and sold at the market. At that my jaw dropped. Never in all my months living near the market had I heard anything about trade in babies or children, although for months my staff and I had been quietly addressing the issue of trafficking in women.

In my view, both men had been wildly misinformed, probably by their headquarters' staffs—few of whose members had sympathy for or empathy with the Brčko arbitration process. Neither Klein nor Barry seemed open to the possibility that the Arizona Market could become a golden egg for the *opština,* which was soon-to-be reunited as the Brčko District. I was further caught off guard when High Representative Petritsch rather hastily threw in with Klein and Barry. Had Short not picked up on his sentiment either? Only SFOR, which had steadfastly supported the Brčko mission, remained neutral; its commander, LTG Ronald Adams, abstained from taking a position. Striving without success to make my case against minds already set, after twenty minutes I reluctantly came around to Petritsch's view that in order to address Klein's and Barry's concerns we needed to flesh out our proposal with a more in-depth study of criminal activities at the market. Petritsch suggested I come back to the principals in a month with my findings. Swallowing hard, I rose from the table and headed back to Brčko to initiate a second report on the Arizona Market.

The next day I reconvened what we were by now calling the Arizona Market Working Group (AMWG). This time, however, we cast our net wide, inviting members of the Brčko branch offices of UNMIBH, UN/IPTF, SFOR, and Customs and Fiscal Assistance Office (CAFAO),[8] as well as members of my own staff, to take part. Once again, Tim Yates led the effort, which eventually consumed over two hundred person-hours and resulted in a thirteen-page report, complete with appendices. The data we used in the second report were, as before, based on interviews and heretofore unseen documents unearthed by the AMWG. The AMWG's intent this time was to focus more carefully on the type and level of criminal activity associated with the Arizona Market without ignoring its projected economic impact—both positive and negative—on the future Brčko District. The market's footprint now covered more than twenty-five hectares of land immediately south of the IEBL, some fifteen kilometers southwest of Brčko *grad*. The AMWG counted more than a thousand trading stalls as well as 150 lorries (trucks) from which goods were being sold directly off the tailgates. One observer described the Arizona Market as having more the air of a bazaar than of an organized commercial enterprise.

Actually, the AMWG found two markets developing: the "original market" and the "new market." The original market was comprised of 1,011 trading stalls that sold everything from animal feed to textiles and employed some twenty-five hundred people. The AMWG report estimated that an additional seventy-five hundred people were dependent on market activities for a major portion of their livelihood—the so-called "ripple effect." SFOR Civil Affairs officers reckoned that between fifteen thousand and twenty-five thousand people visited the market on weekends during the summer. The original market's annual turnover was estimated at a hundred million KM (US$50 million, at the then prevailing exchange rates). About 65 percent of the stalls were officially registered with Ravne-Brčko and paid a monthly rental fee—but no taxes. Croat mayor Mijo Anić declared receipts in 1998 of seventeen thousand KM from registration and parking fees, and nine-month receipts to October 1999 of seventy-two thousand KM.

The second, or new market, planned to open seven hundred additional vending outlets, but only four shops were found to be operating. In early 1998, the ethnic breakdown among traders was determined to be 65 percent Bosniak, 30 percent Serb, and 5 percent Croat—but the Arizona Market's management was 100 percent Bosnian Croat, with collected revenues unevenly split between the then HDZ-controlled Ravne-Brčko and HDZ-controlled Mostar. The report noted that the removal of the IFOR/SFOR tank, or checkpoint, had created a security vacuum that allowed for exploitation of the market by criminal elements. According to SFOR and the local UN/IPTF, however, no evidence surfaced to suggest that the criminal activity involved trafficking in human beings including, most significantly, children. Since no businesses were registered for tax purposes, the AMWG judged the main crime in the Arizona Market to be economic in nature: the failure to pay taxes to the appropriate authority.[9] Yates concluded the second report with three recommendations, that:

- The Arizona Market be made subject to a regulatory regime that addressed all aspects of economic and other criminality.
- The regulatory regime be established *within three months* of the formal creation of the Brčko District.
- The case for the Arizona Market be reviewed by the principals *nine months after* the imposition of the complete regulatory regime under the soon-to-be-established Brčko District.

As part of the AMWG's fact-gathering, Tim Yates asked then commander of Brčko's UN/IPTF, Ken Johnson, a retired police officer from Houston, Texas, to prepare an ancillary report focusing exclusively on crime and criminal activity at the Arizona Market. In keeping with the close collaboration that characterized relations between our offices, Johnson readily agreed. He quickly set about sifting through police statistics, not only those in the jurisdiction of Ravne-Brčko, but also those on file in the BiH Federation's Ministry of the Interior in Tuzla. Johnson's report was revealing. Opening with a general disclaimer about weaknesses in the statistical base, he addressed the central question posed at the principals' meeting: Was the level of organized criminal activity so overwhelming as to make regulation of the market infeasible? With respect to organized crime, Johnson found that while it was widely suspected that criminal enterprises were actively trading in illicit goods and demanding protection money from small vendors, these suspicions could not be substantiated by the available evidence. Acknowledging that some well-known criminals such as Ramiz "Ćelo" Delalić operated nightclubs in the market,[10] Johnson found, through vendor interviews, that the conventional wisdom about rampant criminal activity at the market was not supported by the facts. Further, nearly all the vendors with whom he spoke wished to see the market regulated in a manner that would permit them to continue to operate. They all depended on it for their livelihood and would willingly register their shops and stalls to stay in business. Johnson concluded that while a few vendors and business operators might in fact threaten action should market regulators attempt to eliminate the flow of untaxed goods, the great majority would comply with rules for taxation and/or revenue collection if they were imposed fairly and equitably. Yates appended Johnson's report to the body of the second AMWG study.

Working from the AMWG's second report, our team developed a six-step plan for regulating the market from the supervisor's office once the Brčko District was announced officially and in place, which we expected to happen by early March 2000. As previously, of course, we emphasized that the plan would depend for its success on the full cooperation of all relevant international agencies in BiH. The one-page plan is reproduced below in its entirety:

The Supervisor's Plan for Regulating Economic Activity at Arizona Market
Step One:
Seek views of a representative group of vendors at Arizona Market concerning regulation, registration, and taxation.
Step Two:
Take their views into account in developing, in cooperation with SFOR and UN/IPTF, an information campaign using all media outlets. Distribute a simple, clear, one-page statement of intent referring to the Brčko Final Award to all vendors at the Arizona Market in advance of taking action.
Step Three:
Establish a multi-ethnic Arizona Market Management Board under the District's (multi-ethnic) Department for Economic Development. The Management Board, overseen by OHR, would first hold hearings and then meet to impose basic procedures on the market, such as hours of operation, traffic controls, sanitation standards, and the like.
Step Four:
Establish a sub-station of the Brčko District (multi-ethnic) Police Service *in situ*. Increase SFOR random patrols around and through the market. Locate an office of the BiH Customs Service at the Arizona Market, perhaps collocated with the District Police.
Step Five:
Develop, in collaboration with the Brčko District Government and in line with District-wide laws on tax and revenue, a process for collecting registration fees, taxes, and for enforcing sanitary standards, including a system of fines. Establish a fund, drawn from collected taxes and fees, to improve Arizona Market infrastructure (sewage, water, electricity, lights, parking facilities, etc.) under the control of the Arizona Market Management Board.
Step Six:
Address the criminal element in two phases. First, close down shops that are violating Intellectual Property Rights (i.e., selling pirated CDs and tapes, etc.). Once that is accomplished, move next against the six operating houses of prostitution, closing them one at a time. (When two or three are shut down, the others may well get the point and up stakes for friendlier climes. If they choose to remain, however, then they, too, will be shut down).
Comment: This plan (1) minimizes the likelihood of violence, (2) holds out the promise of capturing critical revenue for Brčko's coffers, (3) saves the livelihoods of some 2,500 persons directly employed at the Arizona Market who have dependents numbering perhaps 4–5,000 persons. Violence, if any, is more likely to come from legitimate vendors whose livelihoods are at stake than from criminals and pimps who can simply relocate.

On January 31, 2000, Tim Yates and I appeared once again before the principals in Sarajevo. During the intervening weeks, I had called on OSCE's Barry about the baby issue and he agreed to drop his active opposition to my plan, while withholding his support. In effect, he would fall silent. Klein, however, remained adamant in his opposition to regulating the market. If anything, his opposition had stiffened. And the High Representative—for reasons I was never able to discern—refused to take a stand. Following our second failed appearance before the principals, the standoff over the Arizona Market dragged on for months: Klein and his subordinates could not make good on the threat to plow the market under without my concurrence, and I could not implement our plan to regulate without the SRSG's cooperation. Despite sporadic attempts to break the impasse during my few remaining months in Brčko, a workable solution was beyond our grasp.

In the end, my successor, Gary Matthews, High Representative Petritsch, Barry, Klein, and SFOR's head, LTG Michael Dodson, reached an agreement on October 26, 2000 to clean up the market. Matthews promulgated a "Supervisory Order on Arizona Market" on November 16, 2000. All business licenses previously issued to vendors were deemed subject to revalidation and reissuance by the Brčko District government. Those businesses operating without a license were given thirty days to apply or be closed down. Further, business activities were to be conducted only between 6:00 a.m. and 6:00 p.m. A week later, Chief Kokanović submitted to the supervisor an "Operational Plan of Stamping out Crime in the Arizona Market." The Brčko District government gathered together an expert team to address relocation of the Arizona Market to a more suitable location.

Another supervisory order was signed February 17, 2001, shutting down two public enterprises operating illegally in the original market, as well as invalidating contracts issued by the vendors. By March 26, 2001, the Brčko District's expert team had adopted a master plan for regulation and development activities. The Brčko District government, Department for Urbanism, Property Affairs, and Economic Development reported 1,654 licenses had been granted, with another 126 being processed. The Revenue Agency of the Brčko District estimated that the payment of tax obligations for these 1,780 businesses amounted to 2,617,356 KM, as well as for the utilization of land and park space in the amount of 1,696,479 KM. This represented 13.5 times more in relation to the realized income at the Arizona Market before the establishment of Brčko District.

On August 7, 2001, an open invitation for submitting bids to finance, design, build, and manage the structures and infrastructure of the Arizona Market was advertised. Two serious bids were received. A commission to review the bids met on November 19, 2001, and selected the bid of the international consortium Italproject. A contract was signed on December 21, 2001, anticipating investments of 250 million KM over a period of seven years and allowing Italproject to manage the market over a period of twenty years.

Afterwards, the Arizona Market was to be returned to the Brčko District. Initially, implementation of the contract was slowed due to the Brčko District government's failure to coordinate activities, as well as obstruction by local landowners. The new buildings opened in the summer of 2004.

CONCLUSION

Let me end with a matter close to my heart. In order to bring a war-scarred economy back to its feet in a manner that will endure and be self-sustaining, you must *first* establish the rule of law throughout the territory. Until an effective local police force is up and running under a coherent body of law, and an independent court system is in place and capable of adjudicating commercial disputes in a timely manner, the process of economic redevelopment will depend almost solely on outside taxpayer-generated funds. All such monies are subject to their disbursers' rules, processes, and programmatic interests. The bottom line for a civilian decision maker when faced with the prospect of a Brčko-like mission is, therefore, to insist upon a clear understanding of existing financial-support mechanisms that will be attentive to their exceptional needs once in theater. Preferably—no, necessarily—such an understanding should be put in writing. The content of the written communication should

Photo 7.2.   Bimal Following Privatization, 2005 (Photograph by Allison Frendak-Blume)

then be shared widely with top officials in donor organizations, both official and unofficial.

Nor should the prospective administrator leave NGOs out of the survey of potential donors to be called upon for support, as and when needed. In my experience, however, left to their own devices, NGOs will go their own merry way, either blithely ignoring or claiming no knowledge of priorities set by policymakers either locally or in far-off capitals. It took a long time for me to recognize that many large and influential NGOs were actually avoiding the task of becoming involved in my mission because of the perception that Brčko was a dangerous place to operate. Indeed, for many NGOs, Brčko was off-limits. Prominent exceptions were Catholic Relief Services, Norwegian People's Aid, and Mercy Corps.

Encouraged by our institution building, one Serb-American investor from Chicago decided to take a chance on the new district and entered into exploratory discussions during my final months to open a cement-block factory on the site of a former VRS facility made vacant by Brčko's demilitarization. That investment was in fact actualized within weeks of my departure. More outside investment, including the opening in Brčko of seventeen branch offices of European banks—a dramatic sign of growing community stability—and the privatization of some fourteen factories and plants has taken place since; but that is a story for another chronicler.

Chapter Eight

Conclusion

My thirty-eight months in Brčko were by far the most trying—and *rewarding*—of my career. In conversation with two of my successors, Henry Clarke and Susan Johnson, I found they felt much the same way about their tenures as supervisor. I offer, in this concluding chapter, my thinking about just what peculiar mix of skills and life experiences might best qualify a person to take on post-conflict civil administration missions and what factors can influence one's degree of success in doing them.

WHAT IT TAKES TO SUPERVISE A COMMUNITY DEVASTATED BY WAR

Much is said and written these days on the issue of competence in the conduct of peace and stability operations. Understandably, the elusive attribute of "competence" is more often noted by its absence than by its presence. Once a peace operation flounders or is seen to be failing, the search for someone to blame—to accuse of *incompetence*—begins. Such an indictment, if you happen to be on the receiving end of it, can be devastating. When one looks hard at this phenomenon, however, it is difficult to avoid the conclusion that not enough up-front effort goes into the selection and training of persons tapped to undertake these highly unorthodox—even hybrid—challenges. As in my case, professional diplomats, for example, are simply not groomed to take on civilian leadership roles in such unusual and often dangerous assignments. Nonetheless, the career diplomat is routinely tagged—along with the occasional retired military officer—as the default candidate to undertake a leadership role in these highly problematic and perplexing operations.

From time to time people ask—sometimes a bit pointedly—just what qualifications I brought to the task of supervising an unstable city like Brčko in a
war-torn land like Bosnia. They are curious to know why I was tapped for the
Brčko job and why, once tapped, I thought I could do it. They wonder what
it was in my experience and background that prompted the State Department
to task me with this highly unusual off-line assignment. Good questions all,
particularly since the Brčko challenge represented a sharp change from the
substance and rhythm of diplomatic work, in which up until then I had spent
my professional career.

As noted earlier in this account, I had agreed on but a few hours' reflection
to leave Saudi Arabia, where I was leading a team inspecting our embassy
and consulates, and return immediately to Washington for a hurried round of
high-level briefings on Brčko and the critical role it had come to play in the
prospects for peace throughout Bosnia and Herzegovina. It quickly became
clear to me that in three decades of diplomatic service, I had yet to encounter a tangled web of ethnic hatreds and war-induced wounds—physical and
psychological—like the mess awaiting me on the Sava River in northeastern
Bosnia. Nor had I ever contemplated being asked to oversee—to supervise—
the day-to-day governance of a community of any kind or shape in the world.
The subject had simply never come up in all my years in the business; none
of my varying job descriptions had ever envisaged such a possibility, nor, so
far as I am aware, had those of my colleagues.

Without experience in the pragmatics of government, I thought of myself
as an "off the shelf" diplomat, a sort of jack-of-all-trades, somewhat versed
in the ways of the world, with only limited exposure to the Balkans. Much of
what I knew about the art and practice of diplomacy, I had absorbed through
the doing of it and from closely observing senior diplomats at work. In sum,
I had nothing by way of formal training and little by way of experience to
fall back on as I girded myself for the job ahead in the strategically situated
municipality of Brčko.

I am often asked my opinion on what would be the ideal mix of professional
skills, temperament, personality, and so on, which a civilian administrator in
a post-conflict peace and stability operation should possess. As this is written,
our nation is still engaged to varying degrees in stability operations in Iraq,
Afghanistan, and Kosovo. Although it would be foolhardy to predict exactly
when and where, it is a near certainty that we will be engaged in more such
operations in the future. I will therefore attempt in the pages that follow to
render my opinion—and it is just that: an opinion—on that question, mixing
hard facts with subjective observations and hunches. To a considerable extent,
I acknowledge up front that my argument will rest on the questionable, even
dubious, value of dealing in stereotypes. But you have to start somewhere.

My experience in Brčko gave me insights into what seems now to be an emerging consensus that selecting the right person or persons for civilian leadership positions in post-conflict peace and stability operations is sine qua non for success. I therefore suggest several desiderata for policymakers to consider in vetting candidates for these high-profile positions.

First, I begin with a fundamental observation: To be effective, a person nominated for a civilian leadership role in such operations must be prepared to commit to it for a minimum of a year, and longer if need be. Shorter commitments of time—say, six to nine months—simply will not cut it in view of the need to establish interpersonal relations with a wide array of actors as you seek to establish your authority, based, you hope, more on suasion than diktat. Establishing such relationships takes time. Although my tenure in Brčko ran to thirty-eight months, a stretch of time many of those close to me considered excessive, such a lengthy presence on the ground had its good points. I well remember RS prime minister Milorad Dodik saying to me, and I paraphrase: "I have stopped learning the names of international officials who come to see me. No sooner do I learn a person's name and function than he or she departs to be replaced by another short-termer. You, on the other hand, have been around long enough for me to get to know you. I am therefore happy to meet with you whenever you come to Banja Luka." A civilian administrator's readiness to remain in the job for as long as it takes, first, to restore a modicum of order and, second, to launch the torn community on the path to reconciliation, will be seen by the people and their leaders, whether they like you or not, as a mark of serious commitment to, and genuine concern for, the process of restoring peace in the land. As Dodik implied, longevity *by itself* counts for much in the estimation of the local body politic and its leaders. In my judgment, therefore, a candidate's willingness (or lack thereof) to commit for the longer haul should be a critical factor in determining his or her suitability for the job. The overall mission suffers when those in top leadership positions are constantly changing: "parachuting in and out" is the phrase often used to describe the phenomenon.

My second observation has to do with the question of where to look for candidates to fill these out-of-the-mainstream roles, based on professional qualities and life's seasoning. For the sake of argument, I have come up with seven categories of loosely defined "professions"—based on education, special training, unique skills, etc.—that can be usefully, if imperfectly, compared as reservoirs of potential candidates for civilian leadership roles. These categories are: career diplomats, lawyers, academics, retired business executives, military officers (active and retired), international civil servants, and, last but not least, politicians.[1]

Photo 8.1.   Bill Farrand and RS Prime Minister Milorad Dodik, 1999 (Photograph from the author's collection)

One would think right off the bat that members of the Foreign Service—career diplomats—would make excellent, even ideal, nominees for such positions. Indeed, as noted above, the Foreign Service is the category most often looked to by default to provide candidates to fill these jobs. Let us therefore begin this discussion by taking a brief look at diplomats and the professional world in which, as a general rule, they operate. When assigned abroad, the diplomat's highest priority is faithfully to represent, promote, and advance his or her nation's interests and policies in the host country. Diplomats observe, analyze, and report back to capitals—London, Washington, Moscow, Ottawa, etc.—on events and happenings in their country of assignment that are relevant to their *home* government's interests and concerns. With rare exceptions, the weighty decisions are made in capitals with instructions sent to the field—to ambassadors—for conveying to the host government. To be sure, diplomats contribute facts and analysis to the policymaking process, but rarely make the big decisions themselves. Thus, the diplomat's primary function comes down to exerting influence on and persuading host (receiving) governments to act in ways conducive to good relations with the diplomat's (sending) government.

Diplomacy can be a demanding process, requiring of its practitioners a keen understanding of political, economic, and social factors and tensions in the host country, as well as a comprehensive awareness of international forces at play in the host nation's region of influence. Because the diplomat is unable to exert direct influence over a host government's decision-making process, his or her effectiveness will often depend on having deep reserves of patience and persistence. Under accepted tenets of international law and tradition, diplomats are proscribed from meddling in the internal affairs of a foreign nation. Indeed, one of the prime tenets of diplomacy is never *ever* to interfere in the internal affairs of another country.[2]

Occasionally, a lucky diplomat will be thrust into a high-stakes negotiation in the field that will demand long and unrelenting hours. (Even here, however, the diplomat is likely to be relegated to a supporting role since, increasingly, teams of substantive and technical negotiators are dispatched to the field from home, especially to deal with high-profile issues involving extraordinary legal and technical complexity.) But such heady assignments are hardly the norm. For most diplomats the "norm" is a quiet, steady routine of interacting with the host government bilaterally on a gamut of issues, among them: making *demarches*[3] to protect your nation's trade and commercial interests, securing over-flight rights for aircraft, supporting Washington-directed negotiations, visiting fellow countrymen ensnared in local laws or in hospital, attending official ceremonies, and so on. All these efforts are carried out through discussions with host government officials and do not involve interacting or communicating with private persons—the people—of the host nation.[4]

The agenda I was to carry out in Brčko as the international supervisor differed sharply from the above description of diplomatic work. Consider the language of the First Award on the supervisor's four main objectives: "*to ensure* freedom of movement," "*to establish* a program *to govern* the . . . return of former residents," "*to ensure* [conduct of] . . . free and fair elections," "*[to] issue* such regulations and orders as may be required *to enhance* democratic" multiethnic government, "*to assist* . . . international development agencies *to . . . implement* a[n] . . . economic revitalization program" [emphasis mine]. Nothing passive about the verbs used here, nor about their meaning. Clearly, as supervisor, I would be actively engaged in the life of the Brčko municipality—in my defined area of supervision—far from the operating norms of diplomacy to which I was accustomed. To be sure, like all diplomats, I had made decisions on many matters over the years, but such decisions were of a different order from the sorts of issues I would be forced to address and decide on in Brčko. Indeed, the First Arbitral Award gave the supervisor virtually free rein in supervising the city and its outlying local communities.

It is hard to point to exact precedents for such a remarkable conferring of power on an appointed international official in such a high-stakes, post-conflict environment. Weak parallels can be drawn with the bestowal of power on a five-member "Governing Commission" in the League of Nation's exercise of authority over the Saarland in post–World War I Germany

(1920–1935). The League also engaged in the administration of the Free City of Danzig (1919–1939), although the high commissioners assigned to the area did not exercise authority in the manner we are speaking of in this discussion. They served more in a "mediating" role. And the United Nations had assigned single administrators to West Irian (1962–1963) and South West Africa/Namibia (1967–1990), but the political context was more in the realm of decolonization than in war's aftermath. (Postwar administration of Germany and Japan involved foreign intervention on a scale so massive as to be beyond comparison for the purpose of this discussion).

All of this begs the question: Does a training facility or basic course exist where a career diplomat—a Foreign Service officer—might be sent to learn the fundamentals of civilian leadership and hands-on governance? Well, no, as it turns out; such a focused training regimen does not currently exist in the Foreign Service. Remember, we are talking about a service that prides itself on having well-educated "generalist" officers who, as professional jacks-of-all-trades, are considered to be trainable (read: self-trainable) on the fly. So where was I to look for guidance as I prepared to shift from a comparatively passive to a decidedly proactive mode of management? For the fact was that when it came to the hands-on management of large organizations, I, like most diplomats, had only a vicarious notion. As a rule, a diplomat's managerial experience is limited to overseeing the work of but a handful of other diplomats with correspondingly small-to-tiny clerical staffs.

I imagine that Foreign Service officers reading this may, and likely will, take sharp exception to my boiled-down description of the diplomatic trade. They may with complete justification point to the fact that most diplomats work longer hours and with less recognition, both abroad and in Washington, than nearly all other groupings of federal employees. Indeed, the record is replete with examples of career diplomats taking bold initiatives to defuse crises in a host country. But such behavior, while worthy of high praise, is the exception that proves the rule. Since entry into the Foreign Service is still relatively selective—in a typical year, some three hundred applicants out of more than ten thousand are welcomed into the service—diplomats are assumed to be highly motivated and disciplined in representing the United States to the rest of the world. Consequently, diplomats tend, as a profession, to view the need for continual in-service training as unnecessary and less than vital to their careers. Indeed, because of the time it would entail away from their work, many diplomats even look upon training as *harmful* to their professional advancement. (Professional military officers, on the other hand, view exposure to regular training courses as crucial to their advancement in rank.)

With the Brčko experience still fresh in my mind, I would argue that my Foreign Service colleagues who think that way are dead wrong—especially when circumstances arise, as they are doing with increasing frequency, that will require a career diplomat to perform in a role that comports hardly at all with the standard diplomatic mold. To be fair, however, and for a variety of reasons, the U.S. Foreign Service has been decidedly understaffed in recent years, which translates to heavy workloads for its members deployed around the globe. So I do not wish in the slightest to diminish the enormous contributions diplomats routinely make to our nation's well-being and security. I was one of them, after all. I am trying to draw a distinction here between the working world of a diplomat, who deals primarily with government officials, and that of a municipal supervisor (or city manager), who must frequently deal with people at first hand. As one who has played both roles, I can assure you there is a major distinction here: not dissimilar to that between a wholesaler and a retailer.

So if diplomats are not my ideal candidates to lead a post-conflict peace effort, where then might we turn to find civilians with the skill sets necessary to fill leadership roles in such high-profile operations? In the discussion that follows, I have chosen, in an admittedly stereotypical fashion, to lump together members of various professions and occupations into different pools where policymakers might look for candidates. I make no pretense at socioscientific rigor here, nor do I presume there can be no overlapping skills between these candidate pools. My purpose, quite simply, is to set up straw men so I can knock them down one by one before reaching my preferred pool of potential civilian leaders.

Let us next examine the legal profession. Few would quarrel with my broad observation (remember, we're into stereotyping here) that lawyers are trained primarily as advisors and interpreters of the law, which is why they are called "counselors." In the first place, lawyers tend to think differently from the rest of us: more analytic, less susceptible to impulse, more cautious in reaching conclusions than the common run of humankind. Observing State Department lawyers over the years, for example, I found them more inclined to look for reasons why something could *not* be done than why it could be done. My close association with international lawyers in Brčko leads me to observe that in their approach to governance, many lawyers, not all, tended to be wary and a trifle stiff (not to say rigid) in insisting on legal precedent before proceeding to act. Excellent qualities all, but not necessarily those you need in a fast-moving crisis that calls for bold action/reaction. In the immediate aftermath of war it is a fact of life that local law effectively disappears as if into a void that can and may persist for a very long time. Earlier, I argued that instilling (or restoring) the rule of law must be the civilian administrator's highest priority on which, to one degree or another, all other priorities will depend. While civilian administrators (supervisors) engaged in this large effort ignore at their peril advice and counsel from their legal staff, they (the administrators) need not, indeed should not, be lawyers themselves. Taken as a class, therefore, lawyers would not be my first choice for civilian leadership positions in the sort of unsettled, post-conflict contexts we are discussing here.

Next, let us consider academia as a potential source of civilian leaders. With utmost respect for the operational—yes, operational—value of intellectual discourse on issues relating to peace, how it is lost, how best restored, etc., I hazard the opinion that the academic mind is far more adept at research-ing, analyzing, and theorizing about ways to fix a broken society than it is at actually managing the corrective process itself. The academic expert's strength, as I see it, lies in thinking reflectively and teaching effectively on these large issues, rather than in engaging hands-on in all the practical aspects of undertakings as, say, city governance.[5] Thus, while professors of relevant academic disciplines can certainly bring invaluable scholarly insights to peace operations, they should not as a rule be considered candidates for leading such operations unless they have proven themselves as successful practitioners in the field. Such experience is, however, hard to come by in the academic world.

We turn now to the suitability of another potential category of candidates for civilian leadership roles: retired business executives and their hardheaded pursuit of the "bottom line." Let me begin by observing that while the art of governance does indeed have a "bottom line," it is of a different type and kind from that which famously drives the business world. The bottom line for gov-ernment is to be measured by the successful delivery of public services—law enforcement, defense, education, health protection, sanitation, water, etc.—to the citizenry and not, as in business, in the delivery of goods and services to the marketplace where they are intended to generate profits (or losses) for shareholders. To be sure, both spheres of activity require knowledge, skill, and patience—but they differ fundamentally as to means and ends. I suggest that business executives—however clear-eyed and forceful they might be in the world of commerce—would find it exceedingly difficult to function in the near-chaotic context of an environment in which normal conditions for doing business have been swept away.

As the experience of the American businessman Claude Ganz showed, the time for entrepreneurs to arrive on scene is after the mess has been largely cleaned up, investor-friendly laws are on the books, and a functioning court system capable of quickly resolving disputes is in place. Only in this rela-tively benign atmosphere would business executives find their comfort zone. So I do not see in retired business executives a particularly fruitful pool of talent from which to draw civilian supervisors for the early phase of a post-conflict operation. Quite apart from professional considerations, moreover, is the question of whether a business executive, active or retired, would agree to work for the relatively low salaries offered to would-be administrators in postwar crisis zones.

Next we consider active-duty military officers and their potential to serve temporarily in the role of civil administrators. In early post-conflict settings like Brčko, where military officers can and do find themselves thrust into dual roles as civil governors, they must adjust habitual modes of thinking and doing as war-fighters to a radically different mode of functioning. Simply put, the governing of a civilian populace is a calling for which most military officers, as with most diplomats, rarely have a natural aptitude. Civil governance calls for a vastly different set of skills than military maneuvers require—skills that emphasize construction over destruction, peace over war, the nonkinetic over the kinetic. It is thus far from easy for professional soldiers trained to destroy the enemy in battle to throttle back from the edge of combat to a less intense and more nuanced plane of action. To restrain the propensity to employ force first and ask questions later requires a conscious change in the military officer's rules of engagement, which guide the behavior of soldiers deployed in the field. For the military professional, the transition from "hot" war-fighting to comparatively "cool" post-conflict operations (policing, repairing infrastructure, providing community services, etc.) can be a disorienting experience, especially when feelings of hostility and fear from combat operations remain paramount, not only within the military itself but, more importantly, among the indigenous populace.[6] My deputy and friend, retired brigadier Ian McLeod, once remarked how difficult it was to manage this balancing act when he commanded British troops in Northern Ireland during the 1980s and early 1990s. "I was trained to blow up villages, not rebuild them!" he exclaimed one day as he and I pored over plans to restore Brčko's flattened neighborhoods.

Brčko is a case in point. Before my arrival on scene, the task of overseeing and attending to the needs of Brčko's rump civilian populace had been, for all intents and purposes, placed firmly in the hands of a U.S. Army lieutenant colonel who commanded the eight-hundred-strong SFOR battalion at Camp McGovern. This highly competent and energetic army officer had all he could do to perform his primary mission of restoring a safe and secure environment in which the local populace might begin to sort through the wreckage of war. Added to this primarily military mission were the largely civilian functions of reinvigorating the Brčko police force and establishing a rudimentary framework for local government. Here was a military officer attempting to run a city, a task for which he surely had no prior training, with an indigenous police force comprised of remnants of the VRS—none of whom he could trust.

Furthermore, messy post-conflict environments do not lend themselves to the setting of precise objectives and the crisp planning that are hallmarks of

military operations. To operate in a world without classified intelligence—
where orders, once given, may or may not be carried out; where ambiguity
reigns; where little goes as planned; and where resources are hard to come
by—is the very antithesis of the military world. Were a military officer to find
himself appointed as a civilian peace implementer, the frustration engendered
by some or all of these factors would, I suggest, put their patience and sense
of order to the severest test.

Despite its commitment to training, the U.S. Army, like the Foreign
Service, has no fixed site where the fundamentals of peace and stability
operations are routinely taught to officers—commissioned and noncom-
missioned—before they deploy to a crisis zone. The army's Peacekeeping
and Stability Operations Institute (PKSOI), located in Carlisle, Pennsyl-
vania, is devoted to the research, study, and dissemination of information
on peace operations—the so-called "Phase IV" of a military intervention.
West Point, too, has recently incorporated a new course for the cadets on
the principles of reconstruction and stability. These educational initiatives,
while certainly welcome, are once-removed from the urgent need to incorporate these concepts operationally in current training for troops about to
be deployed into post-conflict war zones.

The army does, though, make a good-faith effort to include stability and
reconstruction "events" into military readiness exercise (MRX) scenarios
conducted before major units deploy—or redeploy—into post-conflict
environments. An MRX lasts for approximately two weeks and focuses on
classic war-fighting: how the commander is to maneuver against armed resistance in his area of responsibility. The point here is that a military commander is duty bound to keep his unit ready for war—a simple matter of
professional and practical survival. Training activities, therefore, that did
not improve war-fighting skills—like, for example, training for reconstruction and stability operations—were, until recently, clearly subordinated to
the maneuver (war-fighting) mentality. Again, this is a long way of saying
that most military officers spend their time—as their profession rightly
demands—preparing for war, not peace.

What then about senior military officers who, steeped in this warrior mindset, are called from retirement to serve as civilian administrators in Phase IV
operations? How are they likely to fare in such an unaccustomed role? Two
factors stand out: First, the old adage "Once a marine, always a marine!"
applies in varying degrees to military officers across the board. Having
spent their careers in disciplined service to their nation, military officers not
surprisingly carry into retirement a lifetime of respect for and deference to
rank. This phenomenon, unremarkable by itself, takes on operational significance when, as "civilian" administrators, they must interact with a military

commander whose rank is higher than the rank they attained before retiring. Second, the often ambiguous and frequently blurred lines of authority among civilians can be frustrating to a person habituated to hierarchy and to clear, step-by-step decision making rooted in settled doctrine, unambiguous objectives, and unambiguous timelines.[7]

What about the international civil servant? Here we have, or should have, a pool of experienced persons, many of whom will have been schooled or practiced in the fundamentals of peacekeeping. In the United Nations, for example, a real effort has been made in the Department of Peacekeeping Operations (DPKO) to train a cadre of personnel for moving in on a complex postwar contingency operation of the sort we are talking about here. Okay, so in the wide pool of international civil servants we seem to have found the Holy Grail; we need look no further, yes? Well, no. As it happens, this entire category of professional civilians was removed from consideration for top peacekeeping posts in BiH because of the UN's poor performance in protecting Bosniak citizens during the war, especially in the wake of the Serbian massacre of seven thousand Muslim men in Srebrenica in July 1995. While all involved in the debacle hope fervently that this onetime happening would be unlikely to recur, the fact it happened once could not be ignored. Other international organizations are often hampered by the lack of a robust mandate for peace *operations*, per se, and by internal personnel policies that restrict the length of time their members can serve in-country. The Organization for European Cooperation and Development (OECD), for example, functions largely with staffs that are seconded from member countries for periods not to exceed six months.

So where does that leave us? Putting aside, for the sake of simplicity, all the thousands of other professions that have nothing at all to do with peace operations, I come down squarely on the side of professional politicians— yes, politicians—as the preferred candidate pool for such civilian leadership roles. Despite the widely accepted canard that politicians are irredeemably dishonest, untrustworthy, unprincipled and so on, the fact is that without dedicated politicians we would be adrift in our public life. Politicians are quintessentially human; the Yiddish word *mensch* comes to mind. The politician is often driven by ambition, pride, the desire for power (or all three in combination): base motives to some, positive motivators to others, but, in any case, motives widely shared by their fellow man. The best politicians are moved to make a difference, to get things done, to improve their communities—and, most important, are not deterred by obstacles they find in their way: personal attacks, unending hassle, negative odds, and all the rest. Most politicians are, at least when they start out, optimists and risk takers capable of creating a vision and living by it.

In fact, very few of us are called to activism in the political world. To those who take up the challenge of elected office, however, we owe a large measure of gratitude. Half a century ago the eminent sociologist Max Weber had this to say about politicians: "Only he has the calling for politics who is sure that he shall not crumble when the world from his point of view is too stupid or too base for what he wants to offer. Only he who in the face of all this can say 'In spite of all!' has the calling for politics" (Weber, Gerth, and Mills 1946, 128).

Politics demands personal qualities and skill sets that differ in significant degree from those that predominate in the other professions we have examined. As a rule, politicians are less hidebound, less rigid, and more prone to doing what is possible in an imperfect world under adverse conditions. They are, by nature (and self-selection), people who find deep satisfaction immersing themselves in the complexity of human affairs. For the most part, they genuinely like people and do not, indeed cannot, shy away from human contact. Politicians are less likely to be thrown off stride by ugly surprises; they know what it is like to be under continual attack from this quarter or that, fairly or unfairly, for what they are trying to do. They are not hothouse flowers with brittle egos as academics and even diplomats sometimes are. Politicians know what it is to be in the arena, down and dirty, where little goes according to the book and mud spatters all the players. This is the kind of person that a post-conflict civilian administrator needs to be: tough, resilient, hard to throw off balance. While elements of Weber's definition of a politician can be found in both the diplomatic and military professions, neither of these callings captures the full essence of what it means to be a successful, durable politician.

Harlan Cleveland (1985), a noted educator and diplomat now deceased, made points similar to Weber's. He focuses on the overriding importance of attitude over skills in a leader. In Cleveland's words, "Attitudes . . . are indispensable to the management of complexity." Furthermore, a true leader embraces:

- The notion that crises are normal, tensions can be promising, and complexity is fun;
- A realization that paranoia and self-pity are reserved for people who don't want to be executives (leaders);
- The conviction that there must be some more upbeat outcome than would result from adding together the available expert advice; and
- A sense of personal responsibility for the situation as a whole. (1985, 5)

Although written for the business executive, I found in Cleveland's formulation an exceptionally accurate description of the mindset needed by anyone seriously contemplating the kind of leadership challenge that is the topic of this book.

Carl Bildt, the first high representative in Bosnia, was a consummate Swedish politician who taught me the value of getting out of the office, going in front of cameras and microphones, and rubbing shoulders with the people. High Representative Irish Lord Paddy Ashdown was also a seasoned politician who by all accounts preferred to be on the road rather than sitting behind his desk in Sarajevo. Both men, at different times and in different ways, managed to convey an image of caring about the people of BiH as much as about their factional leaders. As politicians, they understood the power game and how to roll with the punches. For all their acknowledged flaws and excesses, politicians are accustomed to the rough-and-tumble of public life and revel in it. Successful politicians know how to communicate with people. Diplomats, academicians, and civil servants, on the other hand, tend to favor the written over the spoken word, the press statement over the public speech, wholesale over retail. While there is certainly a time and place on the team for both, who would seriously quarrel with the proposition that a spoken word delivered in person before a live audience is a more powerful way of communicating than a written communiqué?

Politicians have two other attributes that set them apart from other professionals: First, having been elected to public office from the ranks of the community they serve, they have an independent power (and career) base. That very power base would bestow on the politician-cum-administrator a degree of independence that would translate into a greater willingness to take risks, a necessary attribute in such unstable and high-stakes circumstances. Secondly, life experience has taught politicians that any initiative they might embrace will depend for its success on the availability of funding. Without funding, little can be achieved. The best politicians know instinctively how to go after—and keep after—the funds necessary to fulfill their mandate. Career diplomats and military officers are largely shielded from the necessity of pursuing funds for their work. They are often able to leave that chore to others in their organization who may not share their perception of the larger mission. This phenomenon is especially characteristic of the diplomatic service, where political officers routinely go about their work in splendid isolation from the administrative officers' need to be concerned about resources. I found the constant need to pursue funding for the Brčko mission a huge drain on my energy, time, and patience. Part of the problem was I simply did not know how to go about it. I am quite confident that an able politician/operator would have had a surer grasp of how to go about attaining baseline funding more efficiently and with less frustration than I experienced. For a politician, the pursuit of funds with which to operate is second nature.

Thus, in my judgment, a politician, either temporarily out of office or retired from political life altogether, would be the preferred candidate to consider as leader of the civilian side of a peace operation. I believe an ex-mayor of a large- or medium-sized American city—preferably one with high rates of crime, drug use, crumbling infrastructure, poor health care, lagging schools, inner-city flight, and so on—skilled in the all-important art of coalition-building among feuding parties and groups (police vs. firefighters, Republicans vs. Democrats, social services vs. business interests, and the like) would be a far better choice to govern a collapsed, post-conflict municipality like Brčko, Mostar, Sarajevo, Mitrovica, Baghdad, or Kirkuk than the usual suspects who are normally tapped for such functions. Indeed, I ran across a news item in the *Washington Post* reporting a conversation between then senator Joseph Biden (D-DE) and Senator Richard Lugar (R-IN) in which Biden was quoted as saying: "Lugar had it right five years ago. . . . We needed to send 600 mayors to Iraq to get that country functioning again" (Broder 2008, par. 10). A perceptive insight. Is it not likely that former mayors of such cities as Los Angeles, Atlanta, Chicago, Baltimore, and others of similar size and complexity, who faced during their tenure in office every kind of urban ill, would bring to the table every tested and proven skill necessary to tackle the manifold issues in post-conflict situations? The trick, of course, would be to persuade them to join the game, an issue beyond the scope of this discussion.

HOW TO SUCCEED (POSSIBLY) OR FAIL (SURELY)

Another generic question that keeps cropping up when I appear before audiences is what practical advice I would have for a civilian person about to assume leadership of a post-conflict war zone. What pearls of wisdom might I pass along that might conceivably make such a person's task a little easier, a little less daunting? At first, I dodged this question, since I had not sat down and thought it through. But as time passed, I came around to the idea that this was an exercise worth doing, if only to sharpen my own thinking on what sort of behavior would help—and what would hinder—a civilian leader in advancing the mandate for peace. Serendipitously, I had a chance to confer with my respected colleague, Ambassador (ret.) John McDonald, who happily shared his insights with me on this question. Having engaged in several peace operations himself, John thought the key ingredients of successful peace implementation lay in the traits and attitudes the implementers themselves exhibited in addressing local players. McDonald reduced his chosen attributes to three: *humility,* a *willingness to listen,* and *patience.* These qualities closely echoed my own experience in Brčko—in particular the need to listen. It is trite, but true, that you learn when you are listening, not when you are talking. Often the very fact you are willing to listen to what your interlocutors are saying is enough for the moment. They will give you credit for listening to their plight even if you are unable to offer a solution on the spot. Most local people with whom you will meet know full well that a speedy resolution of their problems is not in the cards, but they need desperately to vent their frustrations to higher authority. In sum, you gain enormously by simply listening, even though your petitioners are unlikely to acknowledge that fact on the spot.

To the Ambassador's three attributes, I would add the following rules for success or failure. Here goes:

Do
1. Take your mission—*not yourself*—seriously
2. Plan for all contingencies
3. Meet separately *and often* with the factions—on their turf
4. Be human—radiate energy, optimism, good humor
5. Be open and accessible—engage directly with the populace
6. Embrace the media—they can be your best friends
7. Promise only what *you* can deliver—not what others might (or might not) deliver in your name
8. Keep higher-ups *and donors* in the loop as to your plans
9. Encourage—*indeed, insist upon*—dissent on your staff
10. Drink the local beer—they'll love you for it

Don't
1. Move without a plan
2. Be aloof
3. Surround yourself with "gatekeepers"; close your office door
4. Dominate every conversation—listening trumps talking
5. React to first reports—they are likely to be wrong
6. Cut and run when the temperature rises
7. Succumb to despair—reverses are only setbacks, not defeats
8. Ignore the center; fail to protect your back
9. Forget to feed the media maw
10. Turn up your nose at plum brandy (or whatever local libation your host offers you)

Additionally, I must emphasize in the strongest terms the importance I attached to having a clear mandate—embodied by the three arbitration awards—both to vest me with the requisite authority and to guide me in my work. To underscore this point, permit me to compare Brčko with BiH's other highly contested and dangerously unstable municipality—Mostar.

Located on the River Neretva in Herzegovina 120 kilometers southwest of Sarajevo, Mostar was a city of approximately 120,000 residents before the war. Muslims and Croats were divided more or less equally between the two banks of the river. As was generally the case throughout Yugoslavia, the two communities had lived side by side in relative harmony for decades. Indeed, Mostar boasted one of the country's world-renowned landmarks: a four-hundred-year-old stone bridge across one of the Neretva's deeper and narrower chasms near the center of town. The bridge stood for centuries as a reminder that genius may be found in every corner of the world. In November 1993, with animosity running white hot between the two communities, Croat gunners in an act of breathtaking stupidity trained their artillery on the old bridge and sent it plummeting into the river. This callous act, along with the senseless killing of civilians on both sides, was emblematic of the mindless hatred inflamed by Milošević and Tudjman, who conspired in the early 1990s to carve up BiH between their two ethnically dominant spheres in an effort to put Bosnia's Muslims in a geographic vise. Their scheme fell apart, though, and by the end of the war the Bosnian Croats were cooperating, at least tactically, with the Bosniaks in a joint military stand against the Serbs.

Despite this wartime convergence of interests, and the subsequent shoehorning of Bosniak and Croat political structures into the shaky Federation of Bosnia and Herzegovina by way of the May 1994 Washington Agreement, tension over the political status of Mostar remained an open wound, not wholly unlike the situation in Brčko. What made Mostar different from Brčko, though, was that while Brčko sat astride a strategic corridor on the very littoral of BiH, Mostar lay well within the country's borders. Mostar's wider significance, therefore, lay in the fact that as a running sore left over from the war it symbolized the Federation's fragility for all to see. It was an open question as to how much weight the Federation could be expected to carry on inter-entity dealings while Mostar remained divided and at war with itself. Mostar, in a word, had become a festering ulcer and remains so today.

The European Union was first to take a concrete interest in doing something to address the ethnic divisions in Mostar. In 1995, they assigned a highly respected German politician, Hans Koschnik—once the youngest mayor of the city of Bremen—as civilian administrator of Mostar. Over one quarter of a million euros were placed at his disposal to engineer a turnaround in the city's fortunes and muffle the ethnic differences that were tearing the city apart. Despite Koschnik's best efforts, however, the violence continued unabated. What Koschnik lacked as civilian administrator, of course, was an arbitration agreement to hang over the heads of Mostar's wreckers and spoilers.

It did not take long for media representatives, particularly the Serbs, to begin comparing circumstances in Brčko and Mostar. They would tackle me with questions like: "Mr. Supervisor, how is it you think you can come waltzing in and expect to solve Brčko's problems when the Europeans, who have been hard at it in Mostar for a much longer time, have failed miserably in making peace stick down there? In Mostar only the Bosniaks and Croats are involved, in Brčko you face all three ethnic groups. Who are you to think you can succeed in Brčko, when the Europeans have not succeeded in Mostar?" Such questions, with variations on the theme, followed me for months. My stock response was this: "Thank you for the question. I am no expert on Mostar or any other municipality in BiH. My job is to restore order and calm and multiethnic institutions in Brčko. All of my energies are directed toward that end. But let me say it is hardly fair to say that efforts to restore peace in Mostar have failed while they are still in progress. No one I know in the international community would make such a judgment. Next question."

Duncan Bullivant, my first media spokesman, suggested early on that I visit my counterpart from the U.J.C., Sir Martin Garrod, who had succeeded Hans Koschnik as the administrator of Mostar. A former lieutenant general in the Royal Marines, Garrod had already established himself as a fresh new force in Mostar. Because our mandates were operationally similar, as were the constituencies we faced—angry, divided communities in need of every conceivable form of help and assistance—I agreed with Bullivant's suggestion to meet with Sir Martin in Mostar as soon as possible.

On a sunny morning, my helicopter set down on Mostar's vacant airfield, which had been closed to commercial flights since the war. Our armored vehicle passed through burnt-out neighborhoods on its way to Sir Martin's headquarters in the Forum Hotel downtown. After a brief get-acquainted session, my host sent me off on a program of briefings by his veteran staff, followed by introductions to key players in OSCE, IFOR/SFOR, and NGOs that lasted well into the evening. Late in the afternoon, Sir Martin himself took me on a whirlwind walking tour of the ravaged parts of the city, ending up at the destroyed bridge. One lesson I took away was the openness and friendliness Sir Martin showered on people he met along the way. He obviously believed, as did Carl Bildt, in the efficacy of pressing the flesh with the people so their leaders would find it difficult to paint him as an aloof and uncaring outsider.

Over dinner that evening, Sir Martin answered my questions into the night. He was greatly concerned that my time be well spent in Mostar; and well spent it was. Sir Martin understood the nature of the challenge he faced and was under no illusions as to how rapidly his work would progress in Mostar given the deeply entrenched hatreds on both sides. Nonetheless, he had every intention of staying the course and, through patience and persistence, wearing down the local hard-liners and obstructionists with a reform program that he hoped would in time go far in reconciling the city's two ethnic factions. The process, however, would be anything but easy, especially since the Croatian government in Zagreb was guiding their Bosnian brethren in the ways of opposition. The only feasible path was to go forward, since to falter or retreat at this stage would weaken the Dayton peace process, and not only in Mostar.

I returned to Brčko not only with a fresh perspective on my work but also with a comrade-in-arms with whom I could consult when times got hard. In retrospect, though, despite Sir Martin Garrod's outgoing and fearless approach to the challenge that faced him, he was hampered in his mission by the fact that OHR had no plan tailored especially for Mostar, as I did in Brčko. Sir Martin had to look to the DPA itself for authority and guidance. But as an action plan, the DPA fell short, lacking in textual precision and action deadlines. As I later learned, there is nothing that enables a civilian administrator more in maintaining pressure on local power brokers than a public deadline set by a higher authority.

Because the state of affairs in Mostar was not seen as make-or-break for the Dayton peace process, it was consequently accorded little attention from the top in OHR. In fact, as I would learn from a drop-in visit to OHR's Mostar office two years later on my way back from Dubrovnik, the staff there was starved for information about what was going on, not only in Brčko but in Sarajevo as well. It was clear from their warm welcome and flurry of questions that they saw themselves on the periphery and fairly ignored by OHR headquarters. Neither High Representative Westendorp nor Petritsch were prone to visit Mostar as frequently as the situation there seemed to demand. Thus, the deputy high representatives that succeeded Sir Martin Garrod when he departed Mostar in 1998 to become civilian administrator of the city of Mitrovica in Kosovo were left largely to their own devices in confronting the violent interethnic strife between Mostar's Bosniaks and Croats.

Thus, in comparing Brčko and Mostar, while the challenge of pacifying the populations was more or less the same, the civilian administrator in Mostar did not have powers such as those the First Award and its two successor awards bestowed on me in Brčko. The awards were the primary sources of my authority, to which I constantly turned for legitimacy and guidance in the perplexing task of restoring civil society and fusing the parts of the Brčko prewar *opština*—which had been controlled by the RS and Federation territorially, socially, and politically—into a new unit of local self-government called the Brčko District of Bosnia and Herzegovina.

It is worth noting here that as the peace implementer goes about the business of reintegrating and multiethnicizing disputed territories, they should keep uppermost in mind that the process, as seen through the eyes of those being acted upon (and often displaced), will be reviewed as anything but positive and benign. No matter how high principled and well designed your plan, no matter how humanely and carefully you try to execute it, the hard fact is that those in whose interest the plan is putatively created will resist you, imputing to your best efforts and to the plan itself dark implications and hidden motives. Only through patience, persistence, and, yes, humility, will you be able eventually to overcome such deeply ingrained skepticism and fear. As I explained in more detail earlier, until a modicum of trust is established between you—the peace implementer—and the fractionated local populace and its often obstructionist leaders, you will be spinning your wheels. Such trust will form, if it ever does, only when you have shown a scrupulous attention to truth in your dealings with, and a genuine respect for, your interlocutors; without question that includes delivering on what you say you will do. Regrettably, this is far easier said than done and will require a time commitment longer than the usual one-year term for most international civilian contracts. I am presuming here that these vitally important jobs will continue to be looked upon as non-career enhancing by active-duty Foreign Service and U.S. military officers and other professionals—a great pity, really, given the potential of these high-visibility jobs to stretch a person's capacity for executive leadership to the limit. As I said before, nothing in my Foreign Service career, including my stint as a chief of mission simultaneously to three small developing nations, compared to the professional demands of Brčko. Nothing.

Faced with all that needs to be done, a civilian administrator could be forgiven for occasionally throwing up his or her hands in despair—a facile thought, but in practice you have no choice in the matter. The only real choice you have is to put your head down and get on with it. In the case of Brčko, I found, to my not inconsiderable surprise, that solutions, or hints of solutions, would often present themselves in the process of simply engaging on the issues: In other words, where a solution had not been evident before, one would appear as a consequence of tackling problems head on. Call it serendipity in problem solving. I leave the reader with this last story.

The Balkan tradition of male dominance over public life was alive and well in Brčko. For some time I had been concerned that I had not been hearing directly from women in the community. So, without a coherent strategy in mind, I began randomly calling on the few women's organizations we were able to identify. While I did this ostensibly as a courtesy, I was also eager to learn about women's programs, if any existed. It was a scattershot affair, driven as much by opportunity as by plan. During each call on a women's group, however, I would let drop my hope that women from all three communities might find a way to come together *for the sake of their children* to share experiences and, hopefully, to begin a dialogue about how to mend the wounds of war. Given the relentless pace of events, though, I was not able personally to follow up on these random visits. I left that to our bright and capable human rights officer, Sacha Crijns.

Then, one day, out of the blue in early 2000, an organization calling itself the Brčko Women's *Kola*[8] invited me to be guest of honor at a gala evening in the Revena Hotel in downtown Brčko. With dinner and music on the program, a rarity in Brčko those days, I readily accepted although I knew nothing about the host organization. So when my Serb interpreter, Dragica Todorović, and I showed up a bit late we were surprised to find the hotel's cramped ballroom filled with Bosniak, Serb, and Croat women—maybe a hundred in all—talking, laughing, and already dancing to the *kola*. A five-man band was at full throttle. As we settled in at the head table, a waiter filled our glasses with *sljivovice*. A few minutes later, the band fell silent and Adela Božić, Croat judge on the magistrate court, rose to propose a toast. To my astonishment, she turned my way as she raised her glass to proclaim me as "founder of the Brčko Women's *Kola*"! Caught totally off guard, I asked Dragica if I was hearing right. After conferring with Judge Božić, Dragica replied, "Yes, you are being recognized as founder of this organization because you initially suggested that women from the three ethnic groups needed to get together. They took you at your word and now, two years later, they've done it, thanks to you!" Wow! And I had nearly forgotten making those suggestions.

The point to take away from this little story is: *Never underestimate the power of suggestion*, especially if you happen to be a supervisor. Another point: Rather than wait until you have a "perfect" solution to a problem—in this case, the lack of contact between women—get going by sharing your thoughts around, including with the target audience. Maybe in this case the women's groups were just waiting for a catalyst to come along and nudge them into action. Who knew? Looking back, I can easily imagine one group of women broaching the idea of getting together with another by saying: "The supervisor thinks it would be a good idea if . . ." Wherever the truth may lie, I can only say that after nearly three years of butting my head against the walls of ethnic hatred and suspicion it was a rewarding moment for me to be able look out on a room full of women dancing to the heady rhythm of the *kola*. True, I could not be sure that Serb and Croat and Muslim women were actually intermingling on the dance floor—they may in fact have subtly circled themselves into groups. If that were the case, however, an outsider would have never detected it. In any event, for me the evening was a milestone in empowering citizens to participate in the rebirth of their community. In peacekeeping, as with other departments of life, when women are given full opportunity to use their intelligence, skills, and innate sense of family and mutual support— in sum, with women integrated into the communal rebirth—there is no telling how far you can go!

Someone once said: A job half done is a job not done at all. In the end, the success or failure of the type of peace operation we have been considering in these pages will depend on the readiness of the outside intervening powers to stay the course, to finish the job, whatever that hard-to-define milestone may require in terms of resources and time. It is an unfortunate accident of history that democratic governments, arguably best suited to act as agents of benevolent change in conflicted circumstances, are also—for domestic political reasons, frequency of elections, and so on—the most likely to be pressed by their electoral constituencies to hurry along the process of reconciliation and healing at a pace considerably faster than local culture and conditions will allow. Such pressure from outside donor nations can be, simultaneously, both a help and a hindrance to the work of the peace implementers on the ground. A help, in that it stresses the need for forward progress, which implementers can point to as cover for their actions; a hindrance, in that it signals impatience with the peace process, an impatience that plays into the hands of the adversary whose goal it is to outwait the international community and reimpose its version of control—often the status quo ante—over the populace.

The fact is that post-conflict peace interventions are complex affairs that will not be successful unless the possibility of a potentially long and involved engagement has been openly and fully addressed up front. This is especially true when, as in the Balkans, ethno-religious tensions—not to say hatreds—are in play. In ethnically diverse regions like the Balkans, which not only have a long history of ethnic tension but of periods of surprising harmony—for instance, the Yugoslav region of Bosnia and Herzegovina during the interwar years where Bosnian Muslims, Croats, and Serbs lived side by side and intermarried in significant numbers—peace intervenors need to be keenly aware of the potential for long-term involvement numbering years, even decades, to enable passions to cool. The hope is that as lives slowly improve—as the economy revives and jobs are to be had (and lost)—the impulse to war and violence will gradually give way to the dawning realization that more will be lost than gained from a return to open conflict.

All of this presupposes on the intervenors' part a serious level of commitment, patience, and persistence tied to an unwavering vision of a better life for all of the people whose future is so inevitably and deeply tied to the success of the peace operation. For when all is said and done, it is *not* about us, it is about *them*.

Appendix

U.S. ARMY CIVIL AFFAIRS OFFICERS

I refer in the foregoing pages to activities in which U.S. Army Civil Affairs officers (known in NATO as Civil/Military Corps, or CIMIC, officers) contributed to our overall mission and think it important to mention the names of these highly dedicated men drawn almost entirely from the ranks of the Army Reserves.

The normal pattern in Brčko was for the U.S. Army under COMSFOR to assign two CA officers at a time for tours of, as I recall, nine months each. These two-man teams were seconded to my staff in fulfillment of the military's mission to assist civilian peace implementers in doing their job. These remarkable officers, of which I counted ten teams during my time, were permitted, at least in the beginning, to live in apartments in Brčko *grad* and, at my insistence—since I did not want the supervisor's office to be seen as a front for the army—to shed their military uniforms in favor of civilian garb when in my office or on their daily rounds in the community.

In seeking to optimally utilize these CA/CIMIC officers, I simply relied on what they had to say about their professions and pursuits in civilian life and point them in that direction in Brčko. For example, COL James Perlmutter had been a hospital administrator. It thus was a no-brainer to ask Jim to take the local hospital under his wing and suggest ways in which we might most rapidly bring the hospital up to standards from its war-devastated condition: broken windows, decrepit heating system, lack of basic surgical equipment, and total absence of medical supplies of any kind.

LTC Thomas Molina was a city manager in real life. Imagine that! Another no-brainer: Down to the municipal building he went to help sort out the tangle of practical issues with which the "mayor" and his sidekicks were trying to cope. And many were the evenings in which I asked Tom to sit down and share with me the fundamentals of his trade. A godsend.

And so it went.

Needless to say, I became a strong supporter of the army's civil affairs effort, even as its senior officers were having difficulties in figuring out just what it was that civil affairs brought to the table (or, as they were more likely to say, "to the fight").

My apologies to the officers whose names I have included in the accompanying list for whatever errors may have slipped through my efforts to be factual and complete.

LTC James Rogers, 350 CA Command, 1997–1998
MAJ Robert Bishop, 431 CA Battalion, 1997–1998
MAJ Cole Cartledge, 1997–1998
MAJ Thomas Molina, 1997–1998
MAJ David Bennett, 1997–1998
LTC Kevin McAleese, 358 CA Brigade, 1998–1999
MAJ Roland de Marcellus, 354 CA Brigade, 1998–1999
MAJ Brooke Allen, 354 CA Brigade, 1998–1999
COL James Perlmutter, 354 CA Brigade
CAPT Alex Rodriguez, 350 CA Brigade
COL Robert Sundberg, 322d CA Brigade

OFFICE OF THE HIGH REPRESENTATIVE—NORTH BRČKO, 24 APRIL

In accordance with the Peace Agreement for Bosnia and Herzegovina, the Award of the Arbitral Tribunal for the Dispute Over the Inter-Entity Boundary line in the Brčko area of 14 February 1997 and the Conclusions of the Brčko Implementation Conference of 7 March 1997, the Deputy High Representative for Brčko has, under the guidance of the High Representative, decided on 24 April 1997 to establish the following Procedure for Return to Brčko. This Procedure shall enter into force on 24 April 1997 and shall remain in force until amended or canceled.

PROCEDURE FOR RETURN TO BRČKO

Introduction

1. In accordance with Annex 7 of the Peace Agreement, all refugees and displaced persons have the right freely to return to their homes of origin.

This right to return encompasses the right to reconstruct. The right freely to return to homes of origin has to be exercised in a peaceful, orderly and phased manner. The rights of displaced persons, temporarily housed in homes of returnees, must be respected.

2. This document sets forth procedures and principles to be followed by refugees and displaced persons wishing to return to their homes located in the Brčko area. For purposes of this Procedure alone, the area comprises the territory of the prewar Municipality of Brčko. This Procedure defines the role of the Return Commission for Brčko and the principles which will guide the work of the municipal housing administration.

The Return Commission for Brčko

3. The Deputy High Representative for Brčko, or his designated representative, shall chair the Return Commission which receives, using the form provided by the Commission for Real Property Claims of Displaced Persons and Refugees (CRPC) (hereafter: the form), notifications of refugees and displaced persons wishing to return to Brčko. The Return Commission also receives the form from displaced persons currently occupying homes in the Brčko municipality wishing to return to their home of origin elsewhere in Bosnia and Herzegovina.

4. The Return Commission is composed of representatives of OHR, UNHCR, SFOR, UN, IPTF, and the Mayors of Brčko or their designated representatives, as well as a representative of the Commission for Real Property Claims of Displaced Persons and Refugees (CRPC). Representatives of the municipal housing administrations will participate in the sessions of the Return Commission as observers. Participation of members in the proceedings of the Return Commission is obligatory.

5. Proceedings of the Return Commission require a quorum of four. The Return Commission takes decisions in consensus. However, if no consensus can be reached, the Deputy High Representative for Brčko or his designated representative can decide. The decisions of the Return Commission are binding.

Notification

6. Persons intending to return to their homes of origin shall notify their intention to the Return Commission with the attached declaration and form. The form shall be filed with the CRPC. The declaration shall include names and number of returnees, address of the home of origin and all other information requested. The information will also include the earliest intended return date and an indication whether the home of origin is currently inhabited or uninhabited (the earliest intended return date is requested for planning purposes only and will not predetermine the decision of the actual date of return).

7. By signing the declaration, the claimant expresses his/her intent to

return to the home of origin and acknowledges the commitment of the returnees indicated in the form to abide by existing laws and regulations, provided these are in accordance with the General Framework Agreement for Peace (GFAP). Returnees are not subject to military service for a minimum period of 5 years.

Clearance for Return

8. Whenever a claim has been submitted, the CRPC will render its decision and inform the Return Commission as rapidly as possible whether the claimant has a prima facie right to ownership, lawful possession or any other right to reoccupy the home. The Return Commission may also request the CRPC to render an advisory opinion. The Return Commission shall verify the obtained information and, in particular, check whether the intended home for return is inhabited or uninhabited.

9. If the CRPC has given a positive advisory opinion—which does not prejudice its final decision—and if the intended home for return is inhabited by other persons as temporary occupants, the Return Commission will inform the competent Brčko municipal housing administration. The municipal housing administration will, under the direction of the Return Commission, take the appropriate measures by applying the following provisions:

a) The municipal housing administration shall, within three working days, move to terminate the temporary occupancy of the present occupant and give him/her a time limit of 60 days for vacating the home. If the claimant indicates a date for intended return which falls after the expiration of the 60 day period, the time limit for vacating the home will be determined in accordance with that later date.

b) If the temporary occupant intends to stay in Brčko, the municipal housing administration will provide him/her with a reasonably sufficient accommodation within the period determined for vacating the home.

c) If the temporary occupant wishes to return to the home of origin in another municipality in Bosnia and Herzegovina outside Brčko, Paragraphs 12 and 13 below will apply.

10. When the intended home for return is vacated, the Return Commission will inform the claimant without delay and give clearance for return.

11. The Return Commission will take its earlier decision under review if the CRPC reverses its decision or its originally positive advisory opinion or if new material or facts are presented.

Returns from Brčko to Other Municipalities

12. Whenever a displaced person currently living in Brčko and intending to return to his or her home of origin elsewhere in Bosnia and Herzegovina has presented a claim to the CRPC, the CRPC will submit a copy of its decision

to the Return Commission, in accordance with Paragraphs 6, 7, and 8. The Return Commission will promptly pass the decision of the CRPC on to the receiving municipal authorities, which will facilitate the return of the displaced persons to their homes of origin through UNHCR.

13. The governments of the Federation of Bosnia and Herzegovina and the Republika Srpska guarantee that the municipal authorities will vacate the home of origin of the claimant with priority by applying the provisions of Paragraph 9 above.

Orderly and Phased Return

14. In order to ensure that the process of return proceeds in a peaceful, orderly and phased manner, the Deputy High Representative for Brčko may issue, as appropriate, regulations, including establishing priority for certain areas for return and for certain categories of returnees, or, if the situation so requires, he may limit or suspend the return process.

Interpretation of this Procedure

15. In case of dispute, the Deputy High Representative for Brčko is the final authority regarding interpretation of this Procedure, the authentic language of which is English.

Brčko

24 April 1997

OFFICE OF THE HIGH REPRESENTATIVE—NORTH BRČKO DECLARATION

The undersigned, Mr/Mrs...................(hereafter: the claimant) and the returnees listed hereafter, declare that

(1) he/she will abide by existing laws and regulations, provided these are in accordance with the General Framework Agreement for Peace in Bosnia and Herzegovina;

(2) the answers to the questions in the attached form are correct and in accordance with the truth;

(3) in case fraud is subsequently detected or the CRPC reverses its decision or its originally positive advisory opinion, he/she will vacate the home, if the Return Commission for Brčko decides so.

The claimant: Mr/Mrs .... Signature ....

Date of birth ....

No. of ID Card ....

Name of the Father ....

Current Address ....
Address of home of origin ....
Number of Returnees ....
Names of Returnees .... (1) .... Signature* ....
                                  (2)   "
                                  (3)   "
                                  (4)   "
* if a minor, the claimant will sign in his/her place
  Date of birth of returnees .... (1)
                                    (2)
                                    (3)
                                    (4)
  Nos. of ID Cards .... (1)
                                    (2)
                                    (3)
                                    (4)
  Name of the father .... (1)
                                    (2)
                                    (3)
                                    (4)
Earliest date of return ....
Brčko, ...……......... 199

SUPERVISORY ORDERS

Date	Order
August 12, 1997	Order on Identity Cards for Returnees to Brčko
August 12, 1997	Order on Return Procedures to Brčko
August 12, 1997	Order on Participation in Chiefs of Police Meetings
August 30, 1997	Brčko Implementation Conference, Supervisory Order
August 30, 1997	Order on Collection of Fees at the Brčko Bridges
September 19, 1997	Supervisory Order
October 9, 1997	Supervisory Order
October 10, 1997	Order on Judiciary in the RS Municipality of Brčko

October 10, 1997	Order on Multi-Ethnic Administration in the RS Municipality of Brčko
October 13, 1997	Order on Multi-Ethnic Police in the RS Municipality of Brčko
November 10, 1997	Addendum to Order on Multi-Ethnic Police in the RS Municipality of Brčko of 13 October 1997
November 13, 1997	Amendment to Supervisory Orders on Collection of Fees at the Brčko Bridges
November 15, 1997	Addendum to Order on Multi-Ethnic Administration in the RS Municipality of 10 October 1997
December 4, 1997	Order on Privatization
December 5, 1997	Addendum to Order on Judiciary in the RS Municipality of Brčko
December 31, 1997	Second Addendum to the Order on Judiciary in the RS Municipality of Brčko
July 13, 1998	Brčko Arbitration Supervisory Order
August 24, 1998	Order on Return to Unoccupied Property in the RS Municipality of Brčko
November 3, 1998	Order on Outstanding Cases of Article 17 of the Republika Srpska Law on use of Abandoned Property, Internally Displaced Brčko Residents, and Cases of Multiple Occupancy
November 3, 1998	Order on Return of Non-Serb Members of the Municipal Assembly, Administration, Police, Judiciary, and Others to their Pre-War Homes of Origin in Brčko
November 3, 1998	Order on Outstanding Cases of Article 17 of the Republika Srpska Law on use of Abandoned Property, Internally Displaced Brčko Residents, and Cases of Multiple Occupancy
November 11, 1998	Order of Ravne-Brčko
November 16, 1998	Second Addendum to the Order on the Multi-Ethnic Administration in the RS Municipality of Brčko of October 10, 1997

December 3, 1998	Order Suspending Councilor from the Ravne-Brčko Municipal Council
June 26, 1999	Supplementary Order on Privatization
September 10, 1999	Addendum to the Orders of November 3, 1998–September 10, 1999
January 20, 2000	Order on the Establishment of the Brčko District Police Service and the Appointment of the Chief and Deputy Chiefs of Police
March 8, 2000	Order on the Establishment of the Brčko District of Bosnia and Herzegovina
March 8, 2000	Order on the Appointment of the Members of the Interim District Assembly of the Brčko District of Bosnia and Herzegovina
March 21, 2000	Order of the Establishment of the Interim District Assembly of the Brčko District of Bosnia and Herzegovina
April 14, 2000	Order of the Financial System of the Brčko District of Bosnia and Herzegovina
May 26, 2000	Addendum to the Supervisory Order on the Appointment of Members of the Interim Government of the Brčko District of Bosnia and Herzegovina

Notes

1. INTRODUCTION

1. Many refer to the latter as the Federation of Muslims and Croats.

2. The UN General Assembly established the United Nations Commission on International Trade Law (UNCITRAL) in 1966 to reduce or remove obstacles to international trade caused by disparities in national laws governing trade. Ten years later, a UNCITRAL working group charged with matters concerning international arbitration and conciliation put forth a comprehensive set of procedural rules for the conduct of arbitral proceedings. These were adopted by the commission and, although intended largely for commercial disputes, have also been used widely in ad hoc international arbitrations.

3. I consider this so crucial that relevant portions of the awards and annexes have been incorporated into this text rather than in an appendix. Those readers seeking complete copies of the documents may find same at: www.ohr.int/ohr-offices/brcko/arbitration/archive.asp?sa=on.

4. The parties to the GFAP agreed by Annex 10 to the designation of an international High Representative to implement the civilian aspects of the peace settlement in BiH.

5. The North Atlantic Treaty Organization (NATO)-led peace-enforcement operation ensuring stability in postwar Bosnia.

6. A Peace Implementation Conference was held in London, U.K., on December 8–9, 1995, to garner international support of the Dayton Accords and established a Peace Implementation Council (PIC) to integrate the activities of fifty-five countries and agencies assisting in the peace process by financial, troop-contributing, observer, and/or operational means. The PIC Steering Board—comprising Canada, France, Germany, Italy, Japan, Russia, the U.K., the United States, the presidency of the European Union, the European Commission, and the Organization of the Islamic Conference (represented by Turkey)—provides the High Representative with political guidance.

2. SUPERVISOR'S AUTHORITY

1. Ian McLeod is a retired brigadier who had served in the British Army's Parachute Regiment. He was a veteran of Northern Ireland's "troubles" and before joining our team in Brčko had been on the ground in Bosnia with the European Community Monitoring Mission.

2. Ambassador Gennadiy Shabannikov had been with the Ministry of Foreign Affairs since 1967. Notably, he represented the Soviet Union and Russia between 1991–1993 in the Joint Commission on Compliance and Inspections under the first Strategic Arms Limitation Treaty.

3. This was also done because I wanted their respective governments to know that as an American I had no intention of unilaterally running roughshod over Brčko—more pointedly over the Serb residents of Brčko—and aimed to preside over an open operation without a hidden agenda.

4. Camp McGovern was the largest of the U.S. base camps for American troops serving with the NATO force in Bosnia under Operation JOINT ENDEAVOR. It was established in December 1995 approximately four kilometers south of the *grad* in a minefield straddling the IEBL. The camp was closed in 2004.

5. The Civil-Military Cooperation (CIMIC) units are part of the civil-affairs component of the military and had been tasked with interfacing between NATO and local and international civilian organizations operating in Bosnia. See the appendix for a list of the U.S. Army Civil Affairs officers who were active in Brčko during my tenure.

6. A few days earlier, I heard Carl Bildt say it was "not so much an exit strategy we should be concerned about, but an *entry strategy* . . . for Bosnia and Herzegovina into the family of nations" [emphasis mine].

7. Pale had been one of the sites for ski competitions during the 1984 Winter Olympics.

8. At the time, BiH had been divided into three divisional boundaries and Brčko was situated in the U.S.-controlled MND-North sector. Headquarters was at "Eagle Base" (or "Tuzla Main") set outside the Federation city of Tuzla.

9. I gave the LNO carte blanche to report through his channels on anything he saw or heard in my office during the day or night.

10. These regular meetings devoted to strategy, although migrating to other days in the week, remained a fixture of the Brčko scene until my departure.

11. Ahmed and Scheye were civil affairs officers within the UN system. Functionally, they served as political advisors within UNMIBH. On the one hand, they provided political reporting to the head of civil affairs of UNMIBH, and therefore to the SRSG and UN headquarters. On the other, as CIVPOL advisors, they assisted UN/IPTF with its work and situating policing activities within the politics of BiH and the international community.

12. Bosnia's equivalent to a small, plain hamburger wrapped in pastry and normally eaten at midday.

13. Unlike the SDS, directed from Pale, the SRS was controlled by Serb firebrand Vojislav Šešelj in Belgrade. Šešelj's minions in Brčko were caricatures of the two-dimensional Serb who hates all others, has no original ideas, and is—first and last—a docile foot soldier.

14. In the former countries of the Communist world, checkpoints were the preferred mode of policing to control movements along highways. Policemen would stop their patrol cars alongside the road and then either randomly, or by plan, pull motorists over simply by holding up a stick with a circular stop sign on the end of it, known popularly as a "lollipop." It had the overall effect of needlessly slowing traffic and, at the same time, offering endless opportunities for bribery. Checkpoints were anathema to freedom of movement.

15. Westendorp's reaction to the announcement of the Final Award was telling. In his judgment, it was premature and should have been delayed sine die. This was in direct contravention to Owen's point of view—embodied in the language of the Final Award—that further postponement of a final decision in the dispute over the IEBL in the Brčko area, the only unresolved issue left over from Dayton, would impede the development of BiH as a whole.

3. FREEDOM OF MOVEMENT

1. In fact, a prewar intermarriage rate of 27 percent insured that most local communities within Brčko *opština's* boundaries were indeed far less than ethnically homogeneous.

2. It was widely accepted that the Serbs accounted for 97 percent of the *opština's* inhabitants north of the IEBL, up from a high of 21 percent before the war. A very few Croats and Bosniaks, mainly elderly spouses of Serbs, lived through the war in the Brčko *grad* itself; but they numbered in the low hundreds. And they were frightened, so they said nothing, nothing at all.

3. The U.S. Army temporarily had restored the two spans by installing Bailey bridges across each in 1996, but at the time I arrived traffic was still restricted to the NATO force.

4. I include this point here because it fits within this context. But, actually, the point about needing police security plans in advance of planned public events that might trigger violence took time—a matter of a week or two—for me, a newcomer to city management, to fully recognize and embrace. Of equal and concurrent importance, of course, was the explicit agreement of the chief of police to carry out the plan. In the case of the two buses, I had personally called on the chief and informed him of the necessity to protect the buses. I had wrongly accepted his silence as a positive response—a potentially tragic mistake I would not repeat.

5. Plavšić, a woman in her late sixties, had for years aligned herself with Radovan Karadžić and, in fact, had helped him form the SDS party. She had studied biology at the University of Zagreb, spent two years in the U.S. as a Fulbright scholar, and taught prior to the war at the University of Sarajevo. Her views on genetics caused many eyebrows to lift among non-Serbs in the Balkans. In the summer of 1997, however, Karadžić and his political theorist, former history professor Aleksa Buha, chose to attack her in the crudest way. They labeled Plavšić a "whore of the West" because of her less strident position on several issues of importance to the Serbs, thus earning her undying enmity while at the same time enhancing her reputation among the international community.

6. A cross with the Cyrillic letter "C" interspersed four times between the arms represented the belief that "only unity saves the Serbs" (*samo sloga Srbina spašava*).

7. Along with the crescent moon, a traditional Muslim symbol in Bosnia.

4. REFUGEE AND IDP RETURNS

1. Statistics on PNG's spoken languages derive mostly from research done by the Summer Institute of Linguistics (Wycliffe) in Dallas, Texas. For many years following World War II, the institute has sponsored Christian Protestant missionaries to go among the clans in PNG to decode their unwritten tongues and, once decoded, to translate the New Testament from English into those languages. Incidentally, the number 832 represents some 16 percent of all the known languages in the world!

2. This policy had the salutary effect of sparing the two communities enormous physical and psychological damage, as well as muting postwar animosity between them.

3. Nearly five years later, while attending a workshop on official and nonofficial responses to conflict at the University of San Diego in California, Regina Larson, who had served for eighteen months as a democratization official in the OSCE's Brčko office, told me that Serb residents of the town confided in her that they had taken great solace from the supervisor's commitment not to evict them from the houses in which they were living until they, or others, could arrange identifiable onward accommodations for them. Larson, I think unrealistically, attributed the relatively peaceful returns process in Brčko entirely to my public promise.

4. We opened the doors of the Return Commission proceedings to observers from SFOR, UNHCR, OSCE, UN/IPTF, and resident NGOs with return-related mandates.

5. In truth, several Bosniak families had already begun to return to the village of Omerbegovača close to Camp McGovern in the ZOS as part of SFOR's program of return prior to my arrival.

6. Translated as *miran, postepen i metodičan* in the local languages.

7. In fact, when the Return Commission met initially, I was disappointed to see there were no Bosniak applicants for homes who had shown up from the CRPC registration process. Therefore, no cases were passed forward for residences in the MZs Omerbegovača or Brod. I thus was put in the position where I could only approve the Croat villages of Ulice and Vuksić Gornje, along with Stari Rasadnik (just north of the ZOS). This went against my basic principles, but I simply had no other applicants for return. Predictably, the Serbs were unhappy and started saying they wanted five days of advance notice for such lists. I said that was the old ZOS procedure which had not gone well and caused lots of difficulties; I was determined to avoid that. Also, the Serbs wanted twenty days to look over the list. That would just give them more time for vicious troublemaking. Finally, they said there were municipal plans to build a superhighway through their community, or railroad. Utter nonsense!

8. As a general rule, matters should be handled at the lowest level of authority and responsibility.

9. In fact, we had nicknamed Ljerka "the Valkyrie" because of her long, jet-black hair which gave her the appearance of the witch in German operas who selects heroes to be slain.

10. At that time, by nearly every economic indicator within Bosnia, the Federation was better off than the RS. Ljerka was using this widespread knowledge to intimidate and hopefully dissuade the Bosniak woman from returning.

11. The definitive account of Serbs driving non-Serbs from the latter's homes in the Brčko *opština*, or, indeed, from other places in BiH, has yet to be written. My comments about what happened during that campaign therefore can only be conjectural. I am confident, however, after scores of conversations with people who lived through the war, that my speculation as to what actually took place is not terribly wide of the mark.

12. Roughly two hundred houses had been totally demolished and were what we were eyeing for future returns.

13. This ex-banker was elected in November 1997 to succeed Miodrag Pajić as Serb mayor of Brčko.

5. DEMOCRATIC GOVERNANCE AND MULTIETHNIC ADMINISTRATION

1. This not atypical comment captured the prevailing attitude toward elections in Brčko and elsewhere in BiH at the time.

2. The 1991 census results for Brčko are contained in the first chapter of this volume.

3. Although my motives for maintaining some wiggle room on the numbers were purely tactical, I cannot resist quoting from Conor Cruise O'Brien on the subject of ambiguity: "The successful wielder of ambiguity has a certain high imperiousness in his attitude to facts and inclines to a magician-like confidence in the overmastering power of language" (1966, 270).

4. Years later, a member of the OSCE team told me that Frowick's initial visit to Brčko, while ostensibly to work out election procedures with me, had been largely window dressing. Driven by election technicians who were loath to introduce exceptions to the countrywide electoral model, the visit had been organized largely to mollify me over such concerns as I might have regarding the election process. In short, there was no serious intent to change OSCE's overall approach in light of what my advisors and I might have had to say about the Brčko scene.

5. OSCE technicians had slipped us advance word that the names of nearly twenty-six hundred actual Serb voters had gotten lost in the computer because of a "glitch." When I reacted with shock and incredulity to this staggering news, they simply shrugged: "What had happened had happened and nothing more could be done about it." Sophie Lagueny, a young French woman on OSCE-Brčko's staff, however, had been so frustrated by the inexplicable loss of the twenty-six hundred names that she took it upon herself to painstakingly review all computer inputs from Brčko to the voter database in Sarajevo. By dint of sheer persistence, Lagueny was

able, working around the clock and *counting by hand*, to restore each of the lost names to the Brčko voters list. Her self-directed effort, unparalleled in my experience, so impressed us that in December when she let it be known she would be interested in working on my staff, we snapped her up. A year later, Lagueny contributed greatly, with her uncommon knack for systems management, to the analytic work necessary to form the multiethnic administration. Her clearheaded and logical approach to recruiting, interviewing, and selecting candidates for positions in the new Brčko District government helped whittle that mind-numbing and potentially disaster-laden task down to size.

6. Actually, I was prepared to argue either way. If Ellerkman had said the rule flowed from a high policy decision, I would have pushed for a change in that decision.

7. Besides, I had consciously made few requests for "air lift," as the army called it, and so SFOR's internal bias may have been to approve such requests as I did make. In this, I was helped enormously by Supreme Allied Commander Europe General Wesley Clark, who frequently visited Camp McGovern and Brčko and let his in-country commanders know of his strong support of the Brčko Award. As an original member of Richard Holbrooke's negotiating team at Dayton, Clark well understood the hazards of road travel in Bosnia. During our first meeting at Camp McGovern, he asked me point-blank if I needed better access to helicopter lift. When I replied that I did, Clark turned to his aide and said, "Make it happen." Despite the general's helpful intervention, however, I tried to avoid asking for travel assistance very often so as not to wear out my welcome. That said, the difference between a forty-minute trip to Sarajevo by air and a three-hour trip by road was, depending on the weather, substantial.

8. While claims of Anić abusing his office were not beyond the realm of possibility, especially given the shady nature of the notorious Arizona Market (to be discussed in chapter 7), over which he exerted considerable influence, he was nonetheless a more moderate and pro-Dayton figure than anyone the HDZ had put forward. Furthermore, at this early stage in the peace process, charges of abuse of office could be, and often were, liberally sprayed on officials across the political spectrum whenever it served a particular party's interest.

9. Years later, back in the United States, I took special interest in Vermont Senator James Jeffords's decision to move from the Republican Party to independent status while in office. The Republican Party's reaction to the move was not wholly dissimilar to that of the HDZ in Ravne-Brčko in the fall of 1998. In a curious way, the Jeffords affair helped justify in my mind the untutored decision that I, as Brčko supervisor, had made back then.

10. For instance, at one point before he left for good, Ian McLeod recounted to me a conversation he had with Munib Jusufović. The Rahić-Brčko mayor indicated that he had learned a lot from just watching the supervisor's office operate. He had, for example, stopped doubting our every word, casting all we said in the worst light for his people. Instead, he had come to realize that we really were trying to improve the lot of all three ethnic factions in Brčko, which he conceded was not an easy task. Jusufović confided to Ian that he had come around to trusting us.

11. Known locally as the "Chetniks" for their slavish devotion to the memory of Drazhe Mihajlović, Tito's guerrilla rival during World War II.

12. Not surprisingly, Mijo Anić took my rejection badly with the result our paths never crossed again. Some few years later, however, I was pleased to see his name emerge in press reports (which I followed from afar) as BiH minister of defense. By all accounts, he performed well in that important post.

13. We even made provision in our institutional changes for a category of "Other" in order to leave the door open for the small, but real, number of persons who resisted ethnic labeling or who were members of unique groups such as Roma. In this, I can safely say we were well ahead of changes OHR was trying to put in place in other parts of BiH.

14. The named young man was indeed romantically involved with a Serb woman, who also worked on my staff. Today, they are married and living happily as husband and wife in another country. How's that for a lurid story?

15. Although Osmić surely played a key role in triggering the attacks on me, such a coordinated assault on a highly visible international official like me could only have been carried out with the concurrence of the SDP top command: Lagumdzija in Sarajevo and Djapo in Brčko. Of the two, I hold the former primarily responsible for attempting to smear my name.

16. In coming months, I learned a great deal about this fascinating career of which I had been blissfully unaware over a lifetime of living in and out of the United States.

17. For a more thorough and detailed narrative of the DMT's program and accomplishments in Brčko, see William Sommers (2002).

6. RULE OF LAW

1. This phenomenon is rife in the corporate world, too, as CEOs set aside long-term strategic goals to satisfy stockholders' insistent demands for quarterly profits.

2. Robert M. Perito (2005) provides a much more detailed description of the turbulent events that took place on August 28, based on extensive interviews, conducted a few years after the fact, with persons and organizations that either had a role in or were observers of what happened in Brčko that day.

3. Old hands on my staff told me later that during the war the Serbs called their people to action with sirens.

4. In recounting these stories, I must recognize that most of these householders would want to express at least pro forma regrets to their tenants in any case, since the latter were lucrative sources of hard currency. To have treated their UN/IPTF renters with indifference or, worse, callousness in the wake of the violence would have courted the possibility of the renters moving to other quarters and leaving the landlord high and dry, at least temporarily. That said, Maddox was given to understand the landlords' (and neighbors') outpourings of concern for the safety of the UN/IPTF monitors living among them went beyond narrow concerns over money. In the judgment of the monitors who reported these incidents to her, there was a genuineness about it all that could not be glibly explained away. In the monitors' view, that genuineness reflected a community not wholly consumed by hatred and fear, but one capable of normal human emotions, even to foreigners in their midst. Wherever the truth lay in these anecdotes, I took from them a measure of optimism.

5. And here I emphatically state that I am of the school that holds war to have been visited upon BiH as part of Serbian strongman Milošević's strategy to drive all non-Serbs from a territory he and his Bosnian Serb cronies in Pale unilaterally declared as belonging to Serbs.

6. Selecting a Croat for the job was out of the question given the relatively small number of Croat returnees to the area of supervision.

7. The standards included a functioning kitchen and bathroom with running water, and a living room/bedroom, all with plastic-sealed windows.

8. This phenomenon was exhibited not only among legal experts, but also among medical practitioners, policemen, teachers, and members of other professions who had long been denied the opportunity openly to discuss professional topics with their ethnic counterparts.

9. Concerned about the BLRC and its future, I called upon a senior advisor to the administrator of USAID shortly after my return to the United States. Upon hearing what had happened, my interlocutor said USAID could have made additional funds available to keep the BLRC up and running until all laws essential to the new district were in place. I brought this, what I thought to be good, news to the attention of my successor-plus-one, Ambassador (ret.) Henry Clarke. To my disappointment, Clarke said he had agreed at OHR-Sarajevo's behest to shut down the BLRC. He therefore considered it unwise to go back on that agreement. Sometime later I learned that funds sufficient to meet BLRC's operating expenses for another six months remained in its budget at the time of the shutdown. The BLRC had not, in other words, run out of money at all.

7. SETTING THE STAGE FOR ECONOMIC REVITALIZATION

1. During the war, this plant was allegedly used by the Bosnian Serbs to dispose of the bodies of non-Serbs executed either in the notorious Luka camp or in murderous sweeps through the northern part of the *opština*. By at least one sober account, as many as three thousand bodies may have been fed through the plant's meat-processing machines. Although this grisly story has never been proven, the fact it even exists as a rumor is an indication of the depth of tension, suspicion, and hatred still unresolved in the community.

2. I wish to acknowledge here my great debt of gratitude to a German economist and management consultant, Dr. Herbert Schmidt, whose clear thinking on the issue of how best to privatize publicly owned enterprises from the Communist era across the vast domain of the former Soviet Union greatly influenced my own.

3. Then U.S. President William "Bill" J. Clinton had a circle of financial contributors during his 1993–2001 administration who were referred to as FOBs, or "Friends of Bill."

4. In a Foreign Service career spanning more than three decades, I had spent five years in the field reporting on the economies and commercial practices of Eastern Europe and the then USSR.

5. Nicky's father, Count Otto Lambsdorff, served as Germany's Minister of the Economy from 1977 to 1984.

6. I debated whether to use this word or the verb "to install," and decided we were in fact creating something new in Brčko.

7. The IAPG served as a venue where midlevel experts from each of the international policymaking agencies routinely vetted proposals and initiatives for possible consideration by the Principals' Group—the international community's highest coordinative body in Bosnia and Herzegovina. The Principals' Group met weekly and comprised five members: the SRSG, at the time, Klein; the head of the OSCE, Barry; SFOR commander Lieutenant General Ronald Adams; and the high representative, Petritsch, in the chair. A representative of the UNHCR normally attended as well.

8. Some detail must be provided to the reader about this body and its director. Prior to my arrival, CAFAO had established a branch office in Brčko and named as its director one of the more diligent and creative international civil servants with whom I had the pleasure of working. His name was Eamonn O'Riordan, a professional customs agent from Ireland. As I understood it, CAFAO's primary mission was to help plan, fund, and install a modern, transparent, and accountable customs service in BiH. The goal was to insure the national treasury would reap full benefit of customs charges collected at border crossing points so that, in the not-so-distant future, BiH would be eligible for entry into the European Union's (EU) open-trading system. O'Riordan had particular responsibility for overhauling customs procedures and practices at the Brčko vehicular bridge, which, once its war damage was repaired, would be expected to carry a large and growing volume of commercial truck and lorry traffic headed from EU countries to the southern Balkan region: Montenegro, Albania, Macedonia, Greece, and others.

The Brčko District's halting success in financing its own way can, in significant part, be attributed to the CAFAO director's energetic approach to the recruiting and training of local customs officers in the ways of modern customs practice. O'Riordan understood that in a dynamically changing trading environment, involving the movement of large volumes of goods by road to and from Europe and the Near East over traditional trade routes through the Balkans, the time-encrusted practices of rampant bribe-taking at border crossing points to enable shipments of contraband and illegal goods, including human trafficking, had to change. CAFAO sought to establish laws and regulations leading to "clean" border operations that would rid the system of bribes and incentivize customs officials to treat vehicles and persons crossing into the Brčko *opština* with courtesy, respect, and a uniform and transparent schedule of fees and tariffs.

O'Riordan hung on stubbornly as Brcko's security environment gyrated through its ups and downs, piloting CAFAO's reform program through to the point where the new customs dispensation became a solid part of the landscape. To achieve this objective, however, he had constantly to push CAFAO headquarters in Sarajevo to provide the necessary technical and financial means. One cold December day in 1999, I dropped in on O'Riordan in his office—serendipitously located just across the street—to inquire about his program and to offer my help. He indicated he was experiencing resistance from Sarajevo toward his initiatives in Brčko. Basically, he was asked: "Why should Brčko succeed, when we are failing in our efforts to improve customs programs and facilities elsewhere in Bosnia?"

This attitude in no way deterred O'Riordan from his enormous task. On the contrary, he doggedly plowed ahead, making incremental improvements day by day and, although I had to leave Brčko before it came to full fruition, in the end delivered to the community and to the Posavina region a gleaming, brightly lit customs house staffed by well-trained, smartly uniformed officers who, quite uncharacteristically for the Balkans, treated lorry drivers and busloads of travelers with uniform politeness and respect. Word spread, and within a very short time, the new Brčko customs point became a magnet for commercial road traffic from Western Europe, easily eclipsing the larger, but "dirty," border point, controlled by the government of Croatia, some ten kilometers upriver at Slavonski Šamac.

9. In fact, an IAPG paper on the Arizona Market produced in January 2000 concurred that the international community could not continue to ignore the criminal elements of the market, and on balance, the best option would be to try for as successful a regulatory regime as possible.

10. Police investigators under Johnson's close supervision identified nine nightclubs in the Arizona Market, three of which were closed, leaving six in operation. No one held that these nightclubs were not involved in prostitution; clearly, they were.

8. CONCLUSION

1. These professional groupings, of course, are not mutually exclusive: Academics may become diplomats, lawyers may become politicians, and so on. For purposes of this unscientific, subjective analysis, however, I will deal only with a person's current calling, not its antecedents.

2. An even bigger "no-no" is to get *caught* interfering in the internal affairs of another country. Such a frightful thought, however, is beyond the scope of this discussion.

3. From the French, meaning "a diplomatic representation or protest."

4. Of course, diplomats involved in public diplomacy, especially those who worked in the old U.S. Information Agency before it was disbanded in 1999 under pressure from then senator Jesse Helms (R-NC), do in fact make it their business to reach out to host-country publics, but in an informational mode only.

5. A tip of my hat, in this connection, to the scores of academic theorists on peace and governance who contributed to the collection of some forty papers published by the U.S. Institute of Peace Press (Crocker, Hampson, and Aall 1996). The six-hundred-page tome is a rich assortment of think pieces on topics ranging across the spectrum from maintaining the peace, to resolving international and intranational conflict, to illuminating the power of democracy and the rule of law around the globe. This volume had a special place on my reading stand. I spent many an hour thumbing its pages looking for guidance in theory and practice. In my isolated corner of Bosnia, since I had no one in a similar situation to which I could turn for an exchange of views on operational matters, I found comfort in consulting works like this for larger ideas that were germane to my work.

6. That said, intuitively speaking, the war-fighter should be better able to ratchet down to a peace operation than the peacekeeper to ratchet up to war-fighting. But intuition does not always serve us well. The issue here is far more complicated and depends on the level of training and experience of soldiers and the quality of their leadership. To military commanders, the war-fighting "edge," once attained by troops under their command, is an asset to be prized and protected against missions, such as peacekeeping, that would tend to attenuate (soften) the unit's combat readiness.

7. The U.S. Army refers to it formally as the "Military Decision-Making Process," or MDMP for short. Military officers, active and retired, are likely to be more than a little baffled by the less formal way in which civilians arrive at decisions—often opaquely and indirectly. The reverse can also be true, if perhaps to a lesser degree, for civilians working alongside military officers in post-conflict theaters. The former are likely to perceive the latter as somewhat hidebound and rigid in their thought processes. Despite these differences, however, in my experience both avenues to arriving at workable solutions can be synergistically employed to good effect in a peace operation.

8. The word *kola* in Balkan languages means wheel, or "circle," as when people dance in a circle.

References

Acheson, Dean. 1969. *Present at the creation: My years in the State Department.* New York: W. W. Norton & Co.

Arbitral Tribunal for Dispute over Inter-Entity Boundary in Brčko Area (Arbitral Tribunal). 1997. Award.

Ashdown, Paddy. 2002. What I learned in Bosnia. *New York Times*, 28 October.

Broder, David S. 2008. Foreign policy's best hope. *Washington Post*, 19 June.

Cleveland, Harlan. 1985. *The knowledge executive.* New York: Truman Talley Books.

Crocker, Chester A. 1996. The varieties of intervention. In *Managing global chaos: Sources of and responses to international conflict*, ed. Chester A. Crocker, Fen Osler Hampson, and Pamela Aall, 183–196. Washington, D.C.: United States Institute of Peace Press.

Crocker, Chester A., Fen Osler Hampson, and Pamela Aall, eds. 1996. *Managing global chaos: Sources of and responses to international conflict.* Washington, D.C.: United States Institute of Peace Press.

De Tocqueville, Alexis. 2000. *Democracy in America.* Ed. J. P. Mayer. Trans. George Lawrence. New York: Perennial Classics.

Doyle, Michael. 2000. Peace piecemeal. *New Balkan Politics*, no. 1. www.newbalkanpolitics.org.mk/oldsite/issue_1/tekst.asp?id=doyle_eng (accessed July 17, 2005).

Farrand, Peter C. 2001. Lessons from Brčko: Necessary components for future internationally supervised territories. *Emory International Law Review* 15, no. 2 (Fall): 529–91.

Friedman, Thomas L. 2000. Foreign affairs: One country, two worlds. *New York Times*, 28 January.

Gladwell, Malcolm. 2000. *The tipping point: How little things can make a big difference.* Boston: Little, Brown & Co.

Karnavas, Michael G. 2001. *Brčko Law Revision Commission: Chairman's final report.* www.esiweb.org/pdf/bridges/bosnia/BLRC_ChairmansRep.pdf (accessed April 4, 2005).

O'Brien, Conor Cruise. 1966. *To Katanga and back: A UN case history.* New York: Grosset & Dunlap.

Perito, Robert M. 2005. *Where is the Lone Ranger when we need him? America's search for a postconflict stability force.* Washington, D.C.: United States Institute of Peace Press.

Rehn, Elisabeth. 1996. *Situation of human rights in the territory of the former Yugoslavia: Periodic report submitted by Ms. Elisabeth Rehn, Special Rapporteur of the Commission on Human Rights, pursuant to paragraph 45 of Commission resolution 1996/71.* www.hri.ca/fortherecord1997/documentation/commission/e-cn4-1997-9.htm (accessed October 22, 2002).

Sommers, William. 2002. *Brčko District: Experiment to experience.* unpan1.un.org/intradoc/groups/public/documents/NISPAcee/UNPAN003596.pdf (accessed July 17, 2005).

United Nations. 1994. *Final report of the United Nations Commission of Experts, Annex VIII–Part 1/10: Prison camps.* www.ess.uwe.ac.uk/comexpert/ ANX/VIII-01 .htm#III (accessed August 20, 2002).

U.S. Congress. House. 2001. *Foreign operations, export financing, and related programs appropriations bill, 2002.* 107th Cong., 1st sess. H. Rep. 107-142. www.fas .org/asmp/resources/govern/H-Rpt-107-142.txt (accessed April 4, 2005).

Wayne, Leslie. 2002. F. Kenneth Iverson, 76, dies: Reshaped the steel industry. *New York Times*, 17 April.

Weber, Max, Hans Heinrich Gerth, and C. Wright Mills. 1946. *From Max Weber: Essays in sociology.* New York: Oxford University Press.

Index

279

Index

About the Author

In 1997, Robert William Farrand was sent to the disputed city of Brčko in Bosnia's northeastern corner to supervise a multinational team in restoring freedom of movement across the ceasefire line, returning thousands of families to their burnt-out homes, and rebuilding multiethnic government bodies. By early 2000, Farrand was able to proclaim Brčko's new status as a "district," which would answer to the state rather than to either of Bosnia's rival entities, the Serb Republic and the Muslim/Croat Federation. Today, Brčko is considered one of the more successful post-conflict peace operations in the world.

Farrand's diplomatic career encompassed tours abroad in Malaysia, the Soviet Union, Czechoslovakia, and Papua New Guinea. In the State Department he served in the bureaus of economic affairs, European affairs, and human rights/humanitarian affairs. A graduate of the National War College, Farrand later served as international affairs advisor at the Industrial College of the Armed Forces. Farrand is a graduate of Mount St. Mary's College in Maryland (B.S.) and Georgetown University in Washington, D.C. (M.A.).

Farrand is a senior distinguished fellow at George Mason University's Peace Operations Policy Program and a member of the Cornwallis Group. He lives in McLean, Virginia.